D1541438

Quickies

Also by Douglas Flemons

Of One Mind: The Logic of Hypnosis, The Practice of Therapy

*Writing Between the Llines: How to Compose
Riveting Social Science Manuscripts*

Completing Distinctions

A Norton Professional Book

Quickies

The Handbook of Brief Sex Therapy

Shelley Green, Ph.D.
Douglas Flemons, Ph.D.

REVISED AND EXPANDED

W. W. Norton & Company
New York • London

Copyright © 2004 by Shelley K. Green and Douglas Flemons

All rights reserved
Printed in the United States of America
First Edition

For information about permission to reproduce
selections from this book, write to
Permissions, W. W. Norton & Company, Inc.,
500 Fifth Avenue, New York, NY 10110

Production Manager: Leeann Graham
Manufacturing by Haddon Craftsmen, Inc.

Library of Congress Cataloging-in-Publication Data

Green, Shelley K.
Quickies : the handbook of brief sex therapy / [edited by] Shelley K. Green &
Douglas Flemons.
    p.   cm.
"A Norton professional book"—P.
Includes bibliographical references and index.
ISBN 13:978-0-393-70527-0
1. Sex therapy—Handbooks, manuals, etc. I. Green, Shelley K. II. Flemons,
Douglas G. III. Title.

RC557.G735 2004
616.85'8306—dc22   2003070185

W. W. Norton & Company, Inc., 500 Fifth Avenue, New York, N.Y. 10110
www.wwnorton.com

W. W. Norton & Company Ltd., Castle House, 75/76 Wells St., London W1T 3QT

5 7 9 0 8 6 4

In memory of Gary Sanders (1950–2002)

Contents

Foreword

I WAS QUITE MOVED by Douglas Flemons's and Shelley Green's decision to dedicate this book to the memory of Gary Sanders. Having known him for over 30 years and having shared the same daily workspace with him for the last 20 of these (Tomm, 2003), I am very confident that he would have felt deeply honored and extremely grateful. Gary was a dedicated clinician: a psychologist, a psychiatrist, a sex therapist, a couples therapist, and a family therapist. He was also an academic scholar and an extremely talented teacher who loved educating medical students, colleagues, clients, and others about sexuality. Throughout his career he actively participated in generating the kinds of therapeutic "quickies" described here, and he would have been delighted to read this wonderful collection of chapters.

Quickies clearly reflects the respectful and resource-oriented values that Gary held so strongly. The authors clarify and creatively apply many of the clinical ideas and methods he used and taught (Sanders, 1995). Indeed, the whole book is a wonderful acknowledgment of what Gary, with all his characteristic passion, lived and worked for. I can easily imagine him smiling, chuckling, bursting out laughing, and occasionally even exclaiming "yes! yes!," as he read these pages!

Many years ago when Gary talked and wrote about the "Five Sexy Words" (*volition, mutuality, arousal, vulnerability*, and *trust*) to define "best sex," he was already striving toward a second order perspective that clearly gave the experience of sexual intimacy priority over sexual activity (Sanders, 1991). He often used a strategic question to help his clients recognize and acknowledge the importance of this: "If for some reason you could have only one aspect of sex in your life, intimacy or intercourse, but not both, which would you prefer?" His focus on sexual experience rather than sexual behavior enabled him to easily bridge the domains of homosexuality and heterosexuality, and to respectfully validate a wide range of human sexual experiences and events (Sanders, 1993).

One particularly empowering aspect of his work, especially with adolescents, was to give permission for freedom of thought and feeling, while opening space for them to choose to act or to not act upon those thoughts and feelings. He found that simply giving permission, within a cultural context of prohibition and judgment, was incredibly healing. He told many stories of so-called "sexual deviance" that melted away as clients were liberated to imagine freely, to understand what was most important for them experientially, and to choose freely to not act on certain thoughts. Indeed, some of the most bizarre fetishes in teenagers and young adults simply dissolved and evaporated as they internalized ramifications and consequences without duress (Sanders, 1996). With committed couples he was often fond of saying, "It doesn't matter where you stimulate your appetite, as long as you eat at home." And for them, he added *love* and *commitment* to his five sexy words.

Gary was acutely sensitive to the important issue of the abuse of power in the relationships and experiences of clients (Sanders, 1988). He thought of "sexual assault" as an oxymoron. For him, any imposition or abuse was out and out violence and had nothing to do with sexuality. He often used a baseball analogy to clarify this, pointing out that "sexual assault has no more to do with sex than smashing someone's head with a baseball bat has to do with baseball" (Liske, 1993). Usually he embellished the analogy quite a bit to make it incredulous and shocking for the listener. I have certainly learnt from him that clearly separating the notions of sex and sexuality from any experiences of abuse is extremely liberating for clients who have suffered not only from the abuse but also from a debilitating conflation of the incompatible experiences of sex and violence (Sanders, 1990). Gary was unusually gifted in his ability to tease these sensitive issues apart and did so with a marvelous combination of humor and respect.

Yet, despite his extraordinary clinical skills, I suspect Gary would readily agree that there is much that even he could learn from the chapters in this book. There is a certain rigor here—in the conceptualization and implementation of systemic, solution-focused, brief therapy, and narrative ideas and interventions—that makes one sense a significant maturation in social constructionist and second order systemic approaches to therapy. Indeed, I consider it quite an achievement to successfully apply these new and innovative therapy methods so effectively in the domain of human sexuality. Thus, I happily join Gary in applauding the sensitivity, thoughtfulness, and creativity of all the contributions in this fine volume.

Karl Tomm, M.D., LMCC, FRCP(C), CRCP(C)

REFERENCES

Liske, C. (1993). Gary Sanders on sexuality and loving intimacy. *The Calgary Participator,* 3(1), 22–31.

Sanders, G. (1998). An invitation to escape sexual tyranny. *The Journal of Strategic and Systemic Therapies,* 7(3), 23–35.

Sanders, G. (1990). Violence, sex, and therapeutic healing. *The Calgary Participator,* 1(1), 1–7.

Sanders, G. (1991). Five sexy words. *The Calgary Participator, 1*(3), 33–34.

Sanders, G. (1993). The love that dares not speak its name: From secrecy to openness in gay and lesbian affiliations. In E. Imber-Black (Ed.), *Secrets in families and family therapy* (pp. 215–242). New York: Guilford Press.

Sanders, G. (1995). Sexuality, power, and empowerment: One man's reflections on sex therapy. *The Canadian Journal of Human Sexuality, 4,* 289–298.

Sanders, G. (1996). Recovering from paraphilia: An adolescent's journey from despair to hope. *Journal of Child & Youth Care, 11*(1), 1–12.

Tomm, K. (2003). Acknowledging the work of Gary Sanders. *AFTA Newsletter, 87,* 25–26.

(A complete listing of Dr. Sanders' publications is available on the University of Calgary Family Therapy Program website: http://www.familytherapy.org)

Contributors

Barbara Anger-Díaz, Ph.D. Barbara is a Senior Research Fellow at the Mental Research Institute (MRI). Co-founder of the MRI's Latino Brief Therapy Center and a member of its Brief Therapy team for 13 years, she continues to be part of its teaching faculty. She now resides in Miami, Florida and is Adjunct Professor at Barry University's Counseling Program. A writer, lecturer, and trainer both in the U.S. and abroad, she is interested in further articulating and expanding the application of brief therapy to fields beyond psychotherapy.

Monte Bobele, Ph.D. Born in Galveston, Texas, Monte completed his undergraduate and graduate work in psychology at the University of Houston. After a short stint in private practice, he returned to Galveston to begin a postdoctoral fellowship in family therapy at the Galveston Family Institute, where he studied with Harry Goolishian, Paul Dell, George Pulliam, and Harlene Anderson. Since 1981 and except for four years spent teaching with Brad Keeney at Texas Tech University in the mid- to late-1980s, Monte has been at Our Lady of the Lake University in San Antonio. He is currently Professor of Psychology and the training director of an APA-accredited doctoral counseling psychology program.

Robert E. Doan, Ph.D. Until his recent retirement and move to New Mexico, Rob was a tenured, full professor at the University of Central Oklahoma, where he taught for eighteen years. His interest in narrative therapy began during his doctoral internship in Calgary, Canada, when Michael White visited the Family Therapy Program at Foothills Hospital. Since that time, Rob has refined his narrative skills and has published widely on the narrative approach, including a book coauthored with Alan Parry, *Story Re-Visions*. He has worked in private practice, acted as a family therapy consultant with several agencies, and served as a staff psychologist in an adolescent prison.

Karen M. Donahey, Ph.D. Karen is Associate Professor in the Department of Psychiatry and Behavioral Sciences in the Feinberg School of Medicine at Northwestern University. She is also the Director of the Center for Sex and Marital Therapy in Chicago, Illinois.

Douglas Flemons, Ph.D. Director of Student Counseling and Professor of Family Therapy at Nova Southeastern University, Douglas is a Clinical Member and Approved Supervisor of the American Association for Marriage and Family Therapy (AAMFT). Author of *Of One Mind*, *Writing Between the Lines*, and *Completing Distinctions*, Douglas offers seminars and workshops internationally, maintains a private practice in Fort Lauderdale, Florida, and is co-director of Context Consultants.

J. Scott Fraser, Ph.D. Scott is Professor, former Director of Clinical Training and former Internship Director at the School of Professional Psychology of Wright State University in Dayton, Ohio. He served for 14 years as director of the Crisis/Brief Therapy Center at the Good Samaritan Hospital in Dayton. In addition to his teaching, he directs and supervises at a community-based Brief Therapy Center, supervises trainees at primary care healthcare training sites, and consults with juvenile courts and intensive home-based intervention programs. Author of numerous articles and chapters, Scott's most recent book (with Andy Solovey) is *Second-Order Change in Psychotherapy*.

Shelley Green, Ph.D. Associate Professor of Family Therapy at Nova Southeastern University, Shelley also serves as co-director of Context Consultants in Fort Lauderdale, Florida. The Reviews Editor for the *Journal of Marital and Family Therapy* (*JMFT*) and an editorial board member of both *JMFT* and the *Journal of Feminist Family Therapy*, she has published widely in the areas of sexuality, HIV/AIDS, and clinical training and supervision. Shelley is a Clinical Member and Approved Supervisor of AAMFT and a member of the American Family Therapy Academy. *Quickies* is her first book.

Carol Hicks-Lankton, M.A. Carol is a licensed marriage and family therapist who operates a private practice in Pensacola, Florida. Interna-

tionally recognized for her role in the development and growth of an Ericksonian approach to family therapy and clinical hypnosis, she is the
coauthor of three books and author of numerous chapters. Carol conducts
training for mental health professionals worldwide. She is passionate in
her desire to rapidly facilitate therapeutic transformation that is both brief
and deeply healing.

Mark A. Hubble, Ph.D. A psychologist and national consultant, Mark is a
graduate of the postdoctoral fellowship in clinical psychology at the Men-
ninger Clinic in Topeka, Kansas, and an emeritus member of the editorial
advisory board of the *Journal of Systemic Therapies*. Founder and former
director of the Brief Therapy Clinic at the University of Missouri–Kansas
City and a former faculty member at the Dayton Institute for Family
Therapy in Centerville, Ohio, Mark is a cofounder of The Institute for the
Study of Therapeutic Change, a think tank in Chicago. He has served as a
contributing editor for *The Family Therapy Networker* and has published
four books with Scott Miller and Barry Duncan. He is coauthor of *Psy-
chotherapy with Impossible Cases* and *Escape from Babel* and coeditor of
Handbook of Solution-Focused Brief Therapy and *The Heart and Soul of
Change: What Works in Therapy*.

Suzanne Iasenza, Ph.D. Associate Professor of Counseling at John Jay
College–City University of New York, Suzanne is on the faculties of the
Institute for Contemporary Psychotherapy and the Institute for Human
Identity. She also maintains a private practice in psychotherapy and sex
therapy in New York City. Suzanne is coeditor (with Judith Glassgold) of
Lesbians and Psychoanalysis as well as the forthcoming *Lesbians, Feminism
and Psychoanalysis*, and she has published extensively on sexuality and
sexual orientation in professional journals and books. Suzanne is also a
contributing editor for *In the Family*, a magazine for lesbians, gays, bisexuals, and their relations.

Martha Laughlin, Ph.D. Martha is Associate Professor and Director of
Clinical Training in the Family Therapy master's degree program at Valdosta State University. Interested in Batesonian systems theory and all
things relational, she has published articles addressing relational approaches to anger and creativity. She is a Licensed Marriage and Family
Therapist in Georgia, and a Clinical Member and Approved Supervisor of
AAMFT. In addition to supervising students' clinical work, she sees clients
privately in Valdosta, Georgia.

Janie K. Long, Ph.D. A Clinical Member and Approved Supervisor of AAMFT, Janie is a licensed marriage and family therapist and Director of the Center for LGBT Life at Duke University in Durham, North Carolina. She has written numerous articles and book chapters on sexual minorities and has been a sex educator for twenty-five years. Her current research interests include the familial acceptance and integration of sexual minority youth who have come out while still living in the home.

Scott D. Miller, Ph.D. Scott is the cofounder of the Institute for the Study of Therapeutic Change, a private group of clinicians and researchers dedicated to studying "what works" in treatment. He is the author of numerous papers and eight books, including *The Heart and Soul of Change* (with Mark A. Hubble and Barry Duncan) and, most recently, *Staying on Top and Keeping the Sand Out of Your Pants: A Surfer's Guide to the Good Life* (with Mark Hubble and Seth Houdeshell).

Thorana S. Nelson, Ph.D. Professor of Family Therapy at Utah State University in the department of Family, Consumer, and Human Development, Thorana is the author of articles on training and supervision in marriage and family therapy and editor of several books, including *101 Interventions in Family Therapy* (with Terry Trepper), *Tales from Family Therapy* (with Frank Thomas), *Education and Training in Solution-Focused Brief Therapy*, *Handbook of Solution-Focused Brief Therapy* (with Frank Thomas) and *Solution-Focused Brief Practice with Long Term Clients in Mental Health Services* (with Joel Simon). She and her husband, Victor, live in Mendon, Utah.

Bill O'Hanlon, M.S. Bill has authored or co-authored 27 books, including, most recently, *Pathways to Spirituality*, *Change 101: A Practical Guide to Creating Change*, and *Thriving Through Crisis* (winner of the Books for a Better Life Award). He has published 54 articles or book chapters, and his books have been translated into 15 languages. A certified professional counselor, licensed mental health professional, and licensed marriage and family therapist, Bill is a clinical member of AAMFT and a Fellow and Board Member of the American Psychotherapy Association. He has appeared on *Oprah* (with his book *Do One Thing Different*), *The Today Show*, and a variety of other television and radio programs. Since 1977, Bill has given over 1500 talks around the world. He lives in Santa Fe, New Mexico.

William Rambo, Ph.D. An expatriate Texan currently living in Florida, Bill did his initial family therapy training at the Galveston Family Institute with Harry Goolishian and Harlene Anderson in the early 1980s. He is the founder and clinical director of the Fifth Street Counseling Center in Plantation, FL, where he has worked primarily with adult male sexual offenders for the past 16 years. He is a Clinical Member of the Association for the Treatment of Sexual Abusers and a Clinical Member and Approved Supervisor of AAMFT.

Wendel A. Ray, Ph.D. Licensed as a marriage and family therapist, clinical social worker, and professional counselor, Wendel is a Senior Research Fellow and former Director of the Mental Research Institute (MRI) in Palo Alto, California. Founder and first Director of the Don D. Jackson Archive, he is Professor of Marriage and Family Therapy at the University of Louisiana at Monroe. He conducts training nationally and internationally on systemic and brief therapy and communication/interactional theory. Dr. Ray is author or editor of numerous publications, including, most recently, *Selected Papers of the MRI Brief Therapy Center* (with Richard Fisch), *Insight May Cause Blindness & Other Essays of Paul Watzlawick* (with Giorgio Nardone), *Don D. Jackson: Selected Essays at the Dawn of an Era*, and *Propagations* (with John Weakland).

Ursula Pietsch Saqui, Ph.D. A graduate of the MFT program at Purdue University, Ursula is currently Visiting Professor of Psychology at Purdue University Calumet. Her clinical and research interests include abuse, affect regulation, attachment, couples, and MFT supervision and training.

Andy Solovey, ACSW, LISW Andy is clinical director at Scioto Paint Valley Mental Health Center in Chillicothe, Ohio, where he operates a brief therapy training program, established in 1985. A specialist in couples therapy, he is also in private practice at Solutions Counseling in Dublin, Ohio. Andy is a former senior faculty member at the Dayton Institute for Family Therapy, and he is coauthor of *Changing the Rules* and several journal articles on brief therapy. He offers training on state and national levels. His most recent book (with Scott Fraser) is *Second-Order Change in Psychotherapy*.

Tracy Todd, Ph.D. Tracy is President of the Brief Therapy Institute of Denver, Inc. He has appeared in print interviews with such media as *USA Today, Wall Street Journal, Glamour Magazine, Parenting*, and *Psychotherapy*

Finances. He has been honored with many awards, including Outstanding Practice Award, Innovation Award, and Best Practice Award. Tracy conducts seminars nationally on client-based practice building and best practice standards. He holds a doctoral degree from Iowa State University in Marriage and Family Therapy and a master's degree from Texas Tech University in Family Studies. He is a licensed marriage and family therapist and a Clinical Member of AAMFT.

Kate Warner, Ph.D. Kate is Associate Professor of Marriage and Family Therapy and program director of the MFT Program at Valdosta State University. She conducts research and publishes in the areas of family preservation, resilience, violence, juvenile justice, therapy with the homeless, and sexual abuse. She is a licensed marriage and family therapist in Georgia, and a Clinical Member and Approved Supervisor of AAMFT.

Preface

WHEN WE STARTED TEACHING COURSES on human sexuality and sex therapy to graduate students almost 20 years ago, Gary Sanders inspired us with his brilliantly funny, respectful, and passionate approach to working with clients' sexual issues. It seemed at the time (and perhaps not too much has changed) that no one in the field was talking about sex. Gary, bushwhacking through new territory, offered a unique systemic understanding, splashed with his playful and liberating tone and informed by his ongoing clinical work.

By introducing our students to a primer Gary had written on human sexuality (Sanders, 1990) and to Gary's and Karl Tomm's application of cybernetics to clients' sexual dilemmas (Sanders & Tomm, 1989), we gave them a new way to appreciate and understand sex and sex therapy. These writings helped us encourage our students to apply their developing expertise in brief, systemic, and family therapies to their work with couples dealing with sexual issues. With our course and their other training under their belts, they didn't need to refer such cases to a "sex therapist"; they could handle such cases themselves.

It was in part because of the solitary nature of Gary's voice that we decided to create this handbook. Year after year, we struggled to find readings for our students that didn't land them in the midst of a medicalized, pathology-based approach to sex therapy. Coming up with precious few such readings, we finally decided to search out therapists who, like Gary, would be willing to write about their fresh ideas. How delighted we were to discover, as we suspected, that creative therapists *are* working systemically with clients' sexual issues! As you'll soon find out, the work these therapists are doing is brief, strength-based, and often playfully humorous—reflecting the values that Gary embodied so well.

Already undergoing treatment for cancer when we told him of our plans for *Quickies*, Gary kindly declined our offer to contribute a chapter. But though his words are missing from this book, his spirit is very much in evidence throughout. His appreciation for context, his notion of "mutualist" relationships, his ability to deeply honor his clients, his generous invitation into understanding and valuing gay and lesbian relationships, and his irrepressible sense of humor echo through these pages, and you'll read a delightful tale of his clinical work in Rob Doan's chapter on narrative therapy.

We dedicate this book to Gary's memory, with grateful thanks for the gifts he shared with us all.

REFERENCES

Sanders, G. (1990). *Issues of sexuality: A guide to clinical therapeutics*. Unpublished manuscript, University of Calgary, Alberta.

Sanders, G., & Tomm, K. (1989). A cybernetic-systemic approach to problems in sexual functioning. In D. Kantor & B. Okun (Eds.), *Intimate environments* (pp. 346–380). New York: Guilford.

Acknowledgments

IN THE LAST LITTLE WHILE, we've been joking with our contributors that given how long it's taken to finish the book, we should have renamed it *Slowies*. Our authors were generous and patient, and we're grateful to all of them for illuminating their brief therapy innovations with their clients' sexual issues.

Deborah Malmud's eyes lit up when we first approached her with the idea (and title!) for this handbook, and her good humor and editorial acumen helped establish its initial shape and direction. More recently, Michael McGandy's encouragement and guidance have been invaluable in bringing it to completion. Casey Ruble offered thoughtful responses and meticulous copyediting. Kristen Holt-Browning was an excellent midwife to the revised edition.

Our clients and our students provided the inspiration necessary to conceive of and develop the manuscript. Without their questions and stories, we couldn't have made this journey.

Of all our supportive and enthusiastic friends and family (whom we appreciate tremendously!) we feel compelled to single out Erik Bieck, who so cheerfully volunteered (a few gazillion times) to be privately interviewed at Starbucks (by Shelley, of course) on his personal approach to sex. Thanks anyway, Erik, and thanks to the rest of you for your off-color jokes, your suggestive suggestions, and your unsolicited expertise.

Our lovely children, Eric and Jenna, told us tonight that they're excited that we are done. We are, too. Thanks, kids, for hanging in there with us.

Introduction

WE HOPE THE TITLE OF THIS BOOK tickles your sense of humor *and* your therapeutic imagination. If you've read many sex-therapy texts or listened to many couples struggling with sexual issues, you could easily form the impression that solving sexual problems is an excessively serious business, requiring of you, minimally, a white lab coat, grim determination, an extensive background in behaviorist regimens, and psychoanalytic gravity. We and our contributors believe that you and your clients needn't check your humor at the door when touching on sexual issues. Indeed, it might be the very thing that helps turn around a serious, relationship-threatening situation.

The title is also meant to underscore our conviction that the best therapy is often (but not always) the briefest. As soon as possible and when appropriate, we reassure our clients that they are no longer in need of *extended* "professional help." We don't want to abandon them before they have experienced a significant shift in their complaint, but neither do we want to linger, insinuating ourselves into their sexual lives. (An exception to this can be found in Chapter 13, where William Rambo offers excellent contextual reasons for an extended treatment protocol with convicted sexual offenders.) We and our contributors strive to work efficiently, effectively, and respectfully.

Despite these and other commonalities among the authors in this volume, the chapters also display a refreshing array of different practices and strategies for dealing with sexual problems. Whether you're interested in getting ideas on how to approach a specific difficulty (the index can help you search in this way), or you want to sample the range of possibilities offered by particular authors, you will find collected here a creative compendium of brief, client-focused approaches to working with sex-related cases. Informed by theory (regarding both sexuality and systemic thinking) but geared toward practice, each chapter includes clinical case material that offers innovative ways to help clients resolve sexual concerns so that they may celebrate, rather than fear, their sexuality.

In our combined 35 years of experience training systemic therapists, we have often encountered students and colleagues who assume they need to (or perhaps simply prefer to) refer to other clinicians those clients who raise sexual issues in therapy. We think this is unfortunate, given that a systemic framework offers a unique and generative foundation from which to create positive sexual change for clients. Additionally, many brief therapists have been trained to never consider as a clinical issue a topic that clients themselves do not raise; this path unfortunately may give clients the impression that we are unwilling to address issues of intimacy. Because sex is both a physical expression and a passionate one, we may indeed be uncomfortable entering the bedroom with our clients. After all, we don't "know them that well." As one student commented recently, "What do you expect me to do? Just ask them, 'How's your sex life?' I can't do that!" However, the dramatic potential for sex to enhance intimacy and create new layers of passion renders the topic an enormous resource.

A number of different approaches to sex therapy have been proffered since the 1960s, from behavioral (Wolpe, 1966), cognitive-behavioral (Ellis, 1966), quasi-behavioral (Masters & Johnson, 1966), and multimodal (Lazarus, 1988), to psychodynamic (Kaplan, 1979), Bowenian (Schnarch, 1991), object-relations (Scharff, 1982), hypnotic (Araoz, 1982), pharmacological (Kaplan, 1987), and systemic (LoPiccolo, 1989; Sanders & Tomm, 1989) orientations. However, prior to the publication of *Quickies*, few authors working in the Ericksonian-influenced tradition of brief therapy[1]—for example, the Mental Research Institute (MRI; Watzlawick, Weakland, & Fisch, 1974), strategic (Haley, 1976), or solution-focused (deShazer, 1988) approaches—have specifically discussed the treatment of sexual difficulties (see, though, Erickson, 1991a, 1991b; Haley, 1986; Hudson & O'Hanlon, 1991). The previous absence of a well-delineated brief-therapy contribution to sex therapy may have had to do with the brief-therapy assumption that an interactive approach is simply applicable to all problems.

We weren't surprised, then, that when we first approached many of our contributors—guiding lights in the brief therapy world—and asked them to write about their brief, systemic work with clients' sexual issues, they

---

1. Brief therapy as we know it today owes much to the confluence of Milton Erickson's therapeutic techniques and Gregory Bateson's theoretical ideas about communication and change. It would be too unwieldy, but more accurate, to refer to "the Batesonian/Ericksonian-influenced tradition of brief therapy." Jay Haley and John Weakland originally contacted Erickson while engaged in communications research with Bateson in the 1950s.

replied, "But I'm not a sex therapist." Precisely! Just what we were looking for! Brief therapists have unique skills and clinical understandings that offer nonpathologizing, liberating possibilities for clients experiencing sexual difficulties. The authors included in this volume demonstrate personal and clearly contextual ways of understanding sexual concerns, which allow them to honor and utilize their clients' realities and resources.

What this book will not offer is a rehash of standard sexual diagnoses and treatment interventions. There are many conventional tomes that address this in a traditional, and to our ear, pathologizing way. This book, rather, is about freedom and creativity—for you and your clients, alike. We agree with Leonore Tiefer that "it is never the wrong place to recommend ignoring the DSM" (1996, p. 54). The authors in this volume share a passion for accessing the expertise and wisdom of their clients. This points them consistently away from seemingly terminal diagnoses and toward creative conversations that can allow new understandings of their clients' sexual desires and behaviors.

Bill O'Hanlon, in his inimitable style, invites us into Possibility-Land, challenging conventional clinical assumptions, and offering clear guidelines for working collaboratively and inclusively. Yet he advocates that we hold his assumptions lightly, too, always being ready, at a moment's notice, to give them up if they aren't fitting for the client.

Suzanne Iasenza integrates clinical ideas from Ericksonian and narrative traditions, incorporating them in a multicontextual framework for working respectfully with lesbian couples. Suzanne heightens our awareness of the heterosexist and heteronormative attitudes suffusing our culture, and she demonstrates how to use an expanded sexual history to track the sociopolitical influences on clients' lives. She then illustrates techniques for empowering clients who have been marginalized and stigmatized, demonstrating how to find and utilize talents and competencies.

Drawing on the work of Prochaska, DiClemente, and associates, Scott Miller, Karen Donahey, and Mark Hubble point out that people not only experience differing stages of arousal when having sex, but also differing stages of readiness for therapeutic change. What therapists often take to be "resistance" is, in fact, a disjunction between their interventive suggestions and the clients' level of arousal for change. Scott, Karen, and Mark help us see that a good therapist is like a good lover, focusing more on the relationship than on specific techniques.

Using her expertise in Ericksonian hypnosis to explore private worlds, Carol Hicks-Lankton illuminates her clients' potentials with an unwavering, but soft, light. In a sensitive and compelling way, she reaches into the most vulnerable areas of her clients' lives, finding interconnections that allow them to explore and embrace their relationships more fully.

Tracy Todd's provocative chapter challenges much of what passes today for conventional sexual wisdom, pushing us to new awareness of the cultural mythologies that our clients may bring with them to the therapy room, particularly including diagnoses of sexual addictions. Tracy responds respectfully, but also humorously, to these client dilemmas, allowing us entry to his refreshing self-reflexive approach.

Thorana Nelson's chapter offers a kaleidoscopic array of family therapy ideas, refracted through Thorana's warm and engaging presence with her clients. We know no one else who can think and act so comfortably and clearly within and between diverse approaches, attending to her clients' anxiety while she's looking for solutions and monitoring boundaries and problem-saturated stories.

With his laid-back style and soft Texas accent, Monte Bobele is an unhurried and patient therapist. But the pace of his mind is infinitely faster than his speech. Putting the spin of second-order cybernetics on the theoretical premises of MRI practices, Monte shows how to make quick and significant therapeutic progress by honoring the uniqueness of clients' sexual dilemmas, understandings, and interactions.

In our chapter, we explain and illustrate how we invite clients into a different relationship with whatever's troubling them. As they find ways to comfortably connect with their sexual problem, leaving behind their efforts at controlling or eradicating it, clients discover new possibilities for intimacy and pleasure, and the problem is freed up to drift into the periphery of their experience.

Rob Doan seriously questions the appropriateness of the medical model as a bedfellow for sex therapy, persuasively arguing that an eclectic approach to narrative therapy offers a far better choice. By objectifying *problems* rather than *persons* and by working *with* clients, rather than *above* them, Rob is able to invite trust in his therapeutic conversations and help his clients define and claim their preferred ways of being sexual.

Janie Long and Ursula Pietsch Saqui incorporate a social constructionist framework into their work with gay and lesbian couples and provide specific contextual recommendations for assessing and treating same-sex couples. They also remind us of the limited nature of training and education for working with these couples and offer much-needed information to help sensitize us to special client considerations.

Treating MRI and solution-focused therapy as variations of the same process-based orientation, Scott Fraser and Andy Solovey integrate them in their "catalytic" approach to brief therapy. They then demonstrate how these ideas and techniques can be transported to sex therapy, which, they note, has been criticized for lacking an overarching theory. Scott and Andy focus on introducing changes in or exceptions to problematic sexual interactions, finding ways to then support and amplify the resulting shifts in their clients' understandings and actions.

In the first edition of this book, Wendel Ray and Barbara Anger-Díaz completed our tour of brief models by returning us to the beginning—highlighting and explicating the clinical work of one of the original architects of brief therapy, John Weakland. Providing a full-length case study of Weakland's conversation with a severely depressed gay man, Wendel and Barbara illuminate the principles and techniques underlying Weakland's therapeutic method. In this new edition, the conversation doesn't end here. Wendel and Barbara's chapter is followed by two new ones—both remarkably innovative and each a fascinating complement to the other.

In the first new chapter, William Rambo details his therapeutic work over two decades with court-mandated, felony-convicted sexual offenders. Although he sees his clients in treatment groups for an average of five years, Bill still considers himself a "brief therapist," fully embracing Batesonian ideas and MRI assumptions and techniques. His context-sensitive and profoundly respectful approach eschews the "easy relief afforded by condemnation," and, in so doing, he turns traditional treatment models on their head and challenges us all to rethink the comfortable habits of thought that allow us to separate "us" from "them."

Martha Laughlin and Kate Warner share many of Bill's values and therapeutic assumptions, but they bring them to the other side of the sexual abuse equation, working with victims, rather than perpetrators. Scrupulous and creative in orienting relationally to everything they do (and how they describe it), Martha and Kate introduce the notion of "re-membering relationships" as a goal of sexual abuse treatment, as opposed to the more typical commitment to clients' "remembering traumas."

Martha and Kate point out that in the United States, "the treatment of sexual offenders is almost always conducted separately from that of those they abused." This reality only heightens the importance of creating dialogue across the gulf between these two therapeutic arenas. We are delighted to be initiating such an exchange through the inclusion of these two chapters in this updated edition of our volume.

Combined, the authors in Quickies present a wealth of clinical wisdom that we hope will energize your own clinical work and invite you into a new relationship with your clients' sexual concerns. In this sense, this is very *hopeful* book. We are optimistic that as you develop faith and curiosity about clients' sexual lives, your clients will benefit from a more elastic sense of what is possible for them sexually. We hope you will close the last page with an increased understanding of how and why clients present with sexual concerns, with specific skills and ideas about how to address those concerns, and with a new appreciation for the benefits to be gained from exploring the wisdom inherent in clients' sexual choices. We anticipate that your curiosity and your interest will be aroused by the ideas offered within each chapter, but also by the juxtaposition *between* chapters.

REFERENCES

Araoz, D. L. (1982). *Hypnosis and sex therapy.* New York: Brunner/Mazel.

de Shazer, S. (1988). *Clues: Investigating solutions in brief therapy.* New York: Norton

Ellis, A. (1966). *Sex without guilt.* New York: Lancer Books.

Erickson, M. H. (Speaker). (1991a). *Sex therapy: The female.* (J. Haley & M. Richeport, Eds.). (Cassette Recording). New York: Norton.

Erickson, M. H. (Speaker). (1991b). *Sex therapy: The male.* (J. Haley & M. Richeport, Eds.). (Cassette Recording). New York: Norton.

Haley, J. (1976). *Problem-solving therapy.* New York: Harper & Row.

Haley, J. (1986). *Uncommon therapy: The psychiatric techniques of Milton H. Erickson, M.D.* New York: Norton.

Hudson, P. O., & O'Hanlon, W. H. (1991). *Rewriting love stories.* New York: Norton.

Kaplan, H. S. (1979). *Disorders of sexual desire and other new concepts and techniques in sex therapy.* New York: Brunner/Mazel.

Kaplan, H. S. (1987). *Sexual aversion, sexual phobias and panic disorder.* New York: Brunner/Mazel.

Lazarus, A. (1988). A multimodal perspective on problems of sexual desire. In S. R. Leiblum & R. C. Rosen (Eds.), *Sexual desire disorders* (pp. 145–167). New York: Guilford.

LoPiccolo, J. (Speaker). (1989). *The reunification of sexual and marital therapy* (Cassette Recording No. 89-08). Minneapolis, MN: National Council on Family Relations.

Masters, W. H., & Johnson, V. E. (1966). *Human sexual response.* Boston: Little, Brown.

Sanders, G. & Tomm, K. (1989). A cybernetic-systemic approach to problems in sexual functioning. In D. Kantor & B. Okun (Eds.), *Intimate environments* (pp. 346–380). New York: Guilford Press.

Scharff, D. E. (1982). *The sexual relationship: An object relations view of sex and the family.* Boston: Routledge & Kegan Paul.

Schnarch, D. M. (1991). *Constructing the sexual crucible.* New York: Norton.

Tiefer, L. (1996). Towards a feminist sex therapy. In M. Hall (Ed.), *Sexualities* (pp. 53–64). Binghamton, NY: Haworth Press.

Watzlawick, P., Weakland, J. H., & Fisch, R. (1974). *Change: Principles of problem formation and problem resolution.* New York: Norton.

Wolpe, J. (1966). *Psychotherapy by reciprocal inhibition.* Stanford, CA: Stanford University Press.

Quickies

one

Come Again?
From Possibility Therapy
to Sex Therapy

Bill O'Hanlon

I CALLED THIS CHAPTER "COME AGAIN?" not only to be in keeping with the punning title of this compilation, but also to highlight two important aspects of brief sex therapy. First, the title points to the collaborative nature of the approach. Not unlike sex itself, therapy works best when the people involved touch base with one another about preferences and experiences throughout the encounter. I'm forever checking in with clients, making sure I've heard them correctly.

Second, I often meet with clients only a few times—even when we're addressing sexual issues—never assuming that they'll need to make another appointment (unless they tell me). At the end of each session, I ask, "Do you want to come again or have you gotten what you came for?" As a brief therapist, I consider myself an expert on helping people make changes, but I don't consider myself one when it comes to the choices they make or the preferences they hold. Clients are the experts on their lives.

I used to refer to my particular style of working as "solution-oriented therapy," but I've changed it to "possibility therapy," in large part to distinguish it from "solution-focused therapy," with which it shares some but not all values and methods. Although this chapter applies some of the basic premises of possibility therapy to sex therapy, a more thorough discussion of "possibilities" is articulated elsewhere (O'Hanlon & Beadle, 1999; O'Hanlon & Bertolino, 1998; O'Hanlon & Bertolino, 1999).

PREMISES OF POSSIBILITY THERAPY

People are influenced, but not determined, *by the past.* Possibility therapy challenges the all-too-common assumption that the past causes the present and future, holding that people have choices about what they do—choices that are not predetermined. That is, people may be influenced by what happened in the past or by their genetic or biochemical makeup, but they also have some freedom to make choices within those influences and constraints.*

People are influenced by their sense of what is possible for their future. Some approaches, like cognitive therapy, start with the assumption that thoughts cause feelings. Others, like psychodynamic or emotionally focused approaches, espouse the notion that feelings (either unconscious and unrecognized or within awareness) drive or determine behavior. Possibility therapy holds that people can be strongly influenced (but not determined) not only by thoughts and feelings in general, but also, more specifically, by their sense of their future (or futures). What they believe is possible and what they think is likely are both powerfully and experientially connected to the future they can create.

At any moment, unless physically compelled by someone who holds power over them or unless they are prevented by physical incapacitation, people choose the actions they take. Feelings sometimes come unbidden and are not controllable, and thoughts and fantasies are often automatic. However, actions, as the existentialists recognized, always have an element of choice. People are able to choose what they do with their bodies.

People are more likely to cooperate when they and their feelings and points of view are validated and respected. It is crucial that we therapists validate, respect, and take seriously our clients' "negative" or "resistant" feelings, responses, or points of view. Because people tend not to change in the presence of blame and invalidation, we need to take the time and make the effort to ensure that our clients feel listened to, accepted, and understood.

Therapists can never know the truth about people, because we are always influencing what aspects of that truth get spoken and heard. Because we always bring perceptual and assessment biases to the therapy process, therapists can never be truly "neutral," and we can never precisely determine

---

* Masters and Johnson (1970) similarly focused more on the present and future than on the past. Their psychotherapeutic model was one of the first to do so.

what is really happening for our clients. We are always present and influential in bringing forth the particular "truth" or image of the problem that emerges from our therapy conversations.

This is both bad news and good news. The bad news is that we give our clients problems. What they say and what we assess is strongly influenced by our questions, by what we attend to, by what we fail to notice or respond to, and by our theoretical bias. The good news is that in the process of giving our clients problems, we have an opportunity to co-create problem definitions that are inherently solvable.

No one knows for certain what causes behavioral, psychological, emotional, or relational problems, although there is no shortage of people who claim to know. Whereas almost every psychological or psychotherapy model claims to possess the truth about what causes problems, possibility therapy remains causally agnostic. That is, it proposes no grand theory about the origins or driving forces behind problems and, therefore, no grand theory about how they should be resolved.

I find it quite comforting to realize that nobody really knows what causes or drives human behavior. But even though the jury is still out, an amazing number of individuals are afflicted with what might be called "delusions of certainty," believing and wanting to convince others that they have, indeed, discovered the answers and the truth.

In this chapter, I provide some working ideas for interventions, but I consider none of them to be universally true or applicable, and I'm quite willing and happy to abandon them if they do not yield results or if other methods or ideas work better in a particular situation.

What we do in therapy either works or doesn't work. If it doesn't work, it's best to first try something different rather than deciding the person, couple, or family is unmotivated or unable to change. If an individual, couple, or family is not changing, I initially attribute it to a limitation in my approach or in my flexibility. Obviously, if new methods or approaches consistently yield the same lack of results, I may begin to entertain hypotheses about "resistance" or lack of motivation or "secondary gain." But I only do this in the spirit of helping people make changes they say they want to make, not to blame them or to justify my lack of results.

There are many pathways to change. No one technique, method, or philosophy works for everyone, despite many claims to the contrary. If there is no universal truth or method, then therapists are best off remaining flexible. Recognizing that clients are almost always more complex and variable than any psychological theory or psychotherapeutic method, I try not to get too attached to any particular idea or way of working with them.

What helps create change is not necessarily an indication of what caused the problem. Sometimes my clients and I find and put into place a solution without ever determining the original cause of the problem. Other times we agree on the probable origin, but the solution bears little or no relationship to it. Still other times, we discover a solution that is clearly related to the problem.

All experience is okay. Actions are either okay (ethical, safe, and acceptable) or not. I distinguish between what people do—which may be right or wrong, helpful or unhelpful, good or bad—from what they think, feel, or fantasize. I consider all automatic and internal experiences (feelings, thoughts, fantasies, sensations, imaginings) to be acceptable and okay, so I don't expend any effort trying to get rid of or "fix" them. Accepting and supporting clients and all their experience, I focus treatment on their actions and on points of view and contexts that aren't supporting the change process.

METHODS OF POSSIBILITY-INFORMED SEX THERAPY

Please bear in mind that the above assumptions are just that: assumptions, not truths. I hold my premises very lightly; I'm ready to drop them in the face of evidence that they are not working, are invalidating people, or are blocking the change process. I am constantly on guard for assumptions and hypotheses holding me, rather than the other way around.

In treating people's sexual concerns, I put my assumptions into practice through five basic moves:

- Normalizing;
- Validating and giving permission;
- Changing actions;
- Changing patterns (of viewing, doing, or context);
- Inclusion and permission.

Normalizing

A man who had just been diagnosed with high blood pressure came to see me for hypnosis. He had begun exercising during his lunch hour and eating more healthy foods, and his doctor had suggested he seek some form of stress reduction like hypnosis. During the first session, he mentioned in passing that, over the last year, he had been experiencing some impotence, possibly due to his blood pressure problem.

We worked together for several sessions, spread out over three months, at which point he told me that his blood pressure had been back in the "normal" range for a month or so and that his doctor thought everything looked good. He attributed a certain part of his progress to the hypnosis we had done, so I thanked him and asked if we had accomplished his goal. He said we had.

"Anything else I can help you with?"

"Well, actually there is. You remember that I mentioned that I had had some impotence. Well, even though the blood pressure is better, nothing has changed in that regard."

"Oh," I replied. "So is that something you would like to work on here?"

"Yes," he said.

I asked him if he had had any discussions with his wife about the issue and he said he had. She assured him that she was okay with his impotence and that it didn't bother her and she didn't take it personally. She liked sex, but wasn't desperate for it and gave him lots of room. Sometimes they engaged in oral or manual sex when he didn't get or maintain erections, and sometimes they just stopped.

"Do you think she would be willing to come in here and help us work on the problem?"

"Yes, I think she would."

I told him I thought that would be best, because she could give me more information and perhaps be part of working out a plan to help the situation. He agreed to speak to her and bring her in for the next session.

"Meanwhile," I said, "I just want you to know, since you seemed pretty embarrassed when you brought this up, that many men suffer from occasional bouts of impotence. In fact, it has happened to me. I lost my erection with my partner, and when I tried to make myself get hard, it only made matters worse. I kept trying, but nothing was happening. I told my partner what was going on and explained that I was putting too much pressure on myself, and we both agreed that, in order to take the pressure off, we would not expect any intercourse or erections. Finally I began to get erections again, but I often found myself self-consciously watching myself and wondering whether I would maintain the erection. Gradually, over the course of the next year or so, that self-consciousness diminished and finally went away. So one of the areas I would want to talk to you and your wife about next session is all the ways you experience internal or external pressure. We'll try to find ways for both of you to take the pressure off."

He arrived at my office for the next session alone. I was surprised and asked him why he hadn't brought his wife along as we had agreed. He told me, "Because the problem is gone."

"Gone?" I said.

"Yes, just hearing that you had the same problem made me realize it wasn't all that bad and I stopped worrying about it. Once I stopped worrying about it, I was able to get erections easily."

This story illustrates how helpful it can be to normalize and give permission for sexual desire, feelings, and fantasies (or the lack of any or all of them)—in short, for whatever happens in the person's experience. However, as I mentioned earlier and will illustrate later, I don't always normalize or give permission for *behaviors*.

Validating and Giving Permission

I'd like to use two cases to illustrate the importance of validating experience and giving permission. At first blush, the cases seem to be opposites, because their outcomes were 180 degrees apart, but they both illustrate the principle of change though validation and acceptance of feelings, fantasies, thoughts, and any inner experience of sexuality.

A man asked for an emergency appointment, and when he arrived, he said in an urgent voice that he wanted some help because he was a latent homosexual. I asked him what had led him to think this. With shame in his voice, he explained that during sex with his wife over the past few months, he had begun seeing images of naked men. I told him I wasn't sure that this made him a latent homosexual. In therapy, I explained, I was privy to the inner life of many people, and what I had learned is that human beings have a lot of strange things floating through their minds, not all of which are meaningful. I asked him what he would think if, while having sex with his wife, he had images of fire trucks in his mind. Would that make him a latent fireman? He laughed and said he guessed not.

I use humor a fair amount in therapy, seeing people, as do many brief therapists, as resilient, not fragile. Humor can indirectly communicate this view to clients, which may reassure them that they aren't crazy or broken and that the problem isn't as overwhelming as they might have feared.

"Let me guess," I ventured. "When these images first happened, you tried to get rid of them, right?"

"Yes," he replied.

"And the more you tried to get rid of them, the more frequent and intense they became, right?"

"Well," he said, "what I didn't tell you is that they have started to haunt me at various times during the day, even when I'm not having sex with my wife."

"Maybe you are homosexual and haven't come to terms with it," I allowed. "But I don't think we can know that without doing an experiment. For the next while, I'd suggest that you deliberately fantasize about naked men as often as is feasible. Sometimes, the more we try to get rid of a feeling, thought, or fantasy, the more it grows in intensity. Let's see what happens when you stop trying to get rid of it."

In saying "Maybe you are a homosexual," I wasn't trying to be paradoxical, and when I asked him to deliberately fantasize about naked men, I wasn't "prescribing the symptom." I genuinely considered it possible that he would discover he was gay, at which point he'd need to come to terms with it. But I also thought his attempted solution could be responsible for creating his intrusive thoughts, in which case the experiment would take care of them. As a brief therapist, I'm interested in changing things rather than in spending months analyzing clients' internal experience. Often the results from an experiment can make the focus for intervention clearer.

As it turned out, the experiment made sense to the man, and when he tried it, he discovered that the images gradually disappeared, as did his concerns about his sexual orientation.

Another client, John, was brought in by his family after he'd threatened to kill himself. A developmentally disabled adult, he lived independently in a subsidized apartment, handling his own money and even balancing his checkbook. Occasionally he would overspend, become panicked, and call his parents, who would give him a lecture on being more responsible and give him some money to make it through until his next paycheck. He would then begin to complain that his disability prevented him from making enough money, gradually working himself into a state in which he would threaten to kill himself.

The family and I worked to ensure that when John called, they neither rushed into giving him money nor gave him a lecture. John agreed to work with his mother to create and stick with a budget so his parents would see him as more capable (something he wanted very much, because he complained that they treated him like a child). We also had some discussions about John's hopes and dreams, which elicited much fear from his mother. It so happened that 10 years earlier, just after high school, John had enrolled in a college and failed all his classes.

His mother was afraid that if John were to once again fail community college classes, he could again become suicidal. John assured his mother that he'd matured and become more emotionally stable in the last decade and that at first he'd only audit his classes. With this reassurance, his mother reluctantly agreed with John's plan, and John became more hopeful about his future.

After a few family sessions, I thought we were about done with therapy, but John surprised me by requesting that we meet individually. During the session, I asked him what he was there for, and he answered by asking me in a very loud voice, "Do you think it is okay if someone is gay?"

"It's okay with me," I replied.

"Well, I'm gay, and a lot of people in my family wouldn't accept that."

"Have you ever told anyone in your family?"

"No."

"Is it important for you to tell them?"

"Well, none of them know. You're the first person I've ever told. I think it's important to be honest."

"Well, is there any one family member you can tell who you think would accept your being gay?"

"Maybe my sister." We went on to make a plan about how John could tell his sister.

Finding out that John hadn't yet had a romantic/sexual relationship, I discussed with him various strategies for getting a date, dealing with rejection, and practicing safe sex. After we made a plan for how he could tell his sister, he came out to her. She was very accepting and agreed with him that the rest of the family wasn't safe to tell. She became his trusted adviser and confidant, and he never again threatened suicide. When I later asked him, he said that not coming out had played a large part in his suicidal feelings. Telling me, his sister, and some people at work had relieved his sense of desperation.

Both of these cases illustrate the importance of helping people accept and validate their feelings and fantasies, freeing them from shame or intrusive, compulsive obsessions. I consider *all* inner experience to be okay, but I am clear and firm with my clients that although some actions are okay, others aren't. It is okay to fantasize about rape. It is *not okay* to rape. It is okay to have the impulse to have sex without protection. It is *not okay* to have unsafe sex.

I once saw a client who found herself swept away in the passion of her sexual encounters and failed to insist that her partner use a condom. In the cold light of the next day, she suffered terribly from fears that she was pregnant or had been given a sexually transmitted disease. However, the next time she was faced with a partner who wanted unprotected sex, she'd once again sacrifice her safety for his pleasure.

During one particular session, we made an agreement for the following evening, when she anticipated seeing her current condom-hating boyfriend. If she felt that she was about to give in and have unprotected sex, she would excuse herself for a moment and call me, so I could remind her of her intention to stop the pattern. Just the thought that she would have to confess that she was doing something stupid and self-destructive was enough for her to insist that her partner use a condom.

Changing Actions

Most people think they have to *feel* sexual before they can *act* sexual, but because sexuality is such a mixture of the inner (feelings, desire, fantasies, sensations) and the outer (actions, techniques, body positions, patterns of relating), taking sexual action can stir sexual feelings. For example, sometimes, late at night, I am tired, but if either my partner or I initiate foreplay, it often sparks desire and arousal. So instead of having my clients wait for sexual feelings to spontaneously arise, I often suggest they take action to jump-start them.

An empty-nest couple, Jake and Lorraine, came to see me, concerned that the passion had gone out of their marriage. Together they had raised a blended family of several children who had grown up and, in recent years, left home. They were both successful in their careers and they considered themselves friends, but they hadn't had sex for many years. They had never really talked about this issue, but when they finally spoke about it in my office, they speculated that because of their weight gain, they weren't as attracted to each other as they had been.

Both of them had recently begun fitness programs and healthier diets that had resulted in small weight losses and promised more, but this would probably take months, if not years. Lorraine said that Jake's weight, although certainly making him less attractive, was not really an issue for her, but she assumed that he had a problem with her size. Jake reluctantly confessed that her weight was an issue, but this didn't seem fair to him, given his own gains. Still, it was true.

They told me that their sex life had once been "hot" and frequent. Their relationship had begun as an affair, which had led to the breakup of their previous marriages. Even when the kids were around, they had found the time, energy, and creativity to have frequent sex in various places in the house.

Wanting Jake and Lorraine to move into action as soon as feasibly possible, and knowing that taking action and feeling desire are often intertwined,

I asked them if they were interested in trying an experiment. If willing, they should take some time to talk about the "hottest" sexual encounters they'd shared and to try to recreate the actions involved in those incidents, regardless of their initial level of excitement and without waiting for any further weight loss. I told them that they might have to start slowly, with back massages, just to find a level of comfort with each other's bodies again. But to my surprise, they went home and had sex (for the first time in about 10 years!) that evening. They decided that weight wasn't as much of an issue as they had thought, and they continued to create (or recreate) a passionate and creative sex life with each other.

Changing Patterns (of Viewing, Doing, or Context)

Alison and Ryan came in, complaining about their constant bickering. They had five children and couldn't imagine ever breaking up, but they drove each other crazy. Alison worked in the evenings, and when she returned home at 11:30 or so, she usually liked to unwind by sitting in the living room, watching television. Ryan, hoping she would come to bed in time for them to have sex, would begin a nightly ritual of opening the bedroom door, looking out pointedly at his wife, and tsk, tsk, tsking at her.

Livid at the pressure Ryan put on her, Alison, despite enjoying sex herself, would ignore him, silently vowing that hell would freeze over before she would have sex with him. The standoff would turn into bickering, with Ryan complaining about her avoiding him.

I searched for other issues between them, but this nightly interaction seemed to be the main cause of their problems. After getting Alison to tell Ryan that he was off base about her lack of interest in sex, I discovered that he didn't have a clue that his tsking was the main catalyst for the bickering and lack of sex. I patiently explained that he could have more sex with his wife and decrease the bickering if he would just stop opening the door to the bedroom and tsking. For one week, he ceased and desisted, and, lo and behold, his wife initiated sex several times. Amazingly, he fell back into the tsking habit again for several weeks, but finally gave it up after further discussions.

One might ask why he fell back into tsking. But that is precisely the type of question I try to avoid. I might have asked Ryan about it if had he persisted despite its being clear that his actions didn't work. But I don't speculate or hypothesize about the underlying cause. Instead, I engage in conversations and suggest experiments that are designed to break unhelpful sexual interactions.

A woman who had been sexually abused began to have flashbacks while having sex with her husband. She would experience herself once again being raped by her father, who had both molested and raped her when she was a child. While discussing the circumstances in which the flashbacks were likely to happen, we discovered that the couple always had sex with the lights off. The simple change of keeping a small light on in the bathroom off their bedroom helped her to realize that she was having sex with the man she loved rather than being abused by her father. Experimenting still further, the couple discovered that having the wife touch her husband's face while they were having sex also helped keep her grounded in the present. Rather than analyze or speculate about the causes of the flashbacks (beyond the obvious connections to the abuse), we explored ways of differentiating the present from the past.

Another couple were so upset after the wife experienced a flashback of a rape that they stopped having sex for several months. Checking on their pattern of interaction, I discovered that it had begun when the man held onto his wife's upper arms during intercourse. The rapist had restrained her in a similar way. Changing the pattern of their interaction—ensuring that he didn't restrain her and starting with her being on top during intercourse—helped them reclaim their sex life from that past.

Inclusion and Permission

Another element of possibility therapy is to help people embrace whatever they might be experiencing, including seemingly contradictory feelings and beliefs. This reflects the earlier emphasis on validating feelings and desires but takes it a bit further.

A woman came to see me after doing something that surprised and perplexed her. Engaged to a man she'd lived with for several years, she had trouble staying aroused when they had sex. They liked and loved one another, and she enjoyed having sex with him, but within several minutes of beginning she would feel unaccountably scared and would just "shut down."

Sexually abused for some years by a much older cousin, starting at the age of six, she had spent five years in therapy as an adult. Her fiancé knew about what had happened and they had discussed it many times, but this hadn't resolved the situation. After shutting down, she would usually go ahead and finish intercourse for the sake of her partner's pleasure, but she herself wouldn't feel much.

Precipitating her seeking help from me was an experience she'd had while attending a conference in a distant city. The second night of being there, she happened to get into the elevator at the same time as an attendee to whom she'd felt attracted. A spark passed between them, and they ended up having intercourse in the elevator. Having always been faithful to her fiancé, she was troubled and surprised by her actions and perplexed that she'd had an orgasm despite the obvious brevity of the encounter.

During the course of treatment, she confessed that for years she had not considered herself to have been sexually abused because she had "enjoyed" what occurred with her cousin. When I asked her to elaborate, she told me that she'd experienced pleasure and orgasms during the abuse and had felt excited by doing something she knew her controlling mother wouldn't approve of. In her early adult years, she became involved in S&M (sado-masochism), deriving great pleasure from being hurt during sex. She finally left the scene when it became too violent and dangerous.

I usually use hypnosis when working with automatic and experiential symptoms, so we started with that. She realized that she found it hard to be treated kindly *and* have sexual pleasure and orgasm, so we worked toward her being able to include feeling connected and loved at the same time she was experiencing sexual pleasure. She also worked on noticing when she began to get scared during sex, allowing herself to tell her fiancé and let him know that they needed to stop.

She discovered over time that it was okay not to have sex when someone else wanted to (a new realization for her emotionally, although she'd known it intellectually) and also that it was okay to feel connected *and* have an orgasm. She also learned that she didn't need to be "bad" (as in being punished in the S&M scene or having forbidden sex with a stranger in an elevator) to feel good.

In helping people with sexual concerns, I make it possible for them to include and feel permission for what were previously incompatible or contradictory feelings, experiences, or beliefs (e.g., I am this weight and I am attractive; I can feel attracted to someone and not have sex with him or her; I can be attracted to both men and women even though I have decided to live a gay lifestyle). I join with them, validating any "negative," resistant, or troubling experiences (along with, of course, any that are positive, hopeful, and cooperative), and I help them articulate and name the complexities of their experiences and selves.

Life is rarely black and white, all or nothing. "Anger and tenderness, my selves," wrote Adrienne Rich in her poem "Integrity," "And now I can believe they live in me as angels, not as polarities." Part of what therapists can do is look around, explore, and shine a light on the territory surrounding the problem to notice and name the complex reality that has been unnoticed and unnamed. We can also make liberal use of the word "and," inviting clients to experience two seemingly contradictory feelings or states without putting them in conflict.

- "You can feel tense *and* you could relax."
- "You might think you can't change *and* you might be surprised to discover that you are changing."
- "You want to change *and* you are afraid to change."

This contrasts with how most people put things together:

- "I have to feel this *or* feel that."
- "I feel this, *but* I should be feeling that."

Language and time steer us towards one-dimensional definitions of our experience and ourselves. By being inclusive, therapists invite clients to experience polar opposites simultaneously, going beyond mere acceptance of contradictions to a more expansive embracing of the self. Such widening of clients' sense of self can break inner logjams.

I remember being in the midst of a difficult treatment with a woman who had been severely and persistently abused as a child. Because she lived a 6-hour drive from me, we met every month or so for a 3-hour session. She had struggled with suicidal impulses for many years and the work we were doing was leaving her emotionally raw. She called one day and told me she couldn't go on with the therapy. "You are getting too close and I feel too vulnerable. Plus you are too far away, and I can't come easily for an emergency appointment if I need one."

"I understand," I replied, "and I think this isn't a good time to end treatment. So let's talk for a minute and see if we can get you through until the next appointment. You can find a way to be vulnerable and protected. And you can modulate the distance and closeness to make it work for you. I can be right there with you while I am here. You can be right here with me while you are there. I can be as far away as you need me to be and as close as you need me to be. And I can be far away and close at the same time."

I went on in a similar vein for a few minutes, trying to establish in her a *feeling* sense that she could in some almost magical way have her cake and eat it, too—she could want me *and* not want me, feel herself very close to me *and* very far away, and, somehow, in this profoundly ambivalent frame of mind, *still move forward* with therapy. It seemed to work. "Okay," she said, "that was helpful. You're right. I can do that. I'll see you next appointment."

Many people in therapy seem to get stuck with an either/or experience. This client thought she had to be either vulnerable *or* safe, but there were situations in which she'd be able to be vulnerable *and* safe. She said she felt that I was getting too close, and the opposite also seemed true—she felt I was too far away, both emotionally and physically. So I included both possibilities, instead of one or the other.

When people first come to therapy, they often seem to have two or more aspects of themselves trying, and failing, to squeeze through a small doorway at the same time. Unable to simultaneously accommodate, say, a desire to change and a fear of change, they stay stuck. Inclusion expands the doorway, leaving room for both aspects—and perhaps others—to move freely. Merely articulating this double reality is often enough to free clients to move on.

A FINAL NOTE: WAS IT GOOD FOR YOU?

I have given some general brief therapy strategies that can be used with sexual issues, but taken out of context, they could seem rather directive. In my work, I usually let my clients lead me. I have some ideas of what I could do, many of which I have detailed here, but I find that the clients usually have better ideas or, at the very least, responses to my suggestions, possibilities, and ideas that lead me to continue in the direction we are proceeding or to change course entirely.

I listen closely to their concerns, trying not to add any of my own theories about why they are struggling, and then I let their preferences, ideas, and responses guide me. Because it is so hard to capture this collaborative process on paper, writings about therapy are much more structured than the sessions themselves. I thus offer the ideas put forth in this chapter as tentative hints and possibilities rather than definitive strategies.

REFERENCES

Masters, W. H., & Johnson, V. E. (1970). *Human sexual inadequacy*. New York: Little, Brown.

O'Hanlon, B., & Beadle, S. (1999). *Guide to possibility land: 51 respectful methods for doing brief therapy*. New York: Norton.

O'Hanlon, B., & Bertolino, B. (1998). *Invitation to possibility-land: A teaching seminar with Bill O'Hanlon*. Philadelphia: Brunner/Mazel.

O'Hanlon, S., & Bertolino, B. (1999). *Evolving possibilities: Bill O'Hanlon's selected papers*. Philadelphia: Brunner/Mazel.

two
———

Multicontextual Sex Therapy with Lesbian Couples

Suzanne Iasenza

A s a clinician who works with many lesbian couples, I've observed that they often enter sex therapy carrying the unrecognized poisonous effects of familial and societal sexism and homophobia. Many of them are hard-pressed to specify how their adult sexuality, in particular, contains beliefs, feelings, and behaviors influenced by antihomosexual and sexist biases. Nevertheless, many know something about the mental health field's woeful history of characterizing homosexuality as perverse, immature, or abnormal—enough, at least, to be rightfully wary of coming to a therapist for help.

Given these historical contextual variables and their powerful effects on the lives of lesbians, I believe that effective sex therapy with lesbian couples needs to incorporate a multicontextual perspective (Carter, 1993; Carter & McGoldrick, 1999)—one that not only views presenting problems from an individual or couple perspective, but also includes an appreciation of the familial, community, and societal influences that contribute to presenting problems. Such a perspective gives lesbian clients the immediate message that I, as their therapist, am aware of and appreciate systemic contributions to problems and that I do not assume they are solely responsible for having or being the problem. This is a particularly important stance for therapists to take when working with client populations who have historically been marginalized and stigmatized.

15

In this chapter I will present a rationale for why I incorporate a multicontextual perspective in my sex therapy with lesbian couples, and I will also discuss how I integrate well-established techniques such as White and Epston's (1990) externalization process and Erickson's utilization approach (Zeig, 1994) to amplify the effects of therapy. Clinical cases will help demonstrate how this integrative approach creates positive changes in the sexual lives of lesbian couples.

THE MULTICONTEXTUAL PERSPECTIVE

Developed by Carter (1993) at the Family Institute of Westchester, the multicontextual model provides a framework that attends to all systemic levels in assessing and understanding couples and families and their problems. Based on Bowenian (1978) family therapy concepts, the model looks at the "self in context," including how an individual develops within the web of interpersonal and societal relationships. Individual beliefs, feelings, and behaviors are considered within the context of larger systems: the immediate family (including the couple), the extended family, the community and social connections, and the larger society. Carter and McGoldrick's (1999) later work incorporated the multicontextual perspective within a family life cycle frame, providing a comprehensive understanding of the complexities of human developmental change at every systemic level over the lifespan.

Carter and McGoldrick achieve two significant things with this expanded model that I find particularly relevant in working with lesbian couples. First, they redefine the family to include and celebrate cultural diversity and diverse family forms. They acknowledge the limited nature of couple and family models that focus only on one family form: the "white, Anglo, middle-class, nuclear family of a once-married heterosexual couple, their children, and their extended family" (1999, p. xv). They go on to explore how race, ethnicity, religion, class, gender, and sexual orientation influence stages and development of family life. As Carter puts it, "what we're talking about here is not just listing differences— different races, different ethnicities, different genders, different sexual orientations. . . . It's a power hierarchy in which added power and access is given to some, and others are excluded. . . . After we get a handle on the basics, we focus on where this family or person's place is in society, and if they don't have much power in our society, how does that affect their relationships?" (cited in Markowitz, 2001, p. 14).

Second, Carter and McGoldrick (1999) "widen the lens" of therapy beyond the traditional levels of individual, couple, or family units, assessing both stressors and resources and intervening at every systemic level, from the individual to the community and beyond, including sociocultural, political, and economic contexts. They pay homage to the power of language by intentionally changing the language of systemic levels to reflect contemporary family forms: The "nuclear family" becomes the "immediate family," which covers nuclear, single-parent, unmarried, remarried, and gay and lesbian households. Further, they use the term "couples therapy" rather than "marital therapy" to acknowledge unmarried heterosexual couples or, in the case of gays and lesbians, couples who are denied the option of marrying legally.

A multicontextual perspective acknowledges the developmental challenges facing lesbian individuals, couples, and families, attending to how sexism and homophobia affect relationship functioning, and how familial, community, and societal forces affect development (Iasenza, Colucci, & Rothberg, 1996; Laird, 1993, 1996; Martin, 1993; Roth, 1989; Slater, 1995; Slater & Mencher, 1991). In theory and in practice, I strive to learn about and incorporate the unique experience of lesbian women, including how their sexual interactions may differ from those of gay male or heterosexual couples, and how familial, political, and social forces affect their sexual behavior (Iasenza, 2000; Schreurs, 1994).

THE EXPANDED SEXUAL HISTORY

One way I bring a multicontextual perspective into my practice is by taking an in-depth sexual history from my clients. I prefer to do this when I first start working with a couple, meeting with each partner separately. If I were to gather the information with them together, I could help them increase their understanding and empathy for each other; however, I want to give them the opportunity to share information with me without having to worry about the impact it may have on their partner. I do, however, ask couples to share their "history highlights" with each other, which encourages mutual appreciation.

I also take time when I meet back with the couple to identify how sociopolitical contexts have influenced their sexual identities and feelings, helping them to grasp the cultural pressures they experience. I often ask, for example, "How do you think growing up and living in a homophobic and sexist society has affected your relationship?" Such questions make overt my assumption that being gay or lesbian in our culture often affects the development of intimate relationships and a positive sense of one's sexuality.

Below is an expanded version of a standard sexual history (Wincze & Carey, 1991) that includes attention to larger systemic issues (shown in italics). I should point out that I take care to inquire into these areas not by posing lists of questions, but by engaging in a fluid therapeutic conversation.

Childhood

I ask about family members/relations; parents' relationship; *religiosity, race, ethnicity, and class*; first memory of sex; messages about sex; how affection was shown; how nudity/body issues were handled; *how boys and girls were treated*; *gender identity/role*; peer relations; *first sexual feelings (same/opposite sex)*; masturbation; peer sexual play; sex education; any unpleasant or disturbing sexual experiences; medical treatments in self or family members; sexual/physical/emotional abuse or neglect; and substance use.

Adolescence

I explore peer relationships; experience of puberty, body image, and menstruation; pregnancies or abortions; wet dreams; dating; self-esteem; *sexual experiences (heterosexual and homosexual)*; *coming-out experiences*; first intercourse/sexual experiences; fantasies; substance use; school experience; and hobbies/interests.

Adulthood

I take a medical history (including psychiatric treatment or psychotherapy) and ask about relationship histories; sexual experiences; masturbation; fantasies; dreams; sexual problems (in self or partners); sexually transmitted infections (STIs); HIV and safer sex; birth control; children; menopause; medications; substance use; occupational history; peer/family relations; and *coming-out experiences at home and work*.

Community Contact

I want to learn about *friends and neighbors (heterosexual/homosexual)*; *involvement in religious, educational, and government institutions and self-help groups*; *political activity (past and present)*; *recreation/cultural groups*; *volunteer work*; *and any connections to the gay/lesbian community*.

Societal Influences

I attend to *political, social, and economic issues*; *and effects of biases based on race, ethnicity, gender, class, sexual orientation, religion, age, disability, and family form*.

Current Sexual Functioning

I always attend to details about current sexual functioning and difficulties (including any changes therewith); sexual preferences; likes and dislikes about the partner or self; monogamy, extrarelationship sexual experiences; gender *identity role*; *sexual orientation*; nonsexual activities (individually and as a couple); communication about sex; intimacy; affection; and other relevant relationship issues.

A MULTICONTEXTUAL PERSPECTIVE AND BRIEF THERAPY

Brief therapy (de Shazer, 1988, 1991, 1994; O'Hanlon & Weiner-Davis, 1988; Weiner-Davis, 1995), whether for sexual problems or more generic ones, is based on assumptions that are highly compatible with a multicontextual family therapy perspective. Perhaps the most important commonality is the focus on empowering couples to find ways to improve their lives. An antidiagnosis, antipathological stance is essential in working with lesbian couples, many of whom are sensitive to possible pathologizing by mental health professionals who, consciously or unconsciously, communicate beliefs that lesbian relationships are inadequate compared to heterosexual ones. I work to maintain a basic respect for clients and attempt to build an equal and collaborative therapeutic relationship that encourages agency and activity from the couple. Women clients need as many experiences as possible that support them as subjects rather than objects of therapeutic change.

Both brief therapy and multicontextual work emphasize the need for a good fit between therapist and client; such a fit requires the therapist to be flexible in the timing and direction of the work. A multicontextual perspective permits me to gradually develop goals and interventions, as initial sessions consist of gathering information on multiple systemic levels. I may vary the level at which I intervene, depending on the comforts, needs, and resources of a particular couple.

Multicontextual data-gathering may seem antithetical to a brief therapy process, yet the opposite is true. My attention to the ways that various systemic levels help create or maintain problems permits me to rapidly and efficiently help a couple make positive shifts that might not be possible if I focused only on the presenting problem at the level of the couple.

CASE EXAMPLE

Jan and Sue came to see me, complaining of sexual infrequency and loss of sexual desire. They hadn't had sex for eight months, and prior to that they had made love approximately once a month, which was okay with Jan but not with Sue, who had initiated the therapy. Frustrated and angry about their "dead sex life," Sue accused Jan in the first session of being too sexually passive and insecure, despite the fact that neither of them was initiating. This was the first time Jan had heard about Sue's sexual dissatisfaction, so she was understandably defensive and confused. Both wondered if they just weren't sexually compatible anymore. A therapist who focused only at the level of the couple would have diagnosed Jan and Sue as suffering from sexual desire disorder and proceeded to explore how they could revitalize their sexual relationship. But my initial history-taking revealed a more complex picture.

Each growing up in alcoholic families, both women were alcoholics in recovery—Jan had been sober for 10 years and Sue for six. They met in an Alcoholics Anonymous (AA) group, where Jan had been Sue's sponsor. A very intense therapeutic bond had shifted to friendship and ultimately to love. As the relationship developed and they moved in together, they decided to attend separate AA groups, which initially worked well for both of them. From the beginning of their getting together, their social lives had revolved around AA meetings and friends, most of whom were heterosexual and did not know that they were anything more than just "roommates."

A major shift began when, four years into the relationship, Sue decided to switch to a gay/lesbian AA group that met at the local Gay and Lesbian Community Center. This switch became possible as a result of Sue's having explored, in individual therapy, her internalized homophobia and its contribution to her choice of living an almost completely closeted life. She made new friends in her AA group, many of whom were open about their homosexuality to family, friends, and people at work, and these friendships intensified her desire to come out more at home and at work.

Sue's coming out process, supported by her newfound gay/lesbian community, began to cause tension between the partners. Sue wanted to be more open with their friends and family about their relationship, whereas Jan wanted things to remain the same. This imbalance in their coming out process meant that Sue, instead of feeling safe by Jan's desire to be closeted, now felt angry and rejected by it. In addition, Sue realized how secrecy about her lesbianism had dampened her own sexual desires over the years. The changes stimulated by Sue's engagement in the gay/lesbian community were seemingly invisible to the couple. They were only aware of the increased tension and unhappiness that had left them wondering if they were hopelessly sexually incompatible.

As I talked with them, using the information I'd gathered in the expanded sexual history, they began to understand and appreciate the enormous impact that Sue's coming out process had had on their relationship and sex life. After careful assessment of the community and societal contexts of their lives and how these contexts were influencing their development as individuals and as a couple, we could begin to explore how they could proceed in working through their sexual difficulties.

EXTERNALIZATION AND UTILIZATION

To help couples like Jan and Sue shift from blaming each other to working as a team, I enhance my therapy with two well-established techniques—White and Epston's (1990) externalization process and Erickson's (Zeig, 1994) utilization approach.

Societal and internalized homophobia and their effects—stigmatization, secrecy, sexual shaming—are among the most powerful cultural influences in the lives of gay men and women. Lesbians, like all women, additionally have to deal with the privileging of male definitions of sexuality and the perpetuation of sexist myths and attitudes about women that affect the development of self-esteem, body image, sexual assertiveness, and sexual agency (McCormick, 1994; Rose, 1994; Tiefer, 1995). I help couples identify beliefs, feelings, and behaviors that are byproducts of societal prejudice so they may be externalized rather than internalized or projected onto the relationship.

White and Epston's (1990) approach of "externalizing the problem" acknowledges how cultural practices "objectify" and "thingify" persons and their bodies. By locating the problem outside of the couple, partners work together against the problem instead of against each other, a "counterpractice" that deobjectifies and empowers the partners and helps them to transcend societally induced shame.

In my work with Jan and Sue, I normalized their feelings of low self-esteem and shame, as well as their secrecy about their relationship. These were understandable feelings and behaviors that often accompany the denial and rejection of people's sexual identities. The "problem" was then understood as societal homophobia, rather than as a deficiency in them as individuals or as a couple. Hearing this, Sue felt less angry with Jan, and Jan became less defensive. Both described their pain about growing up lesbian, feeling invisible in their families, and being rejected by loved ones who wouldn't accept their sexual orientation. They also recognized how seldom they'd been encouraged by their families to assert themselves as girls. As a result, they stopped blaming and shaming each other, feeling joined in the struggle against the effects of homophobia and sexism. As a team, they were now ready to explore ways to enhance their sexual life.

I often use Erickson's utilization approach to help lesbian couples identify strengths, resources, and competencies, developed throughout their lives, that can be put to therapeutic use in the present. Erickson's term "utilization" referred to making therapeutic use of clients' involuntary mental processes, behaviors, thoughts, and feelings—some of which might even be seen by the client (or other therapists) as problematic—for the purpose of creating positive change.

When used together, externalization and utilization help lesbian couples shift the effects of oppression and prejudice from within themselves to between themselves and society. Rather than feeling depressed and victimized, they become empowered.

I made the argument with Jan and Sue that *surviving* as a lesbian in a homophobic world brings with it its own set of skills and resources. After they laughed at the idea (how could anything good come from being oppressed?), they were able to identify strengths that came with the territory, including a greater appreciation of differences, sensitivity toward others who are marginalized, greater empathy for people's pain, an awareness of social privilege, and a greater commitment to social justice.

I emphasized how their abilities to appreciate differences and feel empathy for the pain of others were resources they could use with each other as they explored different ways they each might (or might not) choose to come out to friends, family or coworkers. Sue was at an advantage in this, having been in more intensive individual therapy, where she had examined her internalized homophobia. Sue, who worked for a small graphic design company, also had an easier employment environment in which to come out. Jan, in contrast, was a corporate attorney. She felt less equipped and more vulnerable about coming out than Sue, who needed some reminding of what it feels like to make major changes in one's life and how helpful it is to get support in doing so. We discussed Jan's exceptional skill as an initial guide in sobriety when Sue felt most vulnerable in the beginning of her recovery process, noting that now Sue could return the favor.

Competence transfer, an additional intervention based on the utilization approach (Lamarre & Gregoire, 1999), provided further identification of resources for navigating the challenging waters in their life. Early on in the sessions, they had reported that one of their favorite recreational activities—and one at which they were both quite competent—was rowing. Early on in their relationship, they had purchased a two-seat boat, and when they went out together, taking turns at resting and leading, the rowing flowed effortlessly. Sometimes, if one of them was too tired or caught up with a different activity, the other would take the boat out alone.

We discussed in detail exactly how such proficient rowing was accomplished—how they dealt with changing directions and how they managed rough waters. They realized as we spoke that through all the ups and downs of their relationship, they'd always been able to get into their boat and row well. We discussed applying their rowing talents to their coming-out process and their sexual life, sharing needs along the way about pace and direction, working together, and sometimes going it alone.

Rowing became as critical relationally as it had been recreationally. They began to share their needs, desires, and fears about coming out, deciding which people to jointly come out to, which to come out to separately, and how to support each other in doing so. Sue more calmly accepted Jan's immediate need to stay closeted in certain contexts, like work, despite the differences from her own needs, and this helped her "row alone" in some contexts.

As they began to work together on coming out more, their sexual desire resurfaced. Their talent at negotiating pacing and direction helped here as well. They had enough self-confidence through utilization and competence transfer to examine together how to co-create a more erotic environment at home. They coauthored a sexual menu, consisting of each of their favorite items, which they took turns experiencing. Like lesbian film critics, they watched and playfully reviewed two woman-focused sex education tapes, one by Betty Dodson (1991) and one by Annie Sprinkle and Joseph Kramer (1999). Jan, the shyer of the two, even accompanied Sue on a shopping visit to a local erotic boutique. Jan was able to remind herself of her competencies as an AA sponsor and co-rower, places where she was able to assert herself, in order to help her to express to Sue what she wanted or didn't want sexually. Both Sue and Jan were delighted at the reduced tension, improved communication, and reengaged sexual life they were experiencing. They rowed out of therapy, knowing that they possessed all the skills they needed to keep the boat moving.

CONCLUSION

My work with Jan and Sue illustrates the importance of assessing community and societal influences on the sexual experiences of individuals and couples, making it possible to identify and diminish the effects of homophobia and sexism. This is why a multicontextual orientation is such an effective and expedient way of intervening in problems that are often created and maintained by a variety of systemic influences. Information from an expanded sexual history helps my clients and me identify not only multiple levels of influence on their sexuality and sexual identity, but also the resources, talents, and competencies they already possess that can be applied to solving their presenting sexual problem. The wonderfully complementary techniques of externalization and utilization ensure that the pressures of oppression and prejudice do not become opportunities for shame-based behavior and feelings but rather winds and currents to row against and through.

REFERENCES

Bowen, M. (1978). *Family therapy in clinical practice*. New York: Aronson.

Carter, B. (1993). *A multicontextual framework for assessing families* (Videotape: *Clinical dilemmas in marriage*). New York: Guilford Press.

Carter, B., & McGoldrick, M. (1999). *The expanded family lifecycle: Individual, family, and social perspectives* (3rd ed.). Boston: Allyn and Bacon.

de Shazer, S. (1988). *Clues: Investigating solutions in brief therapy*. New York: Norton.

de Shazer, S. (1991). *Putting differences to work*. New York: Norton.

de Shazer, S. (1994). *Words were originally magic*. New York: Norton.

Dodson, B. (1991). *Self-loving: Portrait of a women's sexuality seminar* (Videotape). New York: Betty Dodson.

Iasenza, S. (2000). Lesbian sexuality post-Stonewall to post-modernism: Putting the "Lesbian Bed Death" concept to bed. *Journal of Sex Education and Therapy, 25*(1), 59–69.

Iasenza, S., Colucci, P. L., & Rothberg, B. (1996). Coming out and the mother-daughter bond: Two case examples. In J. Laird & R. J. Green (Eds.), *Lesbians and gays in couples and families* (pp. 123–136). San Francisco: Jossey-Bass.

Laird, J. (1993). Lesbian and gay families. In F. Walsh (Ed.), *Normal family processes* (4th ed.), (pp. 282–328). New York: Guilford Press.

Laird, J. (1996). Invisible ties: Lesbians and their families of origin. In J. Laird & R. J. Green (Eds.), *Lesbians and gays in couples and families* (pp. 89–122). San Francisco: Jossey-Bass.

Lamarre, J., & Gregoire, A. (1999). Competence transfer in solution-focused therapy: Harnessing a natural resource. *Journal of Systemic Therapies, 18*(1), 43–57.

Markowitz, L. (2001, Fall). Thinking outside of the symptom: A conversation with Betty Carter. *In The Family Magazine, 7*, 12–19.

Martin, A. (1993). *Lesbian and gay parenting handbook: Creating and raising our families*. New York: Harper Perennial.

McCormick, N. B. (1994). *Sexual salvation: Affirming women's sexual rights and pleasures*. Westport, CT: Praeger.

O'Hanlon, W. H., & Weiner-Davis, M. (1988). *In search of solutions: A new direction in psychotherapy*. New York: Norton.

Rose, S. (1994). Sexual pride and sexual shame in lesbians. In B. Greene & G. M. Herek (Eds.), *Lesbian and gay psychology: Vol. 1. Theory, research and clinical applications* (pp. 71–83). Thousand Oaks, CA: Sage.

Roth, S. (1989). Psychotherapy with lesbian couples: Individual issues, female socialization and the social context. In M. McGoldrick, C. M. Anderson, & F. Walsh (Eds.), *Women in families: A framework for family therapy* (pp. 286–307). New York: Norton.

Schreurs, K. M. G. (1994). Sexuality in lesbian couples: The importance of gender. *Annual Review of Sex Research, 4,* 49–66.

Slater, S. (1995). *The lesbian family life cycle.* New York: Free Press.

Slater, S., & Mencher, J. (1991). The lesbian family life cycle: A contextual approach. *American Journal of Orthopsychiatry, 61,* 372–382.

Sprinkle, A., & Kramer, J. (1999). *An intimate guide to female genital massage* (Videotape). San Francisco: Erospirit Research Institute.

Tiefer, L. (1995). *Sex is not a natural act and other essays.* Boulder, CO: Westview Press.

Weiner-Davis, M. (1995). *Divorce busting: A rapid and revolutionary program for staying together.* New York: Summit.

White, M., & Epston, D. (1990). *Narrative means to therapeutic ends.* New York: Norton.

Wincze, J. P., & Carey, M. P. (1991). *Sexual dysfunction: A guide for assessment and treatment.* New York: Guilford Press.

Zeig, J. K. (Ed.). (1994). *Ericksonian methods: The essence of the story.* New York: Brunner-Mazel.

three
___

Getting "In the Mood" (For a Change): Stage-Appropriate Clinical Work for Sexual Problems

Scott D. Miller, Karen M. Donahey, and Mark A. Hubble

> The readiness is all.
> —*Shakespeare* (Hamlet, act 5, scene 2)

I N 1966, RESEARCHERS MASTERS AND JOHNSON reported that the physiological response to sexual stimulation progressed through a series of stages that were the same for *all* human beings: excitement, plateau, orgasm, and resolution. Prior to their pioneering research of human sexual behavior in a laboratory setting, studies had been limited to what people said rather than what they actually did. Although perhaps difficult to imagine now, the identification of the stages of arousal revolutionized the scientific understanding of the human sexual response cycle and opened the door to understanding differences in and developing therapies for sexual difficulties.

A less well-known but equally revolutionary finding in the field of psychotherapy is that people progress through a series of "stages of arousal" while "getting in the mood" to change. Although a number of systems for classifying these stages have been proposed (see Berg & Miller, 1992; de Shazer, 1988; Fisch, Weakland, & Segal, 1982; Miller & Berg, 1991), none to date compares to the Stages of Change model developed by Prochaska, DiClemente, and associates (DiClimente & Prochaska, 1982; Prochaska, 1995, 1999; Prochaska & DiClemente, 1982, 1983; Prochaska, DiClemente, & Norcross, 1992). For more than 15 years, these researchers have been piecing together "the puzzle of how people intentionally change their behavior" by studying how people change naturally, spontaneously, and on an everyday basis (Prochaska et al., p. 1102). Along the way, these pioneering researchers have not only been able to identify the various stages, but have also found that "at different stages people apply particular processes to progress to the next stage" (Prochaska, 1999, p. 228).

Throughout most of the history of psychotherapy, motivation for change has been dichotomized: People in treatment were considered either motivated or unmotivated. Those falling in the latter category earned the label "resistant." In 1904, Sigmund Freud placed the concept of resistance to change at the center of his evolving theory of therapy. Based on his observation that clients would frequently and often vigorously reject the interpretations he offered, Freud concluded that "patient[s] cling to [their] disease and . . . even fight against their own recovery" (1904/1953a, p. 67).

Although the concept has seen many modifications over time, the belief that people sabotage or otherwise subvert the change process survives (Anderson & Stewart, 1983; Singer, 1994). Therapists still commonly view *resistance* with Freudian eyes, thinking in terms of the clients' *secondary gain* (Freud, 1909/1953b; Weiner, 1975), *habit strength* (Dollard & Miller, 1950), *homeostasis* (Hoffman, 1981; Jackson, 1957), *need for self-protection* (Mahoney, 1991), *lack of motivation* (Malan, 1976; Sifneos, 1992), or *being in denial*. This perspective, as Mahoney noted in his massive and systematic review of psychotherapy process research, has led to "one of the most important points of convergence across contemporary schools of thought in psychotherapy: Significant psychological change is rarely rapid or easy" (p. 18).

Research on the "stages of change" indicates, however, that the whole concept of resistance needs to be rethought—perhaps even jettisoned altogether. All people, the work of Prochaska and colleagues makes clear, have motivation. Although people who do not share their therapist's motivations have historically been assigned one of the aforementioned labels, it may be more correct to say that their "stage of arousal for change" is different from that of their therapists. A number of studies have found that therapists improve the chances of success when the treatment they offer fits with their *client's* stage of change (Brogan, Prochaska, & Prochaska, 1999; Miller, Duncan, & Hubble, 1997; Prochaska, 1999; Reis & Brown, 1999). Stage-appropriate interventions increase client engagement in the treatment process, a factor that over 40 years of research has established to be "*the most important* determinant of outcome" (Orlinsky, Grawe, & Parks, 1994, p. 361).

From this vantage point, even the distinction between long and brief forms of therapy can be seen as a muddle. Indeed, the length of treatment is largely irrelevant to successful outcome. Rather, *efficient* and *effective* treatment results from working cooperatively with people to facilitate their movement to the next stage of change. Prochaska and colleagues (1992) found that people who moved from one stage to the next during the first few sessions of treatment doubled their chances of taking effective action to solve their problem in the next six months. A movement of two stages as much as quadrupled the chances of success (Prochaska, 1999). Other research shows that such movement generally occurs early in the treatment or *not at all*. Nearly all large-scale meta-analytic studies, for example, show that people's response in the first few sessions is highly predictive of eventual outcome (Duncan & Miller, 2000; Hubble, Duncan, & Miller, 1999).

The research of Prochaska and colleagues (1992) shows that stage of change is a better predictor of treatment outcome than the client's age, socioeconomic status, problem severity, goals, self-efficacy/esteem, and existing social support network—variables that continue to be used in spite of their low predictive power. At the same time, the idea of helping someone "get in the mood" for a change by tailoring treatment to their particular stage has the advantage of shifting the guiding metaphor for clinical practice from one that emphasizes therapist power to one that stresses collaboration and facilitation. From this perspective, therapists assume all the qualities of a good lover—that is, "joining with," "working together," and "cooperating" rather than using "techniques, strategies, and other clever maneuvers . . . for the good of the client" (de Shazer, 1986, p. 73). Although rarely stated explicitly, available evidence suggests that experience naturally leads therapists in the direction of attending more to their relationships with clients and less to technical expertise (Duncan & Miller, 2000).

At present, the stages have been successfully applied to the treatment of various compulsive behaviors (e.g., alcohol, food, tobacco, sex, gambling), domestic violence, the management of chronic health conditions (e.g., chronic pain, arthritis), the prediction and prevention of risky sexual behavior (e.g., condom use to prevent transmission of HIV), the improvement of personal decision-making and acquisition of psychological skills, the promotion of health-engendering behaviors (e.g., diet, exercise, routine medical screening), and the management of organizational change (Prochaska, 1999). A review of the PsychInfo database from 1988 to the present, however, turned up no studies or papers directly applying the concepts to the treatment of sexual problems. This chapter illustrates the use of the Stages of Change model in the treatment of such issues.

THE STAGES OF AROUSAL (FOR A CHANGE)

Not everyone needs or wants the same thing, all the time. . . . In my opinion, a responsible psychotherapist respects those desires, is flexible enough to deal with a wide range of them and to adjust his or her services to each client's current concerns.

—Michael Mahoney (1991, p. 280)

Six distinct "stages of arousal" for a change have been identified: (1) precontemplation, (2) contemplation, (3) preparation, (4) action, (5) maintenance, and (6) termination (Prochaska, 1995). Movement through these stages generally happens in one of two ways. First, change may advance linearly, proceeding gradually and step-wise through the stages from start to finish. Relapse and a recycling through the stages characterizes the second and by far most common form of progression. This is the process intimated in the popular saying, "Change is three steps forward and two steps back." Sudden transformations in behavior are possible, too, such as the celebrated overnight conversion of Ebenezer Scrooge in Dickens's *A Christmas Carol* (Miller, 1986). In the material that follows, the various stages are defined and illustrated. For each stage, we offer suggestions for the type of clinical work most likely to facilitate progression to the next level.

Precontemplation

In this first stage, people "are not intending to change or take action in the near future, usually measured in terms of 'the next 6 months'" (Prochaska, 1999, p. 228). Quite often, these are the people labeled "resistant," "in denial," or "character disordered." In reality, however, they may not "have a clue" that a problem exists. Others may feel there is a problem but they typically have not made a connection between this problem and their contribution to its formation or continuation. People in this stage may actually have tried to change. Usually, however, their lack of success has caused them to become demoralized and to stop thinking, talking, or reading about ways to solve their problem. As might be expected, people in this stage are often not interested in participating in treatment (Prochaska, 1995). Most often, they come at the behest or mandate of someone else (e.g., parent, partner, probation officer, or court). As such, they may portray themselves as under duress or the victim of "bad luck."

A fitting example of someone in the precontemplative stage was Martin, a 48-year-old Native American man married for 12 years to Donna, a 47-year-old Caucasian woman. Martin and Donna met in AA. In addition to having a past history of alcohol abuse, Donna had experienced several bouts of major depression as an adult, and Martin suffered from hypertension and diabetes. They entered treatment with Karen Donahey at Donna's insistence.

For most of the last 10 years they had had little to no sexual contact, due to Martin's difficulty maintaining erections and absence of sexual desire. Although disappointed that they couldn't have intercourse, Donna was open to other forms of sexual contact. However, Martin steadfastly refused to consider this, citing his discomfort with oral stimulation and his belief that manually stimulating each other was "just another way of masturbating, which is wrong."

Although distressed that Donna was so unhappy about the lack of sex, Martin felt that she should accept the fact that the medications he was taking for hypertension and diabetes were preventing him from performing sexually. He wanted her to focus instead on how well he took care of her with regard to her depression and in her relationship with her mother. In fact, at one point he said, "I think maybe God put me here on Earth to take care of Donna." Donna conceded that he was a "wonderful husband in all other aspects," but she still craved intimacy. Believing that part of her depression was related to the lack of sexual intimacy in the marriage, she was "hungry for any kind of touch from Martin." Martin responded by telling Donna that in his culture men and women were not affectionate with one another, and that "white women are too demanding sexually." He wanted her to accept him as he was.

To help clients in precontemplation take that first step, a light touch is recommended. This "light touch" means, first and foremost, that the therapist is courteous and willing to listen to the clients' point of view (Miller et al., 1997). The goal is not to *make* clients do something. Rather, in accommodating them in precontemplation, the therapist must create a climate in which they can consider, explore, and appreciate the benefits of changing. This could include, for example, providing information or helping clients become aware of the causes, consequences (positive and negative), and cures of their problems or concerns (Prochaska & DiClemente, 1992). As the word *stage* implies, accommodating motivational readiness requires the therapist to be "in phase" with clients. In the earliest stage, this means that an important first step has been made when clients express an inkling that some action may eventually be necessary.

Karen explored Martin's thoughts about just wanting his wife to accept him. Donna listened without interrupting and then said very sadly that she would try harder to accept him for who he was with respect to his feelings about sexuality. As Karen began to summarize what she had heard from each of them, Martin jumped in and stated, "While I'm not promising anything, if you [Karen] could help me be open to having sexual feelings, I would consider it." He then turned to Donna and told her he wasn't sure what he could do, but because he hated seeing her so sad, he would come to therapy again to see if he could "feel different."

By listening and acknowledging Martin's feelings without pushing him to do anything different, Karen (and Donna) allowed him to rethink his position and consider making a change. On the way home after the session, he held Donna's hand—something that had not happened for some time.

Contemplation

The process of change continues in the second stage, *contemplation*. According to Prochaksa, people in this stage "intend to change in the next 6 months" (1999, p. 229). In traditional treatment approaches, these clients are frequently referred to as the "yes, but" clients—those who earnestly seek out the therapist's help and advice but reject it once it is offered. In reality, however, people in the contemplative stage recognize that a change is needed but are unsure whether it is worth the cost in time, effort, and energy. In addition, they are concerned about the losses attendant to any change they might make.

A 25-year-old woman, Francis, came to see Karen because she was unable to have intercourse with her husband of two months, Tom. She had no history of sexual abuse. During their courtship, Francis had thought that her difficulty was due to guilt over their engaging in premarital sexual contact, but now that she was married, she saw that the problem was more complex. In addition to feeling guilty, she was troubled by many beliefs and fears about intercourse (e.g., it would be painful; her vagina was not large enough; she would not enjoy it; her husband would not be able to stop if she asked him to because he would be too aroused). At the same time, however, she felt badly that she and her husband were not acting "like newlyweds should," and she expressed a desire to be "normal."

Although Tom had been fairly supportive, he expressed growing frustration with what he perceived as her lackadaisical approach to the problem.

Francis: I don't like the way things are right now but I'm afraid to have sex. I think it will hurt. I'm not very big down there.
Karen: You think your vagina is too small for your husband's penis.

Francis: Well, I'm not sure, since I've never tried. It just seems like it
would be really painful.

Karen: Has anyone told you it was painful? A friend perhaps? or your parents?

Francis: No, my friends don't really talk about it very much. I don't like to
hear about it—sex, I mean—but when they do say stuff, they seem to
act like it's fun. And my mother tried to talk about sex with me when
I was a teenager. She told me sex was created by God for married
people and it was beautiful. If you were unmarried, it was wrong. I've
told her about this problem. She keeps telling me it won't hurt, but I
can't get myself to believe her. But I have to, I just have to overcome
this! Tom won't be patient forever.

Karen: You feel pressure to solve this problem.

Francis: Yes, I don't expect to enjoy it but if I can just do it, it would satisfy
Tom. As long as it doesn't hurt, I'll be satisfied.

Karen: That's your goal for now.

Francis: Yes, but I don't know how you're going to convince me that it
won't hurt either.

Accommodating clients in contemplation takes considerable patience,
given their tendency to vacillate and be indecisive. An effective approach
entails creating a supportive environment in which they can carefully consider changing without feeling the pressure or need to take action (Duncan, 1989). In certain cases, the therapist might even actively discourage
clients from taking action and, instead, simply encourage thinking or
observation.

A classic example of accommodating clients who are contemplating
change can be found in the "go slow" injunction from the brief strategic
therapy tradition (Duncan, 1989; Fisch et al., 1982). The advice to "go
slow" (i.e., not change too quickly, postpone, consider how much change is
optimal) is not paradoxical subterfuge. When clients are contemplating
change, allying with their ambivalence is perhaps the most empathic stance
a therapist can assume. After all, by the time most of these clients see a therapist, they have been exposed to all sorts of exhortations to do something—
both from others and from their own conscience.

Karen explained to Francis that she was not going to try to convince her
that intercourse would not be painful (her mother and husband had already attempted this, with no success). Nor was she going to recommend
that Francis go home and try once again to have intercourse with her
husband. Rather, she instructed Francis that "under no circumstances"

was she to attempt intercourse with Tom. Instead, if she was willing, she could practice for the next week inserting a Q-tip in her vagina. Francis was both incredulous and relieved.

Francis: You mean that's all you're going to make me do?

Karen: Well, I don't want to make you do anything you're not ready to do. Does this seem like it's too big a step? Do you need this first week to just imagine doing it?

Francis: [*thinking for a few seconds*] No, I think I could do the Q-tip. I've had Tom's finger inside of me before and it didn't hurt that much. I don't think a Q-tip could hurt.

Karen: Well, if it starts to, I want you to immediately stop. Withdraw the Q-tip, do the breathing exercises again, and then try to insert it again. If it hurts, you're done for the day. You can try again the following day.

Francis: That's all I have to do?

Karen: Yes, I would rather have you take this slow and increase your chance of being successful.

Francis: Will you talk with Tom about this?

Karen: Yes, I think it would be a good idea if the three of us met together next week.

A variation of suggesting that clients "go slow" is to ask them to consider any possible "dangers of improvement" (Fisch et al., 1982). This approach is helpful in accommodating people who have stayed in contemplation for a protracted period of time—clients whose lengthy inaction, multiple false starts, or failures have led them to be labeled "difficult" or "chronic." By taking a conservative position regarding progress, raising possible "dangers of improvement," the therapist is suggesting that change be set aside for some period. Clients are then asked to consider carefully any risks that might be associated with improvement, with no danger too small to contemplate (Duncan, 1989). Overall, it is respectful to show the understanding that change requires time, thoughtfulness, and sometimes radical accommodation. Helping to take off pressure, a therapist adopting such a position gives clients the space and support to commit to change.

Regardless of the particular therapeutic tradition followed or applied in accommodating clients in contemplation, it helps for the therapist to keep his or her finger off the hot button of change. A therapist who attempts to push clients when they are contemplating change will, instead of moving them forward, probably prompt them to dig in their heels. Thus, it is better to listen, agree, provide a small encouraging nudge when invited, and engage clients in an exploration of what they stand to both gain and lose from changing (Miller et al., 1997).

Preparation

In the third stage, clients are preparing to "take action in the immediate future, usually measured in terms of 'the next month'" (Prochaska, 1999, p. 230). The main focus at this stage is on identifying the criteria and strategies for success, as well as on finalizing the development of their plan for change. People in this stage also engage in experimentation with the desired change—trying it on for size, noticing how it feels, and then experiencing the effects. For example, clients experiencing premature ejaculation may purposely spend more time in foreplay or otherwise modify the conditions under which they typically have sex (Prochaska & DiClemente, 1992). In contrast to clients in the two previous stages— where their relationship with change is more tenuous and delicate—those in the preparation phase are rarely assigned negative psychological labels. Indeed, these clients are often considered ideal—their customership is on a surer footing and their intention to take action fits with traditional ideas about the change process (Prochaska et al., 1992).

The therapist accommodates clients in preparation by helping in the sorting through and selection of treatment goals, as well as in exploring and mapping out potential paths that might be taken to reach those goals. At this point, the therapist can assume a more active role in raising possibilities, presenting treatment options or change strategies, and constructively challenging clients' problem-solving abilities. As during all the stages, however, choice is important (Miller, 1986). Clients in preparation need to be active in choosing and designing their own strategy for change. The therapist is most likely to be helpful when he or she presents alternatives or different methods that clients can use to achieve their goals. Implying that there is only one way leads to resistance and increases the risk of clients' terminating treatment prematurely.

In their early thirties, Will and Sandra were a young couple for whom sex sometimes felt "like too much work." Will was working full-time and attending graduate school part-time while Sandra was finishing her undergraduate degree and taking care of their three-year-old son. For the past two years the couple had poured their energy into school and parenting, with the result that they'd been sexual less than once a month. When they were intimate, they enjoyed it and wondered aloud why they "didn't do it more often." Both reported wanting to increase their sexual frequency to three or more times a month.

In the initial session, Sandra and Will acknowledged having let other things "get in the way of sex" (school assignments, household chores, family outings with their son, time with friends and extended family), and each were waiting for the other to initiate. Subsequent sessions focused on exploring the conditions under which sex might be possible (e.g., when their son was in bed or at daycare; when it wasn't too late at night; when they could set aside time for it during the week, including time to think about or anticipate it; and when they were able to watch an erotic video to "get in the mood"). Time was also spent exploring how the couple had let their eroticism decline in the past few years. Sandra, in particular, spoke of her wish for her and Will to "become lovers again." When asked for details, she talked about their earlier days when they were dating and first married, giving each other body massages, cuddling in the mornings before getting up, leaving each other "steamy" notes or voicemails, and "plain, old-fashioned flirting."

Such reminiscing rekindled the couple's interest and creativity. Sandra went out and bought new lingerie and massage lotion; Will bought some erotic videos and sent Sandra several emails telling her what he'd like to do sexually with her. One morning, he joined her in the shower. A few sessions later, they reported having decided to make Wednesdays a "sexual date" night. Sandra would arrange for her parents to have their son over for a few hours in the evening so that she and Will could have the house to themselves. Will, leaving work early, was to stop at a gourmet food shop to pick up some treats, and Sandra was to have the wine chilling and music on the stereo. Talking about and planning the date increased their sense of anticipation, as well as their readiness for change. By specifying steps they could take to revitalize their sexual relationship, the couple successfully set the wheels in motion and attained their goal.

Action

Following preparation, the action stage commences. According to Prochaska, "action is the stage in which people have made specific, overt modifications in their lifestyles within the past six months" (1999, p. 230). Because of a tendency to equate the action stage with therapeutic change, many traditional models erroneously identify this stage as the one in which *the* treatment takes place (Miller, 1986; Prochaska et al., 1992).

Research shows, however, that in spite of the field's historical bias toward action, people are *least* likely to be in this stage at the outset of treatment. This mismatch goes a long way toward explaining the persistence of the concept of resistance in mental health discourse.

Janice came to Scott Miller for therapy, referred by her gynecologist, with a history of dyspareunia, accompanied by complaints of severe genital irritation and infection (Miller et al., 1997). Despite years of medical testing, no physical cause had ever been identified for Janice's complaints, and the latest in a long list of physicians suspected that the problems were psychogenic. She began the first session with some history.

Janice: I have seen so many doctors over the last, well, several years. I have
    had this problem for 30 years. It's serious because, well, you see, I've
    been married twice and both times this problem . . .
Scott: Uh, huh.
Janice: It's a little embarrassing. I've, uh, *had* this redness and infection—
    well, the doctors have all said that I don't, have never had any
    infection—but on my genitals. I'm always swollen and irritated . . .
Scott: Uh, huh.
Janice: . . . and, well, it *has* always hurt to have intercourse, you know,
    because . . .
Scott: [*finishing the sentence*] of the redness and irritation.
Janice: [*with relief*] Yeah. The doctor says I'm psycho . . . [*pauses*].
Scott: Psycho?
Janice: [*nodding affirmatively*] Psycho . . . psychosomatic.

Janice continued for several minutes, elaborating on her story and explaining that she had made the appointment for therapy following a recent visit to a new physician. Unable to find anything physically wrong with her, this latest doctor had said that Janice should consider seeing a mental health professional. Scott simply listened while Janice related these details. Following a natural break in the process, Scott seized an opportunity to highlight a statement Janice had made in the opening moments of the session that indicated that she may have recently made specific, overt modifications in her behavior.

Scott: You say that you have *had* this redness and irritation?
Janice: [*nodding affirmatively*] Mmm.
Scott: Does that mean to say that there have been some changes for the
    better recently?

Janice: [*surprised*] Well, yes.

Scott: What's been different?

Janice: I've tried almost everything. I tried almost every, well, the doctors have tried all the drugs—creams, steroids, antibiotics. Nothing has ever worked, at least not for very long.

Scott: And lately?

Janice: Well, I have been applying a mixture of milk of magnesia and Benadryl, just a few drops topically, to the, uh, red, irritated areas.

Scott: Hmm.

Janice: And it's much improved over the few weeks that I've been doing it.

Scott: Is that right?

Janice: After 30 years, I'd almost given up hope of this ever, well, *changing*.

Scott: Of course. And the mixture is helping?

Janice: Mmm.

Given Janice's long history of unsuccessful treatment, it would have been easy to view her as unmotivated or even resistant to change. Careful attention to her language, however, enabled Scott to highlight a dramatic difference in Janice's perception of her sexual functioning. When clients reach the action stage of change, they are, as we say, "cookin'." Some therapists might think that they should close the case at this point, but spending time exploring and reinforcing the change, providing measured emotional support, and helping clients monitor, modify, or fine-tune the action plan is critical for progression to the maintenance stage.

Scott and Janice continued their conversation, exploring how Janice had managed to discover her new solution, how she knew the "appropriate dose" to use on any given occasion, and how she would know when the "medicine" was no longer needed. Scott also asked about other actions Janice might have taken that had contributed to the improvement.

Scott: Anything else that has been different or helpful lately?

Janice: [*surprised*] Well, yes. Right now, I find myself in a situation, well, with a man that I've known for most of my life and he's quite a wonderful person . . .

Scott: [*pleased*] Hmm.

Janice: . . . and now we, well, have a sexual relationship.

Scott: [*curious*] That is different?

Janice: For the first time, last night, it didn't hurt.

Scott: Is that right?!

Janice: [*proudly*] Yeah, for the first time.

Scott: How do you think that happened?

Janice: Well, for three weeks . . . well, a lot has to do with Steven. We have, well, there hasn't been any pressure. We have gone very slowly and the pain just hasn't been there.

Scott: The pain isn't there?

Janice: I guess it helps that I'm in love with Steven and I don't really think that I was in love with my husbands.

Scott: Sure. What else might be making a difference?

Janice: Well, I'm not as guarded. He is so careful and, well, thoughtful of me. Early on, we talked and agreed that if there was any hurt then we'd stop and, oh, I think we spend a lot of time just, well, you know, touching and just laying there, uh, being together.

The additional steps Janice reported taking—starting a new relationship, communicating with Steven about sexual needs and preferences, and taking the time to become sufficiently aroused prior to attempting intercourse—were clear indications of someone in the action stage of change. For this reason, the remaining time in the session was spent identifying and reinforcing the helpful ways the couple had discovered to communicate with each other about their sexual relationship, as well as developing a plan for monitoring and fine-tuning her plan of action.

Maintenance

In this stage, change continues and stress is placed on what needs to be done in order to maintain or consolidate gains. In contrast to those in the action stage, people in this stage "are less tempted to relapse and increasingly more confident that they can continue their changes" (Prochaska, 1999, p. 231). This is because they have learned from difficulties and temptations they have encountered while passing through the other stages.

Jim and Mary, a couple in their late fifties, sought sex therapy with Karen after a urologist ruled out any medical reason for Jim's frequent problems getting or sustaining an erection. When Jim's penis failed to co-operate, the couple would conclude that sex "wouldn't be happening this time" and refrain from any other sexual contact.

During the initial evaluation, Karen learned that Jim and Mary had very similar, and somewhat limiting, views regarding sexuality. For both, sex equaled intercourse. Sexual foreplay consisted of kissing and a few minutes of caressing. Engaging in oral or manual stimulation to orgasm had not been part of their sexual repertoire. However, in exploring this with them, Karen learned that they were open to considering other possibilities. Jim was particularly surprised at how receptive Mary was to the idea of oral stimulation, having assumed that she would feel self-conscious or uncomfortable. Mary said she'd never suggested it because she'd assumed he wasn't interested. Laughing about their mistaken assumptions, they agreed with Karen's suggestion that for the next month they would focus on stimulating each other manually and orally and abstain from intercourse.

During this time, the couple learned how not to be solely dependent on intercourse for sexual pleasure. With such pressure eliminated, Jim felt considerably less anxious and responsible for the success or failure of their sexual encounters, and, not surprisingly, he had fewer incidents of erectile failure. Together, the couple discovered that by expanding their definition of sex, they were able to enjoy a much more varied and active sexual life than they had ever had in their marriage—with or without an erection.

In the maintenance stage, the therapist accommodates clients' motivational level by helping them anticipate the challenges that might provoke regression or relapse. By identifying such challenges, they can develop prevention plans. For instance, if, in the past, a spouse's work or travel schedule decreased the level of sexual frequency and, eventually, sexual interest, a prevention plan might specify that the couple have a sexual date within two days of his or her return. This way the couple takes active steps to ensure that their sexual relationship remains a vital part of their marriage.

Therapists also accommodate clients in maintenance by helping them design retention plans for the inevitable relapses that accompany any change. Should clients find themselves sliding down the slippery slope of relapse, the retention plan provides handholds for them to grab onto so the slide to the bottom need not continue. For example, if a couple is falling back into old patterns (e.g., not having sex for a period of time), setting up sexual dates may be a way to get back on track.

In Jim and Mary's later sessions, Karen talked with them about any factors that might lead to a setback (e.g., fatigue, illness, anxiety). They were confident that their other-than-intercourse options for pleasuring each other made it possible for sex to continue even through difficult times.

Termination

According to Prochaska, in the *termination* stage, "there is zero temptation to engage in the problem behavior, and there is a 100 percent confidence (self-efficacy) that one will not engage in the old behavior regardless of the situation" (1993, p. 253). So defined, this stage may actually be more of an ideal than a realistic or achievable state of change. Usually most people stay in the maintenance phase, mindful of possible threats and monitoring what they need to do to keep the change in place. For these reasons, when it comes to ending a successful contact between clients and therapists, the best option is to wish the clients well while leaving the door open for a possible return should challenges, setbacks, or a new concern develop.

GETTING IN THE MOOD (FOR A CHANGE): PROGRESSING THROUGH "STAGES OF AROUSAL"

Bill, a 35-year-old software consultant, and Nancy, a business executive, had been married for two years but had never had intercourse. Throughout their relationship, Bill had been able to have strong erections with both oral and manual stimulation, but he lost them whenever intercourse was attempted.

In the months prior to entering therapy with Karen, the couple vacillated between the precontemplative and contemplative stages of change, alternately "fighting about" and "ignoring" the problem. Then, as Nancy described during the first session, "something snapped. We'd go to bed and I'd lay there thinking, 'We need to talk about this.' But nothing would happen. I wouldn't talk. He definitely wouldn't talk. And I just got madder and madder. I started *thinking*, 'How are we ever going to have a family if we never have sex?!' That's when I *decided* that we needed help."

Bill, aware of Nancy's frustration, had alternated between feelings of remorse and anger. "Neither [feeling] changed anything," he said, "so I just stopped talking about it." He then added, "I was, in a way, relieved when Nancy suggested we see someone about our problem."

Nancy and Bill, in the contemplative stage of change, agreed something was wrong and needed to change, but they were uncertain—and even at odds—about what to do about it. Bill, believing that the problem was due in large part to Nancy's "pressuring" him, figured that "things would be better" if she would "just back off." From Nancy's standpoint, "his avoidance of the issue" was the reason she'd felt compelled to bring it up on a regular basis. "Backing off," she said, "was just an excuse to ignore it."

During the first session, the couple described their contrasting views of the situation, arguing over who had the most accurate view. Karen, listening attentively to both, commented that it seemed important for the couple to move steadily (addressing Nancy's concern) but slowly (Bill's concern). Bill nodded in agreement, responding that Nancy had a right to be worried, given his tendency to withdraw and avoid situations in which he might fail. Nancy, in turn, indicated her willingness to "go slow," because Bill seemed willing and interested in addressing the problem.

The session ended with Karen's asking the couple to spend the next week thinking about what they would ultimately like their sexual life to look like—a homework task consistent with a contemplative stage of change. In order to give the pair time to think carefully and thoroughly, a session was scheduled for two weeks later.

When they returned, Bill and Nancy each shared their visions. "I would like us to make love a couple of times a week," Nancy said, "and it would really be stimulating to me if Bill would initiate some of the time, and for sex to become a natural part of our life, together, as a couple. You know, that we don't have to think, 'Okay, are we going to have sex? And how, and who is going to start?'" Bill, in turn, said, "I would be happy if we had sex three or four times a month, and for there to be, you know, no more problems." Karen encouraged each of them to describe their views in more detail, but as the session continued, she sensed that Bill felt troubled. In response to her asking him about it, he confirmed that he was "worried about something."

Karen: Is this something that we can talk about here, now?
Nancy: [*looks from Karen to Bill.*]
Bill: [*looking from Karen to Nancy.*] I think so.
Karen: Okay.
Bill: As I was thinking about our sex life this past couple of weeks, something I kept thinking about . . .
Karen: Uh, huh.
Bill: [*continuing*] Well, in my last relationship, whenever [*looking back at Karen*] Stephanie and I . . . we'd have sex, she'd, uh, it was . . . she said it always hurt. That it hurt.

Because of the pain, Bill and his former partner had stopped having sex altogether after only a handful of attempts, and he was concerned that Nancy would suffer with the same type of pain. Clarifying immediately that she had never experienced pain during intercourse in previous relationships, Nancy attempted to reassure Bill, telling him that she would let him know "immediately" if she were to feel any pain.

Not easily convinced, Bill said that he "needed some time to think about this." At the conclusion of the visit, Karen asked Bill to practice visualizing pain-free intercourse with Nancy, finding discrete indicators that would tell him that Nancy was truly enjoying the experience. Balancing Bill's desire to "go slow" with Nancy's interest in making "steady progress," Karen further asked the couple to engage in nondemand pleasuring activities that did not include attempts to have intercourse.

The couple followed through with both homework tasks. At the next session, Nancy said that their nondemand pleasuring had made her feel more optimistic. For Bill, the sexual contact and the obvious pleasure Nancy derived from it allowed him to feel increasingly more confident as a lover. He watched her facial expressions and physical responses, and he tried incorporating them into his visualizations of pain-free intercourse.

Identifying the criteria and strategies for success and experimenting with their desired change, the couple appeared to be moving into the preparation stage. In spite of their progress, however, Bill continued to feel hesitant about possibly hurting Nancy during intercourse. He knew that his fear was "irrational," but he still "couldn't shake it."

The treatment remained at this stage for several sessions. Although Nancy tried to remain optimistic, Bill, sensing that she was growing frustrated, became increasingly fearful that she would not remain patient much longer. The pressure to resolve the problem only intensified when the couple learned that Nancy's younger sister was pregnant. When Nancy suggested they speak to a doctor about artificial insemination—because it didn't seem like they would be able to "make a baby the normal way"—Bill became angry, refusing to speak for the remainder of the session.

Over the next several weeks, the couple gradually stopped doing the exercises together and Bill stopped visualizing. After canceling two appointments in a row, Bill left a message for Karen that he and Nancy each needed time to "think things over." Recognizing that they had slipped from a preparation stage to a contemplative and then a precontemplative stage, Karen, in turn, left a message for the couple, normalizing the challenging, back-and-forth nature of the change process and indicating her willingness to continue with them.

Shortly thereafter, the couple called and made an appointment, and when they arrived for their session, they brought news of some progress. Nancy had thought "long and hard" about how to help Bill overcome his fear about hurting her, and finally she'd come up with the idea of having him watch while she, without pain, inserted a vibrator (similar in size to his penis) into her vagina. He not only responded positively to her suggestion, but also agreed to help her find a suitable specimen! After choosing one, they practiced together, first with her inserting it and then with Bill. They were once again in the preparation stage of change.

As the couple recounted their progress, Bill indicated that he believed he was ready to attempt intercourse. Consistent with their preparation stage, Karen assumed a more active role, instructing them on how to proceed, raising possibilities, and presenting options and strategies. In the next session, they shared good news: They'd had intercourse twice during the week.

In the two sessions that followed, the couple reported having intercourse, without difficulty, two to three times each week. Karen devoted much time to reviewing and reinforcing their successful strategies. A follow-up call three months later found them doing well and "trying hard to get pregnant."

CONCLUSION

"To every thing there is a season, and a time to every purpose under the heaven."

—Ecclesiastes 3:1

Recent studies indicate that people progress through a series of "stages of arousal" while "getting in the mood" to change. The important issue in treatment, from the perspective of such research, is neither the amount of time involved (brief versus long-term) nor the technique employed (psychodynamic, say, or solution-focused), but rather the timing of the therapeutic suggestions. Clinical interventions that are congruent with the stage of arousal for change facilitate engagement, thereby maximizing both the effectiveness and efficiency of the treatment process. Knowledge of the stages can imbue therapists who are working with sex-related problems with all the qualities of a good lover, chief among them being exquisitely sensitive to the other's needs, desires, and level of arousal.

REFERENCES

Anderson, C. M., & Stewart, S. (1983). *Mastering resistance: A practical guide to family therapy*. New York: Guilford Press.

Berg, I. K., & Miller, S. D. (1992). *Working with the problem drinker: A solution-focused approach*. New York: Norton.

Brogan, M. M., Prochaska, J. O., & Prochaska, J. M. (1999). Predicting termination and continuation status in psychotherapy using the transtheoretical model. *Psychotherapy: Theory, Research, Practice, Training, 36*(2), 105–113.

de Shazer, S. (1986). A requiem for power. *Contemporary Family Therapy, 10*(2), 69–76.

de Shazer, S. (1988). *Clues*. New York: Norton.

DiClemente, C., & Prochaska, J. O. (1982). Self-change and therapy change of smoking: A comparison of processes of change in cessation and maintenance. *Addictive Behaviors, 7*, 133–142.

Dollard, J., & Miller, N. E. (1950). *Personality and psychotherapy: An analysis in terms of learning, thinking, and culture*. New York: McGraw-Hill.

Duncan, B. (1989). Paradoxical procedures in family therapy. In M. Ascher (Ed.), *Therapeutic paradox* (pp. 310–348). New York: Guilford Press.

Duncan, B. L., & Miller, S. D. (2000). *The heroic client.* San Francisco: Jossey-Bass.

Fisch, R., Weakland, J., & Segal, L. (1982). *Tactics of change.* San Francisco: Jossey-Bass.

Freud, S. (1953a). On psychotherapy. In J. Strachey (Ed. & Trans.), *The standard edition of the complete psychological works of Sigmund Freud* (Vol. 7, pp. 257–268). London: Hogarth Press. (Original work published 1904)

Freud, S. (1953b). Some general remarks on the nature of hysterical attacks. In E. Jones (Ed.), *Collected papers* (Vol. 2). London: Hogarth Press. (Original work published 1909)

Hoffman, L. (1981). *Foundations of family therapy: A conceptual framework for systems change.* New York: Basic.

Hubble, M. A., Duncan, B. L., & Miller, S. D. (1999). *The heart and soul of change.* Washington, D.C.: APA Press.

Jackson, D. (1957). The question of family homeostasis. *The Psychiatric Quarterly Supplement, 31,* 79–90.

Mahoney, M. J. (1991). *Human change processes: The scientific foundations of psychotherapy.* New York: Basic.

Malan, D. H. (1976). *The frontier of brief psychotherapy.* New York: Plenum.

Miller, S. D., & Berg, I. K. (1991). Working with the problem drinker: A solution-focused Approach. *Arizona Counseling Journal, 16*(2), 3–12.

Miller, S. D., Duncan, B. L, & Hubble, M. A. (1997). *Escape from Babel: Toward a unifying language for psychotherapy practice.* New York: Norton.

Miller, W. R. (1986). Increasing motivation for change. In W. R. Miller & R. Hester (Eds.), *Addictive behaviors: Processes of change* (pp. 67–80). New York: Plenum.

Orlinsky, D. E., Grawe, K., & Parks, B. K. (1994). Process and outcome in psychotherapy—noch einmal. In A. E. Bergin & S. L. Garfield (Eds.), *The handbook of psychotherapy and behavior change* (4th ed., pp. 270–378). New York: Wiley.

Prochaska, J. O. (1993). Working in harmony with how people change naturally. *The Weight Control Digest, 3*(249), 252–255.

Prochaska, J. O. (1995). Common problems: Common solutions. *Clinical Psychology: Science and Practice, 2,* 101–105.

Prochaska, J. O. (1999). How do people change and how can we change to help many more people? In M. A. Hubble, B. L. Duncan, & S. D. Miller (Eds.), *The heart and soul of change* (pp. 227–255). Washington, D.C.: APA Press.

Prochaska, J. O., & DiClemente, C. (1982). Transtheoretical therapy: Toward a more integrative model of change. *Psychotherapy, 20,* 161–173.

Prochaska, J. O., & DiClemente, C. (1983). Stages and processes of self-change in smoking: Toward an integrative model of change. *Journal of Consulting and Clinical Psychology, 5,* 390–395.

Prochaska, J. O., & DiClemente, C. C. (1992). The transtheoretical approach. In J. C. Norcross & M. R. Goldfried (Eds.), *Handbook of psychotherapy integration* (pp. 300–334). New York: Basic.

Prochaska, J. O., DiClemente, C. C., & Norcross, J. C. (1992). In search of how people change: Applications to the additive behaviors. *American Psychologist, 47,* 1102–1114.

Reis, B. F., & Brown, L. G. (1999). Reducing psychotherapy dropouts: Maximizing perspective convergence in the psychotherapy dyad. *Psychotherapy: Theory, Research, Practice, Training, 36*(2), 123–136.

Sifneos, P. E. (1992). *Short term anxiety provoking therapy: A treatment manual.* New York: Basic.

Singer, E. (1994). *Key concepts in psychotherapy* (2nd Ed.). New York: Aronson.

Weiner, I. J. (1975). *Principles of psychotherapy.* New York: Wiley.

four

Shining Light on Intimacy and Sexual Pleasure

Carol Hicks-Lankton

We are the night ocean filled
with glints of light. We are the space
between the fish and the moon,
while we sit here together.

—Rumi

THIS CHAPTER ELABORATES THE THERAPIST'S role as a kind of spotlight that illuminates without judgment the delicate opening of each client's intimate nature. Using eyes, heart, and soul to generate our "light," we focus awareness upon this universal and yet daunting desire for intimacy. I am using the term *intimacy* to include sex but also to represent any behaviors marked by close acquaintance or familiarity and pertaining to or indicative of one's deepest, essential, and innermost self. The work included in this chapter attends carefully to the intense connection between sex and intimacy.

Complaints and frustrations about sex are hot topics in couples therapy. Clients come to me looking for the quickest fix possible for problems that threaten to undo them, problems that are often embarrassing for them to discuss alone, never mind in front of a stranger. They often want me to make pronouncements—telling them what to do, which one of them is deluded, where they went wrong, how they should act, whether they are compatible or should move apart, or whether they are normal. Sometimes they want me to use hypnosis for some vaguely defined purpose like enhancing sexual arousal, getting the truth from one or the other, or removing destructive impulses via some kind of brainwashing. Before I can assist them in any way, I first have to learn a lot from them, and I need to let them know what I can and can't and will and won't do.

EXPECTATIONS AND ASSUMPTIONS

Although clients expect a lot from me, I enter into the therapy relationship knowing very little about them. I don't know how close they are to the end of their tolerance or their love for each other, how flexible they are in their desires, or how much they want to change things. However, I enter with confidence that together we can put all the pieces of this puzzle out on the table and fit them into a meaningful whole.

I always hope to discover that my clients want to work towards mutually compatible, realistic changes, but my primary guiding principle as a therapist is to be open to, discover, and accept the understandings my clients bring to me. I strive to make sense of whatever unfolds in the moment, so I can assist my clients in having their needs recognized, voiced, accepted, validated, and met. These needs—whether individual or joint, whether insignificant or intensely nonnegotiable, whether sexual, financial, or household—always seem intricately interconnected, regardless of what is first presented to me as a problem.

It is a difficult and complex task for most humans to know what they want and to ask for it in a friendly way, and this is particularly true in the sexual arena. In most cases, both partners will go on record as having the other's best interests at heart; however, rarely do they believe their partner wants the best for them. Instead, they express doubt, misgivings, and downright disbelief in their partner's goodwill. Therapy aimed at resolving the trust barriers that contribute to doubt and suspicion often takes longer than simply negotiating compromises that would maximize sexual pleasure.

In a good partnership, both members believe they are already getting most of their needs met, and thus can appreciate the marriage as a good deal, despite its problems. However, when the partnership is not meeting individual needs, I remain open to the possibility that ending the relationship is preferable to the partners' continued attempts to reform each other. If the couple feels a basic tenderness and acceptance toward each other, I help them determine the viability of their relationship by creating a context in which they can explicitly share their disappointments and desires.

BARRIERS TO INTIMACY

The quest for intimacy is fraught with significant barriers: problematic cultural expectations, a lack of specificity in communicating desires, and shame. Those who can't transcend such limitations risk a sad and lonely isolation.

Cultural Expectations

In Western culture there is a strong prohibition against doing anything that might be seen as selfish. Asking outright for what one wants is often perceived as unacceptably selfish rather than refreshingly honest. As an unrealistic alternative, many clients hope to avoid this dilemma by clinging to the hope that their partner will automatically know what they want. Additionally, many people do not give themselves permission to say *no* when asked to do something they don't feel comfortable doing (particularly something related to sex), fearing conflict or their partner's rejection. Others want to avoid vulnerability, so they express their needs and desires as demands. And though all of these complicating elements are inherently formidable, they become even more hazardous and daunting when the needs are sexual.

Zack and Ellen sat in my office and discussed ending their marriage, despite the deep love they apparently felt for each other. Ellen described Zack as selfish and immature; he strongly disagreed. Given all he did for the family, surely, he argued, it wasn't unreasonable to ask Ellen to clean and iron his uniforms, prepare the meals, take care of the household and children, and be ready for sex whenever he was. I congratulated him on clarifying his needs, pointing out that this was preferable to expecting Ellen to be a mind reader. And I agreed that he had every right to *ask* for anything and everything he desired of her. But was he actually *asking*? His "requests" sounded more like "demands" to me—demands that his wife fulfill the duties he'd assigned to her. If he was looking for a partner, rather than a slave or employee, he'd probably want to find a way to truly ask Ellen whether she was willing and able to satisfy his list of expectations. This would give her a chance to take his requests into consideration, running them past her personal priorities, interests, and other commitments. Some she could no doubt respond to positively; to others she'd probably find it necessary to say no.

Lack of Specificity

Particularly when it comes to sex, many people have great difficulty forthrightly specifying what they do and don't want from each other. Unable to y describe either their wants and needs or what they object to, they nevertheless consider themselves the ultimate authority on their partner's feelings and opinions.

Flora and Mark were experiencing frustration and disappointment in their relationship, but as I sat listening to them describe their concerns, I realized that although their lips were moving, I didn't know what they were really saying. They had initiated therapy to explore and hopefully alter the dissatisfaction they both experienced sexually in their relationship. Flora complained that Mark was not warm and affectionate enough before and during their sexual encounters, and Mark complained that Flora was not fun, playful, or adventurous enough in or out of bed.

I sought to get some kind of "operational definition" for the abstractions they were trading back and forth, but neither of them could elaborate on how "affectionate" or "adventurous" might actually translate into recognizable, doable, yearned-for behaviors. I got the sense that they weren't just reluctant to share the details with each other but that they didn't know themselves. They seemed to be hoping that they'd recognize what they wanted if they chanced upon it.

Responding to my probing, Mark was able to hazard the guess that sex might feel more adventurous if Flora were to diet her way into a "playboy bunny" body and engage with him in a threesome. Flora made it exceedingly clear that a third party would not be welcome in their bed, so I asked him if there was anything she could do in the confines of her current body that would satisfy any little part of his yearning for more "adventure." I wasn't able to help him come up with anything, and I likewise wasn't able to help Flora tease out a meaningful description of what Mark's being "affectionate" would look like.

In ideal relationships, partners are able to tell the truth, take nothing personally, and make no assumptions. However, in many relationships, partners, fearful of rejection, particularly sexual rejection, find it difficult to talk, so they devote much time trying to decipher hidden meanings in their partner's words and actions. I do my best to help clients bring to light their otherwise secret world of fearful interpretations, trusting that such openness can facilitate the development of alternative meanings.

Shame Surrounding Sexual Desires

Sarah and Mack were both struggling with feelings of depression that seemed, for the most part, to be independent of each other, though they each directed a considerable amount of blame for their unhappiness onto the other. Sarah came to see me first, but she talked so much about Mack, I thought it best to include him in our sessions so he could comment on Sarah's assumptions about his various behaviors. Leading the list of her concerns was Mack's recent admission that, in the past few months, he'd been compulsively visiting Internet porn sites. Sarah had concluded that she couldn't trust a "sex addict" with mysterious, shameful, and secret "issues," and she was questioning what to do with a man that obviously didn't find her attractive, didn't really love her, and would probably leave her.

When asked about their current sex life, Sarah said they didn't have sex as often as they would like, due to time constraints and the seemingly constant needs of their only child, an eight-year-old named Denise. Although she loved their daughter dearly, she greatly resented the pressure that Denise so easily placed on her.

Despite her resentment, Sarah was inspired by the congruent and unapologetic manner in which Denise made her demands, and she decided to elevate the status of her own needs so they would at least be equal to those of her daughter, her husband, the dog, or anyone else waiting in line for her attention. I suggested that every time she gave Denise validation for her needs and worth, she tag on a similar transmission to the little girl within herself who had rarely received such messages from her own mother.

In joint sessions, Mack supported Sarah's individual goals, and together they managed to dramatically lessen their overt and covert blaming, listening to each other without becoming defensive, reactive, or judgmental. Sarah stopped taking Mack's bad moods or critical remarks personally, and he tenderly convinced her that he indeed loved and enjoyed her, found her attractive, and wanted and missed her.

Feeling safe and accepted, they became curious to know more about each other, so I suggested it was time to explore the meaning of Mack's forays into Internet porn. Sarah was surprised to learn that Mack's motivation was entirely different from what she'd feared. He described having felt lonely, frightened, and frustrated by the responsibilities associated with a new job, relocation, money problems, and those same incessant needs of Denise that Sarah had described. Pressured and depressed, unable to discuss his distress with her, and afraid of her response should she learn of his Internet activities, he had distracted himself by surfing fantasy sites, where responsibility did not intrude.

Sarah heard and believed this explanation with significant relief. When I was last in touch with them, they were saying no to some of Denise's and the dog's needs and were making time to play with each other, sexually and otherwise, with very satisfying results. They were a little unsettled about feeling so good, but they were willing to deal with it.

HYPNOSIS AND BRIEF THERAPY

I often incorporate hypnosis in my marital therapy, though rarely in the dramatic way it is expected. Being identified as a professional with a hypnosis specialty probably brings me more than the average amount of clients who expect me to mysteriously "fix" some sexual perversion, uncover hidden aspects of the past, or investigate truth as if it were an "X-file." My purposes in using hypnosis are at once more modest and more realistic. I use it to heighten and focus awareness, as well as to promote learning, understanding, goal-setting, resource retrieval, and sometimes the reinterpretation of past events.

I like the Jungian idea of a "spotlight of consciousness" that, though limited in scope, can move freely, bringing light to shadow. When I am facilitating within the hypnotist role, I am the spotlight operator, seeking to illuminate clients' goals, the stumbling blocks that are getting in the way, and the experiences or conditions the clients need to reach their goals.

As Milton Erickson defined it, hypnotic trance involves clients' focusing inward on their own thoughts, feelings, and memories. Irrelevant, external distractions are minimized, while attention is concentrated on needs and desires in the current state. My clients and I don't go on archeological digs to prove or discover what was "really true" in the past but rather to occasion a direct experience of individual truth in the here and now.

Managing Desire Discrepancies

I am often asked to use hypnosis to fix one or the other member of a couple who have differing levels of desire for sexual intimacy. Each person is like the egocentric driver on the highway who defines "normal" in terms of his or her own speed, assessing anyone going faster as a "maniac" and anyone going slower an "idiot." Such a request usually prompts me to suggest that sexual needs aren't right or wrong in and of themselves, but only in relation to the partner's similar or incompatible needs. I remind my clients of the split-screen snippet from the movie *Annie Hall*, in which Woody Allen and Diane Keaton are each in a therapy session with their individual shrinks. Allen laments that they "almost never have sex, maybe only three or four times a week," while Keaton complains, "We have sex all the time, like three or four times a week!"

Karen and Phil were originally seeing another therapist, who inappropriately referred Karen so I could "use hypnosis to help her unblock her sexual expression." Something was apparently mysteriously "wrong" with her, and it was going to take hypnosis to whack it out of her. I did not accept this contract, but I did agree to work, first with Karen alone, to help her explore what she wanted sexually and in the relationship generally. She was furious at what she perceived as Phil's immaturity and explosive temper, which was often triggered by her refusing to have sex.

To help Karen learn more about what she considered necessary for satisfying sex, I invited her to develop a comfortable trance state and to imagine herself and Phil enjoying a pleasurable sexual encounter. When she reoriented from her visualization, Karen said she been repulsed by her fantasy. Angry with Phil, she did not want to see him have any pleasure, yet she claimed that she loved him and wanted to continue their marriage.

During subsequent hypnosis sessions, I sent her on additional internal exploration assignments, each time asking her to delve into a different aspect of the present and the future. What does an ideal marriage look like? What needed to happen for them to approach that state?

Not surprisingly, Karen did not produce many specific particulars in response to these questions, so we decided that she needed to collect data every way she could, including engaging in "experimental sex" with her husband to observe her reactions and awareness of her needs. I recommended she use a "why not?" strategy when considering Phil's daily advances. When Phil would ask her for sex, she was to initially say *to herself*, "Sure, why not?" and then carefully observe her internal response to determine if some really important "why not?" reason should present itself. If one did, she was to reply, simply and firmly, *no*.

If, however, no compelling reason were to present itself, then Karen was to say *yes* and proceed to find out what she could learn. Phil was delighted with this idea, and they starting having sex slightly more often than usual. Karen also agreed to start telling Phil immediately when she was angry at him for his temper or selfishness, but because he was much happier now that he was getting some sex again, she saw less and less of this behavior.

As it turned out, Karen had no "mysterious blocks" in need of removal. She would probably never desire sex as often as Phil did, but her experimenting allowed her to examine and modify her judgmental stance that he shouldn't want it so frequently. Feeling less angry and more in touch with her ability to choose, she was comfortable having sex with him more often, even when she didn't share his degree of enthusiasm.

Exploring Ideal Futures for Goodness of Fit

I'm never surprised when clients, like Karen, aren't able to specifically describe what they want to be different in their sexual relationships. Initially at least, they're able to say much more about what they *don't* want and what they dislike about their partner, so I ask each of them to privately elaborate on this as much as possible. Then they are to take each criticism and turn it inside out until they are able to use this awareness about what they don't want to guide them to an understanding of what they do want. At that point they are ready to directly share only their requests for desired behaviors with each other. Before each partner begins, I ask the other to get into a receptive, nondefensive listening state in which he or she simply receives the transmission about what pleases the partner, whether it currently exists or not. The resulting information can be thought of as "keys to the kingdom" given to a trusted partner whom the person agrees to let inside.

To further facilitate the process, I use hypnosis to help them travel into an imagined future together, a time when they will have accomplished the most ideal relationship they can fantasize, one that includes positive experiences in all vital areas: sex, emotional intimacy, conflict resolution, power-sharing, raising children, managing money, balancing time together and apart, and so on.

While they are fantasizing about sex, I give suggestions for them to experience encounters that allow for deep respect of self and other, verbal and nonverbal communication of their heartfelt desires, and feeling pleasure throughout.

When the couple can picture a nuanced version of a future ideal relationship, I ask them to merge in the present with those "future selves," to feel the pleasures of that accomplishment, and then, memorizing it, to fall into another dream within the dream they are already in and review the steps they "took" to make this happy future become a reality. Finally, I reorient them to the current time frame and invite them to share their newly detailed dream with their partner.

Couples commonly produce fairly different dreams. When therapy goes well, they are delighted and inspired to augment and enrich their individual fantasies with details from the other person's. But when it doesn't, the fantasized territory each person has charted individually overlaps little, if at all, with that of the other person. In such cases, a couple may painfully conclude that their divergent destinations preclude their being able to travel together happily.

Dan and Natalie came to therapy at Natalie's insistence. Complaining that Dan, an airline pilot, had chronically cheated throughout their 20-year marriage, Natalie demanded that major changes were required if the marriage were to survive.

The couple had not had sex at all since Natalie's hysterectomy 6 months earlier, and they had only rarely been intimate for a long time before that. Natalie was sure that Dan considered her unattractive because of the slight pooch of her belly and because he was comparing her to the much younger women with whom he'd had affairs. Dan found sex with Natalie difficult because of lubrication problems and possible pain, but he emphasized that he definitely found her sexually attractive, and he claimed to have sworn off other women. Both agreed that having sex together would help Dan keep his promise, as he said that his estrangement from his wife rendered him somewhat vulnerable to affairs. But Natalie had let him know that sex was out of the question until he took an HIV test.

During a hypnosis session, I asked them to go forward in time to a relationship where they had realized the goals they'd identified in an earlier meeting, inviting them to experience their positive life together with as much action and sensation as possible. Then, after reviewing how they'd gotten to that imagined future, they reoriented to the present time and shared their hopes, dreams, and operational definitions about the relationship they hoped to construct. Both described an active and passionate sex life together as their highest priority. Natalie emphasized the need for absolute honesty from Dan, as well as a test to clear him on possible sexually transmitted diseases. She wanted to stop withholding sex, but she also wanted to be included as an equal on financial matters, something that Dan had never allowed. He was happy about the first part but not about the second. Nevertheless, they both wanted to play together again, in bed and out.

Dan reluctantly but eventually took the blood test and was given a clean bill of health. Natalie, meanwhile, used several individual hypnosis sessions to mentally explore the health and workings of her post-surgery body, remembering its capacity for sensuous and sexual pleasure and appreciating the healing she had accomplished. They were just finishing construction on a new home, so she used the virginal romantic master suite as a background context for mental rehearsals about how they were about to be newly married again, complete with vows to be honest and monogamous. She held constant a feeling of pride about her healthy, fun-loving body while she imagined initiating sexual encounters, letting herself be seduced, flirting, touching, pleasuring, and asking for what she wanted with her newly expressive self. And with very little fanfare about how amazing it was to have so suddenly ignited their passion again, they reported marvelous results.

During a follow up almost a year later, Nancy informed me that despite their satisfactory resolution of sexual intimacy, Dan was still resisting her efforts to become financially equal with him. Guarding his privacy and treating her, in many ways, like one of their children, he was not willing to attend therapy sessions to address her concerns. Nancy was resentful and feeling the impulse to distance and withdraw from him again. Sadly, as successful as the sexual reunion had been, it was only one facet of the true intimacy that remained elusive for this couple.

CASE STUDY

The following case study offers a more comprehensive illustration of my work, demonstrating my efforts to build a strong and trusting relationship, explore patterns of stuckness, reinterpret meanings, and encourage clients to move toward their desired futures while respecting their pace and their simultaneous desires for change and predictability.

Shawn and Savannah, a young navy couple married for almost two years, sat down in exasperation at their first session. When asked what they wanted from seeing me, Savannah announced, "We want to achieve a normal conversation without incessant arguing." I inquired whether there was an identifiable theme to the arguing, to which they both answered simultaneously and in passionate agreement, "Our sex life!"

Before we explored the details of that argument, they summarized that they had gotten married after Shawn returned from a deployment and Savannah had just given birth to their son, Eric. Prior to that, they had known each other for several years as friends who mainly got together for mutually enjoyed sex (though Shawn was officially dating someone else). Shawn described himself as a "jerk" during that period and noted that only when Savannah became pregnant and the other relationship ended did they seriously begin to discuss marriage. Without really knowing each other, they calmly decided to keep the baby and to marry when he returned from the deployment. They entered the marriage with a pledge to release the many accumulated hurts and start with a "clean slate." However, they were also starting with a three-month-old baby and a completely different orientation to sex, despite the fact that it had previously been the only significant bond between them.

Now, over a year and a half later, Savannah rarely desired sex and Shawn was not only sexually frustrated but also deeply hurt by the perceived rejection. When I asked about their patterns of sexual interaction, I learned that Shawn typically asked for sex in a less than friendly manner, through sulking, complaining, and threatening to leave. Savannah, not wanting to get pregnant again and unable to use many contraception methods, was demanding that Shawn wear a condom. This demand was motivated by what Savannah described as "finally beginning to feel good about myself, losing weight, and needing to have some time to figure out who I am." Shawn was offended by her "just springing it" on him without warning or discussion. Though he objected to the condom for all the ordinary reasons, he was additionally offended by the implied rejection and distance.

The second session began with Savannah discussing her new job—a 4 P.M. to 11 P.M. shift that would significantly limit interaction time with Shawn, who was gone each day from 6 A.M. to 4 P.M.

Carol: So I guess that will pretty well put an end to the incessant arguing about sex, or anything else for that matter, because you two will hardly ever be at home and conscious at the same time any more.

Savannah: Actually, we didn't argue much this week except for that one night.

Shawn: [*looking kind of guilty*] Yeah, well . . .

Savannah: We did have sex but it was a big argument first. He didn't want to wear a condom, of course, even though I asked him to very nicely.

Carol: What happened?

Savannah: I gave in.

Carol: You gave in and had sex and he gave in and wore the condom?

Savannah: No, I gave in on both parts. We had sex without the condom.

Carol: What motivated you to do that?

Savannah: Because I didn't want to fight all night and I was tired of him throwing a fit.

Carol: [*to Shawn*] How were you throwing a fit?

Savannah: He starts packing his stuff together like he's going to leave.

Shawn: I just get so tired of her loud-mouthed sarcasm that I just want to go off on my [motor] bike and go fast, doing donuts and stuff.

With the session beginning to spin into insults, despair, and blame, I wanted to intervene with a positive frame and to facilitate a more accurate expression and understanding of their separate stances.

Carol: There is a lot of passionate energy on this matter of the condom. I'm not sure Savannah understands yet what this strong reaction you have really means. I take it that your objections go beyond the normal one that anyone has with condoms when they put up with it anyway because sex with a condom is usually considered better than no sex at all. Of course, in this case, you got the sex without the condom but it doesn't look like either of you feel too good about that. So what does her insistence on this condom thing mean to you?

Shawn: [*with tears in his eyes, to Savannah*] I just feel so hurt with all the rejection for a long time. You used to want me and it just feels so cold now. And wanting me to wear a condom just feels like one more way of getting further away from me, like an excuse you're using. It's not even just in sex, but the whole affection thing. I come up and put my arms around you from behind and you don't even stop what you're doing or act like you notice. It would really mean a lot if you acted like you care.

Carol: [*to Savannah*] Is he reading you accurately or can you help him understand how it is for you?

Savannah: [*to Shawn*] No! I don't want the condom just to be stubborn or get more distance from you! That isn't right. Even though I haven't wanted sex as much as I used to, I do still enjoy it sometimes and I am still attracted to you even when we're not having sex.

Carol: So you still want him sexually?

Savannah: Yes, but I don't want to get pregnant again. I just want him to wear the condom so we can have sex without me worrying about everything that would happen if I get pregnant.

Carol: So, now that you are just about recovered from the last pregnancy obstacle, you want Shawn but you don't want another pregnancy. It sounds like you'd like him to see the condom as a green light for sex with a built-in insurance policy that would guarantee even more sex and other fun together.

Savannah: That's right, and I ask him really nicely but he just gets so mad. And also, I'd like to sometimes have some romance and friendly conversation and snuggle time, but he won't even go in the bedroom together if he thinks we're not going to have sex.

Carol: This is interesting. For two people who claim to be arguing so much, it seems as though you both want the same thing, even down to this affection ingredient. You are both describing feeling hurt when it feels like the other one is rejecting you. You get hurt if it seems like Shawn won't just cuddle and talk in the bedroom when there isn't a chance for sex and Shawn wouldn't take this condom rejection so hard if he weren't feeling like you weren't interested in his touchy, friendly gestures. So it sounds like to me that you both want sex and you both want affection at other times too. I see a lot of basis for hope in that! Where is the disconnect?

Savannah: I guess I'm not a very touchy kind of person and I am so busy with the baby and doing everything around the house that maybe I do seem not very friendly to him. But then he gets so mad and I feel like he won't even come to bed together if there is no chance of sex. I would like it if we didn't have to have sex every night but maybe every other night have sex and the night in between just have a conversation in bed and cuddle.

Carol: So, Shawn, did you hear her say that she would be interested in having sex as often as every other night? Did you know that? Would that be satisfactory?

Shawn: [*mouth open, shaking his head with a look of shock and disbelief*] Oh, yeah, right . . .

Carol: It sounds like good news to me. Would that be okay with you, and cuddle and talk every other night?

Shawn: [*still reeling with disbelief and needing to challenge Savannah*] Tell her how many times we've had sex in the month since you've been back from visiting your family.

Savannah: Okay, maybe twice.

Carol: Wanting it every other night still counts as her goal, doesn't it? Even if things have been radically different in the recent past? You two are good at releasing old hurts. You already told me. So would every other night be enough for you or what?

Highlighting their successes, I attempted to move them toward their desired future by moving away from further talk of frustration and disappointments.

Shawn: Well, yes, that would be great!

Carol: I assume this frequency will be contingent on use of the pregnancy-preventing condom? You wouldn't want to be having that much unprotected sex unless you're willing to make another baby.

I wanted to punctuate the new meaning of the condom—as a pregnancy-preventing pathway to intimacy.

Savannah: Yes!

Shawn: Okay, I guess I could do that.

Despite her lack of interest in sex, Savannah still found Shawn attractive, but he was only able to interpret her loss of desire as a personal rejection. This belief was further confirmed by Savannah's never reciprocating his attempts at nonsexual affection. Looking back at Savannah's history, we discovered that she hadn't received much in the way of modeling or encouragement to be overtly friendly. I thus described her creating interpersonal distance as eminently logical, given her upbringing and her strong tendency to criticize and doubt herself. Her lack of expressiveness didn't mean she wasn't a nice person or didn't love her husband, although he naturally took it that way. Because her actions weren't really about him, he could perhaps begin to appreciate that her recent "breakthroughs" in liking herself more were changes that could benefit both of them.

We talked about the possible benefits of them both clarifying what they wanted and of doing their best to respond positively to the other's expressed need, even if they didn't understand it or didn't, at the time, share the desire. Shawn was not convinced this was a good idea.

Shawn: [*looking troubled*] Yeah, but I just don't know if I could handle it, knowing that she is only doing it because she feels sorry for me or something and doesn't mean it. I don't want her to just fake it.

Carol: Learning doesn't have to end. It's never too late to become the person you realize you want to be, even if you didn't have the opportunity to automatically learn to be that way while you were growing up. And if the two of you as a couple help to inspire each other to grow into those ideal people as a result of the courage you have to express your needs to each other, that is a wonderful thing. I wouldn't want either of you to do anything you legitimately did not want to do just because the other asks you to, but I do hope you can both venture into doing things for each other that are kind of appealing, even exciting, even though it's "not you" typically and it will be a bit awkward for you to go out on the limb and act that way.

When Savannah cancelled their next session, I called to see if they'd gotten all the help they needed (always a possibility I'm hoping for!) or if they had some problem with the therapy. She told me that things were better, but they weren't ready to stop. We rescheduled with the goal of clarifying and specifying how they had "come over some hurdles and were having better sex." This would allow them to take credit for the change and to replicate it in the future.

I asked if "better" meant that Shawn was cooperatively wearing the condoms. Savannah had gone out and bought some for him, which "tickled him so much." She added that she wanted "just to loosen up a little more." Her meaning became clear the next time we met. With both of them smiling, Shawn explained how Savannah had been so much easier to live with during the preceding week. Since she'd started working, she hadn't been nagging him about household chores or getting irritable the way she had previously.

Carol: So that's interesting. You are overextended and tired from working. A person might think you would be more easily irritable about stuff that used to bother you, but you are noticing it is working the opposite?

Savannah: I just don't have time to. I see him maybe 20 minutes a day. I can wake him up to say hi, and he's dead to the world. If he does wake up to say hi to me, he doesn't remember it the next day.

Carol: [to Shawn] You look like you're pleased about something.

Shawn: Actually, I asked her to quit working. I miss her. Whether she nags at me to do this or that, at least she is there to do it. You know? I kind of sit at home lost because no one is telling me to do something. She gives me a list of stuff to do before she goes to work but when she comes home she is too tired to really care either. I used to put on a show pretending to care but I just didn't.

Carol: [to Savannah] When I talked to you last week you said the two of you had "come over some hurdles" somehow. That sounded good and is worth exploring in some detail.

Shawn: I know what one of the hurdles was. She actually initiated some sexual activity. I was dead sleeping. And she's lying—I do wake up. I feel her hand on my leg and I'm here! And I was conscious although I thought I was dreaming.

Carol: So you really liked that?

Shawn: Yeah, it was neat because when I talk her into it, it just seems like she's doing it for me with a reluctant sigh and an "all right, here."

Carol: And that's just not as much fun, is it?

Shawn: Well, no, it's not, because I tell her all the time, it's not the sex. It's really not because it's about me trying to make her feel good and her trying to make me feel good and if I talk her into it, I'm automatically just borderline to not even do it because I don't need the sex. I need for her to feel wanted and me to feel wanted like she really wants me. If I talk her into it I don't get that feeling. I get kind of like "would you hurry?"

Carol: Sort of like an uphill battle to make her feel good since she doesn't really want to do it at that time. You probably get the sense you're making her feel worse?

Shawn: Yeah. I really do. And I didn't feel like that the other night.

Carol: [*to Savannah*] So is that a hurdle you were talking about getting over?

Savannah: Yeah, and that I also went and bought condoms.

Shawn: Yeah, that was neat.

Savannah: And he hasn't been . . .

Shawn: . . . protesting.

Carol: Okay, well that's interesting in a surprising way, too. Tell me how you perceived her buying condoms as "neat." What was cool about that?

Savannah: That he didn't have to buy them, for one thing.

Shawn: Well, I don't know. Did it make you uncomfortable to buy them? Because it would me.

Savannah: I stood there in the aisle reading all the boxes. I mean I never bought them before.

Carol: It almost seems like it was a turn-on, not just something you could put up with but sort of neat.

Shawn: Well, it was kind of neat because I figured she knew I would be hesitant to buy more and she probably had this attitude like, "Yes, we're out." [*laughter*]

Carol: So her buying a bunch of condoms is kind of like another way of her initiating sex. It's like she's saying, "Hey I want to have this much sex," right?

Savannah: Well, I took an interest in it. I think that's pretty much what it is.

Carol: So that's all it took to turn the green light for you to take her up on her request that you have sex but have it with a condom, please?

Shawn: Well, I don't think I'm ever going to give the full green light because that is . . . I don't know. I mean, she's my wife and I'd like to see . . . I mean, I know a lot of people are running around with five or six kids and saying "oops." Out of all the people I know who are married, I just want to ask them, "Hey, what method are you using? Does your wife make you wear a condom?" Because I feel really like minority. I want to be like one of the other guys and not wear one.

Carol: So it represents a pretty big push for you to do it because obviously it is still way less than what you would prefer to do. So, it is a show of your motivation or willingness to cooperate . . . ?

Shawn: Yeah, I don't want to fight with her. Ah, man, at first I thought she was just going to give in and I kept thinking I could stay being a butt-hole just a little bit longer and she'll give in. I mean, how much more could it take? I'm doing a pretty good job. And she never broke.

Carol: So you decided you would go ahead and break or give up the attempt?

Savannah: I think we've both given up a little bit on both ways.

Carol: How did you give up?

Savannah: Well, just us getting along. We haven't really been fighting. We've been getting along pretty good. And then even for me to start sex is a step in the right direction. And I think he knows that, too, so he isn't going to fight about it.

Carol: Because it seems like the condom did stop meaning that she was somehow rejecting you. Because she bought them, she's initiating, she's making it clear she wants you. And now the condom doesn't mean that—it might still be a little irritating is all.

Shawn: It did mean that, but condom or not, she was rejecting me anyway, you know? A lot of those times, even if I wore a condom, she'd still say no. So the condom thing was like icing on the cake—just another form of barrier or something. Now I don't feel so much like that, especially after she initiated it.

Carol: Well, it is a barrier.

Shawn: It is but it is just a small barrier.

Savannah: It's a start.

Shawn: It's a start but I don't think she's ever been rejected by me. She just doesn't know what it feels like to be rejected and the things that come of that. It really hurts me especially since we're married, I always use this phrase "my wife" this and "my wife" that and the whole aspect of everything changes when you get married. When I talked about my girlfriends, I didn't have so much pressure on me to try and make things work. But now that's all I try to do. Like if I get rejection, I'm just sitting back thinking "my own wife doesn't want to have sex with me." That's really to me overwhelming.

Carol: Well, are we talking past tense now? That overwhelmed feeling from rejection you had been feeling and that's one of the things that's shifted? That you're not feeling that rejection any more or that it's a matter of degree?

I wanted to keep the focus on the positive changes and move the discussion away from past hurts and rejections.

Shawn: Yeah, it's a matter of degree really. I can understand that she's tired. Sometimes when I roll over and touch her and she just moans like she's pitiful, she might as well just slap me and say "no."

Carol: Well, do you distinguish between times when she isn't able to be conscious and times when it feels like a rejection of you? Are you at a place where she can say "no," and even though you're disappointed, you don't take it as rejection of you personally?

Shawn: No [*laughing*].

Carol: So anytime she says "no" it's still rejection?

Shawn: Yeah, because it's not like I walk in the door, kiss her, and demand sex every minute.

Carol: So what are you saying? Since you don't ask her every minute, then when you do . . .

Shawn: Then it's kind of hard not to take it as rejection. Because it's not like I'm asking her all the time and have a reason to get turned down.

Carol: You ask a sparing amount you mean?

Shawn: I think so.

Carol: Compared to how often you could ask if you followed all your impulses?

Shawn: Yeah. If she's asleep, and I'm not, I don't try to worm my way in or anything. I let her sleep and I sleep and if we have a day when we're both off which is once a week sometimes, then I'll ask her and she like sighs and says "fine."

Savannah: It hasn't been like that.

Shawn: It hasn't been as bad.

Carol: Well, that's what we're talking about, how things are shifting for the better.

Shawn: And in the two weeks since we've seen you last, we've had sex twice, and like she said, it's gotten better.

Carol: Well, you're moving in the right direction. And that's a good thing.

Shawn: But they were back to back, too, which really showed me a sign of improvement.

Carol: Oh, yeah? You liked that even though it didn't spread them out?

Shawn: [*laughing*] Yeah.

Carol: Well, when you left here, you left with the lofty goal of approaching a frequency of every other night and with off nights being cuddling and talking.

Shawn: Oh, see, yeah, I had brought that up and she goes, "Oh, yeah, that's a goal that maybe someday we will get to" were her words. And then, I want to clarify something else. When you had said last time about there being other alternatives and substitutes for sex like oral stuff. And she's sitting over here nodding and saying "um-hmm" and I brought that up to her and she said, "Yeah, I was nodding agreement that it is an alternative method, but I won't do it."

Carol: Oh. Was that one of the snags or hurdles that you might be moving toward getting over or considering getting over?

Savannah: No.

Shawn: No, because that's not one of my. . .

Carol: That's not one of your pleasures?

Shawn: Well, no, I didn't say that!

Carol: Not one you're getting anyway?

Shawn: Yeah.

Savannah: And never has got used to getting.

Carol: From anyone ever? Or just in this relationship?

Shawn: In this relationship.

Carol: And that's because you don't want to for a particular reason?

Shawn: We both kind of. . . . It's just not a big deal for us.

Carol: Well, it looks like there is some kind of avoidance aspect to it for you. Is there any reason for that to be?

Savannah: No, I mean it's not like it's never been done or anything like that. It's just not something that I'm into.

Carol: Either giving or receiving?

Savannah: No.

Carol: [to Shawn] And you feel kind of the same?

Savannah: [answering for Shawn] No. I mean he would be a happy camper, but he just knows.

Shawn: I don't ever ask, because she would just go "hah," and I pretty much know where that's going.

Carol: Well, that is certainly inconvenient since it would be such a wonderful alternative for a couple stuck with the birth control method of condoms. It would be a nice break from the choice of using condoms or avoiding pleasure, an occasional reward for going along with the condom to have some pleasure that doesn't require a condom. But that won't work if it isn't pleasurable for both people, or at least tolerable.

My emphasis here was on underscoring their successes so that they became established as solid, stable steps in the direction they want to go. Though both were clearly pleased with their progress, Shawn continued to share his ambivalence about the condoms and the overtones of rejection they carried, despite all the evidence to the contrary. Exploring possibilities of their further "loosening up," I learned that Savannah drew the line at oral sex.

However, in the next session, they declared themselves candidates for an even more significant loosening of one of their pervasive and destructive patterns of relating—the chronic sarcasm they frequently directed towards each other. Before proceeding there, I first wanted to explore how it operated and to determine if it was currently working for them in some way. I'm not being "paradoxical" when I check out with clients if they need to continue with something problematic; rather, I'm respecting their pace and their needs as I help move them toward change.

Carol: Well this sarcasm thing is something you have in common, and I don't know but that it's there for a good reason, I guess. Right? I mean you wouldn't do it if it wasn't doing something for you.

Savannah: We feed off of one another because he says something and I say something worse and then he can say something still worse. So it's just something between the two of us.

Carol: Do you suppose it's a way to protect yourselves from hurt? Or do you suppose it's a way to keep a safe distance from each other? Not get too close, even though, at one level, you certainly want to be more intimate than you are?

In response to my questions, Savannah explained that both of them had learned in childhood that keeping your defenses up is a good way of avoiding hurt.

Savannah: And being let down is probably a big thing for me, too, because it seems no matter what in my life, just getting my hopes up, I get let down on something. So yeah, it probably does have a lot to do with it.

Carol: It's just safer to not get your hopes up too much, and to bail out first.

Shawn: We both know that. It's something we've been dealing with for a while now.

Carol: I was really impressed when we first met and you were discussing how you had so rationally made that decision when you got married to erase the old hurts and forgive and start with a clean slate. That's a pretty mature thing a lot of people don't think of to do in their marriage. And now it seems like it might be time to reinstate that or to take that same kind of thing to another level right now. I don't know what would happen. I don't know if it would be a little foolhardy to just stop sarcasm. I don't know how much you really need it, but if you could experimentally make a "no sarcasm" contract for a week, we could see what happens and maybe learn whether you need it or not. So for one week, every time you feel the impulse to start with something sarcastic, you're going to back it up and think, "Wait a minute, what do I really mean and what do I really want to say here instead of some sarcastic cover up?" Because the only reason to refrain from doing that that I can think of is if you had some really good, valid reason not to trust each other to be capable of handling what you are going to say, or to care enough about you to receive the gift of your honesty. And I think you pass that test. I think you do care enough about each other.

Savannah: Oh, yeah, I trust him.

Carol: It's kind of like that sarcasm thing is obsolete. It's a defense mechanism you both know really well how to use from years of past training, but it doesn't seem like it applies. It doesn't seem like you really need it in this relationship. It's like you had a huge bunch of furniture that you've collected that doesn't fit in the apartment or house that you live in now. Why stack it all on top of itself? Just get rid of it with the attitude that this furniture served me well but I don't need it any more.

Shawn: We could probably do that. It would be hard but we could try it.

In the final minutes of this session, as we explored the kind of standard obstacles they could expect to encounter, we talked about the possibility of their taking an honest answer at face value, accepting it and the sender's statement as true.

Shawn made it clear to Savannah that his persistence with requesting sex or getting her to try a new food was not about trying to control her, but about a genuine desire to give her pleasure. When Savannah explained that giving into his insistence usually made her unhappy, Shawn reassured her that he always wanted her "honest to God" answer. I described his intentions as good ones and asked Savannah to explain what they might be.

Savannah: Well, he sees that he likes it and he wants to do it and so he wants me to share the joy.

Carol: And you like that. You just don't want your joy in the particular package that he's having?

Savannah: Right.

Carol: And not just about eating. It can happen about anything—big things too. And [*to Shawn*] it is your biggest thing that you want her to have pleasure. It says how much you love her.

Shawn: Yeah, I do.

Carol: So it's good news for you anytime you can learn how to increase her pleasure, right? Even if it means accepting her answers for what she wants. And you just made clear to her that you're doing that because of how much you value her pleasure. And I wouldn't be surprised to hear that somehow all this leads to more sex and more pleasure all around. See you next week.

In the fourth and last session, Savannah and Shawn pushed to explore tolerance for each other's different needs in areas other than sex, particularly household responsibilities and the distribution of financial power. Savannah said that not making much money and not having her name on the utilities, bank accounts, or credit cards left her feeling "like a nobody." And constantly and unsuccessfully nagging Shawn to help with the house resulted in her feeling like his mother. Shawn surprised her by revealing that he felt "like a nobody" too—"just someone who pays the bills."

These revelations about the similarity of their pain came to light without any mutual blaming, resulting in the generation of significant tenderness and compassion. They reiterated their intention to leave off sarcasm in favor of expressing what they really meant and wanted. Savannah, for example, agreed to simply ask directly for help or understanding when she needed it. I noted what a welcome departure this would be from her previous habit of coming home and complaining that Shawn hadn't cleaned anything up. They jokingly (yet seriously) discussed a possible arrangement in which Shawn would vacuum the house every other day—the same frequency he desired sex. He would happily become a "vacuuming fool," he said, if the two activities could be contingently linked. I didn't even mention to them how far they'd come from their first session, when all they'd wanted to achieve was a normal conversation without incessant arguing. I simply congratulated them on being "on the brink" of an exciting and profound shift in their way of relating to each other, one that included great sex as well as intimate affection and satisfying conversations. They'd found new and important ways to validate how important they were to each other.

DISCUSSION

I am always moved by the privilege of being allowed into the tender and vulnerable zone of a couple's private world. Once there, I proceed with the assumption that everything is necessarily interconnected with everything else. Thus, success in changing problematic sexual feelings and behaviors is more likely when other aspects of the relationship are also addressed and helped along. Whether I'm doing grief work, resolving earlier traumas, or helping the couple locate and express tenderness and kindness, the same guiding principles apply. Focusing on one piece of the puzzle, I always keep the whole in mind.

Couples often find the topic of sex unique, of course, because of the particular awkwardness and embarrassment that comes from discussing in public what's already been uncomfortable talking about in private. As a spotlight operator, I bring objectivity and comfort, holding my light gently but unflinchingly on tender places too long kept in the shadow of shame. I do so from the firm conviction that we are on a quest for treasure together and that the more any area has been hidden away as a weakness or dirty secret, the more we are likely to gain by finally allowing, including, and celebrating its particularly strong power and benefit. As Rumi observed long ago, we reflect and give birth to the value and beauty of another with the respect of our attention and acceptance:

> In your light I learn how to love.
> In your beauty, how to make poems.
> You dance inside my chest,
> where no one sees you,
> but sometimes I do,
> and that sight becomes this art.

five

Premature Ejaculation of "Sexual Addiction" Diagnoses

Tracy Todd

I HAVE A FRIEND WHO HAS A LITTLE HABIT. He spends at least $200 a month on it. Every week he reads glossy magazines devoted to it. Ask his wife about it, and she'll reveal that he loses time with his family because of it. He uses the Internet to explore it, and he does it more when he's feeling stressed.

So what do you think? Does my friend need to attend a sexual addiction group? Nah, he just needs a golf course. Yup, he's a golfer. Like most other duffers, he easily drops $50 for four or five hours of ball chasing and then stops off at the 19th hole for a beer. Nongolfers don't get it, but the time on the course is therapeutic for him. However, if instead of teeing off he were getting it on, the list of behaviors I mentioned in the first paragraph would, in many circles, get him classified as a sex addict.

"Sexual addiction" is one of the newest pathological labels gaining popular attention and acceptance. More and more people are showing up at my door with it branded on their foreheads. "I learned about it from a talk show," one man told me; "My wife's therapist says I am," said another. Clients arrive with a wealth of information obtained from the Internet, where you can find an abundance of self-assessment instruments, recovery workbooks, and advertisements for specialized treatment programs at hospitals. I can predict that if the identified "addict" hasn't reviewed such information, someone else has reviewed it for him (or her) and passed along the diagnosis.

Surf the web, read some program brochures, or peruse other sex addict propaganda, and you'll find virtually no descriptions of healthy sexuality. With fragmented and noncontextual ideas about sexuality inundating popular culture, anyone interested in sex beyond the confines of a predetermined and conventional value system can expect to be questioned, accused, and ultimately labeled. Casting blame on the "sexually disordered," their partners are able to avoid reflecting on themselves, and so-called specialists justify their assumptions and individual treatment myopia by discovering how a sexual problem located inside one of the partners is creating problems for both of them. Failing to notice or care about the contextual complexities of the complaint, everyone involved contributes to premature ejaculation of the sex-addict diagnosis.

DIAGNOSTIC CONSIDERATIONS

I should clarify that you won't find the diagnosis "sexual addiction" in the *DSM-IV.* The closest you'll get in the current version of the revered tome is Sexual Disorder Not Otherwise Specified, which is described as "distress about a pattern of repeated sexual relationships involving a succession of lovers who are experienced by the individual only as things to be used." You can, however, find the diagnosis on the website of the National Council on Sexual Addiction and Compulsivity (www.ncsac.org/definitions.html), where it is defined as "engaging in persistent and escalating patterns of sexual behavior acted out despite increasing negative consequences to self and others."

Considerable debate has been waged over whether a particular set of intractable problems should be considered addictions or obsessive-compulsive behaviors (Coleman, 1989, 1992, 1996). Klein (1998) argued that the addictions model fails to distinguish between sexual addiction and possibly more severe diagnoses, such as obsessive-compulsive disorders or personality disorders, and it often pathologizes sexual behaviors that are nonproblematic. Coleman (1989) further argued that addiction to sex is not the same as an addiction to alcohol or drugs. Generally, even so-called sex addicts hope to avoid giving up sex altogether, whereas a major premise of substance-abuse programs is the inviolability of abstinence.

In respected treatment programs, conference presentations, and refereed publications, clinical issues and treatment modalities are presented as though there were a body of comprehensive research about sexual addiction when, in fact, little exists. People questioning their sexuality or wanting to diagnose themselves, however, can take online self-assessment instruments that will help them realize how messed up they are. The author of the Online Sexual Addiction Questionnaire (OSA-Q), Dana Putnam, at least clarified that her 24-item scale is not a normed psychological test, and she went to the trouble of recommending that people with sexual problems seek out a professional with expertise in the area (www.onlinesexaddict.org/osaq.html). But web surfers are nevertheless able to diagnose themselves or someone they know by answering and scoring questions such as the following:

- Have you ever been caught looking at sexual material on your computer?
- Do you ever masturbate at the computer while looking at online pornography or while engaging in online sexual behavior with others?
- Do you spend money for sexual material or sexual interaction at pay sites?
- Do you ever spend time with online sexual material or engage in online sexual interactions when that time could have been spent with your family, friends, or a romantic partner?
- Have you accumulated credit card debt from fees paid to gain access to Internet sexual material?

Patrick Carnes, the author of the Sexual Addiction Screening Test (SAST), advised that his questionnaire should be considered a screening aid, but he simultaneously presented it as a highly researched instrument (www.sexhelp.com/sast.cfm). He helpfully supplied the phone number of a hospital to be contacted should the web surfer be sufficiently frightened by his or her score, but he also suggested the alternative possibility of contacting a healthcare professional who specializes in *addictions*. Here are some of the items on his instrument:

- Were you sexually abused as a child or adolescent?
- Do you regularly purchase romance novels or sexually explicit magazines?
- Do you often find yourself preoccupied with sexual thoughts or romantic daydreams?
- Does your spouse (or significant other[s]) ever worry or complain about your sexual behavior?
- Has sex or romantic fantasies been a way for you to escape your problems?

Despite the qualifiers offered by the authors of the questionnaires, laypeople seeking to understand themselves better could easily interpret the test results as credible. Therapists and treatment programs are similarly basing clinical decisions on instruments lacking such fundamental necessities as validity and reliability data. I don't know about you, but I'd be afraid to add up my score on some of these assessment variables! I find it alarming that I might be considered a sex addict if, in high-stress times, I let my thoughts return to that cute little redhead I dated a few years back. Alternatively, if I work hard *not* to think of her and I decide to avoid sex, I risk being labeled as suffering from—get this—"sexual anorexia," defined as "an obsessive state in which the physical, mental, and emotional task of avoiding sex dominates one's life" (www.sexhelp.com/whatissexanorexia.cfm).

Klein (2002) effectively criticized the sex addiction approach in terms of its pathology-based assumptions, acontextual considerations, and culturally bound and politically determined biases. Whatever diagnosis my clients present with, I work hard to fully listen to their story. Some are questioning the label that's been attached to them; others have started down the path of completely constructing a sexual addiction identity. Sometimes I'm successful at reigning in my urge to directly challenge their deficit-ridden beliefs; other times I'm not. I'm learning, though, that with patience and a strong commitment to allowing their story to unfold, I can both hear my clients' story of sexual addiction *and* make healthy interventions.

This chapter details a set of therapeutic assumptions that serve as guidelines for my work with clients who present with concerns about sexual addiction. Because the clients in the vignettes obtained their "sex addict" label from a variety of sources, an addictions specialist might argue that they hadn't received a thorough assessment and were thus not necessarily true "addicts." However, all of them, convinced that their story of addiction was accurate, were significantly distressed either by the diagnosis or by someone else in their lives who had accepted the truth of their "condition."

WORKING ASSUMPTIONS

*Assumption 1: The So-called Sexual Addiction is an Attempted
Solution for a Different Problem*

My first and most important premise is that the "addiction" represents a misguided attempt to solve some other problem or challenge. In some cases, the behavior can be construed as an attempt to show sensitivity to a partner.

One couple, both convinced that the husband, Terrell, was an addict, came to therapy after he had solicited sex from an escort service. A few years earlier, the couple's relationship had become distant, and Terrell had started exploring pornography. Terrell's wife, Juanita, suffered from a physical ailment that fatigued her so much that she didn't have energy for sex. Terrell became isolated, feeling selfish because of his sexual desire and the burden it could place on Juanita. His involvement with pornography continued to increase in proportion to the growing distance between him and his wife. Such gradual intensification is viewed in the sexual addiction literature as confirmatory evidence of addiction (Carnes, 2003; National Council on Sexual Addiction and Compulsivity, 2000).

Terrell's solution *not* to place a selfish burden on Juanita created a classic double bind. Approaching her for sex created distress, and seeking alternative sexual relations did the same. My first therapeutic step was to ask, "What are you trying to solve by exploring other avenues of sex?" Terrell responded, "Not to pressure my wife with my selfish needs." This simple sentence, when teased apart, contained two very poignant messages. He was conceiving sexual advancement as "pressure" and sexual desire as "selfish."

Rather than focusing on Terrell's "sexual addiction," we explored how to solve these two concerns. Significantly, the solutions we came up with almost exclusively focused on enhancing emotional closeness rather than increasing sexual frequency. At termination, both partners were amused that they were able to use some of Terrell's pornography endeavors to enhance their sex life. Although Juanita continued to feel hurt by Terrell's solicitation of sex from an escort, she disclosed that it may have ultimately strengthened their relationship.

Sometimes "sexual addiction" can be viewed as an awkward attempt to improve a relationship—an attempt that has, instead, undermined it. Brett explained that he'd wanted to "hint" to his wife, Suzie, that he was interested in a more dynamic sex life with her, so he'd started viewing pornography on the Internet and purchasing pornographic books, magazines, and videos. Suzie, unaware of his intent and feeling inadequate, withdrew from him, which had suggested to Brett that he needed to be more brazen with his hints. Their escalating cycle resulted in Brett's watching more and more porn and Suzie, not participating in any sexual relations with him, going for counseling. Her counselor never met Brett, but she diagnosed him as having a sex addiction (based on Susie's account of his gradual increase in pornographic involvement) and recommended he seek immediate help.

When they arrived for the first appointment, Brett was angry about the label he'd been given, and Suzie felt vindicated that it was "not her inadequacy" but Brett's addiction that was to blame for their situation. Both were surprised when I asked, "What do you think Brett was originally trying to solve by introducing sexual material into the marriage?" Because the situation had evolved over years, both were contemplative. Finally, Brett explained that his original efforts had been intended to enhance their sex life. Suzie recalled some of his more subtle hints and acknowledged that she thought he was "just joking." They both made insightful observations about their interactions and explored the possibility that communicating about their sexual relations would have helped them avoid this painful situation.

Single people identified as "sex addicts," concerned as they must be with safe sex and safe relationships, often come up with a different answer to my question about the problem they were originally trying to solve. Linda, a highly successful saleswoman in her late twenties, had "intimacy" issues. With a six-figure salary, minimal debt, and a strong financial portfolio, she was proud of her disciplined career and financial decisions, as they would allow her to be independent should she need to divorce the man she hoped to eventually meet and to raise alone the children she hoped to have.

Not wanting her plan disrupted by an unsatisfying and premature relationship, Linda met her sexual needs with a vibrator and videotapes. Her friends accused her of avoiding relationships out of fear, and one of them teased that she was fonder of her vibrator than of a real penis. Linda didn't buy the "fear-based avoidance" concern, but, acknowledging that her masturbation had increased in frequency and in involvement of videotapes, she questioned her sexuality and wondered whether she was becoming addicted to sex.

Hearing the guilt in her voice as she emotionally described her situation, I asked, "What are you trying to solve through solo sex?" Her response, accompanied by laughter, was succinct: "I want to stay focused on my career and, when I achieve certain goals, then pursue a relationship." She didn't want to be emotionally available or to risk beginning a relationship while still building wealth and financial security, but she was haunted by a question posed on a sexual addictions assessment instrument she'd completed: "Do you spend significant amounts of money on sexual aids or pornography?" A friend had decided that the $50 per month Linda was devoting to solo sex was indicative of addiction, regardless of the fact that the expenditure didn't create any financial hardship. The friend's concern further exacerbated Linda's shame.

I noted that, given how her $50 expenditure was contributing to her accomplishing her financial goals, such an investment strategy should perhaps be used by everyone. When the laughter died down, I asked her how many single people she knew who were spending $50 or more per *week* on golf and what sort of adverse effects such wanton spending was having on their personal lives.

As we continued talking, Linda became more comfortable with the idea that she wasn't a sex addict. Prior to concluding therapy, we defined what for her constituted healthy solo sex, and we set parameters that would help her determine whether she was sliding toward sexual addiction. These definitions and limits were important, as they increased her confidence that she wouldn't disrupt her personal and financial plans because of a sexual addiction.

Brian, also in his twenties, similarly entered therapy because of a supposed sexual addiction. Doing well in his job, he'd taken a career question to a counselor he'd found through his company's employee assistance program. Somehow they ended up talking about Brian's sexual practices, and the counselor referred him to me for sexual addiction treatment.

Brian believed that socializing and meeting women in bars and clubs was a waste of time and potentially harmful. The chance of meeting a compatible partner in such places was quite remote and the potential for contracting a sexually transmitted disease was far too high. Instead, he spent $30 a week on pornography that he used for masturbation. Recognizing how easy it would be to spend this amount for cover charges and drinks, Brian saw no reason for concern. He was also careful—he never, for example, surfed sex sites on the Internet while at work. I asked him about what he was solving through solo sex.

Brian: I'm allowing a relationship to develop that is healthy. I want to avoid any troubles by becoming involved in a sexual relationship that has no future.

Tracy: Is your solution working? Meaning, are you avoiding promiscuous relations and allowing dating relationships to evolve?

Brian: Yes.

Tracy: Good. Are you experiencing any financial jeopardy from the expenses?

Brian: No.

Tracy: Until you were referred, were you feeling guilt or shame about your
    sexuality?
Brian: No. My parents were open and never wanted us to feel shameful
    about sex.
Tracy: Great. Do you want to talk about your career?
Brian: [*with great relief*] Yes. That's why I started counseling.

This case is an excellent reminder of the importance of actually listening to clients. Imagine Brian's shock when a consult for career issues resulted in a referral for sexual addiction.

Assumption 2: The So-called Sex Addict Could be a Scapegoat

Living as we do in a sex-obsessed but simultaneously sex-negative society,
it is easy to have a critical viewpoint toward behaviors related to sex. With
this in mind, I attend to the possibility that those not participating in therapy (family members, friends, etc.), as well as other professionals, may be
scapegoating my client, casting blame as a way of avoiding being construed as part of the problem (and thus in need of therapy). With pivotal
members of a system having settled on a sexual-addiction diagnosis, a
therapist could easily buy into the mindset, focusing attention on only one
person and inadvertently creating further problems. To avoid such mishaps,
I like taking off (in conversation with my clients) for the golf course.

Cindy, fearful that her husband, Blake, was a sex addict, had gone to
a therapist and described behaviors that upset her—his spending up to
three hours at a time engrossed in pornography (time that was stolen from
the family), his spending up to $50 a week on it, and his making no secret
of the fact that he loved it and looked forward to watching it. The therapist
had confirmed her fears with a diagnosis based on the following criteria:
Blake was disrupting family functioning, he was causing financial distress,
and he was avoiding his relationship with his partner. He then referred her
to me, but I took the conversation in a different direction.

Tracy: Cindy, if I replaced *sex* and *pornography* with the word *golf*, would
    you still be as upset?
Cindy: [*Laughing*] No. I enjoy golfing.
Tracy: Let me challenge you a bit. If golf was creating the distress, would
    you want the focus to be on golf or on these other disturbances?
Cindy: Good point. I resent the lack of family involvement and time spent
    without me over golf. So it really isn't about the sex, it's about not
    being involved with the family.

Tracy: Let me clarify then. Is an acceptable goal of therapy to have more
  involvement from Blake?
Cindy: Yes.

At this point, we were able to cocreate goals acceptable to Cindy and
Blake, emphasizing interaction with his family and involvement with his
wife.

Assumption 3: Therapists Need to be Comfortable Talking About Sexual Behaviors

Wide ranges of emotions are usually present when discussing sexual addiction, and the behaviors and values brought forth may fall outside the therapist's comfort zone. Although I may find my clients' disclosures unique
and interesting, I sometimes also feel uncomfortable. I need to be able to
listen to and talk about sexual behaviors that go beyond my experience,
keeping to myself my shock or embarrassment; otherwise, I risk imposing
further embarrassment and blame on people who've had their fill. For example, a few years ago, a "couples club" opened near my practice, prompt-
ing many couples to ask my advice about joining. When listening to the
activities involving member participation, I found myself thinking, but not
saying, "I could *never* do that!"

Experiencing a direct conflict with my values and behaviors is an integral part of working with sexual issues. At these times, I find it critically
important to either staff the case with a colleague or to revisit the presented problem and cocreated goals of therapy. Most often, keeping the focus on goals works well, but at times I need to explore the source of my
discomfort and discuss with a colleague how to best prevent such unease
from minimizing my therapeutic effectiveness.

Assumption 4: Healthy Definitions of Sexuality Require Discussion and Clarity

I have personal ideas about what constitutes healthy sexuality, and my
clients often solicit my views, but I'm committed to respecting and eliciting *their* views, so we can co-create a *shared* understanding.* This stands
in stark contrast to the sexual addiction movement, which, as Klein
(2002) discussed, sets forth a set of "acceptable" behaviors and advocates
public policy decisions regarding the controlling of sexuality. I typically

---

* Although I firmly believe in co-creating healthy definitions of sexuality, I also assume that definitions and subsequent actions cannot result in harm to others (e.g., rape, pedophilia).

begin the co-creating process by asking "exception" and "miracle" questions (de Shazer, 1988):

"When did you have a healthy or more healthy definition of sex?"

"What was going on when your sexual activities were satisfactory?"

"What will be present, in the future, when you have a healthy sexual definition?"

Common responses include:

"We have never discussed it."

"My partner will not talk about it."

"I will 'just know' when it is happening."

"Why would we discuss sex?"

"At this time, my partner is too upset to discuss it."

Exception and miracle-style questions help me to learn the client's language about sexuality and provide a forum for conversation. When clients can identify times of healthy sexuality, they start to relax, perhaps feeling some relief that their sex life has some hope.

Ben suspected that his wife, Lisa, was a sex addict. They belonged to a sex club that had strict rules about not pressuring members to engage in any uncomfortable behaviors. Ben and Lisa had joined a year before coming to see me, interested in watching others having sexual relations, but Lisa had become frustrated with mere voyeurism. She had stopped viewing pornographic videotapes with Ben, desiring instead to make videotapes of themselves and to perform sex at the club for the enjoyment of others.

Noticing Lisa's consuming interest in and continual references to such possibilities, Ben feared she had become an "addict." Prior to our first session, he had drawn a sexual boundary for himself, withdrawing from sexual relations at home and decreasing his attendance at the club. I asked them to talk about the various meanings sex had for each of them. To Lisa's surprise, Ben described a relationship where sex emphasized closeness, bonding, and a decreased emphasis on pleasure. The session became very emotional, and as they negotiated what they wanted from the relationship and how sex would help them achieve those goals, they co-created a new, mutual definition of healthy sex. The new definition involved their attending the club when they felt "naughty" and wanted "to watch." Lisa felt embarrassed, she said, about losing her perspective on the emotional intimacy involved with sex.

As mentioned previously, single clients can find it more difficult to define healthy sexuality because of the many stigmas associated with solo sex. Furthermore, others may assume that if a single person is not dating or pursuing a sexual relationship, they "have issues" or are avoiding relationships. The societal premise is that healthy individuals will always seek a partner. If a single person enjoys pornography or cybersex, he or she may feel guilty because these are not "normal relationships."

Right at the beginning of our first session, Sam blurted out, "I'm damned if I do and damned if I don't." Not understanding, I asked him to enlighten me about his predicament. He explained that because he enjoyed the anonymity, safety, and connected creativity of cybersex, he paid for membership in chat rooms that were exclusively devoted to "partnering off." For the last six months he had been entering such chat rooms three or four times a week, but when a friend suggested he was a sex addict, Sam, concerned, went to his employee assistance program.

The counselor validated the friend's diagnosis and referred Sam to me. Prior to our meeting, Sam had visited websites and obtained significant information about sexual addiction. I wasn't surprised, then, when he said, "I want to be honest with you and not be in denial." Noting that he'd already adopted the lingo, I asked him to say more about his original statement, "I'm damned if I do, damned if I don't."

Sam explained that he was happy with his use of cybersex and the connections he made, and he was worried that if he pursued a relationship with a "real" person before he was ready, he might be doing it for the wrong (yet more socially acceptable) reasons. However, feedback from others indicated that he was avoiding relationships, addicted to online sex, fearful of "real" intimacy, or all of the above. He had concluded that he was indeed an addict and was wrong to be deriving enjoyment from his Internet activities.

Sam terminated therapy, feeling a renewed sense of comfort with his current form of sexual expression, after we determined that the cybersex wasn't creating financial hardship, wasn't negatively affecting other relationships, and didn't differ significantly from an abiding interest in golf. Before he left, however, we discussed in depth how he could approach his concerned friend, who, Sam knew, would regard his discontinuing therapy as a failure to address his problems. Sometimes therapy is complicated and affected by the "presence" of unknown or silent clients.

Assumption 5: Some Clients Aren't in the Therapy Room

It is common for people other than those in the room to be influencing the course and outcome of treatment. Having formed a conclusion about a client's sexual issues, a parent, partner, friend, or other professional can strongly influence the client's own assumptions about the problem. I know that if I disagree with this conclusion or fail to meet some predetermined treatment expectation, the client can be placed in a distressing situation. At such times, therapy can only proceed once the third party's concerns have been allayed.

Ed was referred to me as a "sex addict" by the couple's marriage counselor, who told me (later, on the phone) that he always assigns the "addiction" label to whomever creates disruption and anxiety in a relationship. Ed did not have any of the symptoms typically associated with this diagnosis. Motivated to work on his marriage, he described his sexual activities and interests as attempts to get his wife more actively involved in their sex life. He anxiously wanted "a turn" to contribute to the marital sessions but was not optimistic about getting an objective ear from the therapist. Upon hearing of Ed's attempts to initiate sexual relations and how they disturbed his wife, the therapist had turned to him and said, "You need help with your addiction" and continued assessing the marital relationship only from his wife's perspective.

In an attempt to stay coordinated with the other therapist, I called and submitted an evaluation of my client, quoting popular sexual addiction assessment tools to support my conclusion that he was *not*, in fact, an addict.* My focus then turned to coaching Ed on expressing his voice in the sessions with his wife.

Assumption 6: Therapy Works Best When Blame is Avoided and Solutions are Emphasized

Developing solutions rather than trying to explain situations helps create a more productive therapy environment (Furman & Ahola, 1992). When presented with sexual addiction information, many clients assume therapy will examine causal factors, such as family of origin and addictive processes. Even when done with exceptional skill, discussing these factors may create a mindset that "something or someone is to blame." An alternative is to immediately brainstorm about solutions, helping clients to recognize we are a team, that no blame is being cast, and that the entire

---

* I hoped that using these tools would better fit the other therapist's language and foster more positive communication.

therapeutic system is part of the solution. Such honoring of the client's value system also avoids the establishment of a predetermined definition of healthy sexuality. As Klein (2002) suggested, therapists need to foster clients' personal agency, allowing them to create the change needed in the direction desired.

The following case study illustrates how I weave my therapeutic assumptions into my work.

CASE STUDY

Louie, a man in his late forties, came to me with his wife, Brenda, after he was arrested for soliciting a prostitute in another town. He was referred by the couple's marriage counselor, who was holding off working with them until Louie's addiction was resolved. Brenda, working with an individual therapist to help her cope with her husband's addiction, came to the first session to make sure he didn't deny his problems. Desiring, with Louie, to save their marriage, she agreed to come back occasionally to inform me of any ongoing problems. I took a deep breath, realizing that Louie was beginning with a diagnosis confirmed by their marriage counselor, his wife's therapist, his wife, and perhaps himself.

First Session*

As is typical, I opened the first session by asking Louie and Brenda, "How will you know you don't need to see me anymore?" Both agreed that Louie would have recovered from his sexual addiction, allowing them to return to their marriage counselor. Asked how they had arrived at this diagnosis, both referenced his arrest and noted the conclusions of their other therapists. Brenda added that Louie visited pornography sites on the Internet, watched adult videos, and constantly wanted to have sex.

Louie could recall no history of addictions in his family. I clarified that although I might not agree with the label "sex addict," I was also not rejecting it. When I explained that the *DSM-IV* includes no formal diagnosis for sexual addiction and that some people labeled this way could also be diagnosed as obsessive compulsive, the tone of the session distinctly changed.† Expressing great relief, Louie and Brenda looked at each other

---

* All sessions were scheduled 2 weeks apart.
† Regardless of my theoretical and clinical perspective, I feel an obligation to all clients to inform them of multiple treatment options and perspectives. Because Louie clearly met the *DSM-IV* diagnosis for obsessive compulsive disorder, I chose to offer this possibility, as it could create more treatment options beyond the scope of "sexual addiction" treatment or even my solution-focused approach.

and started listing Louie's uniqueness as "a checker": He double- or triple-checked locks before leaving his house, color-coded and alphabetized everything, refused to go into public restrooms, used tissue to open and close doors in public areas, and so on. Neither considered these tendencies a problem; rather, they were a source of humor for the family.

Asked what problem he was trying to solve by soliciting a prostitute, Louie answered simply: "I wanted to have sex and get some validation." We concluded the session with a scaling question (Miller, 1997) regarding the quality of their marriage. Both scaled it as a 3. I asked them to come back with ideas about what a 5 and then a 7 would look like.

Second Session

We started the session discussing Brenda and Louie's notions and images about a marriage they could scale as 5 and 7. Whereas Brenda's list focused on emotional needs such as security, love, and respect, Louie's was oriented toward action: dating, taking trips, more sex. This produced some conflict, as Brenda believed she could not participate in such activities without first feeling emotionally connected, and Louie believed there was little chance of closeness without first taking action.

Tracy: How many times a day do you think Louie does something to meet your emotional needs?
Brenda: None!
Tracy: Are you sure?
Brenda: Absolutely.
Tracy: Louie, do you agree?
Louie: Pretty much.
Tracy: Okay. Brenda, please do me a favor. Give Louie a head nod or "more of that" information each time he interacts with you without being disrespectful or insinuating sex.
Brenda: Okay.
Tracy: Louie, when Brenda gives you feedback about behaviors she is appreciative of, note the behavior and think of how you can do it more often.
Louie: Okay.

At the end of the session, Brenda reminded me that they were not seeing me for marital counseling but for Louie's obsession with sex. I considered her comment vitally important for two reasons. First, she was right. Second, her language had changed: The goal had become helping Louie with his *obsession*, not with his *addiction*. I thanked Brenda for this reminder and for making clear that, in her view, Louie needed to solve his sexual obsession. Louie and I then set an individual appointment.

Third Session

Louie had learned a great deal, he said, from the homework, but he wanted us to discuss his obsessive tendencies and sexuality. Mystified by his obsessions, he hadn't felt them to be problematic until recently; he'd always considered them comfortable routines that helped him work more efficiently or feel more secure. He also wanted me to know about his sexual history prior to being married, including his first experience, at 14, with an older neighborhood girl, and his being raped by a man. From an early age, he'd firmly believed that sex was only about immediate gratification—no process leading up to it, no relationship, "just something to do" to feel good.

I asked Louie whether there was a link between his obsessive and compulsive tendencies and his sexual preferences. After a long pause, he made an insightful connection. Just as sex had, prior to marriage at least, always been about pleasure, with a routine to follow and no need for consideration of others, so too had he established routine behaviors—how he touched door knobs, for example—that felt good, regardless of what others thought. Revisiting the list of emotional qualities that Louie's wife wanted him to display (respect, caring, sensitivity), we talked about how they involved delayed gratification and how they related to sex. Louie believed that relationships develop in stages, so we decided that Louie would be best off figuring out, before the next session, what his wife or other women might believe are healthy "stages" of a relationship that eventually lead to sexual relations.

Fourth Session

Completing his developmental timeline for a healthy sexual relationship, Louie had realized between sessions that he'd never given much thought to the emotional needs necessary for participating in sexual relations. Rather than looking at how he could create the essential conditions for his partner to consent to sex, he'd examined factors that could create *closeness*. And he found himself, for the first time, thinking about sex not as the defining feature of a good relationship but simply as an added benefit.

Asking himself what he wanted in a relationship *other* than sex, Louis came up with three qualities: fun, laughter, and good company. He worried, however, that since Brenda had "changed so much," she might not be the person to meet these needs. Asked how he went about creating fun and humor with Brenda, he identified times when he was less critical, when he worked at being appealing or desirable to her, and when he didn't expect sex every time they had a good interaction. Given the potential for more such changes, he decided that he needed, and wanted, a "software upgrade" on his relationship thoughts and skills.

For his homework, I suggested that he make four positive statements toward people for every critical statement and that he create a list of non-physical qualities that would upgrade his skills, making him more appealing to his wife and others.

Fifth Session

Louie had taken a "self-esteem" seminar a few years earlier, and he had noticed that when the participants were asked to describe themselves, everyone but him had detailed several personal qualities, such as having a caring nature or being a loyal friend. Distressed, he had concluded that he was superficial. But now, he was at least able to create an "upgrade list" that included sensitivity, respect, a loving, caring nature, being desirable (conversationally), and taking risks. For homework, I asked him to attach actions to each of these qualities, to establish a workout routine for practicing them, and to find someone who would hold him accountable for doing so.

Sixth Session

Louie had partially completed a chart, similar to a fitness chart, of daily and weekly actions, but he'd had trouble operationalizing some of the desired qualities, such as respect and sensitivity. Together, we brainstormed behaviors that would implement them—listening, inviting challenges, holding back mean or sarcastic statements, and so on.

Considering his family to be a good place to start trying to "upgrade his skills," Louie had taken his 12-year-old daughter and her friend to a concert, something more typically done by his wife, and he'd focused on fun, laughter, and not lecturing his daughter. They'd had a great time together. His daughter invited him to "hang out" with her and her friend, who apparently had found him to be "cool." Overhearing the friend making this comment had a more profound impact on him than anything he could recall in a long time. I suggested he continue undertaking new actions and sharing the results with those who were holding him accountable.

Seventh Session

Louie started the session by letting me know that this would be the last time we'd be meeting. His employer was going out of business. Coworkers were leaving daily, and, stressed, he wasn't sure how long it would be before he, too, was gone. Nevertheless, he'd been using the situation as an opportunity to implement sensitivity, respect, and caring. He'd also decided to post his "upgrade routine" in public places—on his filing cabinet and desk at work and the refrigerator at home.

Brenda appreciated his goals and efforts, and his children, also encouraging, were noticing significant differences. Even acquaintances were offering supportive comments. Such positive feelings felt foreign to him, but he was beginning to understand, he said, how they could intensify sexual feelings.

Knowing that this could well be our last session, we refined his "upgrade routine," identifying his desire to delay immediate gratification, to avoid compulsive/routine efforts to get sex, and to keep his focus on becoming emotionally desirable to his wife.

Outcome

In follow-up conversations via telephone, Louie reported continued gains: He was becoming more emotionally close with his family, and Brenda was no longer avoiding sex. Although he desired more frequent sexual relations, he understood the interplay between this and his emotional behaviors. With an upgrade routine now a full page in length, he no longer felt like a "Neanderthal," and his colleagues were continuing to appreciate his change. One woman in particular had mentioned that she appreciated his listening to her and that she was glad he was no longer "undressing" her and her friends while talking with them. Surprised and embarrassed that they had noticed a behavior he thought had been discreet, he nevertheless felt encouraged.

Discussion of the Case

This case presented many challenges for me. First, I was irritated with the other mental health professionals for making snap diagnoses. However, I understood the necessity of preserving Brenda and Louie's faith in therapists with whom they would be continuing to work, so I restrained myself from divulging my assessment of their pop-psychology clinicians.

Second, as Brenda reminded me, I didn't have a contract with them for marriage counseling. Though I believe Louie could have further enhanced his "upgrade list" with Brenda's involvement in the sessions, I was limited to working alone with Louie.

Third, I needed to remain focused on Louie's sex-related goals, avoiding the temptation to wander off into other issues—his obsessive-compulsive tendencies, his rape as a young man, his general relationship issues. Louie repeatedly validated my belief that clients don't need therapy for all the challenges many therapists consider problematic.

This case exemplifies the integration of my therapeutic assumptions for working with people diagnosed with sexual addictions. Louie clearly identified what his sexual behavior was trying to solve—he wanted more sex and increased validation. This recognition, along with connecting his behaviors to his obsessive-compulsive tendencies, helped eliminate much of his blame and shame. I don't know if Brenda was scapegoating Louie, but both of their therapists were quick to pass the sexual challenges of the marriage onto Louie.

Understanding there were three clients outside of therapy (two therapists and Brenda), I considered it important for Louie to make his therapy goals public, or at least known to Brenda, as she would then be able to confirm whether Louie's therapy was proving effective. I would have preferred to have had Louie more explicitly define his definition of healthy sexuality, but Brenda's feedback had helped him align his understanding with hers.

The most rewarding aspect of this case for me involved the systemic changes. Louie's therapy appeared to help him change how he related to Brenda, his children, and his coworkers, improving his status within the family, his reputation at work, and his self-worth. As a "cool" dad and a respectful colleague, he took pride in the awakening of his emotional life and his coworker's appreciation of his caring and involvement. When he first came to therapy, he didn't care how he got along with his colleagues, as long as the job was completed. Toward the end, he found himself genuinely interested in how they were coping with the transition to unemployment.

CONCLUSIONS

In our sex-negative society, I believe it is critically important to help clients explore and co-create parameters of healthy sexuality. Quickly assessing and diagnosing "sexual addiction" simply adds to a culture of shame and embarrassment. Listening from a strength-based, solution-oriented perspective gives validation to client context, culture, and relational patterns.

Furthermore, this position places responsibility on the client for making necessary changes, satisfying context and relational expectations.

Of course, society's definitions of healthy sexuality will continue to evolve. It is possible, indeed probable, that they will someday include cyber-sex and phone sex. But we as therapists don't need to wait for everyone else to catch up. If we respect our clients' contexts, we can respect sexual behaviors that fit with their predicaments, choices, and goals. Without such respect, and armed with a society-wide fear of any frequent or repetitive involvement in pleasure, we can easily fall into diagnosing sexual addiction.

My working assumptions, my distinct unease with definitive-sounding and too widely available assessment instruments, and my commitment to emphasizing strengths, resources, and resiliencies all come into play when swimming against the current of a pathology-based mental health industry. I'm a brief therapist looking for ways to quickly slow down my clients' (and other therapists') premature ejaculations of sexual addiction diagnoses. If I can get them to discover healthy aspects of their sexual choices, their fear and shame can diminish, and therapeutic change can begin.

REFERENCES

Carnes, P. (2003). Dr. Carnes's resources of sex addiction and recovery. Retrieved July 28, 2003, from: http://www.sexhelp.com/sa_q_and_a.cfm

Coleman, E. (1989). Sexual compulsion vs. sexual addiction: The debate continues. *SIECUS Report*, 14(6), 7–10.

Coleman, E. (1992). Is your patient suffering from compulsive sexual behavior? *Psychiatric Annals*, 22(6), 320–425.

Coleman, E. (1996). What sexual scientists know . . . About compulsive sexual behavior. *Society for the Scientific Study of Sexuality*, 2(1). Retrieved July 28, 2003, http://www.sexscience.org/publications/index.php?category_id=440&subcategory_id=334

de Shazer, S. (1988). *Clues: Investigating solutions in brief therapy*. New York: Norton.

American Psychiatric Association. (1994). *Diagnostic and statistical manual of mental disorders*. (4th ed.). Washington, D.C.: Author.

Furman, B., & Ahola, T. (1992). *Solution talk: Hosting therapeutic conversations*. Collingdale, PA: DIANE Publishing.

Klein, M. (March 1998). *Why there's no such thing as sexual addiction—and why it really matters* (Article 8). Retrieved July 28, 2003, from: http://www.sexed.org/arch/arch08.html

Klein, M. (2002). Sex addiction: A dangerous clinical concept. *Electronic Journal of Human Sexuality*, 5. Retrieved July 28, 2003, from: http://www.ejhs.org/volume5/SexAddiction.htm

Miller G. (1997). *Becoming miracle workers: Language and meaning in brief therapy*. New York: Aldine de Gruyter.

National Council on Sexual Addiction and Compulsivity. (2000). Definitions. Retrieved July 28, 2003, from: http://www.ncsac.org/definitions.html

six

Out of My Office and Into the Bedroom

Thorana S. Nelson

Hilarity is a common response to sexual humor, but when people consider their sexual relationship to be a joke, they're more likely to feel anger, sadness, or despair. Fearful that there is no solution to their frustration and pain, clients often present with other issues: parenting, marital conflict, depression, anxiety, or "communication problems." Some describe a lack of intimacy; most struggle to voice their concerns.

I tend to ignore the *content* areas of therapy—the stuff clients fret and talk and fight *about*. As a systems-trained therapist, I'm more interested in the *processes* of interaction within families than in the content of their conversations. I attend to, for example, the similarities between how partners decide what to fix for breakfast and where to go for the holidays. But when it comes to working with couple's sexual concerns, content is also important. I need to be sure they understand the physiological aspects of their sexuality and be sure I understand their expectations, beliefs, values, and taboos. Having been raised in cultures and families where clear, accurate information was not always available or allowed, they may be battling ignorance, confusion, and anxiety. Thus, the therapy may tack back and forth between content and process, as we focus on all levels of the clients' experience—behaviors, cognitions, emotions, family-of-origin issues, beliefs, meanings, and values—both sequentially and simultaneously.

GOALS FOR THERAPY

My aim, always, is to get clients out of my office as quickly as possible. There are times when "quickly" is a few sessions and times when it is many more. As a therapist, I think of myself as operating mostly *with*, rather than *on* systems; however, I also recognize that I cannot forego completely my expert role, having studied some things a lot (the "deep" in "Piled high and Deep," or Ph.D.) and having had professional and life experiences that could be useful to my clients.

My work is a balancing act between, on the one hand, theoretical ideas about people and relationship dynamics, and, on the other, practical approaches to helping clients change. I have tried, in the tradition of solution-focused brief therapy (SFBT), to ignore causal explanations of people's behavior (de Shazer, 1985); however, this neither suits my obsessive desire to know nor dispels my belief that such theoretical guidance is both efficient and ethical. Similarly, despite my social constructionist leanings (McNamee & Gergen, 1992), I still tend to think about concepts such as *differentiation, boundaries, triangles, sequences, exceptions,* and *anxiety* as if they really existed as things, rather than as a mere abstractions or metaphors. I may not be able to put these notions into a wheelbarrow (a reliable measure of concreteness), but I *can* put them into my *idea* of a wheelbarrow, and that's good enough for me to infuse them with a charming, if deluded, sense of reality. As a systems thinker and feminist, I make sure my wheelbarrow includes ideas about the importance of context and meaning, particularly contexts and meanings of gender, proximity, and power.

I begin with some adequate joining and assessing, and then I contract with the clients for treatment, so they and I know what we are doing. I assist them in changing behaviors and expanding their alternatives, and when things are going well, I look for consolidation and closure, remaining available to them for follow-up sessions. However, because circumstances and client preferences must guide our work together, I don't always follow this path.

I keep track of how processes unfold in the midst of our conversations — how I or my clients build solutions, notice exceptions, introduce information, find and move down good roads, and invent new ways of being. Along the way, I try not to let the concepts get in the way of the processes, and despite my therapeutic focus, I'm still able to delight in the changes in content that clients tell me about ("We did it on the deck! You didn't mention *that* as an option!").

THEORETICAL INFLUENCES

My clinical work grew out of my training, but over the years it has evolved in keeping with changes in my experiences, reading, teaching, training, and life. Several colleagues and I (Nelson, McCollum, Wetchler, Trepper, & Lewis, 1996) developed a systemically informed clinical approach to treating substance-abusing women, and my current therapeutic style continues to be informed by the ideas developed in that context. I utilize assumptions, concepts, and practices from structural (Minuchin, 1974), strategic (Watzlawick, Weakland, & Fisch, 1974), Bowenian (1978), behavioral (Jacobson & Margolin, 1979), solution-focused (de Shazer, 1982), and narrative (e.g., White & Epston, 1990) ways of working. I may incorporate useful practices from other models as long as doing so doesn't violate the basic assumptions under which I operate. For example, I appreciate notions of invisible loyalty from contextual family therapy (Boszormenyi-Nagy & Spark, 1973) and may ask clients whether getting unstuck might show disloyalty to a parent who was unable to succeed in life.

This work is premised on basic systemic concepts of equifinality (there are many ways to undress a partner), nonsummativity (the whole of the sexual experience for the relationship is more than the sum of the different body parts and acts), interaction (your getting aroused by my arousal arouses me), isomorphism (if it works in the bedroom, it just might work in the den), and feedback (I liked what you did last night: Do it again). As a therapist, I must be careful to respond to my clients' needs as I perceive them, sometimes guiding, sometimes staying out of the way, and sometimes "leading from behind" (DeJong & Berg, 2001), that is, encouraging them and cheering them on to do the things they already are doing that work. In this way, I am a part of the system, but a unique part. I must remain aware of my impact and influence in the system, being careful to keep the clients' needs and preferences at the center. I honor clients as experts in their own lives, although I know something different than they do about conversations and about different paths that are more or less likely to lead them toward their desired outcomes. We are collaborators in this game, each with our own complementary role. I look and ask, they notice and answer, and, together, we muddle our ways to something that is rewarding for both of us.

Structural Therapy

Relevant foundational concepts from structural family therapy (e.g., Minuchin, 1974) include *boundaries* and *power*. All of us grapple with the twin forces of separateness and togetherness (Bowen, 1978), struggling to find balance in our needs and desires to have separate selves, to interact with others as unique individuals, and to belong, body and soul, to a group. Culturally, familially, and individually contextualized and socialized, each of us strives to develop an optimal distance with others—some closer, some further. This is proximity in dynamic form, each of us hoping and praying that the biorhythms of our needs get in sync with those of another human being, at least sometimes. As individuals, we need both space and intimacy; as couples, we need contact with the outside world—family, friends, work, community—as well as thick walls that keep the noncouple world at bay. Fundamentally, however, boundaries are dynamic rather than static, changing as relationships and needs require.

Included in this boundaried system is sex. Boundaries that are too thin preclude individual privacy, whether for brushing teeth, changing tampons, passing gas in bed, or having private fantasies. Rigid boundaries keep partners from talking to and exploring each other. Diffuse boundaries around the couple bring the in-laws and former partners into the bedroom like a peanut gallery—popcorn, soda, and all. Rigid boundaries prevent couples from seeking information and exploring new or creative ideas. Cultural mores serve as walls, keeping people away from potentially playful behaviors and reinforcing taboos that each partner may question individually but can't, as a couple, discuss.

Unbalanced power in too many aspects of a couple's life can spill over into the bedroom, preventing the development of an intimate, sexy relationship. It makes sense for efficiency's sake that couples develop delineated and complementary roles: One changes the oil, the other cleans the bathroom; one pays the bills, the other attends to holiday arrangements. However, in healthy relationships, each feels acknowledged and important in these roles. In the bedroom, it is *not* balanced if one person feels compelled to give in to the other's desires and preferences, while the other feels totally responsible for initiating and maintaining the couple's sex life. All sorts of things affect these arrangements and often-unspoken feelings: money, tradition, earning power, social mores, habits, and libido.

James and Clarice had been married for three years. Since the birth of their daughter, Clarice felt exhausted and distant from James; sex was the last thing on her mind after a long day, but she knew that James was unhappy. She wanted to feel closer and sexy, but she resented James's attitude that his job was to bring home the bacon and hers was to cook it and clean up afterwards. They had discussed parenting arrangements and spousal roles early in their marriage, but she had not realized how difficult it would be when there was an actual, resource-demanding infant in the house. She also felt that she should not bring the topic up for discussion because it had been a "joint decision." Clarice did not feel comfortable talking to James about her dilemmas—the boundary *between* them was too thick—and this hurt other aspects of their relationship. And with the boundary *around* them too thin, both were listening too much to others' ideas about babies and about how they should do things. It seemed to me that more closeness between them and more distance from others might help them resolve several issues and come to acceptable agreements about their sex life.

Therapy for Clarice and James included communication coaching so that neither would feel it necessary to give in to the other and both could become responsible for initiating talks. They decided that they still wanted a full-time at-home parent for their daughter and that it made more sense for Clarice to be that person. But they also decided that they needed to take more time for themselves without the baby and to discuss more about what *they*, as opposed to others, wanted for themselves, as well as how their individual and shared goals had changed from when they first got married. Clarice learned that James wanted to be more involved in decisions about their daughter but had felt he couldn't speak up because this was Clarice's "job." Neither had realized how giving over particular power to the other had increased distance in their relationship. Listening more to each other and less to others, they were able to negotiate decisions and tasks that looked traditional but worked well.

Strategic Therapy

Since its inception, strategic family therapy has taken many forms and has been defined in many ways. My work is informed by the tenets and perspectives of the MRI group (e.g., Watzlawick et al., 1974), Haley (e.g., Haley, 1987), and Papp (1983). Strategic therapists recognize that people's problems are unique to each situation, that treatment needs to be individualized, that people get stuck interacting in habitual patterns, and that change in one area can effect change in another.

Frank and Pam presented for therapy concerned that Pam wanted sex more often than Frank. This was perplexing to them, given the messages they heard in the media and from their respective friends about men typically wanting more sex than women. Frank felt embarrassed when his buddies moaned about how deprived they were, seeming to brag about their prowess and excessive sexual needs. Pam, in turn, felt excluded when her friends complained, with subtle tones of satisfaction and bragging, about being "pestered" all the time.

The couple had concluded that there was something fundamentally wrong with each of them as individuals, that somehow their hormones and plumbing were failing them. They had read sex manuals, spent a fortune on self-help books, and listened carefully to their friends' conversations, looking for clues that could help them fix their problem. Nothing had helped.

Interestingly, when I asked them how their search had affected their sex life, they said they weren't particularly unhappy either as individuals or as a couple. Yes, Pam initiated sex more frequently than she liked—she often wished that Frank would be more romantic—and Frank sometimes felt pressured by Pam's requests and feared that if he initiated more, she would expect more. However, sex was fun and satisfying when they had it and Pam did not feel rejected when Frank told her no. She was more likely to simply give him a pat on the butt, snuggle up, and go to sleep. She also enjoyed thinking up ways to get him aroused more easily and this had become a part of the fun in their lives. However, they still thought something was wrong.

I explored potential consequences should things be different. They each discussed the obvious: Frank would initiate sex more often and he would be more a part of the treasure hunt of looking for fun, sexy things to add to their lives. Pam would enjoy being the receiver more often. Neither thought that they wanted to become so "normal" that they fit in with the partner-whining parties of their friends.

People usually think only of the positive results of the change they crave, the ones they hope will, after the therapist has miraculously made things all better, provide relief and allow for a wonderful life. However, sometimes it is better to anticipate the negative consequences of change (Papp, 1983), not as a paradox, but as a realistic anticipation of potential issues that could arise. On occasion, people get what they asked for and wish the genie had not appeared, so I asked Frank and Pam, who seemed to be doing quite well, why they wanted to change. After some thought and discussion, they realized that if they got what they'd been asking for, they might become complacent, losing some of the spark that came alive when both were struggling for intimacy. More frequent sex might become automatic, habitual, and less satisfying, with intercourse and orgasm becoming the only markers of "success."

They decided that what needed changing was not the pattern of their sexual relations, but their discussions with friends and each other about what sex is "supposed" to be like. Problems sometimes are created or maintained by ineffective attempts to solve a difficulty in life (Watzlawick et al., 1974). Frank and Pam's solution attempts—reading, asking for advice, reading more, asking for more advice—had actually made their situation worse. Interrupting sequences of behaviors, feelings, thoughts, and beliefs can free both problems and people from more-of-the-same outcomes.

Pam decided that when her friends started bragging about their partners' desire for them, she'd change her thoughts, change the subject, or brag about *her* desire for her husband. Frank decided that rather than feel embarrassed when his friends complained, he'd experiment with feeling proud of his sexy, adventuresome spouse. They decided they liked things the way they were, for the most part, which, interestingly enough, resulted in their enjoying sex even more (with Frank supplying musk-scented candles). They also found themselves talking differently about other difficulties in their lives, such as possible career changes.

Bowen Family Systems Therapy

Murray Bowen (1978) developed a way of conceptualizing family interaction that ties together intrapsychic processes of thinking and feeling with relational processes of togetherness-seeking and distance-seeking. Bowen realized that people's patterns of relating, learned in their families of origin, are tied into their ability to handle high emotions. If they can't separate their thinking from their feeling or themselves from their relationships, they are more likely to get into trouble and make reactive choices. However, when they are able to balance the pull for closeness with the pull for separateness, they are free to fully feel emotions and make thoughtful choices about actions.

Christy and Sharon were each caught up in a seemingly never-ending cycle of bickering, fighting, making up, distancing, and bickering again. Despite recognizing how the cycle interfered with their work and play, they felt powerless to keep their relationship from disintegrating around them. Because having sex seemed to be creating more distance than closeness, they had stopped showing their passion, affection, or even positive regard for each other.

We constructed genograms of their families, tracing three generations of family patterns and values related to money, education, religion, anxiety, and sexuality. Although Sharon's family was accepting when Sharon came out to them and welcomed Christy as a daughter-in-law, they tended to treat the two of them as "girls" rather than 40-year-old women, and they were privately sad about the difficulties inherent in Sharon's life path as a lesbian. Still, both women felt comfortable relating to Sharon's family.

Uncomfortable with open displays of affection between Sharon and Christy at family gatherings, Christy's parents treated Sharon as their daughter's best friend rather than as her lover and life partner. One of Christy's brothers believed, in keeping with his religious convictions, that homosexual behavior was wrong. He did not allow his children to refer to Sharon as an "aunt," and he wouldn't let them go out with her alone. When Christy had complained to her parents about these attitudes, they told her that she'd made her own bed and now needed to lie in it. I giggled when they told me this, and, for the first time, the two women smiled, too, as though we had a private joke against Christy's family.

Christy's ability to laugh about her parents' unintended double entendre told me that she was sufficiently differentiated to have a sense of humor and not be defensive about her family. When I also acknowledged how painful it must have been to live with her family's attitudes, she said she was willing to divorce herself from them if that would improve her and Sharon's relationship. Bowen (1978) noted that cutting off relationships with families of origin tends to make matters worse, creating unhappiness and stubbornness rather than acceptance and openness to change. I thus looked for other alternatives.

We explored how Christy's family's attitudes could be affecting Sharon and Christy's relationship, which resulted in Christy's talking one-on-one with her mother about her need for closeness, affection, and approval from the family but not at the expense of her relationship with Sharon. This gradually improved their relationship enough that Christy's mother volunteered to tell Christy's brother to treat Sharon with more respect. As the atmosphere changed between Christy and her family, she was more able to disagree with Sharon without picking a fight.

Sharon realized that she'd been willing to secure the favor of her family at the expense of being seen as an adolescent. Talking to her parents about this, she found out that they, not wanting to alienate her, had been avoiding sharing their worries about her. Perhaps discovering that their daughter shared many of their concerns helped them to agree to stop treating her as if she were 16. Sharon, in turn, was able, with Christy's help, to avoid exacerbating the distancing cycles between the two of them. Their relationship and sex life became more enjoyable as the conflicts, hidden and overt, with their families of origin were brought to light and resolved. Free to discuss their differences openly, they could negotiate each of their distancing and togetherness needs.

Throughout my work with Christy and Sharon, I was concerned about the possibility of increased anxiety in the therapy relationship. Because Bowen therapy emphasizes the self of the therapist and therapists' issues, I pay attention to strong feelings in myself. I feel very strongly that society's proscriptions about same-sex orientations are fundamentally wrong, born of societal anxiety related to homophobia and ignorance of how same-sex relationships can be rewarding and truly intimate, not oversexualized choices or ways to offend other people. Important people in my life are gay and lesbian, and this also affects my feelings in these situations as I strive to celebrate these relationships. I must be careful to not rescue people from what I could easily perceive as their own fears and homophobia and must refocus myself on their unique situations, ready to help them separate if that is what they choose to do. Or not.

Behavioral Marital Therapy

When Dorothy and Mike detailed all the things they argued about—kids, money, work, friends, the house, the yard—sex wasn't on the list, so I brought it up. The looks they gave me could have melted a steel beam. Mike was convinced that Dorothy was one of those women who withheld sex for revenge, using her "headaches" to hold him hostage for whatever she wanted. Dorothy claimed that she had enjoyed sex before they were married, but that Mike had since become unromantic and demanding. He'd stopped bringing her flowers, didn't consider personal hygiene important, and thought afterplay included snoring.

Some therapists would view the tensions in Mike and Dorothy's sexual relationship as central to their strife and thus in need of immediate attention; others would point to the cycle of demanding and counter-demanding in all of the couple's arguments and thus treat their sexual difficulties as reflections of their inability to negotiate differences. Such an analysis would suggest the need for behavioral marital therapy (BMT), including communication coaching, caring days (suggesting that couples make lists of nice things they would like the other to do and then each agreeing to do at least one thing from the list each day), and couple dates to help them return to their days of courting and sexual fun (Jacobson & Margolin, 1979).

From my systemic perspective, change in one area of a relationship can—indeed *will*—effect change in other areas. However, I also believe that therapists must take great care in choosing their point of intervention. Rather than jumping into the hottest topic on a couple's agenda, I prefer to begin by changing communication patterns in areas that are neither trivial nor overly intense (Nelson, 1994). Behavioral marital therapists (Jacobson & Margolin, 1979) assume that much strife in relationships is eased when couples learn how to actively listen and constructively talk about their differences. I have found BMT techniques effective in altering communication cycles that preclude satisfying conversations or sex lives. Once the *way* a couple communicates has been altered, they can, without the involvement of a therapist, transfer their new skills to their hot-topic discussions.

Dorothy and Mike learned to interrupt their blame-counterblame cycles by listening to each other, slowing down their discussions, and reducing their interpersonal attacks. Discovering an ability to agree with each other, they easily resolved some minor household disputes (how often each cleaned the kitchen) and moved on successfully to more sensitive topics, such as friends. As Jacobson and Christensen (1996) noted, it helps when couples can agree to disagree, accepting the idiosyncrasies of the other person rather than taking the differences between them personally or trying to get the other to change. Such acceptance enhances pleasure throughout the relationship, including what happens between the sheets.

After learning how to listen better and to avoid making assumptions about each other, Mike accepted Dorothy's fatigue and headaches as genuine, and Dorothy accepted that Mike hadn't been conscious of how his not shaving bothered her. Trying harder to accept each other's differing needs for sex, Dorothy was able to tell Mike about her needs for gentleness, romance, and patience during foreplay. For the first time, he understood that if he didn't ensure that she was sufficiently lubricated before entering her, her resulting discomfort quickly diminished her arousal.

Traditional sex therapists wisely make sure that clients get medical exams to rule out physiological and biochemical problems (hormones, side effects of medications), and they offer them experiments—sensate focus exercises and the "squeeze" technique, among others—to help them better appreciate their bodies and improve their sexual functioning (e.g., Leiblum & Rosen, 2000). My experience, however, is that most couples are pretty good at finding their own solutions. Often the best teachers of human anatomy and sexual interaction are the individuals who are doing the interacting. Of course, an occasional bit of information on the differences in sexual response can be helpful. Explanations about muscle spasms and vaginismus can go a long way toward helping a woman and her partner gently reteach her muscles to relax.

When I suggested that Dorothy make an appointment with a gynecologist, Mike offered to go with her. The doctor prescribed an estrogen cream and a different kind of lubricating gel, which significantly relieved Dorothy's pain. This, of course, led to greater pleasure, which increased the lubrication, and in time, the couple no longer needed the cream.

Solution-Focused Brief Therapy

Solution-focused brief therapy (SFBT) marks a shift in perspective for both therapists and clients, away from problem-solving and toward solution-building (DeJong & Berg, 2001). These therapists assume that they don't need to know much about a problem or its etiology in order to find a solution for the difficulties that arise from it. For example, premature ejaculation may be "caused" by a lack of control over excitement and arousal; however, the solution for a particular couple may not involve "gaining control." Instead, they may learn to enjoy the fast moment as much as possible and then look for ways to bring the other partner to orgasm while the penis is not erect. Similarly, a woman's low sexual desire may be "caused" by previous sexual abuse; however, because the abuse cannot be undone, the solution, found in the present, can be directed toward a future that includes sexual desire and satisfaction.

Esté and Roberto came to me for help with their "intimacy." Shy, quiet, and very proper, they used euphemisms to describe what they feared was an unsolvable sexual problem, one that threatened their ability to have children and thus to gain the approval of their fundamentalist church and their conservative families. When they requested that I diagnose the cause so as to find a remedy, I asked if they were invested in knowing what was wrong or if it might be acceptable to simply fix it. They hesitated, so I offered to explore the cause if we concluded that we weren't getting anywhere or if, after the problem was resolved, they wanted to satisfy their curiosity about it. This reassured them, and they were further relieved to find out that by working this way, I wouldn't necessarily need to know details about their "intimacy"—that they could work on the problem at home in their own way, using suggestions that came from our conversations.

SFBT therapists recognize that clients' responses in therapy must be accounted for within the context of their relationship with the therapist. This means that my clients aren't "compliant" in and of themselves; they are compliant *with me*. Similarly, when they are "resistant," they aren't expressing a character trait or a desire not to change; they are expressing their relationship to *me*. "Resistance" can be seen as a kind of cooperation, because it gives the therapist information about being on the wrong track, not understanding the client's situation, or attempting to force the wrong kind of solutions (de Shazer, 1982).

Such an understanding of compliance and resistance leads to three basic rules: If it ain't broke, don't fix it; if it's working, keep it up; if it's not working, do something different (de Shazer, 1985, 1988). A common technique for gauging the therapist/client relationship and for tracking progress in therapy is the use of scaling questions. Such questions invite clients to rate, on a scale of 1 to 10, the degree to which they feel a "fit" with the therapist, recognize changes in themselves and their relationships, and are making progress toward their goals. As it turned out, the "problem" for this couple was very simple: True to their church values and protected upbringing, neither had any sexual experience, and despite having a sex manual, they weren't sure what to take from it. I began by asking them what would be different in their relationship when things were more the way they wanted them. The question presupposed that they could recognize and describe such a difference and that it would affect more than just their sex life. They were able to talk about several things and to rate the degree to which things were already happening.

Roberto pegged their current situation as a 2; Esté as a 4. We talked about what "2" and "4" meant to them and to each other and how they would know they had moved up the scale a little. We still hadn't touched on sex; we were "merely" talking about their relationship and their pleasure in it. Rather than dwelling on what was wrong, we focused on the times when the problem was not so prevalent. At the end of the first session, I asked them to go home and notice two things: (1) when things in their relationship were happening in the way they wanted, and (2) what else was going on that they wanted to keep (de Shazer, 1988).

SFBT therapists assume that problems don't always occur and don't always occur in the same way. They want to find out about the times when the problem isn't present, when it isn't present in its full intensity, or when its presence is not a problem. Roberto and Esté came to the next session surprised by how much they had enjoyed their relationship during the week and by the various changes they'd noticed in themselves, each other, and the relationship.

I asked them to rate their intimate relationship on a 1-to-10 scale, with 10 indicating "wonderful." They were each two points higher than the previous week, so I proceeded to follow the EARS (DeJong & Berg, 2001) formula:

- Elicit what is better.
- Amplify the change with questions about who else noticed and about how they managed to accomplish the change.

- Reinforce the change with cheerleading and more questions about how they managed to make the change happen or to keep going in the face of difficult obstacles.
- Start over, asking, "What else?" in terms of changes toward goals.

I never got into Roberto and Esté's bedroom, but I didn't need or want to. They were able to move toward their goal without my needing to know who was or wasn't doing what to whom. We stopped therapy when they said that they had reached their goals, that although things were not yet at 10, they were confident that they could carry on without my interference. We talked about things they could do should they find themselves off track, and I reinforced that one of their solutions might be to come in for a refresher session.

Ever mindful of possible medical, religious, or gender-role constraints in relationships, I may challenge restrictive ways of thinking and acting in one-sided or abusive relationships, and I may probe for opportunities than have not been explored. But the couple is ultimately responsible for deciding if they want to seek medical help, discuss with their religious leader alternate ways of being sexual, or develop different gender-role arrangements.

Narrative Therapy

The final assumptions informing my work derive from narrative therapy (e.g., White & Epston, 1990). Like strategic and SFBT therapists, narrative therapists value multiple perspectives of "reality," recognizing that the stories we tell ourselves about ourselves and our relationships provide the perspective or lens through which we perceive life. One person may perceive an obstacle where another sees an adventure or challenge, and the dominant stories of the culture can overwhelm an individual's particular experience. Society's values and beliefs around gender, ethnicity, power, money, performance, childbearing, and childrearing are so much a part of us that we don't dwell on them consciously, yet they have great influence on how we think about and engage in sex.

For example, the inability to achieve or maintain an erection is widely accepted as a sexual dysfunction in our culture, and men spend great amounts of time and money to cure the condition. Nevertheless, I have worked with many people who, after they have understood certain medical conditions such as diabetes, are not interested in using artificial or chemical ways of "getting it up"; they and their partners are quite content to find other ways of expressing intimacy with each other, often to the surprise of their physicians, others, and even themselves!

Narrative therapists also share with their strategic and SFBT colleagues the assumption that problems don't happen all the time with the same intensity and in the same way. When people come to therapy, their stories tend to focus on the negative aspects of their lives, clouding the times when their problems are not or were not so problematic. Whereas SFBT therapists look for "exceptions," narrative therapists look for "unique outcomes" or "sparkling moments" (Freedman & Combs, 1996)—times when the problem could have occurred but didn't.

Allan and Sheila came to therapy as a last-ditch effort to save their marriage. They knew change was essential, but they were each convinced that it was the other person who needed to change first. They staged their battles mostly in the bedroom, with Allan complaining that Sheila's ideas of sex were archaic and not responsive to his needs. Sheila countered by accusing Allan of making excessive and "perverted" demands, demands that were so out of bounds that only wanton women would give in to them.

Despite my curiosity about Allan's behaviors, I limited myself to questions that would establish whether Allan was forcing or hurting Sheila. Although I believe that the only persons qualified to judge the rightness or wrongness of certain behaviors are those who are engaged in them, I can't work with clients who are hurting each other physically, emotionally, or mentality—unless they are invested in changing this aspect of their relationship. On occasion, I have told people that their behavior (short of illegal violence) is their personal business, but that I can't condone it by seeing them in therapy. I then refer them to other therapists.

Sheila said that while Allan's wishes were not hurtful, she did find them "distasteful." We explored the meaning of this word for Sheila, as well as its counterpart, *tasteful*. We discussed at some length the differences and similarities between her and Allan's tastes, and I asked about the flavors she found most and least enjoyable. The conversation illuminated for Allan that Sheila was more open-minded than he'd thought.

In addition to looking for and amplifying unique outcomes or sparkling moments, narrative therapists often attempt to "externalize" the problem and explore times when the client has not been overwhelmed by it. Uniting the couple in their efforts to eradicate the enemy helps them to dispense with blaming each other and to develop a different story about themselves and their relationship, one that includes self-efficacy and a sense of well-being.

After assessing for domestic violence, potential physical limitations, and medical or chemical issues, I asked the couple how "distaste" was getting in the way of their enjoying each other. What sorts of things helped *distaste* to have a larger role in their relationship and what sorts of things diminished its effects? Wondering how *distaste* acted on their lives in many spheres and how they both assisted it and withstood it, I asked *landscape of action* questions (White & Epston, 1990)—questions that explored *sequences* of events.

The couple talked about many aspects of their relationship, as well as the way they each related to their children and at work. Sometimes Sheila was so bothered the day after an argument that she was distracted at work and convinced that she had a scarlet *P* for *perverted* on her forehead. There were times, however, when she was able to push *distaste* into the back of her mind and move on with her work or enjoy her colleagues. We talked about the times when *distaste* was able to do its thing and the times when she was able to ignore it and push it away. Allan had similar stories to tell. Whenever possible, I asked questions about their abilities to move beyond the tentacles of *distaste* and explore their abilities to work together.

A series of *landscape of meaning* questions, which tied the couple's respective behaviors to the meanings they associated with them, led to more conversation about exceptions in meaning, times when certain meanings were associated with other actions, as well as times the actions were tied to other meanings. In their case, *judgment* became a second externalized theme—both the judgment operating between them and the judgment they felt from others.

Sheila and Allan were able to discover and identify a number of ways that they could fight against *distaste* on a daily basis, including their respective ways of judging other people and fighting the judgment of others. The more they were able to accept others, each other, and themselves, the more they pushed *distaste* and *judgment* from their lives. They began to discuss sexual expression as a joint adventure of discovery about pleasure rather than as a battle to be won.

Integration

Assumptions from these varied models are tied to each other through core theoretical ideas and principles of practice. The theoretical core has to do with the management of anxiety—how well my clients and I are able to keep our emotions from overruling our thinking as we explore possible resolutions. The principles-of-practice core has to do with quick and efficient solution-building.

Therapeutic change must attend to both process and meaning. Change in content, or first-order change, is sometimes acceptable in therapy, but most people interested in this level of difference are more likely to access friends, self-help books, or themselves. Clients are usually looking for something more meaningful to happen (as am I). Therapeutic transformation entails second-order change—a shift in the system or the meaning of the problem. Thus, the process of therapy with most clients starts with a shift in paradigm: looking for solutions rather than examining problems.

When the move to a present and future orientation is sufficient, therapy is often over quickly. Sometimes, however, clients' anxiety is so high that they find it difficult or frightening to look for solutions. In such cases, I tend to externalize the problem and to identify the meanings and images they have absorbed from their families, communities, and the media. This can help them lower their anxiety and reduce their feelings of shame and blame, allowing them to enter into solution-building.

When clients don't seem to be responding to my involvement with them, I examine our therapeutic relationship. Do they trust me? Are we clicking? I'm always open to referring people to other therapists. If they decide to stick with me, I explore possible barriers to their reaching their desired goals: boundaries and power, unfortunate cycles and sequences, negative consequences of change, and problem-saturated stories (White & Epston, 1990).

If a couple seems locked in more destructive than constructive interactive patterns, I use genograms to explore their families of origin, looking at possible dysfunctional triangles, problematic gender-role expectations, or unhelpful strategies for managing anxiety. I also examine possible constraints (Breunlin, Schwartz, & Kune-Karrer, 1992), including limiting beliefs and issues of culture, gender, or class. Assuming they're doing the best they can, given their upbringing and their present circumstances, I help them to look anew at their relationship, remove barriers, and change the ways they interact.

The cases in this chapter were all successful, but I've had my share of failures, too. Sometimes one partner is ready for change and the other isn't; sometimes one of them has already given up and left, if not physically, then emotionally; and on occasion, beliefs or meanings don't budge and what I'd hoped would be helpful falls flat. But when I'm able to help couples such as the ones introduced in this chapter, I find it incredibly rewarding. I know that our work has been at the top of my clients' scales when my own scale of satisfaction and pleasure is high and we all leave therapy smiling.

REFERENCES

Boszormenyi-Nagy, I., & Spark, G. (1973). *Invisible loyalties: Reciprocity in intergenerational family therapy*. New York: Brunner/Mazel.

Bowen, M. (1978). *Family therapy in clinical practice*. New York: Jason Aaronson.

Breunlin, D. C., Schwartz, R. C., & Kune-Karrer, B. M. (1992). *Metaframeworks: Transcending the models of family therapy*. San Francisco: Jossey-Bass.

DeJong, P., & Berg, I. K. (2001). *Interviewing for solutions* (2nd ed.). Pacific Grove, CA: Brooks/Cole.

de Shazer, S. (1982). *Patterns of brief family therapy: An ecosystemic approach*. New York: Guilford Press.

de Shazer, S. (1985). *Keys to solution in brief therapy*. New York: Norton.

de Shazer, S. (1988). *Clues: Investigating solutions in brief therapy*. New York: Norton.

Freedman, J., & Combs, G. (1996). *Narrative therapy: The social construction of preferred realities*. New York: Norton.

Haley, J. (1987). *Problem-solving therapy* (2nd ed.). San Francisco: Jossey-Bass.

Jacobson, N. S., & Christensen, A. (1996). *Integrative couple therapy: Promoting acceptance and change*. New York: Norton.

Jacobson, N. S., & Margolin, G. (1979). *Marital therapy: Strategies based on social learning and behavior exchange principles*. New York: Brunner/Mazel.

Leiblum, S. R., & Rosen, R. C. (Eds.). (2000). *Principles and practice of sex therapy*. New York: Guilford Press.

McNamee, S., & Gergen, K. J. (Eds.). (1992). *Therapy as social construction*. Thousand Oaks, CA: Sage.

Minuchin, S. (1974). *Families and family therapy*. Cambridge, MA: Harvard University Press.

Nelson, T. S. (1994). Do-overs. *Journal of Family Psychotherapy, 5*(4), 71–74.

Nelson, T. S., McCollum, E. E., Wetchler, J. L., Trepper, T. S., & Lewis, R. A. (1996). Therapy with women substance abusers: A systemic couples approach. *Journal of Feminist Family Therapy, 8,* 5–27.

Papp, P. (1983). *The process of change*. New York: Guilford Press.

Watzlawick, P., Weakland, J., & Fisch, R. (1974). *Change: Principles of problem formation and problem resolution*. New York: Norton.

White, M., & Epston, D. (1990). *Narrative means to therapeutic ends*. New York: Norton.

seven

Unique Problems, Unique Resolutions: Brief Treatment of Sexual Complaints

Monte Bobele

All happy families resemble one another; every
unhappy family is unhappy in its own way.
—Tolstoy

To PARAPHRASE TOLSTOY, all sexually satisfied couples resemble one another, and every dissatisfied couple is dissatisfied in its own way. This understanding challenges the wisdom of allowing the *DSM-IV* to organize our therapeutic work. Although diagnosing clients has its uses for keeping statistics, doing research, and justifying funding, it also obscures what Tolstoy saw so clearly—that every problem is unique. The case I will describe shortly was chosen because it illustrates how recognizing, respecting, and working with the uniqueness of clients' dissatisfactions—sexual or otherwise—can result in relatively rapid resolutions. Employing the brief-therapy principles of the Mental Research Institute (MRI), I find that my clients are frequently highly motivated to resolve their sexual problems as quickly as possible. This was certainly the case with Bud and Diane, a couple whom I saw in Houston when I was part of a large private practice that specialized in treating marital and sexual problems.

Bud, a 30-year-old college graduate, had been employed as a petroleum engineer since graduating from college. He was the oldest of three children, and his parents were retired schoolteachers. Fit and trim, he exercised regularly and played basketball at the YMCA three times a week at lunchtime. He was soft-spoken and seemed shy, rarely looking up for the first several minutes of the session. Having grown up locally, his speech was tinged with the sound of the east Texas piney woods.

Diane, 29, taught high school English to gifted and talented children. Her father, a lawyer, had died two years previously, and her mother still worked as a bank teller in the small farming community where she grew up. An athletic blond who looked like she'd just gotten off the tennis courts, Diane explained that she played the game regularly with other teachers from work. She was poised and there was little trace of her rural upbringing in either her speech or manner.

Married seven years, Bud and Diane had one child, a daughter, who was six years old and in the first grade. They both said that they did not presently have plans for another child, but they simultaneously lit up when talking about their daughter. It was apparent from their descriptions of their participation in her school activities, her soccer team, and her music lessons that they were enthusiastically involved in her life.

The couple sat close to one another on the couch and frequently looked at one another as they talked. There was little open tension between them, but a faint undercurrent of something was evident. They were polite with me and with one another, rarely interrupting each other, but they seemed a bit anxious and uncertain about how to behave in this obviously new situation.

After spending time trying to set them at ease and finding out some of the facts of their everyday life, I asked about the purpose of their coming to see me. Bud came straight to the point: "I," he said, "have bad orgasms." To explain how I responded to this unique problem, I first need to describe how I approach therapy in general and how I specifically apply this approach to sexual problems.

THEORETICAL FOUNDATION
Mental Research Institute

The work of John Weakland and the Mental Research Institute (MRI) served as a significant influence on this case (Fisch, Weakland, & Segal, 1982; Watzlawick & Weakland, 1977; Watzlawick, Weakland, & Fisch, 1974; Weakland, Fisch, Watzlawick, & Bodin, 1974). MRI essentially conceptualizes a problem as the interactional pattern produced by the social system in which the problem is embedded, and thus focuses on understanding how individuals interact with one another to solve life's ordinary challenges. As Weakland was fond of saying, "Life is just one damned thing after another. Problems are the same damned thing, over and over."

From an MRI interactional perspective, the problems that people bring to psychotherapists are simply exacerbations of ordinary, everyday problems in living. Thus, sexual difficulties can be seen as stemming from regular problems in the relationship. Even in cases where there are clear-cut medical components, the participants' actions and thoughts concerning the problem often lead to an exacerbation of it.

Through experience, we, and those around us, learn how to resolve the everyday difficulties life presents, and often the solutions that worked in the past or worked for someone else can be applied successfully to new difficulties. But according to MRI, we also frequently persist in trying methods that, although successful in the past or in different circumstances, are not now working, and we inaccurately blame our failure on the quality of our effort rather than on the nature of our solution.

Struggling with the failure caused by dogged repetition of unsuccessful solution attempts, people may not only become frustrated, but also lose confidence and become alarmed that the problem is traveling on a worsening trajectory. If they become demoralized, their sense of hopelessness and impotence may spread to other areas of life as well. With this in mind, MRI adapts the old adage "If at first you don't succeed, try, try again" to read "If at first you don't succeed, try again, and then try something else."

Of course, we don't make solution attempts in a vacuum. Each partner in a couple, for example, will understand, define, and perceive a problematic situation differently, and these separate understandings determine how they individually and interactively respond. If they have differing ideas of what needs to be done, they may argue or vacillate over the steps to be taken. The MRI therapist thus begins by tracking clients' interactional patterns and solution attempts related to the identified problem.

From an MRI perspective, the resolution of sexual difficulties in a couple's relationship requires an interactive sensitivity to both partners' understandings of the problem. For example, Rick and Marcia consulted me about a decrease in the frequency and pleasure in their sexual lives, noting that they liked sex and had been mutually satisfied up until recently but were each now angry at the other about their current standoff. Rick's concern that they would never have sex again if not for his frustrated and "desperate" attempts, combined with Marcia's fear of his rejection (which she had experienced before), created a situation in which each was waiting for the other to initiate lovemaking.

Their standoff had spiraled out of control and affected every aspect of their relationship. With each perceiving the other's lack of interest in sex as a lack of love, they had become so allergic to sex that any affectionate talk or touching had become restrained, if not absent altogether. In this atmosphere of mistrust and hurt, rejection had become a self-fulfilling prophecy. The few attempts by either of them to initiate any affectionate activity were rejected by the other as insincere. They each wanted to be approached because the other "wanted to," not because he or she "had to." So, ultimately, any initiation of sexual activity was seen as the fulfillment of some obligation rather than as true affection.

Although several entrees into Marcia and Rick's sequence of "offer-reject-withdraw" were possible, they had both described their fear of rejection as part of the reason for avoiding each other, so I proposed they develop some emotional protection against this danger. I described the rejection that telephone solicitors face, knowing as they do that they may make hundreds of calls before anyone listens to their sales pitch.

At some point, I speculated, telephone solicitors must develop some sort of armor. One solicitor told me (with a primitive first-hand understanding of Skinnerian reinforcement schedules) that he knew that he was not going to get a sale unless he went through about 75 hang-ups first. He thus tried to get those hang-ups out of the way as quickly as possible, so he could get to the sale. "I just realized that the rejections were like a warm-up to the sale," he told me, "so I quit taking it personally. I made myself say 'thank you' even if they had already hung up." I suggested to Rick and Marcia that perhaps one way to develop armor against rejection by the other person was to practice handling it.

After establishing that this idea made sense to them, I asked them each to initiate some affectionate activity a couple of times every day. The partner was in each case to find some creative but gentle way to reject the other's advances. I cautioned them about how difficult it would be, given their recent history, but encouraged them to try. I also asked them not to give in to the temptation to respond affectionately to the other, because each of them needed more practice in being rejected in order to develop "rejection armor."

As I had hoped, when they returned, they had done the homework assignment successfully for several days in a row. Interestingly, the knowledge that their overtures would be rejected had introduced a kind of certainty into their relationship. Before, they had come to count on being rejected but hoped the outcome would be different. While they were doing the homework, they expected to be rejected all of the time, so they didn't get mad at their partner when it happened. As Marcia noted, "I actually felt closer to Rick when he rejected me this week, because I knew he was doing it in our own best interest, kinda." Finally, one of them succumbed and responded positively to the other, and they made love for the first time in months. After a total of three sessions, the couple believed that their relationship was back on track and that therapy had been successful.

The focus of an intervention in this model, then, is the interaction between the problem and the solutions applied to it. MRI has described a number of techniques designed to disengage a problem from its attempted solutions, including changing the meaning ascribed to the problem so that a different class of solutions becomes possible. This shift in understanding of the underlying nature of the problem is referred to in the interactional literature as "second-order change," and facilitating such a shift is an important component of an MRI approach.

Second-Order Cybernetics

Although my work has been influenced primarily by MRI ideas and practices, it is also informed by what some have characterized as "second-order cybernetics," or "the cybernetics of observing systems" (Keeney, 1983; von Foerster, 1982, 2002). Such a perspective underscores the necessity of including the observer in any description of what he or she is observing. Just as subatomic physicists realize that the act of observation changes the object observed (Prigogene & Stengers, 1984), so, too, physiological psychologists have long known that we interpret, or give meaning to, internal feelings based on the external context (Schacter & Singer, 1962). Heart palpitations, sweaty palms, and shortness of breath are interpreted as love or fear, depending on whether we are approaching a lover or being stalked by a tiger. We don't know what to make of a behavior or experience until we've established a context for understanding it.

Therapy provides just such a context for understanding. The definition of a problem is an interactive affair, involving the clients' and my perception of their complaint, as well as the context that brings us together. For example, as clients and I discuss their problem, I am, by virtue of my talking with them in a therapy office, to some extent endorsing the point of view that the problem is psychological in nature rather than medical, educational, spiritual, legal, and so on. If they disagree with this characterization—perhaps because they are meeting with me at the suggestion or demand of someone else—then simply engaging in a conversation about the problem will necessarily put us at cross purposes.

Another contextual component that defines therapy is the decision-making process around the number of sessions conducted. Many therapists, and clients for that matter, believe that the more severe a problem, the more sessions are necessary to remediate that problem. My brief approach to working with sexual problems, as well as other problems, includes communicating progress and hope in several ways.

When clients call for an initial consultation and fees are discussed, I usually quote an hourly fee, followed immediately by an estimate of the number of sessions that will be necessary—usually eight to ten. This picture of the overall length of therapy is often helpful early on in motivating clients.

Related to length is timing. I frequently do not see clients weekly after our first two to three meetings. Spacing sessions further apart, I implicitly and explicitly frame these gaps to clients as signs of their improvement—raising the training wheels, if you will.

Acknowledging the importance of context in interpreting behaviors and recognizing that the observer is part of this context, I have, over the years, moved away somewhat from orthodox MRI explanations. For example, a standard MRI intervention is to ask clients to "go slow" in making improvements. Weakland and his colleagues frequently explained this and other seemingly paradoxical interventions as directed at people's natural tendencies toward resistance. Milton Erickson, the primary influence on MRI's strategies, told the archetypal story of getting a stubborn animal to head toward the barn by pulling on its tail in the opposite direction (Erickson & Rossi, 1975). Frequently, then, MRI developed interventions designed to "pull on the tail" of clients.

A second-order understanding of such interventions adopts a more sophisticated view of the situation. When I encourage clients to "go slow," to "do more of the same," or to "practice their problem"—as I did with Rick and Marcia—I understand that my message is being offered via two channels: the verbal channel ("go slow," "do more of the same," or "practice the problem") and the nonverbal or contextual channel, which is infinitely more complicated and somewhat subtle but just as important.

Delivered in the context of therapy, messages such as "practice the problem," "do more of it," "allow it to occur unimpeded," and so on become therapeutic communications that clients and therapists generally regard as being predicated on change. Thus, such messages are grasped as if I were saying, "I am asking you to interact with the problem in a way that will help you change the situation associated with it." In fact, this is precisely what MRI therapists always do. The rationale, the "frame," that is constructed with clients is always designed to provide a rationale for why, in the service of getting over the problem, it should be practiced more.

From a second-order cybernetics position, the key to this understanding of the intervention is that it takes place in a nonverbalized context of change (psychotherapy), is given by an agent of change (a psychotherapist), and is taken under consideration by a customer for change (the client). This understanding goes far beyond simply pulling the tail of the problem.

An application of all these principles can be found in my work with Bud and Diane, who were suffering, as Bud put it, from "bad orgasms."

CASE ILLUSTRATION
First Session
Description of Problem by the Clients

"I have bad orgasms." I thought I had misheard him, or that he meant he was anorgasmic. At this point, I wanted to get a richer description of the problem.

Monte: Can you help me understand that?

Bud: Well, Diane and I had what you could call a normal, active sex life since we got married. But, a while back, I began having bad orgasms. It's not that I can't come; it's just that when I do, it is not as good as it used to be.

Monte: Okay . . .

Bud: I never have difficulty getting hard, and coming too soon has never been a problem, either.

I turned to Diane to be sure that I included her in the conversation right away. Although I am careful not to overinterpret issues such as who attends sessions and who sits where, I assumed that since Diane had come to this appointment with Bud, the couple at some level understood this to be *their* problem rather than just *his* problem. I wanted to establish a pattern early on that included both of their descriptions of the problem, their attempted solutions, and the meanings each made of the problem. This would ultimately make it easier to enlist both of them in the treatment.

I was still puzzled by what a "bad orgasm" could be, as it seemed to me to be an oxymoron. One of the cardinal tenets of MRI therapy is to avoid using language, labels, and ideas that do not come directly from the client's worldview, so I was prepared to use "bad orgasms" as the problem description.

Monte: Diane, tell me about these bad orgasms. How do they seem to you?

Diane: Well . . . [*looking at Bud*] at first I couldn't understand how an orgasm could be *bad*. I mean, isn't an orgasm something that is good—all by itself? Anyway, I couldn't tell any difference. Everything seemed okay to me. I was shocked when he said that he was not enjoying sex.

Here, perhaps, was an early expansion of the meaning of "bad orgasm"—it had something to do, at least from Diane's perspective, with Bud's not enjoying sex.

Bud: It's not that I'm not enjoying sex. It's that the orgasms aren't good.

More often than not, couples disagree on the nature of the problem, if for no other reason than that their perspectives differ. Rather than resolving this disparity, I decided to begin to try to track the problem's origin and the solution attempts that had been tried.

Monte: Okay. Diane, when did you discover he was having bad orgasms?

Diane: I don't know, I guess it was about six months ago.

Monte: And Bud, when did you first notice you were having bad orgasms?

Bud: It was about a year ago.

Again, I was not surprised that they had different histories of the problem. Instead of trying to resolve a difference in perspectives, I reframed their differences.

Monte: Sounds like you were able to keep the bad orgasms from Diane for a while, Bud. Okay, let's back up a bit. Did you usually have good orgasms up until about a year ago?

Bud: Sure.

I thought that the basis for comparison could safely be called "good orgasms," so I set out trying to expand on "bad orgasms."

Monte: I know this might be tough, but can you tell me the difference between the bad orgasms and good orgasms?

Bud: It's kinda hard to explain. When I had good orgasms, it would be like the fireworks you hear about. And the physical feelings would be very intense—it seemed like I came from everywhere in my body, not just my penis.

Monte: Uh, huh. Anything else?

Bud: Well, I would just feel incredibly close to Diane. Not only when I was coming, but for a long time afterward.

Monte: And now? The bad orgasms?

Bud: Well, first of all there are no fireworks. I mean it feels good, feels like I guess an orgasm should feel, but I don't have that all-over feeling, and that closeness to Diane isn't there like it used to be. It's hard to explain. . . . Just not as good as before.

This was a very helpful description, as it clarified for me that Bud was not anorgasmic. In fact, it did not sound like other orgasmic problems such as premature or delayed ejaculation.

Monte: And Diane, can you tell a difference between the good orgasms and the bad ones?

Diane: Well, at first I couldn't, but now I can pretty much tell from the way Bud is.

Monte: What do you mean?

Diane: He is more distant after sex . . . and we don't cuddle much afterwards like we used to. He doesn't seem as contented. He just rolls over and goes to sleep. That's different. We used to talk for hours afterward.

For both of them, bad orgasms would precede a post-coital distance that was different, although Diane's description did not include observations of differences in Bud during intercourse.

Bud: I know this must sound strange. I mean it's not like I'm impotent or anything. I went to the library and tried to see if there was anything in any of the books about this. I learned a whole lot about problems I'm sure glad I don't have.

It is not unusual for clients, regardless of the problem, to do some research when their initial efforts fail to produce results. The research may involve talking to friends, physicians, clergy, or other authorities; for college-educated clients, library, Internet, or bookstore research is not unusual. To his great relief, Bud's research at the library had certainly helped him eliminate a number of plights that were not his.

Monte: So pain or discomfort isn't a part of what you are dealing with?

Bud: No, it doesn't hurt. In fact, it still feels good when we have sex. . . .

Diane: Well, I used to think it was just because we're getting to be an old married couple [*laughs*]. I've talked some with my girlfriends who have been married longer than us, and they all say that things change over time. They say that things aren't the same for them either. I have tried to tell Bud that.

Here Diane confirmed for me that they had both been invested in understanding their current predicament and searching for solutions. Her research sources included friends who were authorities on married sex, and her comment also suggested that she'd been trying to help Bud by reassuring him.

Bud: Yeah, I thought that might be it, too. But I just think it is something else. I mean, I still love Diane as much as I always have. And in bed I am just as excited before and during sex as I always have been with her. It's just when it comes to the orgasm, it is just not as good.

Monte: So, you both have been doing some research of your own to figure out this problem. Bud, you've gone to the library; Diane, you've consulted with your friends. What else have you found out from talking with your friends?

Diane: Bud didn't like it that I told my friends about this problem. He thinks this is private—and it is, but I wanted to do something to make things better between us. And, well, if my friends had any ideas, I wanted to hear them.

Monte: So, anything else?

Diane: No, I haven't talked to anyone else. Bud told me about what he had read about, and that was helpful to me. At least it was reassuring. I guess I have been pretty lucky. I am usually orgasmic 90 percent of the time with Bud. I like sex, and I feel bad and a little selfish that it isn't as good for Bud, right now.

Monte: Can you tell when his orgasm is good or bad?

I returned to this because her previous description had not addressed her perception of Bud during orgasm. It sounded like both of them were telling me that there were no external signs of a bad orgasm during sex.

Diane: No, not during sex. I have to ask him most of the time, after. But he has gotten to where he doesn't want to talk to me after sex.

Monte: So he doesn't volunteer information?

Diane: Not anymore. That's why I ask him each time. Sometimes he says it was good, but I know he is just being nice. Because later, when we are talking, he will say he doesn't tell me the truth sometimes because he doesn't want to hurt my feelings.

Here was a description, in a nutshell, of the post-coital interactions that probably were contributing to the ongoing problem, although I did not know exactly how. Previously, their relationship had been very open and had included shared intimacy following sex. It was this openness that allowed Bud to tell Diane he was having bad orgasms in the first place. Ultimately, Bud may have been trying to protect Diane's feelings by not telling her about his disappointment. His efforts to protect her included lying to her and withdrawing from her.

I thought it was time to explore additional understandings they might have created around the bad orgasms. One way I did this was by asking about the effect or implications of the problem.

Monte: Okay, well, I have what might sound like a strange question. How have these bad orgasms become a problem for ya'll?
Diane: What do you mean?
Monte: Well, what has changed for the two of you since the bad orgasms started?
Diane: That'll be different for Bud than me, I guess, because I didn't know about them for a long time.
Monte: That's okay; I really need both of your perspectives.
Diane: Well, for one thing, I definitely don't look forward to sex as much as I used to. I feel like I am letting him down.
Monte: Uh, huh.
Diane: But I think it is also beginning to affect my self-esteem. I feel, sometimes, like I am a bad wife.
Bud: I sometimes feel like I am demanding too much of Diane, and myself too for that matter. I think I should be thankful I have such a wonderful wife and family and should just quit worrying about things. I wish I could just be happy with the way things are now.

Description of Solution Attempts by the Clients

Understanding previous, ongoing, unsuccessful, and partially successful solution attempts is essential for resolving the presenting problem. Pragmatically, it helps to protect the therapist's credibility if he or she avoids suggesting solutions that have already been tried and have failed. The variety of failed efforts can often be classified as belonging to the same category of behavior, the same class of solutions—punishment, reward, medication, attempts at understanding, and so on. Understanding the clients' view of the problem is enhanced by knowing what class of solutions has been used, because it points to the class of problems the clients believe their complaint belongs to.

Monte: It sounds like ya'll have struggled with this problem for some time, now. You've talked to friends and looked for answers in the library. . . . What else have you tried?

Diane: Well, I thought that if my friends were right and it was because we were, you know, getting used to one another, that maybe I could try to spice things up some. I bought some new nightgowns, and he didn't even notice, I don't think . . .

Bud: [*finishing her sentence*] I noticed. I felt even worse that you were trying so hard and I was still not having good orgasms.

Diane: Oh, I didn't think you noticed. Anyway . . . I tried to initiate sex more than I had before.

Monte: How'd that work?

Diane: It didn't, at least he didn't seem more satisfied. . . .

Bud: I just thought you were trying too hard, Diane.

Diane: Yeah, maybe I was. Then I thought that I was putting too much pressure on him, so I backed off. I initiated love-making less often.

Her attempts to solve this problem included becoming more sexually aggressive, but when this did not work, she thought that maybe being more passive would help. She described other things she had done to try to solve the problem between them, including several planned romantic evenings and a couple of weekend get-aways to local bed-and-breakfasts. She thought that a change of scenery and a respite from the familiarity of their day-to-day lives would help. She also said that she had tried talking to him before sex about what he liked so that she could be more attentive to his needs and had checked with him while they were having intercourse to see if he was enjoying it.

In addition to going to the library and to bookstores, seeking information that might address his problem, Bud had suggested to Diane that they make love less often, thinking that perhaps the frequency of their sexual activity had taken some of the uniqueness away from it. He added that maybe they had gotten so used to one another that it had become less interesting. He tried cooperating with Diane's strategy of getting feedback and information about what he liked and wanted more of. However, discouraged and demoralized as a result of the bad orgasms, he had returned to masturbation for the first time since he was a teenager. He said that the resulting orgasms were good, but not as satisfying as the ones he used to frequently experience with his wife.

Making Sense of the Problem

Fearing that the bad orgasms indicated that "the honeymoon was over," Bud assumed that perhaps sex just became naturally unsatisfying after several years of marriage. He also had given consideration to the notion that he was losing his sexuality. Worried that he might have something medically wrong with him, he had consulted with his family doctor, who laughed at the idea that Bud could have bad orgasms, but assured him, after a thorough exam, that nothing appeared to be physically wrong.

Diane said that she was invariably orgasmic, but she had become more distracted in recent months worrying about Bud. When he first told her that he was having bad orgasms, Diane became worried that he did not love her anymore. She feared that she had become less attractive and was no longer sexually appealing to him, although Bud reassured her that this was not the case. She had also come to suspect that perhaps he was being too demanding and had become a perfectionist.

It appeared that a cloud of pessimism about their sexual relationship in particular, and their marriage, in general, was hovering over them. In such circumstances, I frequently want to get some understanding of clients' fears, and to learn whether they see the current situation as a harbinger of worse things to come.

Monte: I know this next question may sound off the wall, Bud, but how bad could the orgasms get? How much worse could they be?

Bud: Well, they are pretty bad right now. I guess if they continued to get worse, I would give up wanting to make love to Diane at all.

Diane: That's one of the things I am afraid of. I'm afraid that our relationship will deteriorate because Bud is unhappy in bed.

Bud: I know sex isn't everything in a relationship, but it has been a part of the whole intimacy thing for us, and that is scary for me. That we are losing that. I guess the fun of sex would go away completely, and Diane's right, some of our intimacy might go away, too.

Monte: So you guys have worried about this situation getting worse. Are you already beginning to notice differences in the badness of the orgasms?

Diane: I can't tell about his orgasms, but our relationship is definitely getting worse.

Bud: I think that some orgasms are really worse than others. In fact, sometimes I have just a moment of thinking that I am going to have a good orgasm, usually when we first start making love, and then it turns out bad. But sometimes not as bad as other times.

Monte: What do you notice yourself doing to keep yourself heading toward a "not as bad" orgasm when you get that feeling?

Bud: I'm not sure that I do anything. . . . I guess I try to concentrate on keeping the good feeling and making it last. I try to think about how good things feel, but eventually it turns out being bad.

Monte: Are any of the orgasms ever "good"?

Bud: Sometimes I think it's going to be good and then something happens to spoil it.

Monte: What would you have to do to make your orgasms worse?

This question often provides some clue as to what the participants have been avoiding or are afraid to do. It also helps flesh out their understandings of the origin or cause of the problem and lets me know what trajectory they think their problem is on.

Bud: Sure, I guess they could get worse, but I don't know what I would do to make them worse. As we said, our relationship could get worse. If Diane started blaming me, or I started blaming her for the bad orgasms, they might get worse. I think I have been mainly blaming myself.

Diane: I guess I could be even less attentive to him in bed and start avoiding him altogether.

Formulation

Problems arise from the mismanagement of ordinary everyday difficulties. In this case, perhaps, the chance comparison of one sexual episode with memories of others, and the subsequent conclusion that it was not as fulfilling, had created a lasting problem. Making these comparisons led Bud to assume a spectator role in future lovemaking episodes, becoming a detached critic of his own sexual experience. This detachment altered the context of the experience by changing Bud from a participant to an observer. Monitoring himself was the first step in his attempt to solve the "bad orgasm" problem. Inevitably, each closely monitored sexual experience had to be less satisfactory, because it was contaminated by the act of self-observation.

At some point, Bud shared his disappointment with his wife—another step in problem-solving—and she became recruited into helping to solve the problem. Her participation in sex with her husband was then compromised, as she also became an observer and lost her usual spontaneity. Diane's well-intentioned attempts to help solve this problem, when unsuccessful, increased her anxiety and worry about the relationship. Thus, their initial attempts to solve the problem (keeping close tabs on what was happening) changed something fundamental about their sexual relationship, rendering it less spontaneous.

The couple's solution attempts magnified the original problem, and this perception of a magnified problem brought about magnified solution efforts. Bud and Diane increased their observations and their attempts to return to a satisfactory sexual relationship. Note that each episode of unsatisfactory sex led to a change in perception or meaning of the situation (e.g., "it's getting worse" or "it's worse than I thought"). Sex changed from a spontaneous act of lovemaking to an intense problem-solving activity. Mutual problem-solving involved discussions before and after intercourse; changes in frequency, intensity, and location of their lovemaking; research; and deliberate attempts to act differently.

Masters and Johnson (1970) and others have described couples' efforts to substitute conscious effort for spontaneity and have detailed the resulting problems. Although Masters and Johnson's methods appear on the surface to be different from MRI techniques, both approaches prescribe ways to encourage people to abandon their conscious problem-solving. In this case, Bud was attempting to force himself to have a "good orgasm" and had become hypervigilant about his sexual behavior.

Intervention

In planning a way to intervene in this situation, I was mindful of the connection between the couple's interactions around the problem. The basic strategy was to find a way to interrupt or disconnect the attempted solution behaviors from the couples' sexual activity. In this case, explaining the harmful consequences of taking on a critical spectator role would probably not have been very helpful. In fact, criticizing their performance as problem-solvers might have put more pressure on them, thereby exacerbating the situation. There are several strategies described by MRI, but they all distill down to one of the following injunctions:

- Do less of the solution behavior.
- Do more of the solution behavior.
- Do the solution behavior differently.

The art of psychotherapy, and the active ingredient of any intervention, depends on the therapist's ability to create a context that will enable the client to follow the intervention. MRI describes this context creation as reframing—the process of adjusting the frame or boundaries around a problem so that some of the details of the situation remain in the frame while others that were out of sight before become more prominent. My experience has been that it is easier to reframe a client's picture of the problem than it is to sell them a new picture.

Information about the clients' current frame, or understanding, of the problem and clues for changing the frame arise from the therapeutic conversation and from particular questions. In this case, a number of ideas arose from the interview and offered possibilities for a change in frame:

- Bud and Diane were a close, loving couple.
- They were actively involved in trying to solve their problem.
- They made excellent use of resources like friends and the library.
- They believed that things could be worse.

Frequently, at the end of a first session, I ask clients, as a first step, to gather information about their problem.

Monte: I need a baseline to see exactly what we may be dealing with here. So I need to ask both of you to help me get some information.

Although getting baseline data is common in a number of therapeutic approaches, here it was also deliberately used to appeal Bud's scientific thinking. Not only were his education and career in the sciences, but also one of his early solution attempts had been to do research in the library. This task, although appearing to be an ordinary data-gathering exercise, is actually an intervention. Any time clients are asked to make observations about their behavior, inevitable changes in behavior occur, as the act of observing changes the observations. In this case, the intervention also fit because their problem was so embedded in their roles as observers of Bud's orgasms. I designed the intervention as a means of shifting their observing frame and thus also their observations, ever so slightly.

Monte: Things could have gotten worse in this situation, I suspect. I think that the two of you have been working hard to solve this problem, and trying to keep it from getting worse.

Bud: I don't know, I guess it could get worse. . . .

Monte: Well, I think there are ways. For instance, you still are in there trying, you haven't given up, yet. If you were to give up, things might definitely get worse.

Diane: I guess that's true.

Monte: Well, here's what I need. I need to know how bad these orgasms really are.

Bud: They're pretty bad.

Monte: I realize that, but I suspect that there are things that you may be doing consciously or unconsciously that keep the orgasms from getting worse than they are already. What I'd like for both of you to do this week is to just let the bad orgasms occur naturally. In other words, don't do anything this week to improve your orgasms or make things better. Just go ahead and have sex as you have been, just don't try to interfere with the bad orgasms. I need to see if the orgasms are worse without the benefit of your trying to help.

Bud: You mean, just be miserable during sex?

Monte: Well, I imagine things have been pretty miserable as it is. But yes, I know that it will be unpleasant for this week. But if we are going to get to the bottom of this problem, we are going to need good data to work with. This is not the solution to your problem, it's just a first step in trying to see what is going on. So, while you are having sex this week, I want you to pay attention to what is happening before during and after the bad orgasms, so we'll know what we are dealing with.

Bud: I can understand that. Kinda like doing experiments under standard laboratory conditions, as opposed to in the field.

Monte: Exactly! That's right. We need to see what the bad orgasms are like without any efforts to make them better.

Diane: I'm not sure I have been doing anything different, just trying to make Bud happy.

Monte: That's a good example, Diane. Don't worry about making Bud happy. Just go ahead and have sex like you used to, and we'll talk about it next week. I know that it may be unpleasant for Bud to continue to have bad orgasms, but sometimes things get worse before they get better. Other than that, don't change anything else. Don't have sex more than you think you should or less than you think you should.

Bud: Keep everything standard. . . .

Monte: You got it!

There are several aspects of this homework assignment that are worth mentioning. First, it was an attempt to subtly persuade the couple to stop trying to cure the bad orgasms. However, because the request was rooted in the context of therapy, the message to continue to have bad orgasms was interwoven with another message: "One of the ways you will stop having bad orgasms is to cooperate with me for a time and continue to have bad orgasms."

Second, it changed the perspective of the observers. Gathering data for a baseline allowed the couple to temporarily abandon their problem-solving attempts. In fact, the meaning of the performance of the problem changed from "something to be avoided" to "a necessary step in completing the homework assignment." If bad orgasms were now necessary for information-gathering purposes, then the experience of having them would occur within a different frame, creating the potential for them to feel somewhat different.

Second Session

A week later, Bud and Diane arrived at the office with sheepish smiles on their faces. When I asked how the homework had gone, they said that they had had intercourse on four different occasions. Bud's orgasms had been bad, but not as bad as some of the more recent ones, and, as a matter of fact, they had improved somewhat toward the end of the week. When I asked him how he accounted for this, he had no ideas, but pointed out that there had been some temporary improvement in the past. I agreed with him that if there was any improvement, it was likely to be only temporary. I have found that it is not helpful to become too optimistic when clients report such improvements in the short term.

Diane said that with the pressure taken off her to do anything about Bud's orgasms, she had actually enjoyed sex more during the week. I asked them about their post-coital conversations, as this had previously been a time when they discussed their lack of success. They said that beyond just checking with Bud that he did indeed have a bad orgasm, Diane did not pursue the subject. She also reported that she hadn't felt responsible for his bad orgasms, but had simply made note of it for the benefit of our appointment.

I complimented them on their ability to complete the homework assignment and then spent the remainder of the session carefully reviewing with them their observations before, during, and after their four occasions of lovemaking. Bud said that he had tried to watch for the beginning of the "badness" of the orgasm but had been unable to do so because none of them had been particularly bad. Diane noticed most that they had spent time after sex cuddling and talking about their daughter and the vacation plans they were making.

Diane: I knew that we were not supposed to talk about Bud's orgasms, but I wanted to talk to him about something, so I just talked about things like we had before this all started.

Bud: I noticed that. I mean, that we're talking after sex. I liked that. I missed that. It was easier for me to talk to Diane because I knew that we weren't going to be talking about my orgasm. In fact, I hardly even thought about my orgasms after we started talking.

Monte: What about during sex? What did ya'll do to have a bad orgasm?

Bud: Well, I figured I had to put myself back in the mindset that I had before the bad orgasms started.

Monte: How did you do that?

Bud: Well, before, during sex, I would look at Diane and try to pay attention to how good she was making me feel. It's hard to explain, but I was focusing on Diane like I used to, less on myself. I was just trying to let sex happen. Just trying to let the bad orgasms happen.

Diane: Me too. I mean, I was more focused on me. Bud and I had talked some about the assignment and how to do it. We had talked about trying to go back to having sex the way it was before, rather than trying to improve the way it had been. I don't know exactly how to put it. It's not that I didn't care whether or not Bud enjoyed sex this week; it's just that I never thought about it before this all started. Before, I just assumed that he was going to enjoy it and didn't worry about it. So that's what I did this week.

It was clear to me that Bud and Diane were on their way to eliminating the bad orgasms from their sex lives. There were a number of signs of progress: They had, temporarily at least, abandoned trying to fix the problem by forcing Bud to have good orgasms; they had spontaneously returned to thinking about sex the way they had in the past; and their mood was optimistic. During this visit, although they talked about the "bad orgasms," the focus of the interview was on what they had successfully done differently during the week when they were having sex.

At the end of the second session, I explained that because there hadn't been enough bad orgasms, we were still lacking baseline data. I thus asked them to continue with their bad-orgasm observations. They agreed, but protested that they would prefer to have another week like the last one. I encouraged them to do everything they had done during the previous week.

Follow-up

A couple of days before the third session, Diane called to cancel their appointment, saying that Bud had a business trip that would interfere with their appointment. I asked her if they had some data for me about the bad orgasms.

Diane: You'll have to talk to Bud about that. I think he's going to flunk this.
Monte: What do you mean?
Diane: Well, we had sex. As far as I could tell, Bud had good orgasms again—every time. At least he said he did. And it looked like it to me as well. So he didn't do the homework. I guess he'll flunk [*laughing*].
Monte: Well, what about you?
Diane: It was a great week for me. I didn't worry about Bud as much. And things have been better, both in and out of bed.

Before hanging up, I asked Diane to have Bud call before making another appointment. If things were going well for Bud and they had found a way to get back on track with their lives, I didn't want to schedule another appointment just yet.

Bud called a few days later to tell me, in an upbeat way, that he had been unable to do the homework: "I tried to have bad orgasms a couple of times, but couldn't. A couple of weeks ago I realized that I had forgotten about having bad orgasms. I mean, I guess I was so involved in having sex with Diane that I forgot about whether I was supposed to have bad orgasms or good ones." When I expressed my worry that they had experienced short-lived improvements in the past, he assured me that this seemed somehow different. We agreed to schedule an appointment in four weeks for the purpose of follow-up.

Again, prior to our meeting, they called to cancel, reassuring me that things were back to the way they had been earlier in the marriage. "In fact," said Bud, "even better sometimes." When he put Diane on the phone, she confirmed that things had improved "a thousand percent." We agreed that we would hold off on the last appointment until they needed it.

I waited a year before calling for follow-up information. Diane answered the phone and said that they had not even thought about the bad orgasms again. She happily told me that they were expecting their second child. She put Bud on the phone, and he confirmed that they were doing well and that he had not had any bad orgasms in over a year. "Actually, I don't think I have even thought about them in a long time."

DISCUSSION

This chapter illustrates the application of MRI's brief interactional approach (with overtones of second-order cybernetics) to a unique sexual complaint, showing how a small adjustment in a couple's attempted solution behavior can lead to significant change. I frequently have found that clients can make rapid improvements once some small difference in their ongoing situation occurs. The opportunities for introducing this sort of change are maximized during the first session (Weiner-Davis, de Shazer, & Gingerich, 1987; Talmon, 1990), when the clients' motivation is often the highest. This was certainly the case with Bud and Diane, who had a history of satisfying sexual encounters earlier in their relationship and who, outside of the bedroom, were still doing well. Although I would have liked to have had a final interview in my office with this couple, it would probably have been meeting my needs for closure more than Bud and Diane's needs for moving on.

The success in the case might be attributed to a number of factors. When, following the first session, the couple took a different observational position, they interrupted their pattern of trying to prevent the bad orgasms. In other words, they returned to letting Bud's orgasms just "happen," instead of trying to make them happen in a particular way. As Bud and Diane moved from purposive to accidental observers, their relationship to the problem changed.

Although the nature of this complaint was unusual, its uniqueness stems from the fact that it does not neatly fit into any existing category in current official diagnostic nosology. Some therapists would have attempted to restate or redefine Bud and Diane's problem as an orgasmic dysfunction, for which standardized treatment protocols already exist. A marital therapist might have diagnosed it as a communication problem or as a problem in one or both families of origin and proceeded to put the sexual problem on the back burner, viewing it simply as a symptom or a metaphor of the larger problems in the relationship. An individually oriented therapist, inclined to search for the appropriate *DSM-IV* category for either Bud or Diane, would certainly have conducted a different first interview, and treatment would have been organized around the standard, perhaps "empirically validated," treatments for the arrived-at diagnosis.

The approach I took with this case allowed for idiopathic understandings and custom-tailored treatment. As Tolstoy implied, each client and each situation is different from any and every other. With this assumption in mind, I conduct interviews that honor and make use of my clients' unique circumstances and interactions, rather than going in search of a diagnostic label that can capture their similarities with other, "equally disturbed," "patients." By constantly staying attuned to language, meanings, understandings, abilities, experiences, and culture—that is, to context— I am able to work creatively to help my clients uniquely resolve their problems in as brief a time as possible.

REFERENCES

Erickson, M. H., & Rossi, E. L. (1975). Varieties of double bind. *The American Journal of Clinical Hypnosis, 17*, 143–157.

Fisch, R., Weakland, J. H., & Segal, L. (1982). *The tactics of change: Doing therapy briefly*. San Francisco: Jossey-Bass.

Keeney, B. (1983). *Aesthetics of change*. New York: Guilford Press.

Masters, W. H., & Johnson, V. E. (1970). *Human sexual inadequacy*. Boston: Little.

Prigogine, I., & Stengers, I. (1984). *Order out of chaos: Man's new dialogue with nature*. New York: Bantam.

Schacter, S., & Singer, J. (1962). Cognitive, social, and physiological determinants of emotional state. *Psychological Review, 69*, 379–399.

Talmon, M. (1990). *Single-session therapy: Maximizing the effect of the first (and often only) therapeutic encounter*. San Francisco: Jossey-Bass.

von Foerster, H. (1982). *Observing systems*. Seaside, CA: Intersystems Publications.

von Foerster, H. (2002). *Understanding understanding: Essays on cybernetics and cognition*. New York: Springer.

Watzlawick, P., & Weakland, J. (1977). *The interactional view: Studies at the Mental Research Institute*. New York: Norton.

Watzlawick, P., Weakland, J., & Fisch, R. (1974). *Change: Principles of problem formation and problem resolution*. New York: Norton.

Weakland, J. H., Fisch, R., Watzlawick, P., & Bodin, A. (1974). Brief therapy: Focused problem resolution. *Family Process, 13*, 141–168.

Weiner-Davis, M., de Shazer, S., & Gingerich, W. J. (1987). Building on pretreatment change to construct the therapeutic solution: An exploratory study. *Journal of Marital and Family Therapy, 13*, 359–363.

eight

Just Between Us: A Relational Approach to Sex Therapy

Douglas Flemons and Shelley Green

T HE NAME OF THIS CHAPTER—"Just Between Us"—is suggestive of the sort of intimacy that's engendered when partners share privileged information or tenderness with each other, but more importantly it says something about how the two of us orient to therapy and change. Most clients come to us with the expectation (or at least the hope) that we'll get rid of a problem residing inside their body or head, or inside their partner or other family member. But we don't approach problems, or their resolutions, that way. First, we recognize that any effort to negate something hated or feared only heightens its significance (Flemons, 2002, 2003), and second, we don't consider any problem to be a *thing*, localizable or transformable within a particular person or body part (Flemons, 1991). Our therapeutic imagination is, instead, always focused on how to help shift the *relationship between things*—particularly the relationship between our clients and the relationship between them and their problem. This is where we can make a difference, helping to change how our clients relate to each other and relate to whatever they're struggling to eradicate.

This chapter outlines our general therapeutic assumptions—which differ somewhat from those of other brief therapists—and demonstrates their applicability to sex-related cases. You will no doubt notice compatabilities between our approach and other models both inside and outside the brief therapy domain. Similarly to psychoanalysts (e.g., Henry, Strupp, Schacht, & Gaston, 1994), we focus carefully on the relationship between us and our clients, and like cognitive behaviorists (e.g., Meichenbaum, 1977) and MRI brief therapists (Watzlawick, Weakland, & Fisch, 1974), we recognize the degree to which meaning shapes behavior. We share with feminist and narrative therapists a sensitivity to marginalized voices, to the decision-making processes within couples, and to how each partner "stories" the history of the couple's difficulty (Goldner, Penn, Sheinberg, & Walker, 1990; Penn & Frankfurt, 1994; Roberts, 1994; White & Epston, 1991). And like many brief therapists, we think contextually (Selvini Palazzoli, Boscolo, Cecchin, & Prata, 1978), take interactional processes into account (Watzlawick et al.; Weakland, 1993), and don't consider *DSM* diagnoses to be necessary for bringing resolution or finding exceptions to problems (e.g., de Shazer, 1994).

You will no doubt also notice places where we part company with more established models. We don't interpret to our clients the nature of their relationship with us (Henry et al., 1994), and we don't think in terms of counter-transference (Eisenbud, 1978); we eschew thought-stopping techniques, and we don't try to desensitize or flood anyone (Redd, Porterfield, & Anderson, 1979); we don't attempt to "paradox" our clients (Selvini Palazzoli et al., 1978), and we don't "externalize" their problems (White & Epston, 1991).

We haven't set out to create either correspondences with or divergences from other approaches. Instead, we've gone to the heart of how language and mind work, deriving some general therapeutic assumptions and practices from those ideas (Flemons, 1991, 2002). These are as applicable to sex-related concerns as they are to any other; however, working in the realm of sexuality requires some additional knowledge and sensitivity (Tiefer, 1995). For example, our understanding of sexual desire and response, as well as our knowledge of physiological structures and processes, help us to hold realistic expectations about performance and pleasure and to know when to make appropriate referrals.* Like physicians who can differentiate professional from personal touch without sacrificing interpersonal warmth, we distinguish professional from personal *conversations*—about intimate thoughts and actions—without sacrificing empathic intensity. Clients bring in concerns about a whole range of sexual issues, and our therapeutic curiosity must be piqued by possibilities for change, not opportunities for titillation. Therapists who are distracted by their own reactions (whether of embarrassment or arousal) to their

---

* If clients who are seeing us for a sex-related problem haven't already seen a gynecologist or urologist, we ask them to do so before returning for their next appointment. We get involved once physiological complications (such as diabetes or hypertension) have been ruled out or medical interventions (such as medications or surgery) aren't available or have proven ineffective.

clients' stories risk creating unhelpful, inappropriate, or unethical situations. Such considerations are perhaps not absent from other therapeutic contexts, but the stakes are higher when the subject matter is sex.

THERAPEUTIC ASSUMPTIONS

What is required is precise talk about relations.

—Gregory Bateson

As you walk around, perceiving stuff, you typically distinguish yourself as an observer, separate from what you observe. When the object of your perception lies outside of you, and particularly when it bothers you—a client's too-strong perfume, a driver who cuts you off, a ringing cell phone in the middle of a movie—you tend to experience a *self-other split* between you and it. But you also experience this same gap between observer and observed when you're perceiving something about *yourself*, especially when you're put off or repulsed by what you're noticing—a recurring thought that plagues you, a part of your body that disgusts you, a fear that freezes you.

You, like the rest of us, have the enduring impression (or, more accurately, the Cartesian delusion) that your experience is composed of isolable things or units, each one separate and distinct from other distinguishable things or units, as well as separate from the context in which you find it. And, still more crazy, you, again like everyone else, experience yourself as separate from this experiencing. You sense that the part of you that is aware of itself perceiving—your conscious self or "observing-I"—is somehow set apart, distinct from what you sense and think and feel. But if this were true, then you could easily obliterate objects to which you objected. That horrible memory? Gone! The pain in your stomach? Gone! The anger over last night's argument? Gone!

That your observing-I can't control your perceptions, thoughts, and emotions in this way is a testament to the fact that all experience is fundamentally *relational*. Just as you cannot not communicate (Watzlawick, Beavin, & Jackson, 1967), so too you cannot not be in relationship. When you try to cut off, push away, or control something you identify as other (whether outside or inside yourself), you don't manage to make it disappear or make it less bothersome. Indeed, your efforts at negation only serve to heighten its significance, rendering it more, not less, problematic.

This is why clients experience their out-of-control symptoms—spasmodic contractions of the muscles in and around the vagina, say, or profoundly disturbing sexual images that play out in Technicolor just when sleep beckons—as controlling *them*. Entangled by their Cartesian assumptions and failed efforts to free themselves, they go in search of a therapist who they hope can help them do a better job of negating their problem. But any such effort only makes matters worse. As Milton Erickson once said, a therapist's job "is that of altering, not abolishing" (1986, p. 104).

Recognizing that clients can't succeed at purposefully distancing themselves from whatever's troubling them, we instead look for ways to help them *change their relationship* to it. The problem doesn't exist as a stand-alone object, so it can only transform in keeping with a change in the clients' relationship to it. By helping clients connect to it more comfortably, we help the relationship itself to relax, which allows the problem to take on a different meaning or to become less of an issue. As its significance changes or decreases, other, more interesting, things can grab the clients' attention, and the problem can move into their peripheral awareness.

For example, a man who fails to achieve an erection when he thinks the circumstances warrant it may feel frustrated and afraid of his inability to predict or control his sexual response. When such clients come to see us, we do not offer to help make the problem disappear. Part of the problem is that a "controlled sexual response" is an oxymoron, so success in the way the client is imagining it would necessarily be a complete failure.

One way we facilitate a connection between a man and such a symptom is to make the assumption that his penis is making wise choices about when to become erect and when to keep (or return to being) soft (this, of course, only after a possible medical condition has been eliminated). We invite the man and his partner to join us in our curiosity about this free-thinking penis-wisdom, and we ask them to help us gather further information about how the penis knows when to rise to an occasion and when to hold back for a while. We ask detailed questions about the pattern of the penis' behavior, and, based on that, we ask the couple to experiment with various kinds of sexual activities. We don't tell them not to engage in intercourse; we ask them to help us understand the man's body-logic. All sexual interaction becomes, for a while, a kind of data-gathering, and this changes the couple's relationship to the problem. Instead of recoiling from the behavior of the penis, they, via their curiosity, connect to it in a neutral or even positive way, freeing the man's body to behave in keeping with its sensitive wisdom and its natural ability to get hard. By becoming comfortable with and respectful of the man's penis, regardless of its state of tumescence, the couple make it possible for the symptom to wander away.

Our therapeutic focus, then, is always on relationships—between people, sure, but also between people and various parts of their experience, whether a body part, a physiological response, an idea, an emotion, a behavior, or whatever. We assume that a relationship is most viable when the *relata*—the parts at either end of it—are are free to change or stay stable *in coordination* with each other. Therapy is, for us, the process by which we facilitate, encourage, and enhance the possibility for such *relational freedom* (Flemons, 2002).

In this chapter we discuss the importance of freedom within five relationships that are particularly relevant to the realm of brief sex therapy:

1. The relationship between you and your clients;
2. The relationship between your clients;
3. The relationship between your clients and sexuality;
4. The relationship between you and sexuality;
5. The relationship between your clients and their problem.

RELATIONAL SEX THERAPY

We are primarily concerned here with discussing and illustrating some of the ways we introduce relational freedom in our clients' relationships with their sexual problems. Sometimes a sexual difficulty dissolves without our focusing on it specifically. A change elsewhere in the couple's life, such as their finding a way of feeling/communicating respect for one another outside the bedroom, can change what goes on inside the bedroom. We thus never focus on just one relationship at a time. However, for ease of discussion, we will separately introduce and illustrate (with case vignettes) each of the five therapeutically relevant relationships. Following this discussion, we'll offer a more in-depth case presentation that ties the various ideas together.

The Relationship Between You and Your Clients

Typically, therapists write about their success stories, using the narrative to reveal various clinical enlightenments. We'll do our share of that here, but because we've often learned as much, and remembered what we've learned more deeply, by attending to our failures, we'd like to begin with one of those. We share this failure with you in an effort to highlight the critical importance of developing a respectful and strong therapeutic relationship with your clients.

Shelley once worked with a man, Rich, who had been living with AIDS for several years and was very angry about his diagnosis, his health problems, and his self-described "death sentence." The first several sessions were consumed by Rich's ongoing descriptions of his frequent visits to gay bars, where he would engage in anonymous, unprotected sex with multiple partners. Shelley was, of course, disturbed by Rich's behavior and became more concerned when she realized that Rich had no desire to end or alter these sexual excursions.

Guided by her training and therapeutic assumptions at the time, Shelley repeatedly tried to learn from Rich why these encounters were so important to him, given the potential consequences for his anonymous partners. He, no doubt frustrated by her rather transparent message that he was doing something wrong, told her emphatically, "Someone did this to me, and now it's time for payback." He stressed that his goals for therapy did not include changing his behaviors—he simply wanted to be able to talk with her about his isolation, loneliness, and intense anger.

Unfortunately, Shelley's ongoing negative (and unstated) response to Rich's actions prevented her from engaging with him in a way that would allow her to develop a strong therapeutic relationship. Alienated by his actions and his lack of interest in the consequences, she found herself dreading each session and searching for ways to make him change his mind—not a strong position for therapeutic engagement.

Reflecting on this experience several years later, we now recognize that Shelley could have done more to create a therapeutic connection with Rich that offered possibilities for change. Some much-needed supervision would have helped her to explore her own aversion to his actions and to make sense of them within the context of his isolation and illness. Had she been able to attend more to Rich's pain than to his sexual encounters, it's possible that she could have explored his behaviors in ways that allowed him to reflect on them, consider how they in fact contributed to his isolation, and find other ways to manage his loneliness. Alternatively, she could have talked directly with him about her misgivings and distress. He might have recoiled from such honesty, but at least Shelley's alienation, resulting from her silence, dread, and discomfort, wouldn't have gotten in the way of their working together.

Therapeutic engagement is unlikely if you're invested in stopping or controlling your clients' behaviors. Once you free yourself from such an investment, therapeutic change is possible. We worked together on an Employee-Assistance-Program (EAP) case some years ago involving a man who was close to being fired from his job for various sexist indiscretions.

He came to us because he wanted to stay employed, but he had no interest in becoming a gender-sensitive man. It would have been easy (and smugly satisfying in a politically correct sort of way) to dismiss him as a sexist buffoon, but instead we found it possible to make sense of his manner of relating to women, and we worked within his worldview to help him make the necessary changes for keeping his job.

For example, we complimented the man on his communication skills but suggested that perhaps he had been a little "too cocky" (pun intended) in applying them. We taught him how to insult more subtly, so subtly, in fact, that only he could possibly recognize the sexual innuendo he was of-fering in conversations. We suggested, for example, that he think about all the words starting with *t* and *a* and to use them liberally when talking with women. Who would suspect that the question "Could I Ask you To Take care of A small detail for me?" contained references to body parts? A bright man, he took great pleasure in these exercises and successfully tried them out on us without our realizing it. We looked for and found a way to respect him, and he could tell. The results were positive: Not only did he not get fired, his colleagues voted to make him their supervisor.

Connecting with clients is essential, but therapy is impossible if you and your clients aren't able to feel free within the relationship. Both you and they need to be able to keep separate within the context of your con-nection. Douglas once saw a professional woman, Alicia, who wanted to change her sexual relationships with men. She had not been in a commit-ted relationship for some time, and she was concerned about having too often engaged, over the previous few years, in unprotected sex with casual partners whom she didn't respect.

In the first session, Alicia told Douglas about her experience with a pre-vious male therapist. It had taken her a long time, she said, but she had fi-nally managed to seduce him. She knew she would be able to, and she had succeeded. She took responsibility for what happened and never reported the incident to anyone; however, her trust in the therapist was soured by the experience, and she ended therapy with him a short time later. Doug-las talked to her about dual relationships and ethical breaches, and he made clear that nothing she said or did would ever result in his reaching out to her sexually. Without the trust of that safety with a therapist, he said, any talk about her sexuality was a risk to her integrity. He expressed confidence in her ability to trust herself to decide whether or not she could trust him (or any other therapist), and he noted that because trust should be earned, she might want to exercise some caution in opening up to him. This conversation helped establish the possibility for necessary therapeutic trust, and their work together proceeded well from that point.

The Relationship Between Your Clients

The pattern of intimacy in a relationship between committed partners is woven of many strands, and although a couple's sexual relationship is an important thread, it certainly isn't the only one. Sometimes we find it easier or more efficient to resolve a couple's specific sexual complaint by introducing relational freedom elsewhere in their life together.

Shelley worked with a lesbian couple who had been partners for two years when they entered therapy. Ellen and Carol rarely fought during the first one and a half years of being together, and when they did, they were able to resolve their differences quickly. They each described their relationship as the healthiest, most intimate one they had ever had, but they were concerned by recent ongoing conflict and sexual difficulties. The frequency and pleasure of their lovemaking had dropped dramatically, and each woman was beginning to see sex as an impossible, no-approach issue.

This sexual struggle was going on within the context of Ellen's intense desire to bring a baby into their relationship. Carol was ambivalent about the idea and unwilling to provide Ellen with any guarantee for the future. The resulting conflict had permeated their lives. Ellen feared that Carol would never agree to a baby, and she had begun wondering aloud whether she needed to find someone else with whom she could share her dream. Carol, in turn, heard such musings as evidence of Ellen's lack of commitment to the relationship. Increasingly ensconced in their divergent stances, they had become alienated from one another both emotionally and sexually.

Carol's and Ellen's pulling away from one another had created an uncomfortable distance between them, and each of them had been trying to improve the situation by getting the other to change her position. Thus each of them was both separating from the other and separating from the other's separation: Ellen wanted Carol to stop dragging her feet about the baby, and Carol wanted Ellen to stop threatening to leave.

Shelley commented on the wisdom of each of their positions, thus making it possible for them to connect to—understand, appreciate, and respect—the other's separations. She noted that Carol could have easily placated Ellen by agreeing, hypothetically, that at some point in the future she would be willing to have a baby. However, Carol's desire for an honest relationship had prevented her from taking the easy way out. Although at present it seemed that Carol's stance only alienated Ellen, it also offered them both the opportunity to make any future decisions with integrity and without destroying each other and their future together.

Shelley also observed that Ellen could have chosen to avoid the issue, and thus the conflict, in the hope that Carol would eventually "see the light." However, again, Ellen's desire for an honest relationship meant that she had been willing to keep the issue in the spotlight. Each was willing to risk the relationship for the sake of integrity, and such convictions could well enable them to proceed slowly and cautiously toward the commitment they both wanted.

Shelley's comments connected each woman to her own and her partner's way of staying separate in the relationship, but she didn't comment directly on their sexual struggles. Nevertheless, when they came to the second appointment three weeks later, they reported feeling "closer than ever" and, on at least a couple of occasions, having had "great sex." Shelley continued not to focus specifically on their sexual relationship, attending instead to relationship issues. During the following two weeks, Carol and Ellen approached each other sexually only a couple of times, but they had positive experiences, even turning around a potentially upsetting interaction. Once when things were going badly, they separated as usual, but shortly thereafter Ellen returned and initiated more lovemaking. They had a very intimate experience, including mutual orgasms. As they each connected to the other's way of managing individual integrity, their sexual relationship changed in analogous ways.

Shelley avoided any attempt to separate Carol and Ellen from their conflicts, their fears, or their opposing desires for the relationship. Instead, she encouraged them to connect to those fears and desires, and thus the conflicts, in a way that respected the individuality of each of them. They never had to minimize or ignore either of their sometimes opposing demands. Rather, they embraced them as messages of commitment to the honesty of the relationship, and their sexual relationship changed in keeping with this transformation. When Shelley checked in with them a year later, they had moved to a new city, and Carol had let Ellen know that she wanted her to become pregnant. Sex had also continued to be a positive experience for both of them.

The Relationship Between Your Clients and Sexuality

Melanie requested therapeutic help from us after an upsetting interaction with her boyfriend, Gerry, during sex. Gerry believed there was something wrong with her because she, in the middle of what they both considered to be a time of pleasurable lovemaking, had suddenly started screaming and hitting him with her fists. Gerry had, at the time, been playfully holding Melanie's wrists above her head. This was a new position for intercourse for them, but it had been mutually agreed upon, so they were both initially somewhat mystified as to why Melanie had suddenly become, as they described it to themselves, so violent. After a cooling-down time the two of them talked about what had happened. During their discussion, Melanie recalled having been held down with her wrists above her head by a man who had raped her some 20 years earlier. The similarity between the body positions of the two sexual encounters resulted in her reacting to Gerry in terms of her relationship with the rapist, even though the lovemaking with Gerry did not resemble a rape in any other way.

We normalized the association between the two sexual encounters and suggested to Melanie that her legitimate and appropriate anger was obviously very effective in ensuring that no one violated her again, even unintentionally. We speculated that she could now no doubt be more free, if she wished, to experiment with her lovemaking, knowing as she did that she could trust herself to decide what fit and what didn't.

Our comments were designed to connect both clients to Melanie's surprising reaction to their new lovemaking position—to help them respect it as an integrity-protecting response. Further, we wanted to underscore her trust of her sexuality, both the necessity of her feeling safe and her desire to experiment. The incident could well have resulted in one or both of them becoming spooked; instead, they were able to leave the session feeling confident, respectful of the wisdom of her reaction, and comfortable that they could experiment safely with new ways of enjoying intimacy. In suggesting that she never lose the ability to respond automatically in self-enhancing ways, we helped both of them embrace an experience that they had initially wanted to push away.

The relationship between people and their sexuality is deeply connected to their relationship with their bodies and with their experience of their bodies as sexual. Amber was referred to Shelley because of her strong sense of herself as sexually abnormal. Of African descent, she had been adopted as a toddler by parents who later learned that, as an infant, she had been a victim of female circumcision. Amber's parents determined at the time that the best course of action was simply to pretend all was normal. They didn't tell her anything until, as an adolescent, she started asking questions. Her mother tried to reassure her by explaining that her vulva would be easier to keep clean this way, but when Amber became aware of how "normal" vaginas look, she was devastated by the differences she perceived in herself.

When she entered therapy with Shelley, Amber was in a long-term relationship with a man, Vic, whom she planned to marry, and she had recently consulted with a gynecologist about the possibility of reconstructive surgery to make her "normal." The doctor had told her that apart from a very thin sheath of skin covering her clitoris, her vagina was no different from other women's. And given the high concentration of nerve endings in the area, he thought the risks of the surgery far outweighed any possible benefits. Aware of her concern and of the consultation, her parents and Vic encouraged her to accept the doctor's view that she was fine and move on with her life. She, however, became insistent that she would never have a normal sexual relationship without surgery, despite the fact that she was fully able to orgasm. The gynecologist suggested that she enter therapy and explore the "emotional" reasons behind her desire for the operation, noting that if she still wanted to pursue it after 6 months of therapy, she could contact him again.

Shelley spent several early sessions with Amber examining her commitment to a path that came with no guarantee of satisfaction and involved the risk of nerve damage. Despite the warnings of her doctor and loved ones, Amber remained convinced that surgery was her only viable option. Shelley then began exploring Amber's experience of herself in her relationships with Vic and her parents, discovering that she often felt like they didn't listen to her or respect her voice. This became the focus of the therapy, and, over the course of several months, Amber became more assertive and independent, developing the ability to speak her mind and make her demands known. As a result, her relationship with Vic changed dramatically. Their closeness and trust improved, and their sexual relationship was enhanced.

Six months after therapy had begun, Shelley returned to the issue of the surgery, asking Amber what she had been thinking recently about it. It was no longer an issue, Amber replied, and she wouldn't be contacting the gynecologist again. Surprised by this dramatic change of heart, Shelley asked Amber how she made sense of it. Amber explained that Vic and his previous girlfriend had engaged in daily intercourse, and he had brought this expectation forward into his relationship with her. Not interested in this level of frequency but feeling tremendous pressure to meet his demands, Amber began to feel sexually inadequate and to believe that if she didn't turn herself around, she would lose the relationship. Her sense of herself as a failure became focused intensely on the physical appearance of her vulva and on the sheath that she believed prevented her from accessing her clitoris and from wanting sex as much as Vic. Her focus on altering her physical appearance had been caught up in wanting to feel sexual enough to save her relationship.

This all started to change when Amber found her voice. Becoming more assertive with Vic, she started trying out new sexual behaviors that satisfied both of them and took the pressure off of her to engage in daily intercourse. Her experimentation greatly enhanced her appreciation of her sexuality and her trust that the relationship was stronger and more complex than the previous regimen of daily intercourse had suggested. With her confidence as a sexual woman blossoming, she gleefully offered several examples to Shelley of her expertise in performing oral sex.

The Relationship Between You and Sexuality

While in graduate school, Shelley worked with a man who was struggling to come to terms with being gay. He enjoyed his personal and sexual relationships with men but was upset about conflict with coworkers (he worked in construction) who harassed him for being "a fag."

The therapy room was equipped with a one-way mirror, and near the end of the first session, Shelley, in keeping with the tradition at the school's clinic, returned to the observation room for a consultation with her team—in this case, two men. She talked for a while about her perception of the man's predicament and then invited her colleagues to share some ideas. One of the men, who was religiously conservative, said that as far as he was concerned, there was only one course of treatment: Shelley needed to help the client understand the sinful nature of homosexuality, while simultaneously offering him hope that it wasn't too late to embrace heterosexuality as a proper life choice. Shelley considered this contribution problematic in two ways: It offered a solution to an issue the client hadn't presented as a problem, and it proposed amputation (in this case, of the client's sexual identity) as a means of achieving the therapist's desired goal.

After Shelley fired her team, she was able to assist her client with some of the difficult dilemmas *he* had raised, and she did so in a way that demonstrated her respect for him and his sexuality. Therapists who pass judgement on their clients' sexual orientation or choices risk doing more harm than good. We can only judge from a separated position; when we connect with our clients—by understanding the logic of their actions and empathizing with their pain—we can respond to them therapeutically.

The Relationship Between Your Clients and Their Problem

Shelley was asked to consult on a case involving a 29-year-old man who was, as he put it, obsessed with pictures of nude women. John had spent hours a day over many years looking at such images, first in pornographic magazines and, more recently, on his computer. Sexually and emotionally inexperienced, he lived at home with his mother and father. His parents were aware of his habit, knew about his attending therapy, and were also fully informed about his two failed attempts at intercourse. In both instances, each with a different woman, John had been unable to achieve an erection; nevertheless, he and his second partner had both enjoyed their experience together.

During his daily masturbation, John maintained erections for significant periods of time, but he feared future liaisons with women, as he was certain that his penis would again disappoint him. After 12 sessions of therapy, both he and his therapist felt "bogged down," so they, at the therapist's suggestion, asked Shelley to help them move forward.

John, who described himself as "really abnormal," had tried in the past to control his nude-picture obsession by castigating himself for being "sick." Not surprisingly, this approach had failed dismally. Such attempts to recoil from and control despised parts of ourselves always create a disjunction between the observing I and the negated "thing."

Shelley talked at length with John about normal male interest in visually arousing material. He told her that as a 29-year-old, he had to hurry up and "get normal" because "people who are 30 have to grow up and be real people."

Asking if there had been any recent changes in his situation, Shelley was told that over the previous 2 weeks, John had "gotten interested in real people," developing, in the process, a crush on a woman and a much diminished interest in nude pictures. He saw this as a positive sign but said the waning interest had happened before; he feared his obsession would come back all too soon.

John's attempts to control his interest in the pictures by purposefully distancing himself from them (by telling himself, "I am a horrible deviant and so must stop this") could only turn his relationship to them into an obsession (an uncontrolled desire that wouldn't go away). His heightened interest in "real people" had much more potential for positive change. It is much easier to leave behind something that no longer matters than it is to push away something that matters too much.

Shelley asked John what else he had done in his late teens and early twenties that he had subsequently "outgrown." This question linked John's desire to grow up with his changes over the previous two weeks, and it helped to construct the idea that he was capable of moving beyond behaviors that were no longer relevant to his emerging values and circumstances. As discussed earlier, we consider such developments to be the shape of therapeutic change.

John told Shelley about no longer using drugs, partying, or doing crazy things with his friends, as such activities now seemed boring and silly to him. Shelley asked him about his process of outgrowing these things— did he outgrow them suddenly or over a period of time? Did he ever think he had outgrown them, only to go back and try them out again to see if they offered anything of value? Did those times confirm his boredom and thus his sense of having truly outgrown them? Were they ever still a little bit enjoyable? John said that he had certainly tried outgrown behaviors from time to time and that, in general, these attempts had confirmed his boredom and thus his increased maturity.

Shelley suggested that with John's thirties fast approaching, it made sense that he would now be looking at new soon-to-be-outgrown behaviors, given that he would finally be entering true adulthood. She also reminded him that as with any of the other behaviors he had outgrown, he would probably need to try out the soon-to-be-gone ones periodically, to ensure that they no longer interested him. A strategic therapist would describe this statement as a paradoxical encouragement of relapse (e.g., Haley, 1976); however, we take a different view. We do not try to position our clients to do the opposite of what we suggest; rather, we recognize that unless they can stay comfortably connected to the symptom from which they are separating, they risk having the symptom remaining *uncomfortably* connected to them (see Flemons, 1991, 2002).

When asked how much his parents knew of his situation, John said that he was very close to them and had told them everything. He knew that his parents had always had an "incredible" sex life and that his grandparents had had sex every day until his grandfather's death at age 85. Shelley commented that given this impressive family legacy, it was no surprise that John's penis had so far refused to rise to the call: John's parents, grandparents, and sexual partner were all holding a gun to his penis, shouting, "Get it up!" The absence of an erection posed a problem not only for John and his sexual partner, but also represented his failure to carry on the family tradition.

John anticipated that once he had had erect-penis sex, he would immediately share his success with his parents. Shelley talked about how relationships with parents often begin to change when children move fully into adulthood. She commented that privacy sometimes becomes more important at this stage, and though at first blush this might seem to undermine closeness, often the opposite proves true. John quickly confirmed that he never wanted to lose the close bond he felt with his parents. Shelley underscored the importance of this desire and noted that John could decide over the years how much of his private life to reveal to his parents, emphasizing that decisions for privacy need not disrupt their close relationship. John looked much relieved, replying, "Yeah, I could finally get that monkey off my back!"

As the session was coming to a close, John proudly declared his realization that he was much more normal than he previously thought, and he believed his therapy would have a "whole new direction and focus now." On the way out, Shelley commented on the unique nature of John's sexual experience, noting that many women greatly appreciate a man's ability to focus on the woman's pleasure rather than solely on his own erection, as he had obviously done in his previous positive sexual encounter. John replied, "Sounds like I might be the perfect man!"

Shelley did not attempt to rid John of his obsession with sexual images of women, to amputate the flaccidity of his penis, or to criticize his parents' benevolent concern. Instead, she highlighted the importance of connections and introduced the possibility of freedom in various relationships:

- She normalized the arousal he felt when gazing at pictures of naked women and highlighted his demonstrated ability to outgrow behaviors that no longer interested him.
- She helped him appreciate the wisdom of his body—when someone points a gun at you, you automatically put up your hands, not your penis. This provided him with a way of no longer being held hostage by the family legacy of sexual prowess.
- She linked the ideas of closeness and privacy in his relationship with his parents.
- She offered a more flexible understanding of sexual encounters than the stereotypical one he seemed to have been influenced by.

As a result, John was able to embrace his own potential expertise as a lover and to reengage in therapy "with a whole new focus."

CASE STUDY: "ENLIGHTENED" INTIMACY

Sam had a lengthy history of alcohol, heroin, and cocaine abuse, for which he had been in recovery several times—most recently for a period of two years. A treatment center referred him to Shelley and her practicum team* after he had relapsed on alcohol and engaged a prostitute. His wife of two years, Jill, had known about his substance abuse—they had met in recovery four years earlier (she was six months clean of alcohol and heroin at the time)—but this was the first time she had learned about what Sam referred to as his "20-year sex addiction." After the other times Sam had relapsed in their four years together, he had told Jill only about the substances, not about his having had sex with other women.

Shelley and her team saw Sam by himself for the first session, about three weeks after his most recent relapse. He had already begun a new recovery, he said, and he believed that this would be the first "true" one, for he had started attending to what he considered to be his "core issue"—sex. When asked how he knew he was a sex addict, he described molestation by an uncle as a child, chronic masturbation as an adolescent, and "obsessive" searches for sexual partners throughout his adult life. As he said, "The evidence is there: As soon as I finish having sex with my beautiful wife, I still want to go look for a fix. I get off, and I'm not satisfied seconds later." He said his goal for therapy was to develop a monogamous sexual relationship with his wife and to "get comfortable with the idea that sex is not a bad thing." He also described the intense connection between him and Jill and said they had decided since this incident to commit to developing greater sexual and emotional intimacy in their relationship.

Sam actively participated in different 12-step programs, and professionals involved in them had suggested that he begin attending a 12-step sex addiction group, with a goal of achieving total abstinence. However, as he and Shelley discussed his sexual desires and his therapy goals, they came to a different understanding and thus developed a different treatment plan.

Shelley: How much at risk will you be for a sexual fix when you leave here tonight to go home?

Sam: There is a 99.9% chance that I won't pick up a prostitute. But never say never. I would have said there was zero risk the night I relapsed.

---

* The first six sessions of the case were seen as part of a family therapy master's practicum Shelley was supervising at her university. Because of the nature and complexity of the situation, Shelley conducted the interviews; one of her students (Carol Griffith) joined her as a cotherapist for the first few sessions, and the others watched from behind a one-way mirror.

Shelley: Is orgasm important? intercourse?

Sam: It's important not to cross the fatal line to intercourse. That is one thing I haven't done and I won't do. Once you're over that line, it's all over.

Shelley: It seems to me there's a difference in your addictions. As a drinker and heroin user, you don't say, "I want to drink and use heroin socially." You want to quit completely. But you don't want to quit sex. As you said, you want a monogamous and fulfilling sexual relationship with your wife.

Sam: Right. The paradox is that we don't need cocaine and alcohol. But for a healthy relationship we do need sex. Normal people have a sex drive.

Shelley: In a way, sex has been masquerading as a drug.

Sam: Sex is my core issue. If I don't deal with it I'll never be able to stay clean.

Shelley: So what will be your signs that you're going to be able to stay clean?

Sam: When I'm drug-free and monogamous. Sex, but not sex as a drug. Sex as intimacy and connection. That's what we want. It's the best thing in the world.

Shelley: And how much have you had that with Jill?

Sam: Sex is one thing and intimacy is another.

Shelley: How much intimacy?

Sam: Not much. We're trying.

Shelley: What's helping?

Sam: It's easier once you start doing it. I know she loves me very much and I've never felt this way about anyone before. I trust what I have with her.

Shelley: Who is more afraid of the intimacy you're starting to share?

Sam: She is.

Shelley: She has some reasons to be.

Sam: She's been a sexual victim before; she's had many abusive and controlling boyfriends, and her dad died an alcoholic. I know in my heart that if we don't deal with this issue I'll never be able to stay clean.

Sam had been at war with his sexuality for at least 20 years, trying, and always failing, to control himself. A therapy approach that counseled the necessity of abstinence would risk further deepening the gulf that had grown between him and his desire. He had felt controlled by something from which he had always distanced himself, and which wouldn't go away despite his best efforts. Sam described the previous three weeks as his "most powerful, significant, and honest recovery," as the cards were all on the table for the first time. Jill now knew what had been going on, and this made possible a different orientation to sex, one where intimacy was the goal. If sex could be a means of Sam's connecting with his wife, it could also help his connecting with himself.

Jill accompanied Sam to the second appointment, where she asked many questions about Shelley's recommendation that he not supplement his weekly therapy sessions with attendance at a 12-step sex addiction group. In response to Jill's questions, Shelley talked about her understanding of Sam's relapses, his current recovery, the 12-step approach to solving sexual problems, and her own way of orienting to such cases. She connected with the couple by matching their frank and open way of talking about their sexuality and by engaging with their uninhibited sense of humor. Before the end of the second session, they had committed to working as a couple on their sexual relationship, not just on Sam's "addiction."

Jill explained how she was struggling to balance cautious optimism and fear. She had been "blindsided" by the sexual component of Sam's "illness," and she wanted to avoid that in the future. She described her intense desire for sexual and emotional intimacy with Sam, contrasting it with her "terror of being violated sexually." She said she wanted to be able to look him in the eyes during lovemaking, but at this point she could only let in small amounts of intimacy at a time, and she was trying to gauge how much she could handle. She confirmed Sam's earlier descriptions of her prior abusive relationships and said these had encouraged her to be guarded and emotionally distant before becoming involved with Sam. It had felt like the ultimate violation, then, when she found out about Sam's sexual involvements with prostitutes.

Throughout the second session, the couple sat close together and touched each other continually, showing mutual affection and tenderness; however, Jill's fear remained palpable. Shelley commented on the wisdom of Jill's caution and suggested she carefully monitor her pace in their search for intimacy: It was important, she said, for Jill to protect herself. Shelley also cautioned her about the dangers of taking sexual responsibility for Sam's recovery.

Shelley: Of course it makes sense that you would think of Sam being with a prostitute when you're making love with him, or maybe even more when he wants to make love and you don't. But it will be potentially dangerous to both of you to tie those two together. You can't have great enough sex with Sam to keep him out of a prostitute's bed. As he has said to me and to you, sex with prostitutes is not about relationship—it's about body parts. Making love with you and being with a prostitute are two different animals, and if you try to cure one with the other, you will likely fail.

Jill: I know. I can't save him. He has to do that himself. And I have to be okay telling him "no" if that's what I need to do.

Shelley: Yes.

Sam: As I've said, it's an inside job. No one can do it for me. I just want to be able to love my wife.

From our perspective, no couple can be intimate without freedom in their relationship. Shelley believed that sex could further Sam and Jill's connection only if *not having sex* didn't jeopardize it. If Jill felt the need to offer or agree to sex as way of protecting their relationship, or if Sam used sex with Jill as a way of keeping his desire for other partners at bay, then neither of them could feel safe, never mind comfortable, saying no to the other's sexual invitation. When there is intimacy, saying no to something particular in the relationship (such as a request for sex) is a way of saying yes to the relationship as a whole (Flemons, 2002).

Over the next several sessions, the couple discussed their ongoing efforts to balance their optimism and desire for intimacy with the caution necessary to make it possible. Sam struggled successfully not to relapse with either substances or sex, and Jill's willingness to pursue sexual and emotional intimacy with him grew as he continued to have no "incidents."

Sam began telling Jill and the therapy team about situations that could have triggered him to relapse but did not. Initially, these stories were difficult for Jill to hear, as she preferred that he avoid any potentially risky situations. However, for Sam, telling Jill of his experiences seemed to be a way of ensuring and demonstrating his ability to remain "clean." The team offered the idea that Sam's storytelling served to include Jill in his recovery. They also noted Sam's confidence in Jill's willingness to continue risking increased intimacy with him.

During the sixth session, Jill and Sam described difficulties having to do with how they managed their money, spent their free time, and negotiated their friendships. Shelley commented on how different these problems seemed from the ones with which they came in.

Shelley: Maybe I'm wrong but these seem a bit like high-class worries to me. If you can worry about these things, your lives must be going pretty well.

Sam: High-falutin' problems! Don't you love it?

Jill: I adore it! Beats the shit out of "If I don't have sex with Sam tonight he's gonna go find a prostitute!" Yeah, we've got a real different kind of problem now.

Shelley: What happened to those other problems?

Sam: I told her yesterday I saw a prostitute outside work. It took me only a few seconds to know I wasn't going to follow her. I just don't want to do it.

Shelley: Do you ever expect that initial desire to go away?

Sam: Never a day in my life when a working girl on the street won't kick up some sort of memory. Just like looking at booze and saying it'd be great if I could just drink like an earth person. It will always be with me but the answer to the question is "no."

Shelley: So when he comes to you and tells you about seeing prostitutes on the street, what is that like for you?

Jill: It frightens me. It's never gonna go away and that's the reality.

If Shelley could have asked then what she would now, a different question would have appeared: "As your intimacy with Jill continues to develop, and as you increasingly recognize that sex is a way of achieving such intimacy, I can imagine a time when you would see a prostitute and know *in the moment* of noticing her that you wouldn't follow her. When do you expect that to come about?" A query of this sort could have helped further create the expectation that Sam might someday experience a comfortable freedom between his observing I and his desire—where the sight of a prostitute wouldn't have enough of a kick to become significant for him. At this point, Sam's recovery and Jill's trust in it were still dependent on Sam's distrusting himself. When this turned around—when trusting himself became possible and appropriate—he could start to feel some freedom in his relationship with his sexuality.

Shelley: Does that sexual desire scare you more than his other desires?

Jill: Yeah. I'm rebuilding trust. I'm letting down walls. It's scary and it's wonderful. It's very exciting to me.

Shelley: The first time I met you two, we talked a lot about finding a balance of caution and intimacy, and letting down those walls. It seems like you both are letting down walls. And it's scary and there's got to be caution. You look for balance.

Jill: I think I'm ready to go a little further.

Shelley: Where do you think you want to go that you haven't gone yet?

Jill: Well, this week, I seduced him. I covered him with baby oil and did things to him that are so far from anything I ever say or do. Believe me! I can't believe it. I don't really know where else I want to be because I've never been there. I haven't had this kind of relationship before.

Shelley: Emotional and sexual intimacy combined?

Jill: Yeah, that involves touching and loving. That's not something that's ever been a part of my sex life. It's always been mechanical. But we both value intimacy. We both value monogamy. We had a magic sexual moment this week. I don't think either of us can really describe it well.

Sam: I say it was fun.

Jill: I say it was sexy as hell!

Sam: Well, yeah, that too! You felt like my buddy and my friend and my lover. I could get so loose with you and have fun sexually. It was a "wow" moment. Cool. A moment of freedom—no hangups.

Jill: I felt safe because I realized I've been missing out on a whole bunch of stuff.

Shelley: Like good sex?

Jill: Yeah!

Shelley: But you had to trust first, to feel safe. You have a way of holding people at bay if you need to protect yourself, and that has worked for you, particularly in previous relationships. But right now you don't feel the need to do that with Sam. You feel the need to drop the walls and go toward him.

Jill: Yeah, we're having frequent sex, and good sex. But when I hold back, I know I'm looking for safety; it's empty, but it's safe. But I don't want that, I just need it sometimes.

Shelley: Yeah, if you just wanted safety you wouldn't be sitting here with Sam.

Jill: You got that right! But every time I think about our fun, sexy encounter, I have to smile.

One of the joys of working with couples is seeing how change in one person is occasioned by, and helps occasion, change in the other. In the following session, two weeks later, Sam relayed a new story of how he had seen but not engaged the services of a prostitute, and he described how he had responded at the time. Again, this tale was somewhat frightening to Jill. Shelley discussed with them his decision to share the details of such encounters with her and how she was responding to his descriptions.

Shelley: Do you understand why she's more spooked about this than you are?

Sam: I do, of course.

Shelley: Are you more confident than she is about your ability to resist?

Sam: Absolutely.

Shelley: Cocky?

Sam: Maybe. Some issues never go away completely.

Shelley: I agree. This thing you just described isn't resolved. You resolve it again each time you encounter it.

Sam: Exactly.

Shelley: Every time you see the girl you get another chance to resolve it. There seems to be no one time to resolve it for the rest of your life. The more distance though, the better. And every time you resolve it well, the distance grows.

The kind of distance Shelley was noting here is the comfortable gap engendered by a relaxed letting go, not the anxious separation resulting from a forceful pushing away. Sam was still finding it necessary to keep his potentially destructive desires at bay, but Jill had begun to relax, and the two of them were staying safe through intimacy rather than fear.

Sam: Right, and lots of stuff is going right these days. I just have to keep my guard up.

Shelley: How much is Jill involved in keeping your guard up?

Sam: We do it together. That's why I tell her this stuff.

Jill: I've relaxed a lot.

Shelley: You're not afraid to push him. But he's not afraid to tell you about the scary times. That's a good sign.

Jill: Yeah, this week he thanked me because he went out and I wasn't paranoid. He was showing me he's consistent. A few months ago I would have been crazy.

Shelley: And how's the intimacy?

Jill: We had an amazing experience this week. We were making love and Sam was going down on me. Always when that has happened in the past, with anyone, I find myself going to what I call the "dark place." That's the safe place for me even when I'm with someone abusive, because then I forget about them and just have this incredible orgasm, very powerful physically. But this time, for some reason, and for the first time in my life, I didn't go away. I stayed in the light. I never went to the dark place. And what happened was that I looked Sam in the eyes when I came, and I'm not sure he even felt me come. Because usually he can feel it physically. This wasn't such a powerful physical orgasm. But it was so powerful emotionally.

Shelley: So you had a small but intimate orgasm. Maybe this small one was actually the biggest orgasm of your life. And how did you know, for the first time in your life, that it was okay to stay in the light?

Jill: [*looks at Sam for a long time*] I just knew he loved me. I want to stay there. I don't want to go back to the dark place.

Jill found a way to feel safe enough to experience orgasm *in relationship* with Sam. Soon after this, Sam began timing his orgasms to ensure Jill's pleasure. Subsequent sessions were used to explore the couple's sexuality and intimacy within the context of Sam's ongoing success with remaining clean—from drugs, alcohol, and nonmonogamous sex. And the intimacy they created together went beyond their lovemaking. As Sam explained in a later session, "Jill's the only woman I have ever fallen asleep with while she's holding me in her arms. It's the safest place."

A month later, Shelley saw the couple for a check-in session; this was something they had requested to help monitor Sam's ongoing struggle with addiction. During that session, Sam and Jill described the enormous progress they had made in the face of potentially devastating crises, and they again underscored the intense intimacy that had become possible for them.

Jill: The bottom could drop out tomorrow but we would survive that, too, after all we've been through.

Shelley: Right, you guys have survival skills that most people don't have. You've been through the fire and have come out stronger.

Jill: Whatever happens, we'll find the good in it somehow; I know I will.

Shelley: You said a long time ago that everything you've gone through in your life has brought you to a better place, even if you can't see it in the moment.

Jill: Yeah, but when I do see what I've gained, I trust it. I have become more emotionally prepared; I've grown so much. I see what I have to offer now.

Shelley: Your lives have pushed you to the limit and you've come through. You found the way to get yourself to the other side.

Sam: It's really unbelievable the way our lives have turned out. Who the hell would have thought we could come this far? We're so blessed.

Shelley: I don't think it's only that you're blessed. Of course you are, but you've also done this; you've made the choices. You had a lot of shit in your lives, too. You could have chosen to go down with it.

Sam: I know; it's true. I can't believe where we are.

Shelley continued monthly "check-ins" with Sam and Jill for another six months. At termination, Sam was continuing his involvement in 12-step programs for substance abuse, but he was relating to sex as a choice for intimacy rather than as an uncontrollable addiction. Jill was continuing to explore the exhilarating liberation of "enlightened" sexual and emotional intimacy: Although she acknowledged that the dark place could be "safe and easy," it was not a place she wanted to choose. At a follow-up one year later, the couple's relationship was stable, and Sam's sobriety, both sexual and chemical, was intact.

DISCUSSION

Some sex theorists (Califia, 1986; Newitz, 1994) have decried the normative bias inherent in upholding intimacy as the only desirable goal in people's sexual relationships. We respect any expression of sexual pleasuring as long as there is respectful mutuality (Sanders & Tomm, 1989) and the ongoing freedom for anyone involved to stop at any time; however, most of our clients are in search of some form of intimate pleasure—sex that can express and deepen the connection between partners.

When therapy goes well, clients find it possible to hold their problem comfortably close rather than painfully distant or restrictively in check. And, as a result, the problem (if we can anthropomorphize for a moment) sees fit to release its death grip on their lives. In our work, we commit ourselves to creating, encouraging, maintaining, and supporting freedom in all relationships, and we do this by always inviting a relaxed grasp—one that can provide support without imprisonment and freedom without banishment.

REFERENCES

Califia, P. (1986). Feminism and sadomasochism. In A. Kleiner & S. Brand (Eds.), *News that stayed news* (pp. 206–214). San Francisco: North Point Press.

de Shazer, S. (1994). *Words were originally magic.* New York: Norton.

Eisenbud, R. J. (1978).Countertransference: The therapist's turn on the couch. In G. D. Goldman & D. S. Milman (Eds.), *Psychoanalytic psychotherapy* (pp. 72–90). Reading, MA: Addison Wesley.

Erickson, M. H. (1986). *Mind-body communication in hypnosis: The seminars, workshops, and lectures of Milton H. Erickson* (Vol. 3). (E. L. Rossi & M. O. Ryan, Eds.). New York: Irvington.

Flemons, D. (1991). *Completing distinctions.* Boston: Shambhala.

Flemons, D. (2002). *Of one mind.* New York: Norton.

Flemons, D. (2003, January/February). The psychology of the sandpit. *Psychotherapy Networker, 27,* 32–37.

Goldner, V., Penn, P., Sheinberg, M., & Walker, G. (1990). Love and violence: Gender paradoxes in volatile attachments. *Family Process, 29*(4), 343–364.

Haley, J. (1976). Problem-solving therapy. New York: Harper & Row.

Henry, W. P., Strupp, H. H., Schacht, T. E., & Gaston L. (1994). Psychodynamic approaches. In A. E. Bergin & S. L Garfield (Eds.), *Handbook of psychotherapy and behavior change* (4th ed., pp. 467–508). New York: Wiley.

Meichenbaum, D. (1977). *Cognitive-behavior modification: An integrative approach.* New York: Plenum.

Newitz, A. (1994). Why do you want to get laid? Mapping sexual geographies. *Bad Subjects, 17,* 1–6.

Penn, P., & Frankfurt, M. (1994). Creating a participant: Writing, multiple voices, narrative multiplicity. *Family Process, 33*(3), 217–231.

Redd, W. H., Porterfield, A. L., & Anderson, B. L. (1979). *Behavior modification: Behavioral approaches to human problems.* New York: Random House.

Roberts, J. (1994). *Tales and transformations: Stories in families and family therapy.* New York: Norton.

Sanders, G., & Tomm, K. (1989). A cybernetic-systemic approach to problems in sexual functioning. In D. Kantor & B. Okun (Eds.), *Intimate environments* (pp. 346–380). New York: Guilford Press.

Selvini Palazzoli, M., Boscolo, L., Cecchin, G., & Prata, G. (1978). *Paradox and counterparadox.* New York: Jason Aronson.

Tiefer, L. (1995). *Sex is not a natural act and other essays.* Boulder, CO: Westview Press.

Watzlawick, P., Beavin, J., & Jackson, D. (1967). *Pragmatics of human communication: A study of interactional patterns, pathologies, and paradoxes.* New York: Norton.

Watzlawick, P., Weakland, J., & Fisch, R. (1974). *Change: Principles of problem formation and problem resolution.* New York: Norton.

Weakland, J. H. (1993). Conversation—but what kind? In S. Gilligan & R. Price (Eds.), *Therapeutic conversations* (pp. 135–145). New York: Norton.

White, M., & Epston, D. (1991). *Narrative means to therapeutic ends.* New York: Norton.

nine

Who Really Wants to Sleep With the Medical Model?: An Eclectic/Narrative Approach to Sex Therapy

Robert E. Doan

THE DIVERSE AND COMPREHENSIVE application of a narrative metaphor as a guide for conducting therapy has been well documented over the last two decades (Epston, 1989; Freedman & Combs, 1996; Parry & Doan, 1994; White, 1989; White & Epston, 1990). In this chapter, I outline how narrative ideas can more specifically serve as a sound basis for conducting sex therapy; however, given that there is more than one way to do narrative therapy, I avoid reifying any particular version (Doan, 1998). Indeed, what follows might most accurately be called "eclectic narrativism," as the approach draws not only from the work of Michael White and David Epston, but also from those associated with brief, solution-focused approaches (Berg, 1990; de Shazer, 1985, 1988, 1991; Hubble, Miller, & Duncan, 1999).

After briefly exploring the reasons for avoiding the medically languaged, pathology-based model of therapy that predominates in our culture, I argue that being aware of the common factors of successful therapy is more important than the model used. I then go on to present a discussion for how sexual dilemmas can be handled from an eclectic/narrative approach.

REASONS NOT TO SLEEP WITH THE MEDICAL MODEL

There are two good reasons for avoiding the use of the model of therapy suggested by the medical community, specifically in the context of sex-related issues.

Sex Occurs *Between* People

Working within a system that emulates the successful diagnostic and treatment practices of the medical community, psychotherapists find themselves in the predicament of having to diagnose clients according to the *DSM-IV* schema or be denied reimbursement from insurance providers. Such an individual-focused, pathology-based system fits the world of medicine, but despite its adoption by legions of mental health professionals and agencies, it doesn't work well in a therapeutic domain. Sex therapy is a case in point.

Unless the goal is to help a client masturbate better, a sex therapist typically meets with *partners* who are experiencing difficulties in having sex *with each other.* Even if only one member of a couple is being seen, the therapist's focus is typically relational. Nevertheless, under the current diagnostic schema of the *DSM-IV*, the therapist is required to diagnose *one* of the two partners as having a mental disorder, inferring in the process that the other has no comparable or complimentary affliction. From a systemic/cybernetic perspective, such a practice seems arbitrary, if not violent, undermining the therapist's ability to recognize the interactive nature of sexual difficulties and thus missing the whole point of therapy.

I recall seeing a case in which the husband complained that his wife was "undersexed and sick." Had I been organized by the *DSM-IV*, I could have diagnosed her with "Hypoactive Sexual Desire," but that would have obscured the fact that the husband preferred (demanded) sex on the average of three times a day and became quite angry if his wife turned him down. The *DSM-IV* doesn't include "Hyperactive Sexual Desire" in its pages, so if I had wanted to maintain an individual, pathology-based focus (making the same error as diagnosing the wife, but in the opposite direction), I might have felt compelled to turn to the popular notion of "sexual addiction" to label him. Instead, I chose a third alternative.

The wife had become so disenchanted with her husband's unrelenting demands that she had no desire at all for physical contact with him. And the more she refused to have sex, the more insistent he became. It thus seemed more logical, not to mention kind, to view their problem as an *unfortunate mismatch of desire*, rather than a problem afflicting one or the other partner.

Because sexual desire and behavior are negotiated and constructed *between people*, we are far better off basing our assessment and treatment on the interactions between each particular couple being served. Diagnosing one partner with a mental disorder is not only unnecessary for successful treatment of sexual issues, it may, in fact, make things worse, as the therapist risks being viewed as "taking sides," working to cure one member of the couple while the "well one" awaits the successful outcome.

The "Sex Equals Intercourse" Myth

All *DSM* categories are based upon the fundamental assumption that sex is intercourse and only intercourse (allowing people to testify that they "haven't had sex with that woman" and be telling the technical truth!). All other forms of sexual activity are summarily dismissed in our culture as "foreplay." No matter how successful individuals might be at achieving their own satisfaction, or inducing a partner's satisfaction, via nonintercourse methods, they are still subject to being diagnosed with a mental disorder if they don't measure up on the intercourse scale. For example, a male can be diagnosed with premature ejaculation if he cannot postpone orgasm long enough for his partner to achieve one, although research has indicated that only a third of women consistently achieve orgasm via intercourse (Maines, 1999; Weston, 2001). Can't you picture the poor man who can perform intercourse for an hour and still must view himself as a failure? And what about the woman who, taught that she should be able to reach orgasm during "sex," but finding herself somehow unable to do so, assumes that she has failed?

Under the current diagnostic schema, which define mental disorders in terms of deviation from the majority, wouldn't it follow that the third of women who do orgasm regularly during intercourse could be labeled abnormal? After all, they do fall outside the majority! The most that can be said of such a situation is that the definition of abnormality is being made on the basis of deviation from a socially constructed grand narrative that represents what our culture determines "should" be the case, rather than on the basis of actual experiences and behaviors. I find it ludicrous to label something abnormal when it represents the vast majority of personal experience.

Once again, the medical analogy seems a poor fit in the area of human sexuality, especially when sex is defined so narrowly. Assessing and diagnosing sexual problems is very different from diagnosing a broken arm or an inflamed appendix. Trying to pretend that diagnosis can be done in the same manner used in medicine oversimplifies a very complex issue.

Several years ago, I attended a workshop conducted by Joseph LoPiccolo, in which he presented the most unusual case he'd encountered in his years as a sex therapist. It involved a couple, together for 18 years, who had never experienced intercourse or any form of genital contact. They were quite content with this arrangement until they changed churches and were told that they were "sick" and needed to see a therapist. Dr. LoPiccolo gave them his blessing and sent them on their way. Instead of pathologizing them, he found it remarkable that they'd found each other. He didn't feel it was his right to diagnose them in relation to practices that are embraced by the dominant culture, especially in an area as subjective and relative as sexual relationships and preferences. Indeed, if intercourse were removed as the standard against which all sexual disorders were measured, many of them would disappear! This could result in "quickie therapy," indeed.

THE IMPORTANCE OF COMMON FACTORS IN PREDICTING THERAPEUTIC SUCCESS

Recently, there has been increasing pressure for the mental health professions to define "effective therapy." With the American Psychological Association having issued a list of "empirically validated" therapies, there is much searching within the profession for a suitable definition of "evidence-based practice." Of course, insurance companies sit as interested observers to this process, and it is possible that the time is not too distant when third-party payers will only pay providers who can demonstrate they are trained in the procedures that "make the list." This is creating understandable concern within the therapeutic community, as the socially constructed outcome of such an investigation has widespread implications. There is a growing fear that if the search for evidence-based approaches is limited to an effort to identify specific techniques or models, anyone not practicing cognitive-behavioral therapy will be out of business.

If insurance companies were to take this action, they would be overlooking the findings of the vast majority of all therapy-outcome research, which indicates that all treatment approaches achieve approximately equivalent results (Wampold, 2001). Given this fact, the search for "what works" is best focused on the factors or elements that are "common denominators" in the various models, and the challenge of training new therapists would be best met by directing students' attention to these common factors rather than indoctrinating them into various theoretical ideologies.

Research to identify these factors or "core elements" (Bergin & Garfield, 1994; Hubble, Miller, & Duncan, 1998) has produced the following results:

- Extratherapeutic factors, such as the clients and their view of the process of the therapy, cognitive style, and expectation (theory) of what is necessary for change to occur account for 40% of the variance in successful therapy.
- The core elements of a therapeutic relationship, as defined by Carl Rogers and others, account for 30% of the variance in successful therapy.
- The placebo effect (i.e., the client's and therapist's hope that change will occur) accounts for 15% of the variance. Without hope, what exists other than anxiety, depression, or quiet desperation?
- The structure or model of therapy and the techniques employed account for the remaining 15% of the variance. Some models and techniques are more likely to contain the aforementioned ingredients than others.

It is quite possible that "techniques" that have been empirically validated to produce change do so because they contain (either intentionally or otherwise) the first two factors. For example, to my knowledge, there is no more empirically validated treatment for fears than systematic desensitization. Proven effective across various types of fears, genders, ethnic backgrounds, cultural differences, and religions (Taylor & Arnow, 1988), it considers clients' point of view (by accessing their opinions and perspectives in the construction of a fear hierarchy), and it matches the type of relaxation practiced to the type the client finds most effective. Pairing relaxation and the constructed fear hierarchy, the therapist only moves to new levels of fear when clients indicate readiness, thus providing hope and expectation of change through early successes.

SEX THERAPY FROM AN ECLECTIC/NARRATIVE STANCE

Narrative therapy, as the name implies, is conducted using a literary, rather than a medical, metaphor. Narrative work, informed by social constructionist notions, seeks to liberate clients' voices from the oppression of cultural mythologies and discourses. It does so through the use of dialogues that externalize, rather than internalize, problems, distinguishing between narratives that are socially and culturally prescribed and those that are authored and informed by client "preferences." A complete tutorial on narrative work is beyond the scope of this chapter, but interested readers can find complete and explicit accounts of this model in the reference list. The narrative ideas described in the following pages can be generalized to many types of cases.

Externalizing the Problem

Most, but not all, narrative therapists use problem externalization in their work. Although the concept itself is quite simple, putting it into practice adeptly takes considerable skill. Most therapy training programs are steeped in "internalizing diagnostic conversations" (White, 1989) that place the source of problems inside the person being assessed. Externalizing conversations characterize *the problem as the problem*, rather than *the person as the problem*.

Instead of objectifying the client, defining him or her as having a "problem identity," the therapist objectifies the problem, inviting couples to "take a stand" against it rather than against each other. This is often helpful in the arena of sex therapy, given that by the time a couple see a therapist, they are often blaming each other for the problem. Through problem externalization, the couple are invited to consider the steps they need to take in order to reclaim their preferred sex life from the clutches of the problem.

Richard and Sophia brought a long list of concerns to their first marital therapy session, near the top of which they'd written "sexual issues." Sophia was most urgently concerned about Richard's insensitivity, lack of consideration, and minimal knowledge of her needs. Richard, a career military officer who had been in the service since he was 18, expressed confusion about "what women want and need" and seemed somewhat depressed about his failure to please his wife.

Externalizing "military lifestyle," I inquired how it had been good for them. Both described many advantages. I then asked how it might have been a problem. Richard spoke up immediately, saying that although the military had made him an expert on managing large groups of men and organizing them in defense of our nation, it had taught him absolutely nothing about how to deal with and please women, sexually or otherwise. In the military, he said, he could give women orders and they would follow them, but this didn't work at home. Sophia agreed, adding that his being a great military man and provider had occupied all his time and energy, leaving him with little opportunity to learn other things.

When asked if he would like to be as well trained with women as with military matters, Richard answered very enthusiastically in the affirmative. This opened space for a discussion about female preferences, sexual response styles, and sexual techniques, which we were able to have without his feeling defensive or inferior. The couple were interested in getting to a place where not all sexual activity would necessarily lead to intercourse, that pleasuring each other would become more mutual, and that they would exhibit a wider range of sexual behavior, including reciprocal oral and manual techniques.

Growing up with stereotypical values, Richard had come to believe that women don't desire sex very often, if at all, and that they exist to serve the needs of the male. He was surprised to learn that women are the most sexual females on the planet, as evidenced by the fact that they are sexually receptive 365 days of the year (at least theoretically) and capable of multiple orgasms. This new information, as well as the creation of a nondefensive and nonjudgmental position from which to discuss their differences, allowed Richard and Sophia to find new ways to relate sexually and to enjoy each other in more varied contexts.

Another couple, Adam and Nicole, were concerned about Adam's "sexual indifference." Nicole explained that ever since she had expressed an interest in giving and receiving oral sex, Adam's attitudes toward her had undergone a drastic change. As we talked, I discovered that the two of them had had very different family-of-origin experiences and educations in the area of sex, so I externalized and explored "family sexual beliefs." When asked what these family differences in belief had invited him to do, Adam responded that he had been raised to believe that only whores liked oral sex, and this had caused him to wonder if his wife had a shady past that she had been keeping secret. Nicole, in contrast, had been raised to believe that all types of pleasurable activities between two consenting adults were normal and fine, and she had not understood his reaction. Adam subsequently asked me whether his parents had been correct in their teachings. In response, I gave him an article to read that included research data on the sexual practices of most couples. He came back for the next session quite amazed and feeling somewhat remiss for judging his wife so harshly. The story ended happily, with Adam discovering that oral sex was quite pleasant indeed.

Comparing Prescribed Stories to Preferred Stories

Grand narratives about human sexuality, informed by culture, religion, gender, and family, inform and limit people's behaviors, attitudes, and feelings. Inviting couples to compare prescribed stories to their preferred stories can prove liberating and curative, helping them separate from the oppressive aspects of such problem-saturated narratives. I begin by interviewing couples about the origin and current status of their sexual attitudes and beliefs, using questions such as the following:

- As you were growing up, how did your family influence your sexual beliefs and behaviors? Was sex talked about openly? Were you invited to believe sex was "clean" or "dirty"?
- Were your parents appropriately open with you about their own sex life? What sort of sex life do you believe they had/have?
- How did teachings about gender influence your sexual beliefs? Are the beliefs you hold equally applicable to men and women? If not, how are they different?
- How did marriage affect your sexual beliefs and practices?
- Do you believe sex is to be mutual and shared, or is one partner to submit to the other?
- What have you been taught sex is? Does sex include only intercourse?
- Do other forms of physical touching have to lead to intercourse?
- Are there things you believe are inappropriate for consenting adults to do sexually in the privacy of their home?
- What are the necessary factors for "good" sex? What do each of you require in this regard?
- Which influenced your beliefs about sex the most: family, religion, gender, education, or something else?

Over the years, I've received a wide variety of responses, yet many, at least from heterosexuals, point to strong gender differences between women—

- When I fantasized about sex as an adolescent, it never included having a big throbbing penis in my mouth.
- The only thing my mother told me about sex was that you do it lying down, and that although it's not all that pleasant, it doesn't hurt.

- Every time my husband touches me I know if it doesn't lead to intercourse, he'll be disappointed.

—and men:

- I was taught that sex isn't something women enjoy; it's just something they do to please men.
- Marriage changed sex a lot. We went from doing it all the time to not doing it much at all. I got laid a lot more before I was married.
- I never got any instruction or training in what women like sexually or how to be a good lover.

Whatever a couple's sexual orientation, their answers help me assess their understanding and offer clues for where to initiate interventions. When they still have mutual respect and trust, I may only need to offer some form of "sex education." Often, though, the problem is primarily relational rather than sexual. That is, the couple's sexual difficulties are secondary to a lack of mutuality and to feelings of threat, distrust, and insecurity. A good sexual relationship is very difficult to achieve when trust and mutual respect are absent, so in such cases, I focus on restoring their belief in themselves and the relationship.

After I have a reasonably complete understanding of a couple's current beliefs, I begin discussing their preferences. This can be a somewhat more difficult conversation, as many clients are reluctant to express their opinions in front of their partner. Solution-oriented questions can help them find their voice:

- Would you prefer a partner who chooses to have sex with you out of desire or out of a sense of obligation?
- Has there been a time in your relationship when your sex life was good for you? If so, can you describe how it was then?
- Are there any beliefs about sex you grew up with that you would like to discard?
- Are there sexual activities you would like to eliminate, or add, to your present practices?
- What do you believe would be necessary to have the type of sexual relationship you prefer?
- How important is it for each of you that your partner's preferences be realized in your sexual relationship?

- If a miracle occurred tonight while you were sleeping and tomorrow you began having the type of relationship and sex that you preferred, what changes would you notice?

At this point in our therapy, we now have two stories that can be compared—one that is problem-dominated and another that is solution-saturated. The next step is to determine what is standing in the couple's way of having the type of sexual relationship they prefer. That is, I look with them at whatever is "restraining them" from thinking, feeling, and behaving in ways that they prefer.

Exploring Restraints

Restraints usually take the form of beliefs and obligations that influence clients so strongly that departure from them has never been seriously considered. An excellent example is the previously mentioned assumption that "sex equals intercourse." Judging success or failure in relation to this standard, couples consider themselves to be sexual failures whenever they aren't mutually—or, worse, simultaneously—orgasmic during intercourse, despite the fact that they're able to please each other manually or orally. This can be quite a restraining belief!

From a narrative point of view, it is just as important (and perhaps more so) to liberate clients from what is restraining them as it is to produce change via some intervention. Often, when space and permission are created to explore restraints, change occurs quite naturally, as it did with the husband who believed that only whores engaged in, and enjoyed, oral sex.

I witnessed another example of restraint-loosening change while doing my internship at the Family Therapy Program in Calgary, Canada. An elderly couple seeing Dr. Gary Sanders told a story of a long and pleasurable sex life that had been recently interrupted by age-related physiological changes. Dr. Sanders correctly assessed that their relationship was solid and that what was lacking was "permission" to engage in other forms of sexual activity besides intercourse. He suggested that before continuing with their session, they watch some sexually explicit films in the viewing room. After about 30 minutes, the couple reappeared and asked if what they'd been viewing was normal sexual behavior. Dr. Sanders assured them that it was. They left with a twinkle in their eyes and scheduled no further appointments.

Once restraints have been defined, I gently critique and challenge them in relation to the type of sexual relationship the couple has indicated they desire. I usually have a more difficult time liberating clients from restraining beliefs than Dr. Sanders had with the couple described above, but it always helps when the clients have a mutual and safe relationship to build on. If couples have relational issues, or if the restraints are too large and well engrained to be easily altered, therapeutic change is more difficult to effect.

Generating and Processing Unique Outcomes

The major "intervention" in narrative therapy, as I understand it, is locating instances where clients are already behaving in ways that match their preferences. Narrative therapists call these instances "unique outcomes," because they fall outside of what anyone would predict would happen if the problem were totally controlling the clients' lives. Here are a few of the sorts of questions that can help generate such outcomes:

- When was the last time your sexual relationship was like you prefer it to be?
- Have there been times you could have been oppressed by distrust or fear, but managed to give it the slip and have a good time with each other?
- Are there any special contexts or times within which you recapture the relationship that Trouble has managed to partially steal away from you?
- Are there nonsexual areas in your relationship where trust and mutuality prevail?

When narrative therapists are able to discover instances of liberation, they actively use them in a process of "story revisioning" that is compatible with the couple's preferences. The process generally follows a series of "steps":

- Listening closely and asking questions (such as those listed previously) to generate a "unique outcome of exception" to the problem-saturated story.
- Eliciting from the clients a "unique account" of themselves and their relationship in light of the unique outcome.
- Serving as an interested audience as the clients narrate a "unique redescription" of themselves and their relationship.
- Exploring with the clients the "unique possibilities" that are potentially available as a result of the previous discussion.

Melissa, 45, came to therapy feeling depressed, following the termination of an intense sexual relationship with a 28-year-old man. My conversation with her, reconstructed from memory, illustrates some of what I've been describing.

Melissa: Life has no meaning anymore. He left me for a younger woman and told me I was no longer attractive. I don't care what happens at this point. Romantic attachments and sex won't happen for me anymore.

Rob: What a cruel thing to do! He not only left, but told you it was because you weren't attractive. I understand this would be a very painful experience. Can you say more about it causing you to feel that life has no meaning and that romantic relationships with men are no longer possible?

Melissa: I'm not getting any younger. . . . I gave him some of my best remaining years, years when I was very attractive. I won't be able to attract men, considering my age and how I look. I feel like such a fool!

To help her see the problem, and not herself, as the problem, I externalized "fear."

Rob: So time is running out, and Fear has you believing that you are no longer attractive enough for men to be interested, and believing that you've used your time foolishly.

Melissa: Exactly! I don't even want to go to work anymore. Nothing seems to matter.

The client was experiencing unrelenting negativity, so I posed a question to elicit a unique outcome.

Rob: I'm very curious about something. I can't help but notice that you are very nicely dressed and that your makeup is carefully applied. I can't help but wonder, if he took everything with him—all the meaning in life—how is it you look so nice today?

Melissa: Well [*long pause*], I may have overstated it a little. He took a lot, but not everything.

Rob: I see. He didn't take all your pride, and Fear hasn't managed to get you to stop caring how you look.

Melissa: No, not entirely.

Having established one unique outcome, I went in search of others, but first I added "pain" to her externalized problems.

Rob: So in this way, you're standing up to Pain and Fear. Are there other ways you're standing up, too?

Melissa: I suppose there are. I'm still working out. I swim five days a week.

I then characterized the pain as the "pain of loss."

Rob: Really! So Fear and the Pain of Loss haven't convinced you to give that up, either.

Melissa: No.

Rob: You mentioned dreading going to work. Are you still going?

I was listening for yet more unique outcomes.

Melissa: I haven't missed any work, if that's what you mean.

Rob: So even though Loss and Fear have had quite an impact on you, they haven't been able to get you to stop caring entirely. Is that correct?

Melissa: Well, I suppose you could look at it that way, but I have to do those things.

Rob: Really? Who says so? I mean, you don't literally have to do any of those things [*pause*]. You could have let Pain and Fear convince you to give them all up. How have you managed not to do that?

To answer this question, she would need to come up with a unique account.

Melissa: Well, I still have some pride.

Rob: So on the one hand, Pain and Fear have tried to take over your life and convince you of some pretty depressing things about yourself— but on the other, there's been a part of you fighting back all along and keeping them from taking complete control of you. What do you think it means about you that you've been able to do this?

I was asking her to provide personal attributes to help explain the unique account.

Melissa: Umm [*pause*], well [*pause*], maybe it means I'm not as bad off as I could be. Maybe there's some hope for me [*a slight smile*].

Rob: So, in spite of their best efforts, Pain and Fear haven't been able to get you to give up on having a relationship and a sex life completely. How do you manage to keep looking nice, working out, and going to work? I mean, specifically, how do you do that most days?

Melissa: I'm not sure, let's see . . . I [*pause*] well, I just tell myself I have to, that there will truly be nothing if I stop caring about myself.

Rob: So, you have talks with yourself about it, talks in which that part of you that still has hope tells you to hang in there.

Melissa: I suppose so.

Rob: What sort of person would do this—in spite of Pain and Fear, to continue to hold onto some hope and concern for herself?

This was a unique redescription question, posed in the third person so Melissa could feel freer to describe herself in new ways.

Melissa: One that hasn't given up completely.

Her response allowed me to follow up with a unique possibility question.

Rob: Knowing this about her, what do you predict she'll do in the coming days?

Melissa: [*small smile*] She'll keep on taking care of herself in those ways, [*pause*] just in case.

Rob: Just in case what?

Melissa: That there's [*pause*] uh, that there's a man out there that might notice.

PUTTING IT ALL TOGETHER

The following case example illustrates the eclectic approach to narrative therapy I've been describing and provides specific examples of several of the techniques.* Jared and Andrea, a couple in their late twenties, presented for therapy with concerns about their sex life and how it was affecting their relationship. Married less than a year, they had abstained from sexual relations prior to marriage. When, following the wedding, they attempted intercourse, Andrea found it painful. In talking to Jared about it, she revealed that she'd had previous lovers, with whom she

---

* See Parry and Doan (1994) and Freedman and Combs (1996) for a more in-depth (and general) treatment of the narrative approach.

hadn't experienced pain. He was shocked to discover that she wasn't a virgin and that she liked to both give and receive oral sex. Jared told me that he hadn't married the woman he thought he had, and he considered Andrea's liking oral sex to mean that she was "like a prostitute."

Andrea described herself as someone who had always enjoyed sex, adding that she realized Jared didn't want to hear such statements. He agreed. Feeling like a failure as a lover, he was concerned that his lack of experience put him at a disadvantage, as Andrea had "so many others to compare" him to. I externalized their problem as "Trouble" and asked how it had managed to influence them.

Rob: It sounds like Trouble had been using sexual difficulties to try to create distance and confusion in your marriage.
Andrea: Yes, I certainly agree with that. [*Jared nods in agreement.*]

With their having accepted the externalization, I could then use it to gather further information.

Rob: How has Trouble managed to accomplish this?
Andrea: We have very different sexual pasts . . . not only in terms of experience, but in the way we were raised by our families.
Rob: [*to Jared*] Do you agree with this?
Jared: Yes, even greater differences than I was aware of while we were dating.
Rob: So Trouble has used differences in family teaching about sex in order to create a problem in your marriage?

This externalizing reflection helped me check whether I was tracking with them.

Jared: Yeah, I guess it has.
Rob: Can you describe some of the differences it has used?
Jared: Well, I was raised in the United States and my parents were very conservative religiously. Much of what I believe I learned from the church and them.
Rob: [*to Andrea*] And where and how were you raised?
Andrea: I was raised in Cuba and came to the U.S. when I was a teenager. My mother was very religious, but my father wasn't. In fact, he refused to go to church at all.

Jared: And he cheated on her mother all the time!

Rob: [*to Andrea*] Do you agree with this?

Andrea: Yes, I'm pretty sure that he did . . . although I never knew anything for sure. Mother said that he did, but that she couldn't divorce
him because it was a sin to do so.

Rob: [*to Jared*] So, in your upbringing, sex outside of marriage was wrong,
and you and your parents behaved accordingly. And [*to Andrea*] in
yours, sex outside of marriage may not have been ideal, but it was
tolerated due to religious beliefs.

Andrea: Yes, but it's more than that. He was raised to believe that intercourse in the missionary position is the only way to have sex, that
anything else is kinky and sinful.

Rob: And how were you raised?

I was inquiring about the origin of their attitudes so I could get a sense of
their familial prescriptions (and proscriptions).

Andrea: That sex was best practiced inside of a marriage, but that it was
also to be enjoyed and celebrated in a variety of ways. It was okay to
have manual and oral sex and to experiment with various positions
of lovemaking.

Rob: [*to Jared*] Were you raised to believe that women enjoy sex or just
tolerate it?

Jared: Well, it was never talked about in our home, so I don't really know
for sure. But the feeling I got was that it was done mainly for the
man. I can't really imagine my mother enjoying it all that much, and
I certainly can't imagine her engaging in oral sex.

Rob: Did you discuss these issues prior to getting married?

Andrea: No, not really. I think we just assumed everything would be okay
once we were married. I knew he was more conservative than me,
but thought that once we were man and wife, things would be okay.
I looked forward to having sex with him and pleasing him, [*pause*]
and being pleased myself.

Rob: [*to Jared*] Would it be okay if she liked having sex with you?

I was curious to assess the degree to which Jared's family teachings were
restraining him.

Jared: Yeah, of course, but she doesn't. We can't even do it because it hurts
her too bad. I must be doing something wrong.

Rob: Gosh, Trouble has had lots to work with, hasn't it? The differences in your backgrounds, and also pain when you try to have intercourse—how much of an influence is it having on you, out of 100 percent?

My externalized reflection asked them to scale the relative influence of the problem.

Andrea: It's 100% in our sex life, and it's starting to affect other parts of our relationship, too.

Rob: [*to Jared*] Do you agree?

Jared: Yeah, I think we're both getting defensive, and we argue more.

Rob: So, Trouble used differences in background and pain to gain entrance to your relationship, but wasn't satisfied with just that. Now it's trying to influence other aspects as well? This has to be frustrating and scary for you both—to have something trying to create distance and conflict in your marriage.

Jared: Yeah, that's why we're here.

I typically continue problem-externalizing dialogue until I have a clear picture of a couple's problem and how it is influencing them—one that the clients agree is accurate. But in the interest of not further "creating the problem," I prefer not to linger too long in this process. After one or two sessions of acquiring a "problem-saturated" account, I can move to counteracting it with a "solution-saturated" version.

I began the next phase of the therapy by asking a unique-outcome question.

Rob: Despite Trouble's influence, here you are, still together and seeking counseling. How have you been able to do that?

Andrea: We still love each other very much. We want to be together. There are lots of good things about our relationship.

Were Trouble completely in charge, Andrea wouldn't have been able to offer such a wonderful unique outcome.

Jared: Yeah, I agree. If we can get this sex thing straightened out, we've got a great relationship.

Rob: So Trouble's influence in your sex life hasn't been strong enough to erase the love you have for each other and your desire to stay together?

Andrea: No, it hasn't, although it has been able to affect us some.

I responded to Andrea's comment by attempting to elicit a unique account.

Rob: But despite its best efforts it hasn't been able to totally influence you. How have you managed to stop it?

Andrea: We do things together that we enjoy, like eating out. Both of us really like food and special evenings.

Jared: Our religious beliefs are a big part of this. We both believe we've made a spiritual commitment to each other. Remembering this helps.

I saw this as an opportunity to elicit a unique redescription.

Rob: So you've continued to do things that sponsor closeness and commitment, even though there's one area of your relationship that Trouble has managed to undermine somewhat. What do you think it means about the two of you that you've done this?

Andrea: What does it mean about us?

Rob: Yes, I mean you could be divorced over this. What does it mean about the two of you and your relationship that you're fighting back and are determined to rid yourselves of trouble's influence?

Andrea: We're not the kind of people that take marriage casually. The vows we took are important to us.

Jared: This thing isn't going to get the better of us; our love is stronger than that.

Rob: I see. Trouble is in for a real dog fight with the two of you. You're up to the challenge.

Andrea: [*laughing*] I guess you could say that, yes.

Jared: I hadn't thought about it that way, but I agree.

Their agreement with my comment allowed me to take the next step—to elicit a unique possibility.

Rob: So you're determined to unite against the influence of Trouble. What difference do you think this will make in the outcome?

Andrea: Lots. Otherwise it might do much more harm.

Jared: For sure, our future is going to be a close, committed, one.

Rob: So would it make sense for us to get a clearly outlined plan in order to reduce Trouble's influence even more? Would that interest you?

I thought it might be helpful to formalize their standing up to Trouble.

Jared: Absolutely . . . that's what we need to do.

Andrea: I agree, we've needed to all along; we just haven't known what to do, exactly.

Rob: Yeah, Trouble works that way. It weasels its way in, causes confusion, and gets stronger and stronger if we let it. Instead of letting this happen, you've come in for counseling, reminded yourselves about what's good in your relationship, and remembered the commitment you made to each other. You already have Trouble on the run. We just need to invite it to leave quicker.

Jared: Sounds good to me. [*Andrea nods in agreement.*]

Given that Andrea was experiencing pain, I suggested that part of the plan to lessen Trouble's influence include her getting a thorough physical exam. She agreed to visit a female physician I recommended, who discovered and treated a lesion on Andrea's cervix, eliminating her pain within a month. The couple also agreed to educate themselves with some reading material I offered. Jared, who'd lived a sheltered life with regard to sexual practices, was surprised to learn that many couples engage in oral sex and that some very religious and spiritual people enjoy a variety of sexual behaviors with their partners. Agreeing to explore oral sex with Andrea, Jared soon decided that, in the interest of his marriage and commitment, he wanted them to continue with the experiment! This concluded the therapy.

SUMMARY

I stressed earlier that a therapist's model is less important than his or her ability to access intrinsic client resources and to develop strong therapeutic alliances. However, some models, more than others, underscore the importance of such skills. Narrative therapy is one such approach. It emphasizes the objectification of problems rather than persons; it encourages therapists to work collaboratively *with* clients, not as experts *above* them; and it highlights the familial and cultural influences on peoples' attitudes, beliefs, and actions. I became a narrative therapist more because of the type of therapeutic relationships it sponsors than because I believed it was "the best and truest way of helping people."*

---

* Readers interested in approaching sex therapy from a narrative perspective will need, of course, significant training (via books, workshops, and live supervision), practice, and motivation to become adept at working within the model.

When narrative therapists externalize a problem, they and their clients are in a position to revision the medical model–informed meanings contained in *DSM-IV* mental disorder categories. How profoundly different it is to suggest that clients are "under the influence of depression" than to refer to them as having a "mental disorder called depression." I have found that by placing problems outside of my clients, objectifying problems rather than persons, I'm able to invite trust into our therapeutic conversations, and I can accept the medical model as a houseguest, without finding it necessary to sleep with it. For those therapists who might be tired of the same old medical-model partner, perhaps an affair with narrative therapy is just what the doctor ordered!

REFERENCES

Berg, I. K. (1990). Solution-focused approach to family-based service. Milwaukee, WI: Milwaukee Brief Family Therapy Center.

Bergin, A., & Garfield, S. (Eds.). (1994). *Handbook of psychotherapy and behavior change* (4th ed.). New York: Wiley.

de Shazer, S. (1985). *Keys to solution in brief therapy*. New York: Norton.

de Shazer, S. (1988). *Clues: Investigating solutions in brief therapy*. New York: Norton.

de Shazer, S. (1991). *Putting difference to work*. New York: Norton.

Doan, R. (1998). The king is dead; long live the king: Narrative therapy and practicing what we preach. *Family Process, 37*(3), 379–385.

Epston, D. (1989, Autumn). Temper tantrum parties: Saving face, losing face, or going off your face. *Dulwich Centre Newsletter.*

Freedman, J., & Combs, G. (1996). *Narrative therapy: The social construction of preferred realities*. New York: Norton.

Hubble, M., Miller, S., & Duncan, B. (1998). S.W.A.T.: "Special" words and tactics for critical situations. *Crisis Intervention and Time-Limited Treatment, 4*, 179–195.

Hubble, M., Miller, S., & Duncan, B. (Eds.). (1999). *The heart and soul of change: What works in therapy*. San Francisco: Josey-Bass.

Maines, R. (1999). *The technology of orgasm*. Baltimore: John Hopkins University Press.

Parry, A., & Doan, R. (1994). *Story re-visions: Narrative therapy in the postmodern world*. New York: Guilford Press.

Taylor, C. B., & Arnow, B. (1988). *The nature and treatment of anxiety disorders*. New York: The Free Press.

Wampold, B. E. (2001). *The great psychotherapy debate: Models, methods, and findings*. Mahwah, NJ: Erlbaum.

Weston, L.C. (2001). Webmd Corporation. Retrieved July 28, 2003, http://aolsvc.health .webmd.aol.com/content/article/41/1687_51146.htm.

White, M. (1989). The externalization of the problem and the re-authoring of lives and relationships. In *Selected papers* (pp. 5–29). Adelaide, Australia: Dulwich Centre Publications.

White, M., & Epston, D. (1990). *Narrative means to therapeutic ends*. New York: Norton.

ten

How Do Therapists of Same-Sex Couples "Do It"?

Janie K. Long and Ursula Pietsch Saqui

WHEN I (JANIE) BEGAN MY CAREER as a sex educator within the United Methodist Church at the ripe age of 22, I was completely unprepared for the first question asked of me by a group of junior high kids: "So, how do two men do it?" A recent college graduate with no formal training as a sex educator, I was helping to conduct a sexuality weekend for teenagers and their parents. The question, asked in front of a group of about 20 adolescents and four other trained adult leaders, sent several thoughts racing through my mind: (1) I don't want to be fired from my job; (2) they told us to be honest in our answers; (3) why did I have to draw the first question? (4) don't act embarrassed; (5) don't seem uninformed. From the perspective of 25 years of subsequent clinical work and training, I recognize how woeful my worries were. Had I been less anxious about appearing naïve, my personal thoughts could have been more probing and relevant: (1) Why am I so ill-equipped to answer this question? (2) Why was the question asked? (3) Why, throughout the entire workshop, have no questions been asked about how two women relate to one another sexually? (4) How will my listeners interpret my answer to the question?

Neither of us (Janie and Ursula) have gained our knowledge about gay and lesbian sex through the sex therapy classes and workshops we have taken over the years, but, rather, through our own reading and seeking out of information on the topic with other professionals, particularly sexual minority professionals. We have also learned through our exposure to sexual minority clients and through being more involved in the gay community in general. We presume that few graduate programs are focusing on therapeutic approaches with same-sex couples,* which means that many clinicians are probably in a similar position to that of the junior high kid who raised his hand so many years ago. They want to know, "So how do therapists of same-sex couples 'do it'?" This chapter offers, we hope, a more sophisticated answer to *this* question than the one Janie came up with a quarter century ago. In the following pages, we lay out the theoretical foundation of the work we do, followed by some clinical illustrations. But first we need to discuss some of the general challenges facing clinicians who work with sexual minorities.

CHALLENGES IN WORKING WITH SAME-SEX COUPLES

The foundations of traditional sex therapy are heteronormative (Ritter & Terndrup, 2002). Several authors have pointed out the subjectivity involved in the diagnosis of sexual difficulties and the heterocentric notions that underlie many of the major sexual dysfunctions (Tiefer, 1997). At the same time, the sexual complaints that often bring lesbians and gay men to sex therapy, including oral sex aversions and anal sex difficulties, are largely ignored in the literature (Rosser, Short, Thurmes, & Coleman, 1998). The literature that does exist suggests that female couples may face the stigma attached to sexual and erotic behaviors in women, or alternatively, that woman-to-woman sex can only be a magical experience that is a cure-all for any type of sexual difficulty (Brown & Zimmer, 1986). Women may also be concerned about gender conceptualizations that tend to dichotomize sexual norms, such as the belief that initiating sex is only a masculine role (Slater & Mencher, 1991). It is not surprising then that the most frequently reported sexual difficulty between lesbians is discrepancy in sexual desire (Hall, 1987; Schwartz, 1998).

Gay men are also influenced by gender-role socialization and heterosexist beliefs. They may struggle with the need to split their sexuality from their emotional needs (Canarelli, Cole, & Rizzuto, 1999), or become overly focused on performance, constantly monitoring how their partner is responding and how they are performing (George & Behrendt, 1987).

---

* We use the terms *same-sex couples* and *gay and lesbian couples* interchangeably, intending for them to include persons who identify as bisexual and are involved in same-sex relationships.

How do two gay males, socialized to believe that men should focus on sex in relationships and that a real man has many sexual conquests, handle the idea of monogamy?

Sexual orientation includes not only sexual behavior, but also erotic fantasies and interpersonal affection. We need to be sensitive to the potential historical changes in a person's sexual orientation over the course of a lifetime (DeCecco, 1981), and we need to be informed about the varieties of gay and lesbian sex, working through any discomfort or fascination with practices and couple arrangements that are different from our own (Bernstein, 2000).

Good therapy involves helping couples explore what they want, which may require that we explore possibilities and issues of both commitment and sexual nonmonogamy (Bernstein, 2000; Brown & Zimmer, 1986; Shernoff, 1999). "Clinicians need to understand what issues such as sexual fidelity, sexual dysfunction, and compulsive sexuality mean to each couple, rather than seeing these behaviors through the lens of psychopathology or the values of a heterosexist society" (Ritter & Trendrup, 2002, p. 348). For example, Hall (1987) indicated that women who are sexually involved with each other and also are each other's best friend, political ally, social support, and perhaps business partner may decrease sexual contact in order to create some distance. Is this sexual dysfunction or establishing healthy boundaries?

THEORETICAL AND CLINICAL FOUNDATIONS

Constructivist, social constructionist, and feminist assumptions guide our clinical thinking and actions. We embrace notions regarding the relativity of reality, always maintaining respect for the relationships within which our understandings are constructed, and attending to how our role as observers informs our observations (von Foerster, 1981; von Glasersfeld, 1984). We view client dilemmas as social inventions, created in conversation among clients, others important in their contexts, and therapists (Gergen, 1985; Hoffman, 1990). Thus, we assume that these dilemmas are open to multiple interpretations and understandings. Such a view of the therapeutic process enhances our flexibility and our clients' options, as we encourage the creation of nonpathologizing and change-oriented constructions.

As feminists, we attend carefully to creating the sorts of collaborative, affiliative relationships with our clients that will honor their diversity, their unique competencies, and, at times, their disenfranchised voices

(Avis, 1988; Hare-Mustin, 1994; McGoldrick, 1998). Context is central in our clinical understandings, and, thus, we believe we must always include an awareness of our own participation in the construction of clinical realities. As such, we consider an understanding of ourselves, our authenticity, and our transparency to be critical to the therapeutic process (Johnson, 1996).

Although the theoretical framework just described informs our work with all clients, regardless of sexual orientation, there are pivotal issues that are specific to our work with same-sex couples. The following questions guide our exploration of ourselves as therapists:

- As we sit with same-sex couples in session, are we being real and present?
- Are we staying open to our own experience?
- Are we aware of our own heterosexism and homophobia?
- Systemically, how might we also be contributing to the problem or be involved in the context of the problem (Haley, 1987; Minuchin, 1974)?
- Are we adequately valuing same-sex couples, believing that they are capable of succeeding in therapy and deserving of happiness (Brown & Zimmer, 1986; Long & Lindsey, 2004)?
- Alternatively, are we *over*valuing same-sex couples? Wanting to compensate for the homophobic myth of short, meaningless same-sex relationships, are we emphasizing the *longevity* more than the *quality* of relationships? If so, our clients may protect our image of same-sex couples by underemphasizing their problems.
- Gay men often have an explicit vocabulary for describing sex. Are we able to be comfortable matching it or the language of lesbian lovers (Shernoff, 1999)?
- Are we educated enough in (and comfortable enough to explore) gay and lesbian sexual practices? If not, how can we adequately understand the difficulties our clients may be describing?

In addition to posing questions to ourselves, we pose specific, informed questions to our clients, assessing their unique characteristics and concerns. However, we are careful not to focus on aspects of sexual orientation or sexuality to the detriment of assessing for other issues, such as substance abuse (Bernstein, 2000; Brown & Zimmer, 1986). Exploring the following areas with gay and lesbian clients helps us to better understand the presenting problem and its influence on the couple relationship (Peterson & Stewart, 1985):

- Degree of self-acceptance regarding sexual orientation;
- Coming-out history, including any negative messages;
- Medical concerns, including HIV status and urological or gynecological difficulties;
- Amount of support within the family and the community;
- Openness in their work environments;
- Degree to which partners have come out to others;
- Commitment to monogamy versus nonmonogamy;
- Aversions to specific sexual acts;
- Impact of previous heterosexual relationships/marriages;
- The reaction of children from previous relationships or children who are adopted or born into the existing relationship;
- How the cultural or racial heritage of the couple may influence their sexual orientation. For example, in some cultures same-sex relationships may be seen as a rejection of cultural values or as a form of social deviance that brings shame to the family (Choi, Salazar, Lew, & Coates, 1995);
- Potential drug or alcohol abuse to deal with rejection of self or from others.

CREATING AFFILIATIVE CLINICAL RELATIONSHIPS

In sessions, we move between the center and the edge of our clients' relationships, depending on the couple's ethnic and racial backgrounds, their ages, and the nature of the presenting problem. Working collaboratively, we always maintain a voice in the process, but we also acknowledge the voices of the client system and larger systems that may be involved, and we often solicit feedback about what is helpful and what is not. As clients become familiar with our commitments to them and to the process, they share more in the experience; we attribute this to their sense of comfort that their opinions and thoughts are being respected. Without this respect, a working alliance and a sense of trust are extremely difficult to create.

We must also be willing to open space for discussing our own sexual orientation with same-sex couples. Whereas some lesbians and gay men prefer working with straight therapists (Bernstein, 2000), others report that there have been times and circumstances in which they favored working with a sexual minority therapist (Bernstein; Long, 1996). The issue of our sexual orientation is usually raised at the beginning of therapy, when our gay and lesbian clients are testing the waters for safety (Bernstein).

Encouraging Multiple Perspectives

Our challenge as therapists is to create a context in which new meanings can emerge. We often search for novel ways to view and resolve the problem, thereby legitimizing multiple viewpoints, encouraging critical thinking, and allowing for experimentation with other options. We realize that not every theory or intervention will work for every client and that there are multiple possible paths to change (Hubble, Duncan, & Miller, 2000). In addition, we don't assume that we know the specific content of clients' lives (Freedman & Combs, 1996). Encouraging clients to tell their story helps them feel respected and heard, and it gives room for their resources and knowledge to come forth (Anderson, 1997).

This style of therapy promotes the loss of certainty and calls forth flexibility and spontaneity. By honoring multiple perspectives, we are able to hold and tolerate same-sex couples' feelings about homophobia and heterosexism without responding in a defensive or pathologizing manner (Bernstein, 2000). To balance our own perceptions, we self-monitor and check with colleagues to make sure that our own biases aren't getting in the way (Brown & Zimmer, 1986).

Focusing on Strengths, Resiliency, and Coping Abilities

Borrowing heavily from solution-focused approaches, we ask about and identify strengths and exceptions to the problem. Exceptions may be used to encourage clients to do more of what has previously worked for them, thus highlighting their own coping abilities (de Shazer, 1991). Highlighting exceptions also makes the problem secondary to the successes the clients have already experienced. A solution-focused approach (de Shazer, 1988, 1991) is helpful in cementing change, as we talk about what exactly happened that was different and what things they would like to see continue.

Such tools are extremely helpful in working with sexual minority clients, particularly those in interracial and intercultural relationships, who are dealing with multiple layers of multiculturalism (Pearlman, 1996). Often pathologized by society and deemed in need of "repair" by some even within the mental health field (Rosik, 2003; Yarhouse, 1998), these same-sex couples often demonstrate remarkable strengths—adaptability and flexibility to multiple roles and commitments, increased levels of communication, and greater empathy. Nevertheless, we need to be aware of the many challenges they face: interracial prejudice, antagonism by families-of-origin, adjustments to new cultural mores, and limited connections to the gay community (Long, in press).

Power Issues

We must acknowledge the power we as therapists have over our clients if we are to reduce the chances of its misuse. Downplaying it just makes abuse and boundary violations more likely to occur. Our obligation is to meet the needs of our clients and make a positive difference in their lives.

We must also attend to power issues outside the therapy room. We attempt to increase our clients' awareness of dominant stories created by powerful people and groups in society and to collaboratively examine how these dominant stories—such as those that reinforce homophobia and heterosexism—inform the problems clients bring to our attention (Freedman & Combs, 1996).

The following case example offers a glimpse of our affiliative, collaborative style. In working with Tyra and Meg, I (Janie) considered it important to attend to the complexities of their racial and cultural differences and to challenge the dominant cultural stories that were negatively affecting their ability to create a mutually satisfying relationship.

Tyra and Meg wanted a female therapist who could help them deal with what they described as a problem of roles, including who should initiate sex. Tyra was 28 years old, Hispanic and Catholic, and was employed as a welder; Meg, a 26-year-old social work doctoral student, was Anglo-American and agnostic. Having met through a lesbian social gathering, they had been dating for six months and living together for the previous two months.

During the early part of the initial session, Meg tended to do the talking for the couple. To make sure I heard both voices, I attempted to also draw Tyra into the discussion. Meg described the problem as revolving around Tyra's need to control the relationship. She often felt, she said, as though she were in a relationship with a man who wanted to tell her what to think, how to look, and how to run her life. Vehemently asserting her bisexuality, she said that if she wanted a man, she knew where to get one. Tyra jumped into the discussion at this point, stating that she was through with the relationship because no matter how hard she tried, she was not a "good enough man" for Meg.

Thinking a different perspective might be helpful, I interrupted the couple at this point and asked if they could envision a miracle happening tomorrow, and to consider what their relationship would be like (de Shazer, 1978). Both women seemed shocked by the question, and they remained silent. Finally, Meg said that things would be like they had been when they were dating, and Tyra quickly agreed. When I asked for more details, both partners described a very egalitarian dating relationship, with both partners contributing equally to decisions, finances, and sexual advances.

Meg explained that since they had begun living together, Tyra had become more dominant in all aspects of their life, including the bedroom. Tyra agreed, but explained that with Meg still in school, she felt a lot of pressure from her to be the "breadwinner." And, wondering whether Meg would really rather be with a man, she felt the need to initiate sex enough to "keep her satisfied."

Questioning this dominant story, I asked Tyra if she liked the sexual initiator/breadwinner role. "No!" she replied. I wondered aloud whether they were falling into a sort of butch-femme pattern out of some confusion about what kind of relationship they each wanted. They both protested this hypothesis, calling it antiquated. I commended them for working hard to find a way to hold onto what was good between them, including sex, and I told them that once they regained the balance in their relationship, they would most likely also find it in their sex life.

In order to set up a situation in which Tyra and Meg could possibly behave differently, I recommended something that I anticipated might seem bizarre or perhaps humorous to them (de Shazer, 1985). "Do you have a strap-on dildo?" I asked. Both women gasped and shouted, "Hell, no!" I suggested that they buy one and introduce it into their sex play. I hoped that, if nothing else, the introduction of the dildo would make more overt their struggles around their roles in the relationship.

The next week, the couple came to the session in a very angry mood. Tyra had purchased a strap-on and had tried to use it with Meg, but things hadn't gone well. Meg said that she felt even more preyed upon by Tyra and wanted nothing to do with "that *thing*" or, for that matter, with sex at all. Working interactively with them, I explored the power differences between them, hoping a solution would emerge.

My questions revealed many interesting contrasts. Whereas Meg was out at school and to her family, Tyra was not. Meg was from an upper-middle-class family that was quite liberal, and she had more education. Tyra grew up in a working-class family whose cultural and religious beliefs were particularly homophobic and heterosexist. Although Meg currently made less money, her education gave her, as Tyra pointed out, much more future earning potential. Tyra also noted that Meg was more physically attractive than she was, especially to men. In addition, Meg had more friends and more opportunities for social contact.

I postulated that perhaps all of these differences had something to do with the pressure Tyra felt to be the breadwinner and sexual initiator. At the end of the session, I asked Meg if she ever enjoyed initiating sex with Tyra, and she answered positively. I then asked her if she had ever fantasized about using a strap-on, to which she blushed and giggled, admitting that she had. I responded, "Hmm . . . carpe diem!" Wanting to highlight the exceptions to the problem (de Shazer, 1985), I asked them to both notice the times during the next week when they felt happy and content with the relationship.

The couple came to the third session holding hands. They revealed that Meg had initiated sex with the strap-on, and they had played with it several times during the week. They realized that they were happiest and most content when they were working as a team, rather than when one was trying to take care of the other. We worked for a few more sessions on how to achieve and maintain more balance in their relationship, and they reported no further sexual difficulties.

LETTING GO OF ASSUMPTIONS

As Hartman (1999) pointed out, the United States is experiencing a social revolution of acceptance in attitudes and policies toward lesbians and gay men; nevertheless, widespread tolerance, protection, and equality remain elusive. Heterosexist bias still pervades our culture, our belief systems, and thus our therapy (Long & Serovich, 2003). Homophobia and heterosexism also lurk in the legal and cultural invisibility of gay and lesbian relationships, keeping same-sex couples and families from participating in most traditional life rituals, such as marriage and adoption (Brown & Zimmer, 1986; Long, 1996). We attend carefully to these cultural biases and maintain awareness of how they may be influencing the perceptions of our clients, as well as of our own.

A good example of this is how we think about boundaries in same-sex relationships. Mencher and Slater (1991) suggested that what is often pathologically described as *fusion* or *merger* in a lesbian relationship is rather an adaptive way for the couple to defend themselves against an antagonistic environment. Gay men also must contend with questions of boundaries. Given how males are socialized to focus on sex, it isn't surprising that when gay males meet someone new, sex is high on their list of priorities. However, once the newness wears off, gay men may be at a loss for how to maintain their relationship or what boundaries may be appropriate (Brown & Zimmer, 1986). We do our best to deconstruct myths about masculinity and appropriate male behavior, avoiding homophobic stereotypes of gay males and exploring what kind of boundaries would be most helpful (Brown & Zimmer).

A couple, Charles and Mel, came to therapy seeking help for Charles's erectile difficulties. Although I (Janie) worked hard to avoid heterosexist stereotyping as I explored Charles and Mel's beliefs about sexual exclusivity and commitment, they weren't convinced, initially at least, that I was succeeding.

Both men, in their mid-thirties, were professionals: Charles was an architect and Mel was a pediatrician. They had been in a committed relationship for five years; prior to this, Mel had been in an eight-year relationship that he described as emotionally committed but not sexually exclusive—an arrangement agreed upon by both partners. Charles described several previous short-term relationships in which he had been committed both emotionally and sexually but in which the other partner had not been monogamous. Mel and Charles had agreed to be sexually involved only with each other, and before the onset of Charles's problem, their sexual relationship had been a source of enjoyment for both of them.

I did a brief, solution-oriented (de Shazer, 1985) sexual history with the couple, including questions about the duration of the problem, frequency of contact, sexual practices, health concerns, and so on. Included in the sexual history was a question about recent relationship impasses, which generated a response that seemed to highlight the crux of the situation. During the past year, a new architect, Lynn, had joined Charles's firm and had become social friends with both him and Mel.

Both partners were not only very fond of Lynn, they were also sexually attracted to him, and they'd learned that he was also attracted to them. During our conversation, they revealed that for six months or so, they'd been joking with one another about inviting Lynn to join them in bed. Remembering that the erectile difficulties had started about five months earlier, and feeling comfortable enough to venture a tentative hunch, I wondered aloud if there was a connection between the joking and the difficulty. Both Mel and Charles seemed stunned by the idea, and they rejected it outright, insisting that they were only teasing each other and reasserting how comfortable they were with him. In fact, they said, they were having dinner with him that night.

Letting go of my initial assumption and being open to their view, I agreed with them that I'd probably been too hasty in my suggestion. I complimented them for being able to maintain a friendship with Lynn without becoming threatened by the mutual attraction. And with the end of the session fast approaching, I offered a suggestion for a small change that I thought would take some performance pressure off Charles. I recommended that they might try, over the next week, not having sex together. They agreed.

At the beginning of the next session, Charles and Mel came in with an animated description of what had transpired when they'd left my office the previous week. Frustrated with what they'd seen as my "internalized homophobic" and "unscientific" approach to the problem, they'd had a spirited discussion about my lack of understanding and mistaken assumptions. Perhaps it was homophobia that had caused me to link the erectile difficulties to their relationship with Lynn. Did I believe that they as gay men could not remain in a committed relationship? Was I trying to break them up? They decided to call me the next day to cancel subsequent sessions and find a more gay-friendly therapist. Then they met Lynn as planned.

As dinner progressed, they both felt increasingly uncomfortable with their friend. When they got home, they had a huge fight, with Charles insisting that Mel was "coming on to" Lynn, and Mel insisting that I was to blame for postulating this ridiculous theory. They argued for a long time, finally decided to sleep on it, and made plans to talk again the next evening. They also decided not to cancel the therapy appointment until they had had more time for discussion.

They both thought a lot about the situation throughout the next day, and when they sat down again, they were both able to talk with less defensiveness. This discussion led to the conclusion that I was probably more on target than they'd initially given me credit for, as they both realized that they felt threatened by their attraction to Lynn and what it meant for their commitment to each other.

They seemed happy to report that they'd failed their homework assignment miserably. Each reaffirmed his commitment to the relationship, and they both agreed to continue working with me and to quit teasing one another about the threesome. After a few more appointments, they found themselves less angry at each other, and Charles reported no more erectile difficulties. We ended therapy after eight sessions.

THE CHALLENGES OF COMING OUT

When gays, lesbians, or bisexuals come out to themselves or to others, they begin a process of integrating their sexual orientation and their identity. George and Behrendt (1987) divided the coming out process into three phases: (1) an acknowledgement of one's self as gay, lesbian, or bisexual; (2) an identification with other sexual minorities and the building of a social support system with them; and (3) an acknowledgement of one's sexual orientation to important others.

Coming out is a multidimensional and continuous process (Browning, 1987) that questions and redefines relationships to family, friends, coworkers, present or potential intimate partners, and a person's cultural context (Bepko & Johnson, 2000). Browning detailed pivotal cognitive, emotional, and behavioral elements that are often present throughout. Cognitively, it is a time of identity-shifting and striving for congruence. Emotionally, feelings such as excitement, guilt, shame, fear, and pleasure may be elicited by the awareness of same-sex attraction. Behaviorally, lesbian women tend to act on their feelings only after achieving an intellectual understanding of their attraction.

In therapy, difficulties for same-sex couples may arise when each of the partners is at a different stage in coming out (Brown & Zimmer, 1986). Viewing these conflicts within a developmental perspective may be helpful in resolving them (Bernstein, 2000), but it is also important for therapists not to impose a normative template on clients, expecting or prescribing the process in a particular, predictable fashion.

A strength of many same-sex couples is that they are able to create a social support network of lesbian, gay, and bisexual friends, validating heterosexual friends and colleagues, as well as former partners and lovers. This family of choice can be an important asset to consider in therapy (Bepko & Johnson, 2000; Long, 2003). In addition, many lesbian and gay couples face a lack of acceptance and validation from their families of origin, which may be associated with presenting problems in therapy. Partners who differ in the degree to which they are out to their families of origin face loyalty conflicts when family gatherings take place (Bepko & Johnson).

In the following case study, the therapist had to attend sensitively to the timing of coming-out decisions, family-of-origin versus family-of-choice concerns, sexual behaviors that were both defining and confusing sexual identity, and pervasive social-support concerns. In this case, the therapist's affiliative and nonpathologizing stance was pivotal in allowing the couple to come to their own decisions about coming out, defining their relationship, and pursuing intimacy in ways that were mutually fulfilling.

Mindy called the family therapy clinic where I (Janie) am a supervisor, seeking help for her friend, Joann, whom she described as being anxious and struggling with her recent divorce. Mindy scheduled an appointment, which she said she would also attend, in order to offer Joann support. The case was assigned to one of my supervisees, Jack.

In the first session, the two women explained to Jack that they'd met about three months earlier at the church where Joann worked as a choir director and Mindy served as a counselor for the youth group. At the time, Joann, 44, had just ended a marriage of 24 years, and Mindy, 28, was a week away from her three-year marriage finally ending. They became friends, quickly bonding over their divorce experiences.

Joann had two adult children, a 22-year-old daughter and a 20-year-old son, neither of whom lived at home. Mindy had a one-year-old son, Winston, who lived with her. Mindy was not yet receiving child support, and she'd been out of work for several months before finally getting a sales job in a computer store, so she was struggling financially. Joann's only income was her minimal pay from the church, but, through the divorce, she'd obtained the house, part of the joint savings, and some shares of stock. She described herself as having enough money to get by but not enough to spare in the event of an emergency.

Three months earlier, Joann had invited Mindy to move in with her and share their expenses. This had helped their finances, and they both felt as though they'd found a soul mate. Mindy was happier than she'd ever been, and Joann felt less depressed than she had in a long time. However, in the previous two months, Joann had experienced a significant increase in anxiety.

When Jack asked them to tell him more about what had brought them into therapy, Joann exclaimed, "My children accused me of being a lesbian! They're wrong, of course!" Mindy, looking injured, remained silent, but her eyes filled with tears. Jack asked Joann if her children's suspicions had anything to do with her increased anxiety. "They definitely brought it to a head," she said, but she had started becoming more anxious when Mindy and her son had moved in.

Jack was curious about how Mindy had responded to the speculation of Joann's children. She said that she'd never thought of herself as a lesbian but had grown very fond of Joann in the past several months. She added that she thought it was "kind of cool" that the kids were open to such an idea. Jack ended the session by complimenting the friends on supporting one another through hard times and for being willing to talk openly about the things that had brought them to therapy. He admitted to feeling confused about their goal for therapy and suggested that they do some thinking about what they wanted to accomplish by working with him.

The next session began with what Jack perceived to be a lot of tension.

Asked if they had discussed possible goals for therapy, Joann said that they had, but were unable to reach total consensus. They both wanted to further address Joann's anxiety, but Mindy also wanted to work on defining the nature of their relationship. Jack asked them to help him better understand its development by telling him their story of it, pointing out that it would be normal for them each to have a different version.

Mindy said that while Joann continued to refer to her as "just a friend," she continually touched and flirted with her. They had been sharing a bed in order to allow Mindy's son to have his own room, and they both enjoyed snuggling in it. Joann frequently pretended to nurse at Mindy's breasts, which had recently resulted in their beginning to produce milk. Mindy found herself becoming sexually aroused by Joann's sucking, but she also found their contact to be somehow "warped." She asked Jack if he thought this kind of behavior was normal "or just a little strange."

Jack said that his understanding was that some lesbians did indeed engage in this type of sexual activity, at which point Joann clarified that she considered their behavior to be nurturing but not really sexual. A "full" sexual relationship between them would be impossible, she said, given that they would jeopardize their positions in the church if people thought they were lesbians. It seemed to Jack that Joann's "nursing" was a way for the couple to safely enjoy sexual exploration by not defining it as such. But the price for safety was confusion.

Complimenting the women on the strengths of their friendship and how they had managed to develop such a close bond in spite of the concerns that had brought them to therapy, Jack suggested they spend some time before the next session thinking about this. He also suggested that Mindy might consider getting another bed or cot for Winston's room and sleeping in his room until she and Joann became clearer on what they wanted their relationship to be. They reluctantly agreed to consider the possibility.

At the beginning of the next session, Joann and Mindy said that they had discussed at length the possibility of no longer sleeping together, but they had, together, decided that they weren't willing at this point to give up this way of being close. This decision had led them to seriously question whether they were indeed in a romantic/sexual relationship. Both felt guilty when they went to church and were fearful of being discovered. They cried as they talked about the potential loss of Joann's position and possible expulsion from their faith community. If not for this threat, both would want to pursue a romantic relationship.

When Jack asked how their local congregation, and their denomination in general, viewed same-sex relationships, Mindy said that both were disapproving, though she had heard of "affirming congregations" in larger cities. Although both women disagreed with the church's position, they each felt that they were suppressing/denying their sexual expression because of it. Having grown up in the church, they still considered it an important support, and Mindy said that she wanted to give her son the same experience she had had. Jack acknowledged that the dominant story in their faith community about same-sex relationships seemed to be filtering into their interaction with one another, causing them to question their beliefs.

In response to one of Jack's requests in the previous session, the women had generated lists of their relationship strengths. Believing that they could utilize these lists to help them meet their own needs (de Shazer, 1985), Jack suggested that these strengths and resiliencies held the answers to lowering Joann's anxiety and clarifying their relationship. He asked them to spend some time before the next session coming up with a plan that would allow them to do something different in addressing both issues.

When they came back, Joann and Mindy had indeed come up with a plan and had already begun to implement it. Deciding that postponing a physical relationship, except for friendly hugs, would greatly reduce their anxiety and fear, they had purchased another bed for Winston's room and Mindy had moved in. For the time being, they would continue to develop their friendship and make plans to move to a larger city. Once they had relocated and found new jobs, they would again explore a romantic/sexual relationship and find a new faith community.

When they'd shared their plan with Joann's children, they'd received enthusiastic support. They thanked Jack for pointing out the strengths in their relationship and for not forcing any choices upon them. They liked that he had let them make their own decisions, they were impressed by his being informed about sex between women, and they appreciated that he "had not even flinched" when they'd told him about their physical interactions. Rather than pathologizing their behavior, he had in fact had normalized it. They had subsequently bought a lesbian sex manual and both were enjoying reading it.

It took Joann and Mindy about five months to find jobs in a nearby larger city. They saw Jack biweekly during this time and discussed various issues, including balancing power in the relationship, coparenting, and dealing with stigma. A year after their move, they sent Jack a note, thanking him again for his support during their time of transition and reporting that they'd found a nice apartment in a "gay friendly" neighborhood and were attending an affirming church. They were developing other lesbian and gay couple friends and very much enjoyed the freedom to engage in more than just "snuggling"—free, now, from guilt and fear.

CONCLUSION

Ritter and Trendrup (2002) have recently noted the virtual silence in the professional literature about the sexual expression of same-sex couples. Traditional sex therapy has proven to be no less heterosexist/homophobic than the rest of society. We believe that brief sex therapy, with its emphasis on depathologizing, can help to bridge the gap that has been missing in the literature, providing positive messages and suggestions to same-sex couples. As in other aspects of same-sex relationships, gay and lesbian couples share some sexual problems that are common with heterosexual couples, but, as we have attempted to highlight, they also face many unique challenges. We hope that this chapter has been helpful in identifying such challenges and in providing some direction in how to respond to them.

How do effective therapists of same-sex couples "do it"? They learn about the range and meanings of sexual expression among gays, lesbians, and bisexuals; they challenge their homophobia and heterosexism, examining how such biases may be infiltrating the choices they make and the possibilities they recognize; they reexamine their beliefs about and opinions of issues such as monogamy, boundaries, and gender roles; and, finally, they work respectfully and efficiently, using brief therapy theories and techniques to inform and guide their work.

REFERENCES

Anderson, H. (1997). *Conversation, language, and possibilities: A postmodern approach to therapy*. New York: Basic.

Avis, J. M. (1988). Deepening awareness: A private guide to feminism and family therapy. In L. Braverman (Ed.), *Women, feminism and family therapy* (pp. 15–32). New York: Haworth.

Bepko, C., & Johnson, T. (2000). Gay and lesbian couples in therapy: Perspectives for the contemporary family therapist. *Journal of Marital and Family Therapy, 20*(4), 409–419.

Bernstein, A. C. (2000). Straight therapists working with lesbians and gays in family therapy. *Journal of Marital and Family Therapy, 26*(4), 443–454.

Brown, L. S., & Zimmer, D. (1986). An introduction to therapy issues of lesbian and gay male couples. In N. S. Jacobson & A. S. Gurman (Eds.), *Clinical handbook of marital therapy* (pp. 451–468). New York: Guilford Press.

Browning, C. (1987). Therapeutic issues and intervention strategies with young adult lesbian clients: A developmental approach. *Journal of Homosexuality, 14*, 45–52.

Canarelli, J., Cole, G., & Rizzuto, C. (1999). Attention vs. acceptance: Some dynamic issues in gay male development. *Gender and psychoanalysis, 4*, 47–70.

Choi, K. H., Salazar, N., Lew, S., & Coates, T. J. (1995). AIDS risk, dual identity, and community response among gay Asian and Pacific Islander men in San Francisco. In G. M. Herek & B. Greene (Eds.), *AIDS, identity, and community: The HIV epidemic and lesbians and gay men* (pp. 115–134). Thousand Oaks, CA: Sage.

DeCecco, J. (1981). Definition and meaning of sexual orientation. *Journal of Homosexuality, 6*, 51–67.

de Shazer, S. (1978). Brief hypnotherapy of two sexual dysfunctions: The crystal ball technique. *American Journal of Clinical Hypnosis, 20*, 203–208.

de Shazer, S. (1985). *Keys to solution in brief therapy.* New York: Norton.

de Shazer, S. (1988). *Clues: Investigating solutions in brief therapy.* New York: Norton.

de Shazer, S. (1991). *Putting difference to work.* New York: Norton.

Freedman, J., & Combs, G. (1996). *Narrative therapy: The social construction of preferred realities.* New York: Norton.

George, K. D., & Behrendt, A. E. (1987). Therapy for male couples experiencing relationship problems and sexual problems. *Journal of Homosexuality, 14*, 77–85.

Gergen, K. J. (1985). The social constructionist movement in modern psychology. *American Psychologist, 40*, 266–275.

Haley, J. (1987). *Problem-solving therapy* (3rd ed.). San Francisco: Jossey-Bass.

Hall, M. (1987). Sex therapy with lesbian couples: A four stage approach. *Journal of Homosexuality, 14*, 137–156.

Hare-Mustin, R. T. (1994). Discourses in the mirrored room: A postmodern analysis of therapy. *Family Process, 33*(1), 19–35.

Hartman, A. (1999). The long road to equality. In J. Laird (Ed.), *Lesbians and lesbian families: Reflections on theory and practice* (pp. 91–120). New York: Columbia University Press.

Hoffman, L. (1990). Constructing realities: An art of lenses. *Family Process, 29*(1), 1–12.

Hubble, M. A., Duncan, B. L., & Miller, S. D. (2000). *The heart and soul of change: What works in therapy.* Washington DC: American Psychological Association.

Johnson, S. M. (1996). *The practice of emotionally focused marital therapy: Creating connection.* New York: Brunner/Mazel.

Long, J. K. (1996). Working with lesbians, gays, and bisexuals: Addressing heterosexism in supervision. *Family Process, 35*, 377–388.

Long, J. K. (2003). Interracial and intercultural lesbian couples: The incredibly true adventures of two women in love. *Journal of Couple and Relationship Therapy, 2*, 85–101.

Long, J. K., & Lindsey, E. (2004). The sexual orientation matrix for supervision: Training MFTs to work with sexual minority clients. *Journal of Couple and Relationship Therapy, 3*, 123–135.

Long, J. K., & Serovich, J. M. (2003). Incorporating sexual orientation into MFT training programs: Infusion and inclusion. *Journal of Marital and Family Therapy, 29*, 59–68.

McGoldrick, M. (Ed.). (1998). *Re-visioning family therapy: Race, culture, and gender in clinical practice.* New York: Guilford Press.

Mencher, J., & Slater, S. (1991, March). *New perspectives on the lesbian family experience.* Paper presented at the annual convention of the Association for Women in Psychology, Hartford, CT.

Minuchin, S. (1974). *Families & family therapy.* Cambridge, MA: Harvard University Press.

Pearlman, S. F. (1996). Loving across race and class divides: Relational challenges and the interracial lesbian couple. In M. Hill & E.D. Rothblum (Eds.), *Couples therapy: Feminist perspectives* (pp. 25–35). New York: Haworth.

Peterson, T. L., & Stewart, J. H. (1985). The lesbian or gay couple as a family: Principles for building satisfying relationships. In H. Hidalgo, T. L. Peterson, & N. Jane (Eds.), *Lesbian and gay issues: A resource manual for social workers* (pp. 27–32). Silver Spring, MD: National Association of Social Workers.

Ritter, K. Y., & Terndup, A. I. (2002). *Handbook of affirmative psychotherapy with lesbians and gay men.* New York: Guilford Press.

Rosik, C. H. (2003). Motivational, ethical, and epistemological foundations in the treatment of unwanted homoerotic attraction. *Journal of Marital and Family Therapy, 29*, 13–28.

Rosser, B. R. S., Short, B. J., Thurmes, P. J., & Coleman, E. (1998). Anodyspareunia, the unacknowledged sexual dysfunction: A validation study of painful receptive anal intercourse and its psychosexual concomitants in homosexual men. *Journal of Sex and Marital Therapy, 24,* 281–292.

Schwartz, A. E. (1998). Sexual subjects: Lesbians, gender, and psychoanalysis. New York: Routledge.

Shernoff, M. (1999, March/April). Monogamy and gay men. When are open relationships a therapeutic option? *Networker,* 63–71.

Slater, S., & Mencher, J. (1991). The lesbian family life cycle: A contextual approach. *American Journal of Orthopsychiatry, 61,* 372–382.

Tiefer, L. (1997). The medicalization of sexuality: Conceptual, normative, and professional issues. *Annual Review of Sex Research, 7,* 252–282.

Von Foerster, H. (1981). *Observing systems.* Seaside, CA: Intersystems Publications.

Von Glasersfeld, E. (1984). An introduction to radical constructivism. In P. Watzlawick (Ed.), *The invented reality: How do we know?* (pp. 17–40). New York: Norton.

Yarhouse, M. A. (1998). When clients seek treatment for same-sex attraction: Ethical issues in the "right to choose" debate. *Psychotherapy, 35,* 248–259.

eleven

A Catalytic Approach to Brief
Sex Therapy

J. Scott Fraser and Andy Solovey

L AWRENCE AND TINA HAD BEEN ENGAGED for nearly a year, and their wedding day was a month away. Lawrence had recently lost all interest in sex, and thus they sought therapy with a sense of urgency. During the past month they had been interlocked in an intense conflict over sex, with no resolution. Like most couples, they had revealed their sex histories early in their courtship; they had both appreciated the openness of these discussions and had shared many details. As the wedding drew nearer, Lawrence suddenly became uncomfortable when he and Tina were making love. He explained that during their previous sex-history discussions, he had formed mental images of what Tina looked like when she was with former lovers. Recently, these images had begun to enter his head when he and Tina were making love. He had tried to deal with this on his own by telling himself that these ideas were silly. However, his attempts were futile; he simply would feel himself turn off whenever he and Tina started to become intimate.

When Tina discovered Lawrence's distress and asked him what was wrong, he reluctantly confessed and then asked Tina to describe more of what she had done with other lovers, wondering if she did things with the others that she hadn't done with him. Feeling very uncomfortable, Tina tried to brush these questions off, but this led Lawrence to secretly conclude that she had more of a past than she was revealing. When frustrated with her, the word *whore* popped into his head. He tried turning his anger into sarcastic remarks, but this brought out more defensiveness in Tina, which, in turn, inspired more suspicions, not only of Tina's past, but also of her present.

They came to therapy with several concerns. Tina truly loved Lawrence but was afraid that he had a serious emotional problem. Lawrence realized that he was being irrational; however, try as he might, he was unable to stop the images of Tina with other sex partners. Conversations had only made things worse. Both admitted that they were emotionally and physically exhausted from staying up into the early morning on most nights, trying to resolve their problem. They were hoping that the therapist could help them get out of this "downward spiral," so they could get on with enjoying their relationship and wedding.

Alicia and Dave appeared for therapy with what they thought was an unusual problem—male frigidity. They reported that after 10 years of marriage, Dave had become completely uninterested in sex. He hadn't approached Alicia in six months, and he found excuses not to have sex when she made advances toward him. Dave was puzzled by his lack of responsiveness, as Alicia was extremely attractive, worked out regularly to stay in shape, and was wonderful with their two children. The couple did not argue or fight, although there had been a growing tension over Dave's lack of sexual interest in Alicia.

They initiated therapy after a discussion in which Dave had revealed that he was questioning the possibility that he had fallen out love with Alicia. Considering her more friend than lover, he was spending more time at work. In separate conversations with the therapist, Dave denied that he was having an affair or was interested in other women. Alicia suspected that because Dave was not having sex at home, he must be "getting it someplace else."

Nadia didn't like sex. Married to her husband, Ivan, for nearly 13 years, and mother of their two young boys, ages four and five, she felt numb when they made love. Throughout their marriage she had tried to meet Ivan's needs; however, lately he was becoming increasingly frustrated with her over her lack of desire. Complaining that they did not have sex frequently enough, Ivan didn't like it when Nadia would "just lay there."

Nadia agreed that she wasn't interested in lovemaking and that Ivan was right about the frequency issue. Given her responsibilities with the children, she had been more tired lately, and, consequently, she was having more difficulty forcing herself to have sex with her husband. Not having had intercourse in more than six months, Nadia said that as far as she was concerned, she could live just fine without sex; she loved her children very much and Ivan was a good husband who treated her well. If anything, she felt sympathy for his plight. However, several weeks earlier, they had had an argument about sex, during which Ivan threatened divorce if Nadia didn't get "her" problem solved. This was especially upsetting for Nadia because Ivan had never threatened to leave her before. Ivan always went by his word, so Nadia knew that if she didn't do something, he was likely to leave. Nadia consulted her gynecologist, who, unable to find a medical problem, referred her for psychotherapy.

Had the couples described in these vignettes gone to a sex therapist in the 1950s or 60s, they would have probably found themselves involved in long-term psychodynamic work, with their therapist going in search of the underlying causes of their sexual difficulties. Had they simply consulted some sex manuals, they probably would have encountered prescriptive techniques, heterosexual assumptions, and the idea that foreplay is a prerequisite to insertion and orgasm for both partners (the closer to simultaneous the better)—the universally desired end (Apfelbaum, 2001). The manuals, implicitly suggesting that sexual contact is a "performance" to be judged, would have inadvertently heightened the couples' performance anxiety.

Had the couples gone to a sex therapist in the 1970s, 80s, or 90s, they would probably have worked with someone influenced by Masters and Johnson's pioneering and widely influential work, *Human Sexual Inadequacy* (1970). As a result, their time in therapy would have been much briefer, and it would have been organized much differently. Their therapist would have known much about their sexual response cycles (Masters & Johnson, 1966), and he or she would have assumed that their difficulties were probably based on performance anxiety. As Masters and Johnson put it, "Fear of inadequacy is the greatest known deterrent to effective sexual functioning" (1970, p. 12).* The therapist would have had several techniques at his or her disposal—including "avoiding goal directedness," "sensate focus exercises," "intercourse prohibitions," "nondemand pleasuring," "receptive kissing," "start-stop methods," "squeeze techniques," "masturbation training and self-pleasuring," and "vaginal dilators"—and one or more of these might have been helpful in resolving their problems.

---

* Masters and Johnson (1970) themselves inadvertently played into these fears (among other problems) by the very title of their work, which focused on *inadequacy* rather than on difficulties or problems, assuming that there was some tacit norm of adequacy.

However, it is possible that the therapist's drive toward brevity and efficiency, along with his or her assumptions and biases, might have only exacerbated the couples' distress.

Despite the many improvements to sex therapy offered by Masters and Johnson and others, current approaches are still burdened with significant problems. Peggy Kleinplatz (2001) articulated a telling critique:

- There is no unifying theoretical base for sex therapy.
- Sex therapists' fundamental assumptions are laden with sexual myths and stereotypes (e.g., about gender and "normalcy").
- Current sex therapy practices are based on gender-biased, phallocentric, and heterosexist assumptions. For example, rapid ejaculation in males is seen as a serious problem, whereas rapid orgasm in females is seen as reason for celebration (Reiss, 1990).
- Sex therapy's basic conception of sexuality remains biologically based, rather than offering equal attention to personal and interpersonal processes, cultural norms, and gender bias.
- The field continues to focus on body parts, rather than on the persons attached to them.
- Sex therapists are least successful where the greatest needs are— in problems related to desire.

We concur with these criticisms. The sex therapy field has, historically, paid too little attention to cultural, contextual, theoretical, and interpersonal competence. As Apfelbaum (2000) pointed out, the societal enthusiasm that has greeted the introduction of Viagra highlights a continued emphasis on sustained erections. Delayed ejaculation is considered a blessing, enabling sustained intercourse rather than the troubling dilemma it can often present for those who experience it. Sex for pleasure is left out of the picture, in favor of intercourse-based, orgasm-mandated acts. Sex therapy writers rarely address the positive ways of expressing joyful and passionate sexuality or consider that many men and women prefer same-sex partners.

The treatments of vaginismus or erectile dysfunction mark two additional examples of this focus on performance. The fact that vaginal dilators are used with nearly 100% success to eventually enable intercourse is, on the one hand, good news. However, this news also supports the myth that intercourse is the ultimate desirable goal. The target of treatment is a set of parts in disrepair, and the context for the problem remains irrelevant. Similarly, the treatment for erectile dysfunction tends to be on the penis, with frequency and firmness of erections taking precedence over understanding the contextual pressure of performance on demand. When the focus of treatment is on techniques to enhance performance, clients aren't given an opportunity to discover multiple ways of being in relationships or to understand the contexts in which sex disappoints them.

Too often, sex researchers and sex therapists have (literally) put on the white coat of medical lab researchers to assume an air of medical objectivity and neutrality in their work, to desensationalize their focus on sexuality, and to gain credibility for their research grants. In doing so, they not only have lost the broader contexts of sexuality, but also have overlooked the pure passion and pleasure that sexuality offers. Perhaps this has contributed to the field's limited success in helping clients presenting with low desire* to find the erotic intimacy and fulfillment necessary to fuel their sexuality.

In the face of such critiques, sex therapy appears to be caught in a cul-de-sac, where disjointed and ungrounded techniques are atheoretically applied in service of traditionally defined and medically driven performance criteria. This chapter offers a way out of this dead end. Drawing on the insights and practices of the strategic and systemic brief therapies, as well as the metatheories that have influenced them, we present a "catalytic approach" to brief sex therapy that honors the complexities and particular passions of our clients and their partners, attending not only to their struggles with performance, but also to their levels of desire. This is done with a contextual sensitivity to their cultural understandings, as well as to their sexual identities and expressions.

CATALYTIC BRIEF THERAPY

Before we can describe our approach to sex therapy, we must first explain our brief therapy foundations. We have been significantly influenced by both the strategic model of the Mental Research Institute (MRI) (Fisch, Weakland, & Segal, 1982; Nardone & Watzlawick, 1993; Watzlawick, 1976, 1984; Watzlawick, Weakland, & Fisch, 1974; Weakland, Fisch, Watzalwick, & Bodin, 1974) and the solution-focused model advanced by the Brief Therapy Center (de Shazer, 1982, 1985, 1988, 1991, 1994; de Shazer et al., 1986) and others (O'Hanlon, 1987; O'Hanlon & Martin, 1992; O'Hanlon & Weiner-Davis, 1989; Walter & Peller, 1992).

---

* Years ago, most clients presenting with this problem were women. However, more recently the proportion of males and females presenting with low desire has become essentially equal (Apfelbaum, 2000).

Although many would suggest that MRI and solution-focused approaches to brief therapy should be considered separate models, others have strongly argued that they are best considered two variations of the same process-based orientation (Fraser, 1995; Presbury, Echterling, & McKee, 2002; Quick, 1996). Adopting the latter perspective, we use the term "catalyst" to refer to a blending of the two (Cummings, 1995; Fraser, Morris, Smith, & Solovey, 2001, 2002).

A catalytic approach is organized with a simple focus—to introduce a small but significant shift in the relationship interactions or descriptions around a problem, and then to amplify the subsequent ripples in the system to foster change. Like MRI therapists, we view problems as vicious cycles of well-meaning attempts to solve a perceived difficulty. When the attempted solutions don't work, people tend to try them again and again, which makes the difficulty itself worse, or in fact *becomes* the problem.

Our basic interventions involve finding or creating significant exceptions to the problem pattern, or finding or creating small but significant differences in the vicious cycle of the problem. The first step involves identifying the vicious cycle pattern around the described problem. Like MRI therapists, we then initiate new action by redirecting solution attempts or reframing the problem. Like solution-focused therapists, we also identify and amplify already-occurring exceptions to the problem pattern and build upon them to support change.

Both components of the catalytic approach seek to introduce shifts in the action or conceptualization of the interaction around the identified problem. In this chapter, we describe some of the major ways brief therapists introduce such shifts in the "doing" or the "viewing" of the problem, but first we must elaborate on two metatheoretical ideas that inform this way of working—the systemic concept of *second-order change* and the social constructionist notions of *the coevolution and relativity of reality*, or *second-order reality*.

Second-Order Change

Although the concepts of first- and second-order change are based on rather complex theoretical premises (Watzlawick et al., 1974), they can be explained quite simply. *First-order change* refers to change within the normal definitions, understandings, premises, rules, and practices of a given system. It may be described as change in frequency, intensity, location, duration, and so on of a given practice or action.

For example, a man experiencing difficulties in attaining and maintaining an erection may (along with his partner or partners) initiate a wide variety of actions that would fall under the heading of "first-order change." He and his partner(s) might, for example,

- try to have sex more frequently, while rating his "erection success";
- try to avoid or reduce sexual interactions, thus reducing the frustrating potential of "failure";
- try harder to produce and sustain his erections, while closely attending to the "success" of their efforts in terms of hard penises.

All such solution attempts are first-order changes that either maintain the status quo or exacerbate the very difficulty that the client and his partner(s) are trying to resolve. Based on the shared assumption that the way to solve the problem is to try harder and to attend closely to success and failure, the solutions themselves become the problem. With success measured by the degree to which a sustained erection facilitates an orgasm by the man, his partner, or both of them, the man will be caught up in performance anxiety and continual distraction from the intimacy and passion that leads to arousal.

Second-order change is a change of the premises, definitions, assumptions, practices, and traditions of a given system of relationships. It most often represents a counterintuitive stepping out—or a *reversal*—of the commonly held ideas on the nature of a situation and its logical and reasonable solutions. It has thus often been described as *paradoxical* or *ironic* (Fraser, 1984). Such change tends to alter the premises or corollaries of a given system or, building upon them, to evolve new, different, or opposite solutions.

The man with erectile difficulties could experience a second-order change in many different ways:

- He might question whether his difficulty was actually a problem, or simply a reflection of other circumstances, such as reduced interest in his sexual partner(s) or their sexual practices. In this case, there would be little reason to expect firm and sustained erections.
- He might realize that his difficulty was situational—a result, say, of fatigue, worry, distraction, or illness—rather than an indication of a more severe problem. This could allow him to stop trying to remedy the situation, thus reducing the very pressure and distress that was precluding resolution.
- In an effort to learn more about what was going on, he and his partner(s) might purposefully try to make him lose his erections.

Many of Masters and Johnson's most effective interventions—from "sensate focus" techniques to giving directions for going slow and not engaging in intercourse—introduce the possibility for second-order change. For example, in male-female couples, the therapist reverses compulsions for male direction by putting the woman equally or more in charge of portions of nondemanding pleasuring, or start-stop approaches to rapid ejaculation. The compulsion to reciprocate is reversed in the exercises of receptive kissing and nondemanding pleasuring. And redirecting women away from attempting to achieve orgasm and toward self-pleasuring often reverses their difficulty in reaching orgasm.

The Co-evolution and Relativity of Reality

Both MRI and solution-focused therapists have been significantly influenced by the constructivist and social constructionist position that all of our ideas and constructs are individually and interactively created; they aren't floating "out there" as truths to be discovered. Constructivism (Bateson, 1972; Gergen, 1985, 1991, 1992; Watzlawick, 1976, 1984) refers to the philosophical and epistemological viewpoint that individuals co-create their views of reality through interacting with the world. Social constructionism (Gergen, 1985, 1994; Hoyt, 1994; Mahoney, 1995; McNamee & Gergen, 1992; Neimeyer, 1993; Neimeyer & Feixas, 1990; Neimeyer & Mahoney, 1995) builds upon the constructivist premise by emphasizing the influence of the social context on the making of meaning.

These postmodern understandings emphasize that all interactions should be considered in terms of the contexts of language and culture (Gergen, 1991, 1994). Thus, our ideas of gender roles, sexuality, and normative sexual practices, for example, must be considered within the individual and cultural assumptions from which they have evolved. As the MRI group (Watzlawick, 1976; Watzlawick, et al., 1974) noted, any given action or situation can be described and understood within any number of useful realities or frames of reference. These frames, which both enable and constrain possibilities, are applied not only by clients, but also by therapists and theoreticians.

Such a recognition invites us to examine our implicit assumptions on sexuality and normative practices, reminding us that there are many entirely positive ways of defining and expressing sexuality that don't fall within culturally dominant norms. Further, if all views of reality are created through social interaction and the use of language, then they can co-evolve in new ways through interaction with therapists and homework with partners. Slight shifts in interaction with therapists and others can have watershed effects in altering the path of formerly problematic patterns.

Influenced by these ideas, catalytic brief therapists attend to, respect, and accept their clients' language and conceptual frames (Fisch et al., 1982; Nardone & Watzlawick, 1993; Watzlawick, 1976, 1978; Watzlawick et al., 1974; Weakland et al., 1974), creating pathways to change with interventions such as the following.

Restraining Change

Restraining clients from moving too quickly, or prohibiting them from directly attempting their desired goal, is often a second-order change in and of itself. Catalytic brief therapists employ both "soft restraints," where they give clients the directive to "go slow" in their attempts to rush headlong into some resolution, and "hard restraints," which involve either prohibiting a goal-oriented action or offering challenges to clients.

For example, a catalytic brief therapist may, not unlike Masters and Johnson, recommend that clients refrain from engaging in intercourse or other kinds of sexual interaction. When the couples "slip up" and attempt or successfully engage in their desired sexual pleasure, the therapist may cautiously celebrate their unexpected success. When their slip-up doesn't turn out well, the therapist can use their experience to reinforce the go-slow message.

Normalizing

This intervention attempts to put clients at greater ease by contextualizing their difficulties as normal reactions, given the constraints of their situations. Allowing clients to relax their often-pressured efforts to solve a perceived difficulty, normalizing helps them depathologize themselves and whatever they are struggling with. Sex therapists often accomplish much the same thing through psychoeducation, outside readings, and direct explanations.

Framing, Reframing, and Deframing

Framing involves placing a person, situation, action, or problem in a particular context. Reframing involves putting the same person, situation, action, or problem in an alternate but equally sensible and often more useful context. Deframing refers to deconstructing the context of a particular frame of reference to eliminate it as a cause for a problem, challenge its absolute reality base, or simply point out that it is but a point of view.

Positioning

Catalytic brief therapists adopt a position relative to their clients that is designed to facilitate therapeutic change. They might take a position of "cautious optimism," a "one-down" position, or a position that is significantly different from that of the clients or "helpful" others.

Prescribing Symptoms

Symptom prescription involves asking clients to engage purposefully in some variation of the described problem behaviors, allowing the therapist to learn how they think, act, or react during the problematic cycle, or to learn more about what brings the problem on or what makes it worse. Such prescriptions make the problem pattern less "automatic" or less out of the clients' control.

Predicting Difficulties or Relapses

This technique is often used to deflect clients from being discouraged at perceived setbacks or to encourage them to consolidate their gains by reencountering old perceived dangers. For example, clients might be warned that their first attempts at a new sexual exercise or technique is unlikely to produce instant success or pleasure and that the main objective is to learn something about themselves or their partner. Once they've achieved greater intimacy, they might be asked to see if they can reignite one of their old struggles. If they fail to fight, they further solidify their new patterns. If they succeed at fighting, they learn in what ways they are still vulnerable to the old pulls.

Finding and Amplifying Exceptions, Differences, and Positive Solutions

Once desired goals are identified, clients and therapists jointly look for times in the past and present when the problem hasn't happened. This process of searching for positives and identifying how they've come about is itself a second-order change, a reversal of the common client process of focusing only on problem-saturated stories. As exceptions to the sexual difficulty are identified, the contingencies surrounding them can be identified, and these positives may then be amplified, creating successive approximations of the desired goals.

Adopting a Goal-Oriented Future Position

Catalytic brief therapists help clients identify small, achievable, and relevant goals that are action-oriented and observable. The more clients orient toward a possible future, the more successful they become at realizing it.

With the theoretical framework of our catalyst approach established, we'd now like to discuss some cases. The first two demonstrate our method of working with clients who have medical concerns; the following three further elaborate on the vignettes presented at the beginning of the chapter, illustrating a way of dealing with level-of-desire problems.

"MEDICAL" PROBLEMS

As noted in the first section of the chapter, sex therapy has recently been critiqued for becoming overly biological in its approach to sexual problems and their resolution. Hormone therapies, surgical procedures, and medication have been seen as so successful that clients, physicians, and therapists have begun to view these paths to treatment as the ultimate brief therapy for sexual difficulties. This is despite recent resolutions by world health bodies, who recommend combined medical and psychosocial treatments even when biological interventions are most strongly indicated (Rosen, 2000). For brief therapy to be successful, therapists have a critical responsibility to approach *all* problems within the context of the clients' relationships and worldviews.

Beth and Tom came to therapy complaining that even Viagra hadn't helped Tom with his sexual performance problems. Married for seven years, the couple had had a mutually satisfying sex life until the past year. This was Tom's second marriage and Beth's first; his first wife had left him for another man she'd met at work.

Tom seemed to have lost the ability to have or maintain erections, and he had recently stopped initiating sex or responding to Beth's advances. Their family physician had prescribed Viagra; however, Tom stopped using it when he found it to be inconsistent and rather strange and unnatural.

Two years earlier, Beth had quit her job as a secretary and returned to college to finish her bachelor's degree. Tom, the owner of an auto mechanic shop, thought that perhaps Beth's involvement with her studies had prevented them from paying more attention to their sexual relationship. If so, he would just wait it out until she was finished. Beth was distressed, fearing that either he had some physical problem or he no longer found her sexually attractive. When they had tried sexual encounters, they both had quickly responded to the first signs of an erection, rushing to insertion and attempts at intercourse. These efforts had all ended in failure, and Tom had withdrawn still more.

Respecting the couple's concern that there was some biological basis for their problem, the lead therapist, our colleague Mary Talen, invited a physician (who was also a family therapist) to consult with them. His work-ups revealed some vascular difficulties that had probably initiated some of Tom's erection problems. The couple was relieved to learn of this, but they were also concerned, given that Viagra hadn't worked.

Mary and her colleague saw, in addition to Tom's biological condition, three other interrelated problems potentially contributing to the couple's difficulty. First, Beth's going back to college had resulted in her both withdrawing from Tom and potentially surpassing him in education and aspirations. Second, the couple had become locked in a vicious cycle of demanding and withdrawing. And third, overfocusing on the state of Tom's erections, they had pressed toward intercourse whenever they were apparent.

The therapists recognized that their interventions needed to attend to the biological component of Tom's condition, honor each of their views on sexuality and on each other, and reverse the demand/withdraw cycle. Working within Tom's worldview, they used metaphors of auto repair and maintenance, suggesting that he indeed needed a "new transmission" when it came to enjoying and having sex with his wife. However, he certainly needed instructions from his own "mechanics," or physicians, on what to expect of the new transmission and how exactly to break it in so he could eventually resume the pleasure of the driving experience.

Mary and her colleague told the couple to "slow down" when it came to having sex, avoiding intercourse for the time being. Tom was to learn how to utilize the effects of Viagra through masturbation and then gradually teach Beth what he had learned. In the past, the couple had found each other most attractive when they went out with friends and flirted with each other. The therapists thus asked them to go out on dates with other couples and look for each other's secret flirtations. Beth and Tom would be a little rusty, but it was important to get the "car back on the road." As they got aroused, they were to restrict themselves to some gradual pleasuring exercises, having intercourse only if they absolutely couldn't abstain.

Within the next three weeks, Tom had adjusted to using the Viagra, he and Beth had made time to socialize, and they not only had learned more about each other's pleasure, but also had rediscovered both intimacy and intercourse. By reversing the couple's solution attempts, the therapists were able to resolve Tom's biologically based difficulty and help put the couple's relationship back on a firm foundation.

Couples often hope that there are biological causes and cures for their sexual difficulties, but this is often not the case. Bob and Cheri had enjoyed a passionate sexual relationship until moving in with each other, at which point, much to Cheri's puzzlement and dismay, Bob started to sexually withdraw. He, and all the other men in her life, had always found her "hot," so Cheri figured that he must be experiencing a testosterone deficiency. When this proved not to be the case, they came for therapy, with Bob feeling singled out and accused of being the one with the problem.

The therapist, again Mary Talen, had the couple share some of their sexual history. Bob, when he was young, had walked in on his father crossdressing. After that, he'd strongly affirmed his own heterosexuality in vigorous sexual relationships with women, while remaining sensitive to what might happen to him in a long-term committed relationship. Cheri had a history of drug abuse and prostitution, during which she'd come to believe that her main value was her sexual attractiveness to men.

Mary normalized the changes the couple had been experiencing, mentioning the transition in their living situation and pointing out how it had kicked off a problematic spiral. This reframing helped them attach new meanings to their recent difficulties, allowing them to simultaneously take a step back and draw closer to each other. Bob told Cheri that it was her love of life that made him want to be with her, and she told him that he was the strongest and truest man she'd ever been with. They reaffirmed each other's attractiveness and acknowledged the stresses of moving in with each other.

Mary asked them to make lists of what each wanted to retain of their separateness, while evaluating what they wanted together. During this time, they were to refrain from sexual contact and reinitiate dating, only returning to lovemaking as their transition to living together settled in. These gentle changes gradually got their sexual relationship back on track.

LEVEL OF DESIRE PROBLEMS

As noted earlier, several recent sources have critiqued mainstream sex therapy for not having an adequate way of treating what has now become the most frequent sexual complaint in the offices of sex therapists; differences in desire among partners (Apfelbaum, 2000, 2001; Kleinplatz, 2001). Indeed, "low sexual desire" has been called the sexual dysfunction of the 1990s (Pridal & LoPiccolo, 2000), affecting men as often as women and both heterosexual and same-sex couples.

As we return to the opening vignettes, notice how deframing "low sexual desire," shifting the pattern of relationships, and disrupting solution patterns become the keys to "reawakening desire."

Recall that Lawrence, Tina's fiancé, had lost all interest in sex after learning of her prior sexual experiences. The more he thought of her with other men, the more distracted and distressed he became. When Tina realized why he was withdrawing from intimacy, she was reluctant to share any more information with him. This aroused his suspicions, and they were off on a "downward spiral."

With accuser-defender vicious cycles, one partner typically accuses the other of some type of infidelity. The defender denies the infidelity, but does so in a tentative or defensive manner, which fuels the insecurity of the accuser, leading to more accusations, followed by more defensive denials, and so on. Lawrence's accusations had begun with concerns about Tina's former sex partners, but they'd quickly escalated to speculations about current betrayals as an explanation for her loss of interest in sex.

Catalytic brief therapists seek to interrupt this type of cycle, helping the accuser to stop accusing, or helping the defender to respond in a more definitive way to the accusations. In this case, the therapist, Scott, selected the latter approach. Honoring Tina's concerns about Lawrence's emotional well-being and respecting her frame of reference, he sought to use her language while reframing the situation and normalizing Lawrence's behavior.

Scott explained that the couple had fallen into what some might refer to as a "gender trap," which was being maintained by their deep love and strong passion. Deep love often brings out primitive emotions and a need to mark the relationship as something very special and exclusive. Men and women sometimes do this in different ways. A competitive man may want to be viewed by his woman as the greatest of all lovers. He feels secure, knowing that his virility and skill will keep his woman from wandering, given that the sexual experience he offers is beyond comparison.

In contrast, a passionate woman may like to mark the importance of her relationship by forgetting previous sexual experiences and pretending that her man is her only real lover. Lawrence and Tina's conversation about the past, although understandable, was interfering with their ability to complete their somewhat separate tasks before the wedding. The more that Lawrence brought up the subject of previous relationships, the more Tina was reminded of the past that she was trying to forget. On the other hand, her tentative responses were not providing Lawrence with the assurance that he was seeking.

Scott told Lawrence that he could offer him a strategy for dealing with his unsettling questions, but before proceeding he wanted to answer any questions they might want to pose to him. Tina asked how he could possibly have known exactly what was going on inside of her. Lawrence said he hadn't realized what Tina had been trying to do. Scott acknowledged these reactions, explaining that "love makes us all a bit crazy."

Scott then turned to Tina and explained that there was a good "antidote" for Lawrence's condition. The next time Lawrence asked her about her past, she could simply give him a big Hollywood-style kiss, regardless of where they were—the mall, a family gathering, in bed, or in a restaurant. After the kiss, she should tell him the truth, which was that she didn't want to think about sex with anyone but him, that he was the only one she was interested in.

Upon hearing this, Lawrence burst out laughing. Scott looked at Tina, and, with a smile, told her to "make sure to give Lawrence some tongue with that kiss." They both left the session laughing, excited about the "antidote."

Lawrence and Tina were married on schedule. When they came back for a follow-up interview after the wedding, Tina said that she had followed the prescription once. Lawrence had laughed and dropped the subject, and he hadn't brought it up since. With their sexual relationship back on track, they moved on to discuss other challenges, such as where they were going to live and when they were going to start a family.

By reframing Lawrence and Tina's interaction and by using humor to invite passion, Scott was able to help them interrupt their vicious cycle, moving them beyond jealousy and fear.

Alicia and Dave, the second couple presented at the beginning of the chapter, were also trapped in an escalating cycle, in their case between a pursuer and a distancer.

Earlier in their 10-year marriage, Dave had had what Alicia considered to be a voracious sexual appetite. No longer. They hadn't made love in six months, and Dave seemed to have lost all interest in sex. He considered Alicia more a friend than a lover, and he was concerned that he had fallen out of love with her. Alicia, in turn, suspected Dave was having an affair, despite his sincere denials to her and Andy, the therapist. Their relationship was becoming more and more polarized.

Andy made note of how hard Alicia had been working to attract Dave's interest. She had waited up for him when he was late from work, arranged candle-light dinners, worn sexy lingerie to bed, given him long suggestive kisses, and asked him about what he was thinking and feeling about her. When he'd failed to respond in an assuring manner, Alicia had become tearful.

The more eager Alicia had been for Dave's attention, the more he'd withdrawn, at one point talking about suicide. Convinced he was suffering from depression, he'd obtained an antidepressant prescription from his family doctor, but the medication didn't change the problems with the relationship. He felt especially guilty that Alicia was going out of her way to make the relationship work. Wondering what would happen if his feelings for her didn't return, he considered the possibility that he would have to leave his marriage.

Pursuit-flight cycles may kick off when something tips the delicate balance of initiation in a couple's relationship. When one partner, feeling unwanted, pursues the other partner for affection and validation, it can inspire attempts for him or her to flee or withdraw. Just as pursuit stimulates flight, flight stimulates insecurity and more pursuit. The fleeing partner may read this cycle as a sign that they are no longer in love. If this fear is spoken, the situation is further complicated and may lead to an extramarital affair or divorce.

By the time Dave and Alicia entered therapy, their cycle had become a full-time endeavor. Alicia, spending most of her day dwelling on her fears of Dave's leaving her, had quit her part-time job to concentrate on the relationship. Dave was also devoting considerable time to worrying about his marriage, and his job performance was declining.

Andy's therapeutic objective was to interrupt this cycle by having one or both partners stop or even reverse their part in the cycle. If Alicia were to stop pursuing Dave, he might rediscover his interest in her. Alternatively, if Dave were to reverse his participation and pursue Alicia, she might feel less compelled to pursue *him*.

Dave didn't consider himself capable of making changes, given his loss of feelings, so Andy met with him separately, validating the difficulty of his position and praising his willingness to stay in the relationship. Andy reframed the nature of long-term relationships, talking about how sexual interest naturally waxes and wanes, and normalizing his loss of interest.

Meeting alone also with Alicia, Andy validated her concerns and assured her that Dave's lack of interest did not mean she was unattractive. He explained that sometimes people withdraw in relationships when their partner becomes too predictable or loses some of the uniqueness and passion for life that originally drew them together. He wondered with Alicia about ways that she might make herself a bit more mysterious to Dave, while recapturing her own interests. They agreed that unpredictability should be expressed in subtle yet honest ways. Certainly, she wouldn't want to hurt him.

Alicia had a habit of kissing Dave at bedtime, telling him that she loved him and, when he didn't respond, asking him if he loved her. Because this had sparked recent arguments and bad feelings, Andy suggested that she could forget to kiss him or kiss him and forget to say that she loved him. She might also dress for bed in a way that downplayed her interest in sex. When Dave came home late, she might be so absorbed in some activity that Dave would have to seek *her* attention. Because the renewal of Dave's interest in her couldn't be forced, his free will would need to be given time to express itself by Alicia's getting more involved in her own life, going back to work or, as she was an avid reader, joining a book club.

The outcome of this shift did not appear until two sessions later. Initially, Alicia found it difficult to disengage from Dave in the way they'd discussed; Andy validated her struggle by acknowledging the challenge of trying something different when the stakes are very high. Disengagement came easier after this, as did reengaging in the things that interested her. At the next session, Alicia described what happened after a few nights of not giving Dave a kiss. Coming home late and finding Alicia reading a book, he tried to get her attention. However, she really was absorbed in what she was doing, and when she stayed engaged in it, Dave felt uneasy. Later that evening, he initiated sex.

Reengaged in her own life again, Alicia returned to work. She continued to feel more energy and assurance of her love for Dave and of his for her. Dave reported that his feelings for Alicia were starting to come back, and soon their sexual relationship rekindled. They both admitted that they had fallen back in love with each other. In essence, they had gotten out of each other's way, allowing themselves to rediscover each other.

Sometimes low desire is related to a history of sexual abuse. Such was the case with Nadia, who, you may recall, felt either numb or nothing at all when having sex with her husband, Ivan. Not having had sex in six months didn't bother Nadia, but Ivan was threatening divorce, so, after her gynecologist had told her that there was nothing physically wrong, she came to Scott for help in solving "her" problem.

Nadia realized that saving her marriage would entail her having sex more often with Ivan, but until Scott asked, she hadn't considered the possibility of actually enjoying it. She said that if pleasure was possible, then, yes, she'd like to feel it.

In gathering a sex history, Scott asked about what the couple had tried to make sex a pleasurable experience. This discussion was initially difficult for Nadia, but she was eventually able to reveal some very important details. From ages 13 to 16, she was sexually assaulted frequently by an adult male cousin who was living with her family. Entering her bedroom and forcing intercourse on her, he threatened to hurt her if she ever told her parents.

She kept quiet, and the cousin continued to abuse her until he was killed in a car accident.

During these abuse episodes, Nadia would freeze up and go somewhere else in her head. She learned how to have sex without feeling like she was having it, but her cousin wasn't pleased with this. Trying to make her "get into the experience," he would tell her, while abusing her, how pretty or sexy she was, and he'd sometimes buy her sexy underwear and tell her to put it on.

After the death of her cousin, Nadia felt great relief. She started dating boys and became sexually active, but only because the boys seemed to like it. She continued to "go somewhere else," so for her, it was something of a "dead experience." Still, her lack of interest gave her a sense of power. While guys were losing control over her, she was able to remain cool and collected.

When Nadia met Ivan in her early twenties, his solidity and genuine caring for her made her feel secure. She wasn't sure if she ever really "loved him," because she never felt romantic and her feelings about sex had remained unchanged. Because of Ivan's disappointment in her lack of interest, she made an effort to warm up to the idea, reading romance novels that contained sexual material. They might have done the trick, had it not been for Ivan's habits in bed. When making love, he liked to talk to her and tell her how sexy she was. He'd also brought her sexy underwear, hoping it might spark her interest.

Nadia had told Ivan about being abused, but, afraid she might upset him, she'd never given him the full details. She had asked him to stop talking during sex and to stop bringing home sexy underwear, but he hadn't really responded. Recognizing that he seemed to enjoy these activities, she'd decided to drop the subject and try to make the best of it.

After listening carefully to Nadia's story, Scott reframed her numbness as a "secret power" for disconnecting herself from her feelings of sexual pleasure. This was not only an appropriate way to have handled the sexual abuse, but it also showed a keen sense of inner wisdom: It was her way of fighting back. In essence, she'd been able to say, "You can take my body, but you can't really have sex with me."

Now, as an adult, Nadia had a new need—the need to discover the power of sexual pleasure in a trusting and loving marriage. Scott, expressing his hope that this could be accomplished, suggested that Ivan's involvement in therapy would make it possible for them all to work together on helping Nadia in this discovery. The dilemma was theirs as a couple, not simply hers.

Nadia thought she might be able to convince Ivan to come to the next session, but she was uncertain about how it would turn out, because he didn't believe in "shrinks." Scott normalized Ivan's skepticism as a common reaction among men. He then asked Nadia if it would be okay for him to spend some time trying to help Ivan understand the impact of the sexual abuse as a way of helping her experience sexual pleasure.

Nadia brought Ivan for the next session. In an effort to put him at ease, Scott thanked him for coming and explained his reasons for inviting him: "Nadia has told me about the sex problem that she and you are having. My goal is to help her to experience more sexual pleasure so that you can have a more enjoyable sex life." Brightening up, Ivan said he would do anything to help, and he affirmed Nadia's description of his talking to her while they were having sex and bringing her sexy underwear. Yes, she had told him not to do this, but he figured she was just being modest. Because all women want to know that they are beautiful and sexy, he thought that telling her would turn her on. And if she, with her nice figure, could see how good she looked in the underwear he bought her, maybe it would be enough to get her going.

Over the years, Ivan had become impatient with the whole process of sex, so he'd gotten to jumping into intercourse without much foreplay. This seemed to be what Nadia wanted. He loved her very much, he said, but although he had adjusted to her lack of interest in sex, the frequency of their lovemaking had recently gone to such a low level that he just couldn't handle it. He'd begun thinking that maybe he just wasn't sexy enough for Nadia and that she needed another man.

After carefully helping Ivan to unfold his side of the story, Scott reframed their dilemma, drawing on the information that he had gathered over the two sessions: "Ivan, the problem that Nadia is experiencing is not about your ability as a lover. As you know, Nadia was abused as a young girl. As part of that abuse she became turned off to sex. This is not at all uncommon for women who have been abused, and in fact Nadia's reaction was quite expected. This business of being turned off has to do with the mental associations that Nadia has about sex. Mental associations include her fantasies and a sense that these fantasies are pleasurable. Pleasurable fantasies within a very trusting relationship with you are what Nadia needs to feel turned on. Unfortunately, as a couple, in your efforts to solve this problem, you have done some things that reinforce Nadia's negative images of sex. They set off her triggers. You may not be aware of this, Ivan, but when Nadia was abused, the abuser talked to her and told her that she was pretty and sexy. He also brought her sexy underwear. I know that you have done something similar totally out of your love, but the problem is that these efforts may be too close to what happened to Nadia for her to stop the negative associations that she has with sex. I also know that Nadia's request to have sex without foreplay is well intended. She wants to please you and get the experience over with; however, this is also too close to what happened when she was abused."

Scott paused, and Ivan teared up and began to cry. Nadia, at Scott's request, placed her hand on Ivan, who said that he'd had no idea that his wife had been affected in this way. Scott explained that she had tried to protect him from her pain, which Ivan understood and appreciated.

Scott then proceeded to unfold a plan for therapy that included many elements of Masters and Johnson's work. He explained to Ivan that the course of treatment would involve a sacrifice from him. He was giving them an initial prohibition against intercourse while they engaged in a program of progressive pleasuring, and this could take a few months. It would be key that Nadia not engage in intercourse just to relieve his sexual tension, because this could reinforce her negative mental associations with sex. Masturbation would be perfectly appropriate, though, if he got too frustrated.

The couple's progressive pleasuring started with one-on-one talking, without touching, for 15 minutes a day, and it continued, with assignments given every two or three weeks, for sitting together and touching hands, then hair, and then face and other nonerogenous zones. They progressed to doing this without clothes on and then to giving massages, also without clothes. Scott stressed that Nadia should always take the lead so that she could feel in control and reverse the process that had brought on her negative sex images. She was to direct Ivan's hands when he was touching her and to practice touching him. Scott asked them to talk about which types of touches felt better and what they liked most. In subsequent sessions the three of them talked about the couple's attitudes and what kinds of sex they were most comfortable with.

Nadia began to enjoy sexual pleasure and sensation, but she also had an experience, for the first time in her life, of feeling intensely jealous. It came upon her as she watched Ivan talking to an attractive woman at church, and she didn't know what to make of it. Scott framed it as an indication of their budding romance, and he warned Ivan of the need to reassure Nadia of his love for her. Her jealousy meant that she was making herself vulnerable to him, and she would need protection so that she could continue opening up.

As a parallel development, Scott asked Nadia if she would feel comfortable exploring how to experience sexual stimulation, pleasure, and arousal on her own. She would be in control, and, eventually, she could share her discoveries with Ivan, thus opening a new sexual relationship together. After some hesitation, Nadia agreed to take some steps in this direction. She was referred to the book and video *Becoming Orgasmic* (Heiman & LoPiccolo, 1988) and asked simply to review the materials and consider what it might mean to her to open this part of herself back up. She made excellent use of the materials and exercises, using them to slowly explore her sensuality.

Scott eventually suggested that they were ready to take the step into intercourse. Recommending that Nadia be on top, Scott directed her to be the one to insert Ivan's erect penis into her vagina so that she could feel the power of eventually reducing it to a withering pulp.*

The couple were doing well when they returned for a follow-up a month later. Nadia was experiencing pleasure with sex (both on her own and with Ivan) and Ivan was no longer contemplating divorce. They had two concerns. First, Ivan had noticed that Nadia wasn't consistently having orgasms with him. Second, they were wondering whether it would be okay to have intercourse with Ivan on top. Scott offered some ideas: "Sex usually goes better when the objective is pleasure. Orgasms will happen sometimes and sometimes not for Nadia. Trying too hard can have the opposite effect for her. There are many ways for you to reach orgasm with each other. As Nadia continues to discover these herself, she can help to guide you in helping the two of you to experience this with each other. The mark of a good lover is the ability to nurture a pleasurable experience for one's partner. Unfortunately, the movies rarely get this right."

Regarding their second concern, Scott said they were free to have sex in any way that they chose, as long as it produced mutual pleasure. They could also trade off on initiating. Scott ended with a caution: "You have done a wonderful job of learning to make love. Even so, you should expect that sexual interest will be stronger at times and less strong at others." He invited the couple to check out the women's magazines at the grocery store, noting that they all include features on how to spice up your sex life. Apart from any useful ideas these articles might contain, they attest to the fact that *all* couples ebb and flow in sexual interest from time to time, even when sexual abuse is not a factor in a person's life. Nadia expressed her gratitude to Ivan for helping her to open herself to him and to allow her to discover her own true sensuality. Ivan cried.

---

* This suggestion, taken from a case made famous by Milton Erickson, reflected a reversal of the abuse situation.

Although the guiding ideas for this case, as for all of our work, derive from systemic and social constructionist theory, the interventions were similar to those used by mainstream sex therapists working with desire problems (Pridal & LoPiccolo, 2000) and issues of sexual abuse (Maltz, 2001a, b). What was different in this case, as in each of the others before it, was the therapist's close attention to first- and second-order change and the respect given to the relativity of realities in social relationships. Nadia and Ivan had been locked in a solution-generated problem cycle of well-meaning attempts to negotiate their sexual relationship. The more they'd struggled, the worse it had become. With their worldviews honored in a therapeutic setting, they were able to make small yet significant shifts in their ideas, knowledge, and solutions, initiating the progressive resolution to their shared difficulty.

A CATALYST FOR CHANGE IN SEX THERAPY

The "new sex therapy" has always been a relatively brief therapy, but it has been criticized for lacking an underlying theory. In this chapter, we articulated and illustrated the social constructionist and systemic ideas that influenced the development of the MRI and solution-focused schools, as we believe that they can offer sex therapy the theoretical foundation it has been lacking. A social constructionist view honors clients' contexts and traditions, while also acknowledging the influence of the therapist's background. Such an appreciation helps therapists avoid the tendency to perpetuate dominant and implicit sexual myths, while also avoiding associated gender-biased, phallocentric, and heterosexist assumptions.

Because the theoretical framework of a catalytic approach is *fundamentally systemic*, its biopsychosocial set consistently places people in the larger contexts of their relationships. Thus, even biologically based difficulties and interventions are framed within the clients' social and interpersonal relationships. Instead of focusing on parts (a criticism, you may remember, that has been leveled at mainstream sex therapy), a catalytic approach to sex therapy considers the context of relationships to be of crucial importance. As can be seen from the cases we've discussed, such contextual sensitivity proves very helpful when therapists are addressing couples' problems with desire. The nature of the dilemma becomes clearer, making available a number of effective interventions.

This chapter has been a blend of both theory and practice. The editors of this book, Shelley and Douglas, told us that they wanted to "get inside our heads and our hearts," to learn how we work from our point of view. This chapter demonstrates our thinking and our passion. We believe that therapists who practice without a guiding theory risk losing their direction and abdicating their professional responsibility. Alternatively, theory that isn't grounded in effective clinical practice is lifeless and useless.

As we have demonstrated, the innovations of traditional sex therapy can be integrated with those from MRI and solution-focused therapy. We believe that in bringing the two fields together, using systems and social constructionist ideas as the bridge, practitioners from both can be mutually enriched. The result is an exciting catalyst for effective brief therapy for sexual difficulties.

REFERENCES

Apfelbaum, B. (2000). Retarded ejaculation: A much misunderstood syndrome. In S. R. Leiblum & R. C. Rosen (Eds.), *Principles and practice of sex therapy* (3rd ed., pp. 205–241). New York: Guilford Press.

Apfelbaum, B. (2001). What the sex therapies tell us about sex. In P. J. Kleinplatz (Ed.), *New directions in sex therapy: Innovations and alternatives* (pp. 5–28). Philadelphia: Brunner-Routledge.

Bateson, G. (1972). *Steps to an ecology of mind.* New York: Aronson.

Cummings, N. A. (1995). Impact of managed care on employment and training: A primer for survival. *Professional Psychology: Research and Practice, 26*(1), 10–15.

de Shazer, S. (1982). *Patterns of brief family therapy.* New York: Guilford Press.

de Shazer, S. (1985). *Keys to solution in brief therapy.* New York: Norton.

de Shazer, S. (1988). *Clues: Investigating solutions in brief therapy.* New York: Norton.

de Shazer, S. (1991). *Putting difference to work.* New York: Norton.

de Shazer, S. (1994). *Words were originally magic.* New York: Norton.

de Shazer, S., Berg, I. K., Lipchick, E., Nunnally, E., Molnar, A., Gingerich, W., & Weiner-Davis, M. (1986). Brief therapy: Focused solution development. *Family Process, 25,* 207–222.

Fisch, R., Weakland, J. H., & Segal, L. (1982). *The tactics of change: Doing therapy briefly.* San Francisco: Jossey-Bass.

Fraser, J. S. (1984). Paradox and orthodox: Folie a deux? *Journal of Marital and Family Therapy, 10*(4), 361–372.

Fraser, J. S. (1995). Process, problems, and solutions in brief therapy. *Journal of Marital and Family Therapy, 21*(3), 265–279.

Fraser, J. S., Morris, M., Smith, D., & Solovey, A. (2001). Brief therapy in primary healthcare settings: A catalyst model. *Journal of Brief Therapy, 1*(1), 7–16.

Fraser, J. S., Morris, M., Smith, D., & Solovey, A. (2002). Applications of a catalyst model of brief therapy in a primary healthcare setting. *Journal of Brief Therapy, 1*(2), 131–140.

Gergen, K. J. (1985). The social constructionist movement in modern psychology. *American Psychologist, 40,* 266–275.

Gergen, K. J. (1991). *The saturated self: Dilemmas of identity in contemporary life.* New York: Basic.

Gergen, K. J. (1992). Toward a postmodern psychology. In S. Kvale (Ed.), *Psychology and postmodernism* (pp. 17–30). Newbury Park, CA: Sage.

Gergen, K. J. (1994). Exploring the postmodern: Perils or potentials? *American Psychologist, 49,* 412–416.

Heiman, J., & LoPiccolo, J. (1988). *Becoming orgasmic* (2nd ed.). Englewood Cliffs, NJ: Prentice Hall.

Hoyt, M. F. (Ed.). (1994). *Constructive therapies.* New York: Guilford Press.

Kleinplatz, P. J. (2001). *New directions in sex therapy: Innovations and alternatives*. Philadelphia: Brunner-Routledge.

Mahoney, M. J. (Ed.). (1995). *Cognitive and constructive psychotherapies: Theory, research, and practice*. New York: Springer.

Maltz, W. (2001a). Sex therapy with survivors of sexual abuse. In P. J. Kleinplatz (Ed.), *New directions in sex therapy: Innovations and alternatives* (pp. 258–278). Philadelphia: Brunner-Routledge.

Maltz, W. (2001b). *The sexual healing journey: A guide for survivors of sexual abuse* (Rev. ed.). New York: Harper Perennial.

Masters, W. H., & Johnson, V. E. (1966). *Human sexual response*. Boston: Little, Brown.

Masters, W. H., & Johnson, V. E. (1970). *Human sexual inadequacy*. New York: Little, Brown.

McNamee, S., & Gergen, K. J. (1992). *Therapy as social construction*. Newbury Park, CA: Sage.

Nardone, G., & Watzlawick, P. (1993). *The art of change*. San Francisco: Jossey-Bass.

Neimeyer, R. A. (1993). An appraisal of constructivist psychotherapies. *Journal of Consulting and Clinical Psychology, 61*, 221–234.

Neimeyer, R. A., & Feixas, G. (1990). Constructivist contributions to psychotherapy integration. *Journal of Integrative and Eclectic Psychotherapy, 9*, 4–20.

Neimeyer, R. A., & Mahoney, M. J. (Eds.). (1995). *Constructivism in psychotherapy*. Washington, D.C.: American Psychological Association.

O'Hanlon, W. H. (1987). *Taproots: Underlying principles of Milton Erickson's therapy and hypnosis*. New York: Norton.

O'Hanlon, W. H., & Martin, M. (1992). *Solution-oriented hypnosis: An Ericksonian approach*. New York: Norton.

O'Hanlon, W. H., & Weiner-Davis, M. (1989). *In search of solutions: A new direction in psychotherapy*. New York: Norton.

Presbury, J. H., Echterling, L. G., & McKee, J. E. (2002). *Ideas and tools for brief counseling*. Columbus, OH: Merrill Prentice Hall.

Pridal, C. G., & LoPiccolo, J. (2000). Multielement treatment of desire disorders: Integration of cognitive, behavioral, and systemic therapy. In S. R. Leiblum & R. Rosen (Eds.), *Principles and practice of sex therapy* (3rd ed., pp. 57–81). New York: Guilford Press.

Quick, E. K. (1996). *Doing what works in brief therapy: A strategic solution focused approach*. San Diego, CA: Academic Press.

Reiss, I. L. (1990). *An end to shame: Shaping our next sexual revolution*. New York: Prometheus.

Rosen, R. (2000). Medical and psychological interventions for erectile dysfunction. In S. R. Leiblum & R. Rosen (Eds.), *Principles and practice of sex therapy* (3rd ed.) (pp. 276–304). New York: Guilford Press.

Walter, J. L., & Peller, J. E. (1992). *Becoming solution focused in brief therapy*. New York: Norton.

Watzlawick, P. (1976). *How real is real?* New York: Random House.

Watzlawick, P. (1978). *The language of change: Elements of therapeutic communication*. New York: Norton.

Watzlawick, P. (Ed.). (1984). *The invented reality*. New York: Norton.

Watzlawick, P., Weakland, J. H., & Fisch, R. (1974). *Change: Principles of problem formation and problem resolution*. New York: Norton.

Weakland, J. H., Fisch, R., Watzlawick, P., & Bodin, A. M. (1974). Brief therapy: Focused problem resolution. *Family Process, 13*, 141–168.

twelve

"Don't Get Too Bloody Optimistic": John Weakland at Work

Wendel A. Ray and Barbara Anger-Díaz

INTERACTIONALLY FOCUSED FAMILY THERAPY was but a decade old in 1965 when Richard Fisch, influenced by the ideas of Don Jackson (1955, 1961), proposed the creation of the Brief Therapy Center (BTC) at the Mental Research Institute (MRI) (Fisch, 1965). With the exception of a small number of pioneers, particularly Harry Stack Sullivan, Gregory Bateson, Milton Erickson, Don Jackson, Jay Haley, and John Weakland, few clinicians or researchers had focused on how therapy could be made more effective and efficient.

The problem-formation, problem-resolution orientation set forth by the MRI Brief Therapy Team (Fisch et al., 1968; Fisch, Weakland, Watzlawick, & Bodin, 1972a, b; Watzlawick, Weakland, & Fisch, 1974; Weakland, Fisch, Watzlawick, & Bodin, 1974) is one of the most, if not *the* most, influential brief therapy approaches in use today (de Shazer, 1998; Trepper, 1995). A forerunner to postmodern, social constructionist approaches, the MRI Brief Therapy model evolved directly out of the cybernetic/ communication theory of human behavior set forth by Gregory Bateson and his team during the 1950s (Bateson, 1955; Bateson, Jackson, Haley, & Weakland, 1956; Jackson, 1957; Jackson & Weakland, 1961). Conceptually simple, the orientation takes seriously the idea that it is not so much the difficulties in living that bring people into therapy, but rather their ineffective efforts at resolving those difficulties. Their failed solution attempts inadvertently exacerbate and perpetuate the problem into irresolvable vicious cycles. It makes sense, then, that if the efforts being made to resolve the problem are interrupted, the problem will often dissipate on its own.

Nonnormative and nonpathologizing, the MRI model has demonstrated effectiveness with a wide variety of problems in living, from common marital and family difficulties to acute and chronic problems such as anxiety, substance abuse, delinquency, sexual problems, depression, eating problems, school and work difficulties, and severe emotional illness such as schizophrenia (Fisch, Weakland, & Segal, 1982; Watzlawick et al., 1974; Weakland & Ray, 1995; Weakland, Watzlawick, Fisch, & Bodin, 1974). The Palo Alto Group introduced a body of theoretical premises and clinical techniques that form the prototypical orientation from which most current family and brief therapy approaches derive. This prototype was developed over the past fifty years, originally in Bateson's research team, then in refinements crafted by Don Jackson during the first decade of the MRI, and more recently through advancements by the MRI Brief Therapy team. Fundamental MRI assumptions and practices have influenced present-day brief therapy approaches in the following ways:

- the application of cybernetic, information, and system theory to make contextual sense of human interaction;
- emphasis on the crucial influence of the therapist's perspective;
- the application of social constructionist assumptions to clinical work;
- attention to pragmatics (i.e., who does what when and to whom in the present);
- acceptance and utilization of the symptom and other client behaviors;
- attention to using the clients' language;
- the use of circular questioning both diagnostically and as an intervention;
- prescription of behavior at one order of abstraction to address the organization of the system at another order of abstraction;
- the use of relationship-focused hypothesizing, positive connotation, rituals, and tasks;
- attention to the implications of language, as evidenced in the intentional shift in verb tense from "to be" to "to seem";
- attention to the importance of the referring person.

These are but a few of the ways therapists and researchers at MRI have influenced present-day models of family and brief therapy practice. In addition, many of the technical advances now taken for granted in clinical practice—such as the use of the one-way mirror, audio and film recording of sessions for the purpose of later analysis, in-session and between-session tasks, and therapy teams and live supervision—were introduced by the Palo Alto Group. The implementation of these technical advances carries profound implications for how human problems in living are conceived and treated.

Among the therapists who have been part of the MRI Brief Therapy team over the years,[*] John Weakland was one of the most influential. Although a number of studies have featured analyses of first sessions or short segments of Weakland conducting therapy, a report of an entire therapy case from beginning to end has never before been published.

Using concepts derived from the interactional/communication theory and the brief therapy method Weakland helped to create, this chapter analyzes a successful five-session therapy that Weakland conducted in 1990. The case involved a man who was severely depressed and desperate because he could no longer attain and maintain an erection. Weakland supervised the editing of these five sessions into a two-hour composite film, the video and verbatim transcript of which provided the basis of this chapter.

The process and structure of the MRI Brief Therapy model is well documented in the literature (e.g., Fisch et al., 1982) and therefore will not be emphasized here. Instead, we will focus on some of the finer nuances, underlying logic, and rhetorical devices employed in Weakland's therapeutic method.[†]

First Session

John Weakland: We need to sort of start at ground level by asking, "What's the trouble that brings you here?"

Tom: I always feel like I have to go to the bathroom, but when I go, drops of my urine will come out, but it's like I never really feel like I have emptied my bladder.

---

[*] In addition to Richard Fisch, John Weakland, and Paul Watzlawick, the MRI Brief Therapy Team has included a number of leading contributors to family and brief therapy, such as Don Jackson, Jay Haley, and James Coyne. The team presently consists of Richard Fisch, Paul Watzlawick, Karin Schlanger, Barbara Anger-Díaz, Beth Martin, Joann Watkins, and Wendel Ray.

[†] Verbatim transcripts are of immeasurable value in analyzing interaction, yet they do not convey numerous aspects of discourse vital for understanding, such as timing, voice inflection, pace, intonation, and nonverbal behaviors. For controlled access to the original recordings, contact the MRI Brief Therapy Center, in Palo Alto, California.

John: Let me say first of all, before we go any further, if you have to stop
any time during a session feel free to do so.

From the outset, no assumptions about the nature of the difficulty are implied or imposed. Weakland frames the exchange as purposeful and oriented toward difficulties in the present. Intervention begins immediately in
response to Tom's initial description of the problem—the constant need to
go to the bathroom. Weakland's comment embodies basic tenets of the interactional approach: that one cannot not communicate, and its corollary,
that one cannot not influence (Jackson, 1965; Watzlawick, Beavin, &
Jackson, 1967). By immediately giving Tom permission to interrupt therapy any time he feels the need to go to the bathroom, Weakland accepts
Tom's premise and begins to work within the client's position or frame of
reference. Weakland's injunction is followed by an hour of Tom not having
to stop therapy to go to the bathroom. This sort of intervention was once
referred to as paradoxical (Weakland, 1960).

Tom: Okay. I've been to physicians authorized by my health plan at two
    different hospitals. They gave me different medications and that
    didn't seem to work at all.
John: Presumably, then, they've checked you out physically and don't see
    any physical cause for this?
Tom: Right. They've checked to see if there is any problem with my
    prostate, and there is nothing there. They checked me for sexually
    transmitted diseases and there doesn't seem to be anything. I've also
    tried various other means—a holistic doctor and a hypnotist. I also
    went to acupuncture for about two months but didn't feel that helped.
John: Okay, at any rate, you didn't see any benefit from that during the
    time you were going?
Tom: None at all. I've been extremely depressed by it. Nothing like this
    ever happened to me before. I've always felt I was in good health. It's
    affected my sex life in ways I didn't anticipate.

As would any competent therapist, Weakland makes certain Tom has
seen a physician to rule out physiological reasons for his urinary difficulty.
Tom then provides a review of some of the things he has done to resolve
the problem. The MRI brief therapy approach follows specific stages:

1.   Clearly define, in concrete terms, the exact nature of the problem.
2.   Determine for whom and in what way it is a problem.

3. Obtain information about how the client has been attempting to resolve the problem.

"It is better to make haste slowly from the start rather than to press on toward active intervention before the problem and how it is being handled have been made clear and explicit" (Fisch et al., 1982, pp. 69–70). Weakland continues to work toward obtaining a clear problem definition.

John: Okay. Could you tell me some more about the effect it has on your daily life? You have mentioned two things particularly besides the felt need to urinate more often, mainly the depression and its effect on your sex life. Can you spell that out a little more?

Tom: Well, erections are very difficult for me to keep. I mean it's possible for me to get it; I just need an incredible amount of foreplay. I never had any problems with erections before, because there is always the feeling of running to the bathroom all the time. I should let you know it's more the *urge*. I can hold it in pretty much till it reaches a point where I really have to go. I can restrain myself, but the feeling is always there.

John: Um-hmm. Would you tell me a little more about how this depresses you? I can understand that you would certainly not be happy about this sort of problem, but different people might have that unhappiness in different forms. For example, somebody might be angry or irritated about it, but you said mainly it is depressing to you.

The word *depression* sounds specific, but is vaguely and variously defined, so Weakland, true to his approach, continues to ask questions until he understands what the word means for Tom.

Tom: I guess it has a lot to do with my sexual life. It's the feeling of a lack of confidence. There is a part of me that always felt that that was very important about myself. . . . My sexuality was real strong, and because of the fact that I don't have the erections anymore, I have lost a certain amount of confidence. There are certain days I almost feel castrated.

John: It has restricted, limited, your sexual activity . . . or? Where was it before and where is it now?

Tom: It's now once every couple of weeks, to where it was almost every other day.

The problem is understood to have at least three aspects: (1) an incessant urgency to urinate, (2) a change in Tom's ability to attain and maintain an erection, and (3) related feelings of depression about how much this affects his life. Weakland does not minimize them. As one of his mentors once said, "No one wants a picayune headache; since a headache must be endured, let it be so colossal that only the sufferer could endure it. Human pride is so curiously good and comforting" (Erickson, 1967, p. 422).

Having obtained an adequate, albeit preliminary, picture of the problem, Weakland acknowledges its seriousness and then moves to the next step, exploring how Tom has tried to handle it, paying particular attention to what he has tried that has not worked.

John: Well, that's considerable change. What have you done in your attempts to resolve, or at least mitigate, this problem? What have you done, say, yourself—what have you tried? And let me be clear, obviously in this situation I am not asking for success stories or otherwise you wouldn't be here. But it's important also that I know what you have tried and doesn't work.

Tom: In terms of other than doctors and seeing various people? I have sort of retreated more. I don't feel as sociable as I once was. It's like I am trying to keep busy all the time, which is one way of dealing with it but there is no real chance for me to reflect, because if I reflect I tend to get really depressed about it.

John: Okay, I'm getting it clearer, and by the way, anytime I am misunderstanding you don't hesitate to pull me up on that.

Weakland often invited his clients to correct any misunderstandings he might have. This helped ensure a clear definition of the problem, and it conveyed that both therapist *and* client are responsible for progress in therapy. It also put Weakland in the classic MRI "one down position," designed to help clients become more at ease and expressive.

Tom: Sure.

John: It is, sort of, as if you are keeping busy to keep your mind off the problem?

Tom: That's correct.

John: You mention not staying home. Could you explain that to me a little further?

Tom: Yeah, I tend to be culturally oriented, so movies, theatre. I've been trying to exercise a lot more. And I feel like I need to move around. It helps relax me, makes me feel as though I'm doing something, and also, not giving up hope because I need to find a solution to this. In the past every time I had a possibility of treatment for this and it doesn't work out, the depression seemed to grow worse. So I need some kind of hope.

John: But, since you have had that experience, and, ah, more than once, ah, I think I should suggest to you that, while I am not saying don't be hopeful, [*raising both arms and hands with palms out, gesturing "stop" or "slow down"*] don't get too bloody optimistic this time and build yourself up to possibly a big letdown.

Thus far, Weakland has mostly asked questions to help him clarify Tom's meaning or statements to encourage cooperation. In response to Tom's plea for hope, Weakland does the opposite of what many therapists, working with different assumptions, would do. Instead of reassuring Tom by attempting to convey hope for improvement, Weakland encourages Tom to lower his expectations. Claiming the low ground, Weakland attempts to preempt the possibility of further disappointment, thus allowing the possibility for Tom to experience improvement, should it occur. In this way, Tom is provided with what the MRI team describes as implicit hope—creating a context in which improvement is more likely to occur.

Tom: Well, be grounded a little bit.

John: Maybe if you sort of, when you do think of it when you are away, though you will probably be pretty busy, you could think of this with a sort of attitude of positive skepticism. That would be on the safe side. Do you tell yourself things? This is something people often do with a problem. Give yourself talks of one sort or another?

Having avoided inadvertently helping Tom develop a false sense of hopefulness, Weakland resumes the task of having him describe in detail how he attempts to solve the problem, finding out what Tom tells himself about the situation. Later, the exploration of attempted solutions will expand to other aspects of Tom's life.

Tom: There is a part of me that says, well, this is really nothing compared to what other people, you know, especially AIDS and what our people have to go through. But it's my life and it's very essential to me, so I try to give pats on the back to myself that no matter what happens to me I am still a great person, but . . .

John: Yeah, but, it strikes me, the fact that this is a quote "not a big problem compared to AIDS," in a way, that doesn't make it better, that makes it worse when it's your problem.

Tom reveals many things in this utterance. He reveals one of the ways he has been inadvertently helping to perpetuate the problem—telling himself that things aren't so bad compared to the serious problems others experience. With the statement, "AIDS and what *our people* have to go through," he implies that he is gay. In the video, Tom can be seen closely watching Weakland's response. Following in the footsteps of another mentor, Don Jackson, Weakland conveys the essence of what is meant by a nonpathologizing, nonnormative orientation—the belief that there is absolutely nothing wrong with the client, who is doing the best he can in light of the situation and the relationships of which he is a part. This uncompromisingly nonjudgmental attitude is conveyed subtly by Weakland when, in a low-key manner, he makes overt the no-win consequences of this kind of self-talk.

Tom: I know, I know.

John: Well, ordinarily we ask also whether, what advice other people, or what attempted help they might have given you. But from what you are saying that would probably be not terribly applicable because this is something that you don't talk about to people other than the doctors and hypnotist that you've seen.

This question is structured in a way that elicits a response by discouraging it—a method of inquiry adopted from Erickson and Jackson and pioneered by Weakland and colleagues.

Tom: Well, I am not seeing a hypnotist anymore, that was a once or twice thing.

John: No, no, I meant, ah, that you've only talked with . . .

Tom: I talk to my close friends because I need to share this with them, because it affects me and they know that I am very different in the sense of withdrawing more, more quiet, and I sort of want to be alone more than any time in the past with myself. So I do talk to them, and they say, well, you know, they feel badly for me. And they say, well, maybe something will come up. And, then some will say you just have to live with it.

John: I'm . . . wasn't quite clear, when you do, sort of, talk to yourself or give yourself advice, I wasn't quite clear what the main content of that is?

Tom: When I talk to myself?

John: Yeah.

Tom: That I am still, ah, maybe it's the feeling that I am not, ah . . . because my sexuality seems to be impaired because of this thing I'm, ah, not an attractive and desirable person. And what I am telling myself is that no matter what happens, you know, I will always be a desirable attractive individual.

John: Well . . . let me ask you . . . a . . . question that . . . is certainly hypothetical at this point . . . but quite a tough question; I think it would be useful. Suppose that somehow you came to the conclusion that basically this problem is never going to be resolved. Let's say that it would stay just about the same as it is now. What difference would that make in your daily life? At this point you've got the problem but you're, understandably, of course, hopeful that it would get resolved. Suppose, somehow, that you came to the conclusion it was just going to stay that way?

By naming Tom's worst fear, Weakland makes explicit the presupposition implicit in Tom's attempted solution behavior, setting the stage to inquire about the context within which the problem and attempted solution are made coherent.

Tom: I wouldn't want to live anymore.

John: How long did you say this has been going on now?

Tom: Since June of 1988.

John: Ah, anything in particular happen around that time that seemed relevant to you?

Tom: I was having sex with somebody and, ah, I ejaculated into the person's mouth.

John: Um-hmm.

Tom: And that did it. And, ah, I seemed, it started right at that time.

John: Aside from the . . . not bothering you when you are sleeping, I was wondering whether there might be other, what we might call exceptions to . . . the problem situation. Whether there are periods that you are aware of, that it's okay for a while even temporarily?

Tom's problem has been defined in clear and concrete terms, his efforts to solve the problem have been detailed, and Tom's presuppositions—and the context in which the problem emerged—have been articulated. Weakland now shifts to inquiring about times when the situation is not a problem, a technique now central to solution-focused brief therapy. He seeds the idea that times do exist when the problem is less restricting. By using the phrase "that you are aware of," Weakland invites Tom to contemplate the probable existence of other exceptions of which he is not presently aware. If they find even one, it will imply the presence of others.

Tom: When I get myself busy, you know? So as long as I'm busy it's not as conscious, I am not aware of it at all.

John: When problems change, or are in the process of being resolved, it is usually not a matter of everything becomes resolved overnight. Sometimes there are problems where that can happen, but more commonly it's a matter of step-by-step progress. Ah, so let me ask you what may appear to be a simple question but it's not, not that easy. What would . . . what would be the first sign . . . of progress? What, if you . . . when you see it happen, will lead you to say to yourself, "Well, maybe I'm not all the way out of the woods yet, but I've made a first step in the direction that leads out of the woods." And think small. Is there anything in particular that if you saw happen that isn't happening now that would be a first sign to you?

Tom: [*Silence*].

John: And, first of all, it would be useful if you would, ah, give this some more thought until we meet next time. Don't let it get in the way of your trip to Europe, but if you have some time before then, or just after you get back, think it over a little more, and, one possible further attempt at definition would be, ah, is there anything that you don't do now that if you found yourself doing even once you'd say, "That's a change," and I'd say, "That's a sign of a step in the right direction."

Weakland closes the first session with what has become a standard between-sessions assignment in MRI brief therapy first interviews. The "first sign of improvement" intervention is another legacy of Milton Erickson's influence on Weakland, seeding the idea that improvement is possible and orienting the client to search for small signs of it. This question has also become integral to the solution-focused brief therapy approach.

Tom: Um, well, you know, what I can think about now is actually feeling that I want to go out on a date, or I might be sexual with someone. At some point that would be something that I would want.

John: Okay, I think that certainly that would be a sign, but in a sense, maybe that's still a pretty big sign because, you know, that means almost you are just where you were. So that I still think it can be useful to give a little thought to what would be, ah, a first thing in that direction, before you say, ah, "Well, I want to go out, and I'm confident about it and not worrying myself about it."

Clients almost always respond to a question about the "first sign of improvement" with descriptions, like Tom, of dramatic improvement. Weakland suggests that he think small.

John: That's, ah, you've identified a time how the problem began, but what we are not clear about is, did it begin from there, sort of at a low level and build up, or did it sort of begin all at once?

Tom: Began all at once.

John: Okay.

Second Session

John: Well it's been nearly a month since we last met. Ah, maybe you might fill me in on anything significant that has happened during that time.

MRI brief therapists think *cybernetically*—they attend to how their and their clients' behaviors are recursively connected. Working to foster a cooperative relationship, their choices about how to proceed at the beginning of a new session are contingent on what has happened since the last one.

Tom: Well, as I told you I went on vacation to Europe with my mother, and just the preparation for everything. So, I was there for about three weeks; and then for five days, she lives in Texas, so I spent time with her. So that has been the big event of the last month. It is not often that I get to Europe [*laughing*]. It was a nice trip.

John: Well, it strikes me, considering the nature of your problem, what was it like being on a bus a lot of the time?

Tom: Ah, let me just, the thing I guess that maybe I wasn't clear about is I don't . . . I'm holding it in. It's not . . . I can deal with holding it in. It's not that I have to rush to the bathroom all the time. Ah, so it's not really, it wasn't really a problem on the bus.

John: That does remind me of another thing that we wanted to ask you. You said that usually you hold it in; I was just wondering, have you ever actually lost control and wet yourself?

Tom: No.

MRI brief therapists listen for and accept *any* indication of improvement. Weakland punctuates Tom's success at spending long periods of time on a bus.

John: Okay. Have you found an occasion to give a little more thought to what would be a first sign of progress?

Tom: Um, I guess I haven't really thought about it. You know, like I said, I was real busy, I didn't think about the question. Um, the first sign of progress . . . um, I guess, all I can think of now is I wouldn't be focused on this. It would become natural. It would become the way I was before this whole thing started. So I would be fully unaware.

John: That would be, sort of, the final sign of progress?

Once again, Tom is invited to think small and to focus on the possibility of improvement.

Tom: That would be the final sign, ah . . . I guess the first sign would be not to worry quite so much, maybe that I'd be more relaxed around this issue.

John: I also wanted to ask . . . you mentioned when we met before that, essentially, there are two main aspects of this problem: the urinary urge and the sexual difficulties, or uncertainties . . . lack of confidence that seems to have sort of sprung up in relation to that. Well a couple of points. One of my colleagues was wondering, is this lack of confidence sort of general or widespread, or is it particularly sort of limited to the sexual situation?

Weakland continues clarifying the problem definition by identifying its different aspects—urinary pressure, sexual difficulties, and lack of confidence—and then, with Tom's help, narrows the focus of the treatment.

Tom: To the sexual situation.

John: Suppose, hypothetically, that the sexual side of this whole matter were resolved to your reasonable satisfaction, but there was no particular change in the urinary problem. How much difference would that make to you?

Tom: I'd say it would make, ah, significant difference.

John: Give me a percent. I know it is just an, an estimate at best, but, ah . . .

Tom: I'd say about 75.

John: About 75 percent? Okay. So that is the major concern, at least three quarters of the total?

Tom: Yeah, 75 percent.

MRI therapists often ask clients to estimate, using a percentage, "how much of a difference" a particular change would make (Fisch et al., 1982). Here, Weakland uses the technique to define, with Tom, a clear direction for therapy—the resolution of the "sexual side of this whole matter" to Tom's *"reasonable satisfaction."*

John: Well, particularly, in that case then, I would like to fill in the picture more about how all this all began. I know you gave some information on that, but I, there are a number of things that I don't think I have very clearly yet. You related the onset of the whole matter, the whole problem to a sexual situation in which you ejaculated into someone's mouth. I was wondering what led you to attach particular significance to that.

To gain Tom's cooperation, Weakland needs an accurate grasp of Tom's point of view and explanatory system—what MRI therapists refer to as "client position."

Tom: Number one, that I was aware of, was that I really didn't want to do it. And, ah, the person involved was drunk at the time. I guess I've been feeling a lot of, um, anxiety about the safe-sex situation. I've never been tested for the AIDS virus or anything like that. And there is reluctance on my part to possibly contribute anything that might be transmitted to somebody else. Even though it probably couldn't be done that way, there is always a slight chance there might be some kind of cut, or something like that. I guess there is, was, a part of me that just did not want to do this because this person was not in a state of making, I guess, a lucid judgment. And it was difficult to get out of . . .

Tom's attack of conscience challenged his personal integrity and appears to have manifested physiologically in sexual impotence. An MRI brief therapist probably would not make use of this kind of interpretation directly.

John: Hard to back out.

Tom: Hard to back out, yeah. Actually, right after it happened, that is when I started feeling this urge. And, ah, when I've had that before, it's always been, um, you know, sexually transmitted, gonorrhea, or what is it, unspecified, or something like that.

John: Um-hmm.

Tom: And it's always been one of those two things that caused that. And that's happened in the past.

John: You've had that trouble before?

Tom: Every time it has happened I have always been able to get some kind of antibiotics . . .

John: Okay.

Tom: . . . for it, and it always seems to have worked. I thought something was different. I just was aware that something was different as a result of that. Um, it may not have been right afterwards, but I was aware that, you know, oh, it means, probably it means I've got some kind of gonorrhea or something like that. But it was in, let's say, the first couple of hours after it happened I was worried. It seemed that every time I tried to masturbate, it was just that, well, you know, when you masturbate your mind is focused on one thing. But my mind, every time I tried to masturbate, was focusing on going to the bathroom and I would go to the bathroom to urinate and then it would, I would still need to urinate even though nothing would come out. So my mind could not be focused . . .

John: Um-hmm.

Tom: . . . on an object or something that I can use as a model for my fantasies. And so every time that I tried that, um, I couldn't block it out and as a result I never seemed to have an erection. I was able to ejaculate, um, but my penis was just very soft all the time.

John: And, in that early time, you were, again, seeking some sort of treatment for the urinary part of the problem under the idea it might be like the previous times?

Tom: I kept getting different kinds of prescriptions, ah . . .

John: Yeah, but nothing ever came of it.

Tom: No.

John: In the, what might be called, the development, or the early stages of this problem, you mentioned your initial thoughts and feelings, and your difficulty in masturbating. At about what point did you find out that this was, ah, also seem to be causing difficulties with a partner?

Tom: As a result of my, ah, my, ah, I don't know, I wouldn't say failures about masturbating because I did masturbate.

John: Well, you weren't having great success at that.

Tom: No, no. I didn't want to have any partners at all. And when I finally found a partner, ah, it was still difficult to get an erection, ah, and I didn't ejaculate at all. One of the doctors that I went to gave me some pills. I don't remember the name but they do help give erections. So, as a result, when I went ahead and saw a doctor and he gave me the pills. I think it was anywhere from one to three pills two hours before I knew I was going to have sex. And that definitely helped. So I have been doing that but that has been very infrequent. I just haven't had any real desire to want to have any sexual partner.

Having encouraged Tom to elaborate on the personal and interpersonal consequences of the problem, Weakland now shifts to exploring his efforts to improve it.

John: Some help, ah, how else have you tried to grapple with that side of the problem and do something about it?

Tom: Well, I did mention I went to acupuncture . . .

John: yeah . . .

Tom: . . . at two different clinics. Um, you said grapple, are you asking in terms of sexual?

John: Yeah. I guess I'm thinking first of all, since you didn't come to, "I'll stay away from it for a while," you didn't come to that right away, but only after a considerable time, I was wondering what sort of attempts you made, other than getting pills from doctors, to see if you could improve things. To at least get things to where it was, or at least better than where it was at the worst.

Tom: I didn't make any attempts other than trying to escape in various ways, ah, eating, eating orgies. I like movies a lot, so I can just see movies constantly, reading, music, just barricade myself, and, I guess there's a part of me to make myself as unattractive as possible, ah, and I wouldn't have to deal with the sexual issue. Ah, so, a large part of it, I was running away from. So I didn't really try other than the pills.

John: More running away than, ah, "I'll get in there and give it another try in one way or another to see if I can still get with it?" I thought that you had some reference to, that you . . . I know that you . . . although you were not confident that you could get an erection with considerable foreplay.

Weakland's Columbo-like style of interaction, with the hesitations and detours, embodies a "one down" position, empowering Tom by providing him with an opportunity to fill in the gaps. This is a reversal of the conventional mindset many clients have in therapy. People come to therapy to be helped; Weakland makes it possible for the client to help *him*.

Tom: Yeah, but that's, it happened, it happened once with foreplay on just one time, one occasion, um.

John: Okay, so that was exceptional. Mainly you were staying away? Better to not try than to have a letdown?

Tom: Right, um, pretty much so.

Knowing about Tom's avoidance strategy, Weakland can bring greater focus to the question of "a first sign of improvement," and begin to construct a relevant homework assignment.

John: To go back to that question of what would be a first sign of progress, and, in a way, this is always a more difficult question than it might appear on the surface, but it could be particularly difficult in a situation where, essentially, for very understandable reasons, you are avoiding what would be very much of a test case. So, how would you know, even when you are ready to make another approach? What would be the . . . what, if you were to see it happen, would be a confidence . . . or on the road to getting enough confidence to say, "Look, I think I'm ready to go out there and see how it goes?"

Building on Tom's issue with "confidence," Weakland asks for a more specific, concrete sign of it.

Tom: I guess it might have to do with, maybe, loneliness for myself. I mean, I have gotten used to a certain degree of security and comfort in my trying not to deal with this, 'cause, you know, as I mentioned last week I had some real despondent thoughts about this at times. And I go through a period of really looking to find some answers, or people who are supportive, and I go through a whole thing. And then, after a while, I get real tired of going to doctors all of the time. And there is a part of me that says "enough is enough." Let me just retreat into my little world, which I've made comfortable. But I also know that I get real lonely. But loneliness, you know, after a while, once I really feel that I need more contact on an intimate level, at that point then I know I'll push myself.

John: One question. Ah . . . is there something that you could think of that if it were to occur, that you would say, well that is step one toward regaining my confidence? Or that's a sign I've already made step one, even though I don't know how it came about?

Through elaboration of the "first sign" assignment, Weakland continues to seed the possibility of improvement, now focused specifically on what Tom might notice pertaining to confidence.

Tom: I guess part of it, I think . . . I mean the first thing that I think of is that if I could feel that someone that I am attracted to is attracted to me. I guess because this whole thing is because I feel very unattractive now because of this. I mean it is all internal. I know that. It does not affect how people, who see me on the street, are going to notice that. But I feel very unattractive because of this situation, and I guess if I sense that there is somebody out there that finds me attractive and lets me know about it in some way . . . then I think that would rekindle all, you know, press all the buttons from the past, in terms of how I related sexually with other people.

Weakland once again faces the challenge of responding to Tom's growing enthusiasm, evident in the utterance "that would rekindle *all*." In an article published in 1961, Jackson and Weakland described the nontherapeutic value of encouraging a client at a moment such as this. Later, Weakland and his colleagues (Fisch et al., 1982) explained that such encouragement would simply repeat others' efforts to help the client (i.e., giving false hope by cheering him up).

John: Um-hmm. What I'm thinking is that I certainly see the relevance of that, but, ah, how do you know? And that may, in a sense, be a somewhat unfair . . . question, but I don't think it has ever been . . . spelled out concretely, how one knows, or even thinks one knows that someone else is interested in this area, but I guess I'm bringing it up because if you are feeling in a sort of negative frame of mind, it strikes me there may be a danger that someone might be very interested, but you would write it off, so that either you wouldn't perceive it, or you would say, "Ah, looks like it but it can't be for real."

Weakland restrains Tom from rushing forward by suggesting that his confidence problem would likely prevent him from knowing how to accurately evaluate another's interest in him. In so doing, he indirectly encourages Tom's observation skills.

Tom: Generally I'm pretty good at spotting, um, you know, of course I'm sure I'll miss some signals. I'm in that field where people say to me, you know, I'm nice, or I'm a warm person, and, ah, a lot of people say it, but they say it . . . but they're not necessarily attracted to me. But, um, if there is someone that says something like that, that I am attracted to, then, knowing myself, I would pursue maybe a line of questions to find out if there is more than just that I am a nice person, and maybe they would be interested in doing something outside, with me, outside of work or something to that effect.

John: Okay. So it could involve some exchange of conversation not just, sort of, you sort of, pick up the emanations of . . .

Tom: Right. Yeah.

John: Yeah, I was thinking that, from what you were saying earlier, that before this trip you were sort of cutting yourself off. Ah, and you know, I can see some reasons for that. At the same time, that puts you in a situation where even if there was a possibility now that you would get something positive from other people . . . but it can't happen if you are not around anybody.

What we would like you to do is to deliberately get out some, in any sort of social settings that you would choose, but in a particular way. The idea is that you would be going out with other people, whom you might be interested in, or who might be interested in you, but strictly on an exploratory, observational basis at this time. Ah, to observe and consider two sorts of things: one, any signs that you pick up, verbal and otherwise, as to whether other people are or are not interested in you. But equally, particularly if you observe some such signs that they are, to sort of review yourself and ask, "Am I really interested in getting together more closely with that person or persons?"

The . . . several reasons . . . one we have already been speaking of, to the extent that you keep yourself at home . . . while it may be more immediately comfortable, you are missing the opportunity to check out whether you are making any progress or not. Whether there may not be someone out there that you would be interested in in such a way, that you would feel added to your confidence. So that on the one hand, that makes an important reason to be out in contact with some people.

On the other hand, there are clearly important reasons for going quite slow about anything beyond just observation, gathering some information about others and yourself. On one hand, it probably may not be helpful and it might be quite unhelpful if you proceed on the basis that, "I'll push myself out there and get involved with somebody, even if I'm not confident I'm reasonably ready." Ah, if you try to make too big a jump, you usually fall in somewhere.

The other thing is, it would be important to go slow because there is also the angle that you might, even if the other person is ready, you might go faster than you are ready for. For example, you might become involved with someone that you don't really want to be, but your loneliness can do strange things, and in fact, maybe, some of that was involved in the original event which started this all off. But, at this point, in a sense, your problem can be in a way an asset, in that it will help to restrain you from moving precipitously—while you do move out and gain enough contact to sort of survey both the response of others to you, and you to them, without plunging into any hasty action.

Therapy is now focused almost entirely on the confidence aspect of the problem, relating to Tom's avoidance of social situations, with little or no specific attention given to the urinary or erectile problems. The homework embodies many aspects of interventions pioneered at MRI over the past 45 years:

- an articulation of the assignment using the language and position of the client;
- a request for behavioral change, cast within a suggestion not to change;
- an implication that improvement will occur as a result of this behavioral change;
- the framing of the problem as an asset, in that it will allow the client to proceed with more caution;
- a specific injunction to "go slow."

Following through with the assignment will require Tom to respond to two intentionally contradictory injunctions: (1) implement a 180° reversal of his attempted solution—avoidance of social interaction, and (2) "go slow," or, as Weakland put it, proceed "without plunging into any hasty action." His experiment is to notice, not to get involved.

Third Session

John: Well, I had suggested last time that it could be useful if you would get out of your house some and get among people, particularly some that you could . . . sort of observe their possible interest in you and, on the other hand, your possible interest in them. Have you . . .

Tom: Yeah. I went to a gathering of friends, and ah, I did meet somebody there and, ah, what happened was that we went home and I was trying to be very aware of what you had mentioned to me, but ah, I guess I was sort of curious to see what would happen if I just let myself go, because I had been very guarded since this happened. And ah, eventually things led to something, which I really wish I had more control of, but anyway we ended up, I was able to ejaculate while he was there.

John: Well that's uh, interesting, but moving pretty fast. This, was this the only time that you were able to carry out the assignment? I'm not quite clear on that.

Tom: It was the only time that I've . . . I've been extremely busy for me, and there's just a lot of things that I've had to do, and it was the only opportunity that I had at that time.

John: I think it's obvious I'm a little concerned about the rate of motion that that involves, but ah, perhaps you could tell me what your response was to all this.

As frequently occurs subsequent to assignments that attempt to restrain a client from change, Tom had gone far beyond what was suggested by Weakland, finding himself in a sexually intimate situation. Weakland responds with concern that Tom is moving too fast, implying there are potential disadvantages inherent in moving ahead too quickly.

Tom: I was in a state of shock basically, um, that it happened first of all, because it seemed to move really fast. And what it was, it was with another, ah, well, I, it hasn't come up before and it's not going to make any difference but I'm gay, okay. Um, but it was with another man that I met in a friend's setting and it turned into a mutual masturbation type sequence . . . I just needed to reach out in some way, and that was the only way I could see that he was willing to reach out to me, trusting. I felt detached, because it was the same problem. I kept losing my erection all the time and the more I worried about it, the more it seemed to, um, you know it was like I'm just thinking about it all the time now.

Before it was an instantaneous kind of thing and I'm just concerned about what is going to be his reaction when he sees me with a limp penis.

John: Well, I don't mean to be pessimistic on purpose, but I hesitate to wonder what is going to be his reaction simply when he sees you in any ordinary setting.

When a client demonstrates improvement, many therapeutic approaches suggest that the appropriate response is to praise, compliment and encourage. As he does with Tom, Weakland typically heads in the opposite direction, voicing concern that things are moving too fast and continuing to promote change by restraining it. The logic for Weakland's stance is simple—the client is often surrounded by others who respond with reassurance and praise at the slightest sign of progress. Such advice, unfortunately, helps perpetuate rather than attenuate the problem.

Tom: It was somebody that I probably will not . . . it was just, you know, it was a sexual involvement and it was somebody that probably I have no interest in seeing again.

John: Um-hmm.

Tom: But it was very, it was very, um, exciting at the time I was with him. But at the same time, you know, my excitement usually shows by being erect and I wasn't able to do that. Actually, for a while it was erect, but it just seemed to lose its momentum really fast. I guess maybe because the more I thought about it . . . but I just am not going to be able to help think about it; it's just part of my nature now.

John: The reason was that I was suggesting that not only that you observe some others' potential interest in you, but that you spend time observing your own interest in others as well.

Tom: There have been a number of people that um, you know, that I have made contact with, but just, with their schedules and with my schedules there wasn't time, you know, to really develop, in the sense of getting, you know . . . we talked about getting together. And I'm getting together actually with two different people this week. I guess there was a part of me that was trying to get somebody that I would see again before I came to see you and, you know, I was sort of making, you know, I don't know whether that is good or not. If I really thought about it, I probably wouldn't have involved myself with this guy. But you know, there is a part of it that was something available by today.

John: Correct me if I'm wrong, but I get the feeling that you sort of are trying to push yourself ahead . . . rather than follow the rather gradual
pace that was recommended to you?

Tom: Probably I did.

John: Would it be a fair statement that the outcome of that was sort of
mixed? You mentioned that where the episode was a shock, and what
comes to mind is good shocks, bad shocks, and mixed shocks.

Tom: The good thing for me that came out of this was that there was somebody attracted to me . . . and that I was attracted to. That was very
significant for me to think that there are people attracted to me. So in
that sense, I think something really good came out of that.

    Yeah, I meant actually it has been very easy for me to meet people
this last week or so. I don't know if it has anything to do with my feeling about what happened last week, but you know, I met a waiter at a
restaurant last night that I go to, and then a friend of another friend
that I have started to talk to. We talked about getting together, and this
week, but it's a matter of whether we can find the right times. My
schedule is open but I don't know if he's, if they are going to be able to
get together this week.

John: Am I getting it correct, that you, sort of, have been a little surprised
these two weeks that you mention that it's been easier to meet people
than you had expected?

Tom: Um, yeah, it has been surprising but, you know, I don't mean to put
it down but it just seems that always after a vacation that people . . .
there is a certain glow that people have, you know, and I think part of
it might be that people are curious about my trip.

John: I certainly don't want to make too much of it.

Weakland's manner of inquiry warrants close attention. He believed that
giving direct suggestions was one of the *least effective* methods of influence, preferring to use indirect suggestions, nonconfrontation, and the
implied aspect of messages to influence a client to desist from attempted
solution behaviors. Now that the therapy has progressed to the point
where attempted solutions have been clearly identified, virtually every utterance by Weakland is an intentional effort to indirectly influence the
client, presenting a mixed bag of injunctions and warnings.

- "I'm a little concerned about the rate of motion that that involves."
- "I suggest . . . you spend time observing your own interest in others
  as well."

- "Correct me if I'm wrong, but I get the feeling that you sort of are trying to push yourself ahead."
- "Would it be a fair statement that the outcome of that was sort of mixed?"

When Tom makes light of the change, attributing it to "post-vacation glow," Weakland is quick to overtly minimize the effect as well, saying, "I certainly don't want to make too much of it." He consistently preempts Tom's dismissive thoughts, taking away their power, which, in turn, allows Tom to adopt a positive view of the outcome.

Tom: Right. I mean, it's there but it's also part of, you know. It's nice. It's very nice.

John: Well, the other side of that is you have more power, more attraction than you were recognizing. There is one thing that goes along with that—that you need to give somewhat more thought to where and when you want to exercise it, and that is the aspect that I think we were touching on when I suggested that you also do some observing of yourself in terms of your own interest in whomever you meet. The other thing that I was, ah, worrying about was whether you had any further thoughts as to this experience and anything else that has happened in the last couple of weeks about the question—How will you know when you are really distinctly more confident about your sexual capabilities?

Confidence is a much less threatening topic than impotence.

Tom: I guess when I won't have to worry about erections.

John: The suggestion follows that while you're in bed asleep tonight a miracle happens and in the morning you find it is totally gone. How will you know that that has happened?

Although the miracle question is most often identified with solution-focused brief therapy, Weakland described it as very similar to the first-sign-of-improvement question. They both accomplish the same purpose, but they start at the opposite ends of the spectrum.

The first-sign question immediately orients the client to think in terms of the smallest indication that the situation is improving. Clients typically respond by saying that the problem would be resolved. The therapist acknowledges that such improvement would be a good thing, but then asks the client to think about a sign of improvement that they might notice *even before* that. This is followed up by the therapist's providing examples of possible small signs the client might notice, and indicating that the question is more difficult to answer than it first appears.

The miracle question, in contrast, begins by having the client imagine that the problem no longer exists. The therapist then begins a series of inquiries that involve the client's describing, in detail, small signs that would indicate that the problem is solved. With both inquiries, follow-up questions orient the client to notice and articulate small signs of improvement. They are the most potent aspect of the technique (Weakland, 1991).

Tom: Because I'll know that I won't be thinking about this endless urgency that I have.

John: Okay. So if tomorrow morning it is gone, the problem is over, what will you be doing differently that will tell you it is all over?

Tom: I will, ah, celebrate. Whenever possible, I will.

John: Oh, but that assumes you know it's over. You can't celebrate till you know it's over. I'm trying to ask the question, what will be going on that will tell you it's over?

Tom: I will go out. I will make dates. I will feel comfortable having as much sex or as little sex as I want. I will be a free man.

John: What do you think will be the first thing that will tell you the problem is over?

Tom: I will call up some old boyfriends of mine. Make dates and, depending on how it goes, I will proceed to have a nice intimate relationship with someone, assuming that they are willing on their part.

[*The telephone rings and Weakland consults with members of the team.*]

John: One of my colleagues has a suggestion for a different way to proceed that you might think useful to you, and that would be that you pick someone that you really didn't particularly care about personally. Go out with him, but early on, before you really get down to anything, *do* tell him explicitly that you have a problem with erections. I think what he has in mind—he will correct me if I'm wrong—he didn't explain it very thoroughly, would be something like, you wouldn't have too much to lose.

Tom: Going out with somebody that I don't particularly like?

John: Yes. Somebody that you might, say, have some lust toward but not much possibility of trust, and at least somebody that you would find, ah, at least thinking that you would not establish anything that might be ongoing with, or anything like that. But, to put it badly, the losses are minimal.

Tom: Okay.

This suggestion utilizes and prescribes behavior that is within Tom's current behavioral repertoire (i.e., initiating involvement with someone he doesn't care about), but by directing him to reveal, rather than conceal, his erection problem, it also reverses his previous problem-maintaining behavior. When such a suggestion is carried out, or even thought about, it serves the purpose of bringing the client toward the problem rather than away from it.

John: What I've been, the thought that has been occurring to me in relation to this difficulty of identifying a sort of specific and certainly early sign, is that it reinforces my previous thoughts that it may be desirable for you to take things rather slow rather than pushing yourself ahead. I know the tendency with something like this is charge ahead and get through the barrier, but there are certain indications that that does not work very well. So I think you would be better advised to save time and trouble in the long run to try to take it slowly. A couple of things said that are relevant. Now, both to get a clearer idea of who may be interested in you, and in a way something that I am increasingly thinking, is even more important than that, and that is your interest in other people. For example, I'm assuming, I may be wrong, but I'm assuming that there are people that you would really love, be interested in getting close together with them.

Tom: There are but . . .

John: Even, let's say, if just for a quick fling, there are people who . . .

Tom: Sure. What you are suggesting, if I'm not wrong, is that even though . . . if I'm not attracted to them, if they have some interest in me.

John: Well, what I am suggesting is that you note that, but that you don't automatically respond to it.

Tom: Okay.

John: That you certainly would consider their interest in you, but that you also consider and that you practice considering, till you get tuned-up a little more, "Am I really interested in getting together with that person, or am I perhaps getting a little swept away by their interest in me?"— that sort of thing. My colleague relayed the suggestion to you before, and it would be useful for you to find someone that you are not really interested in, and proceed to see if you can get it on with that person, but within the explicit framework, before you go very far, of, "Look, I've got a considerable erection problem and you need to know about that."

Ah, the thing, more general thing is, we sort of have been arguing from the evidence, that we sort of rushed things during the last two weeks, and the results were sort of expectable. On the one hand, you have made visible steps forward from where you were when we first saw you, and from where you have been for some time, but you still ran into trouble. Ah, it would be better, as much as you can, to go slow and not push things, because there is no real advantage in doing something half way. It is better to take one's time so that you can be prepared to do it the whole way.

And other than trying to restrain yourself some in general . . . the only thing I would suggest is whether you go out and do it deliberately, or whether it's just in whatever situation you find yourself in, it would be good to spend some time surveying other people's potential interest in you and even more, in a way, your potential interest in them.

Tom: The person that, um, if I meet that I'm not that interested in, who I can tell that, you know, I have a problem with erections, and I say there is a problem and he says it doesn't matter to him, um, still say I'm just not prepared at this time?

John: Well, I can't really give you any specific prescription for that situation. I think you would have to sort of have to play that according to how you feel in that particular circumstance. And I can't be sure of that, be-cause I haven't got that situation yet, don't have the data on where would he be and where would you be after you made that explicit statement early on. You'll have to judge for yourself on that. Other than that, the main thing is make the time to observe, particularly observe the extent of the nature or your interest in anyone else. Oh, and a clar-ification from my colleague. He said in that situation, go ahead and go through with it, if possible, but all the way along you keep bringing up the fact that you have a problem. Not just initially but repeatedly.

Tom has made clear progress toward his goal, and has now been given sev-eral suggestions to consider between sessions:

- go slow;
- consider how things would be if a miracle happened and the problem disappeared;

- continue to think about what would be a first sign of change;
- move toward the problem by revealing it to someone;
- consider both other people's interest in him *and* his interest in other people;
- notice what goes on when in the presence of others.

Carrying out any of these suggestions will further interrupt Tom's pattern of attempted solutions, thus solidifying improvement.

Fourth Session

John: It's been three weeks since we met and in addition to suggesting to you that it was best to go rather gradually, we left you a couple of suggestions. The most general was to circulate some but in doing so mainly to keep your focus on observation and judgment, rather than action. To see if they might be interested in you or perhaps even more important, who you might be interested in. And then second of all, a more specific suggestion by my colleague Dr. Watzlawick, about getting together with someone that you really would not particularly be interested in, and in that circumstance make a point of telling about your erection problem. I wonder what you've done with all of this.

Tom: Well, I have made some attempts. It's been frustrating in the sense that there have been two people specifically that I had met and one of them is, it's difficult to try to get together with him, and the other person that I got together with, I met him at the parade. He would plan to get together and I had called to confirm and it turned out that he had a family emergency so he had to go out of town. So he's out of town until, he left last week and he will be back he said some time around the fifteenth and he seemed to indicate that he definitely wants to get together with me. I said that I will call him around the fifteenth to confirm, you know, any specific plans, so that's where the situation is in terms of that.

John: Okay, what would you say about your own sort of both level of interest, and kind of interest in that person?

Tom: I find him an interesting person to be with. He has this problem a lot of people in the gay community have. He is experiencing a lot of loss in terms of friends that have died of AIDS and he may be a little shy about other involvements at this point. That's my sense, but I don't really know. I'll know by spending a little more time with him.

John: In addition to these two specific people, did you take any opportunity to sort of get out and circulate a little bit in general and just form opinions by observation?

Tom: Well, I went to a couple of bars, but bars are such an artificial environment, in the sense that it's always so noisy, and there are always people that pretend that they are not looking at you, and may or may not. There's a rap group that meets—it's going to be held next Saturday and it's a talk session between people who are available for relationships. I have been to it in the past so that's available.

John: Um-hmm. What about that proposal that Dr. Watzlawick made, which is both more specific, and I would say, ah, how can I phrase it, certainly it's a step rather out of the ordinary, to find somebody to get with who you are not really that interested in, but to make a point with that at the beginning that you have an erection problem and then to carry on as far as things can go.

Tom: I was in the bar situation. There were a couple of people that I tried to strike up a conversation with but they were not interested. Their mannerisms and stuff were such that they were not willing to connect with me on that level so I wasn't able to fulfill that.

John: Okay.

Tom: But that is still something that I think is a legitimate thing to follow through on.

John: Um-hmm. I was just wondering, in general, how anxious or uneasy you've been in the three weeks since we've met?

Tom: Well, it's been, I've been real busy, um, and I haven't had a lot of time to reflect. That's always been the situation with this. As long as I keep busy, you know, I'm fine. It's when I don't have things to do that I could get anxious. I haven't really gotten anxious these three weeks. I think a lot of it is . . .

John: Okay, that's good to hear but, as you say, a large part of that may be attributed to special circumstances and that is that you've been busy.

Before Tom can continue to minimize the progress that has been made by attributing the absence of anxiety to "being busy," Weakland interrupts once again. Meeting Tom at his level of skepticism, he preempts his dismissal, defusing it by declaring the situation to be a given. This allows Tom to move beyond this snag, as can be noted in his response.

Tom: And a large part of it is that I feel, you know, my life has come to the point . . . as long as I feel I'm doing something about the problem that I have . . . by coming here, that fills me with a lot of hope. If I don't do anything like this, then I don't have any hope.

John: Okay. I don't like to be discouraging, and I like to hear that for whatever reason you are feeling somewhat more comfortable, but I think it's only fair to warn you that one thing that I don't want to do is give you false hope because, one of the worst things a therapist can do for a client is to build them up for some letdown. So, I hope you will temper your hope with a certain degree of healthy skepticism at least.

Tom: Well, this is my last resort. I mean if this doesn't work out . . . so I am really pretty sure that this is going to work for me.

John: Well, I think it is only fair to say that while I have certainly the intention of being helpful, and I wouldn't be in this business if I didn't think I could help people reasonably often, but then I would say that your degree of expressed assuredness is greater than mine. I would certainly prefer it if you would, a little bit, share the burden of healthy skepticism with me.

Tom: [*smiling*] Yeah, okay, I'll try.

Once improvement has been achieved, the important issue becomes how to maintain it. Weakland accomplishes this not through reassurance or encouragement, but the opposite: by worrying that change has occurred too quickly, discouraging Tom from becoming overly hopeful, and inviting him to share the burden of "healthy skepticism."

John: Tell me a little more about the last three weeks, particularly if anything else were to come to mind that in any way seems different to you from where you were at when you came here. Not necessarily anything that's even immediately connected with the problem that you can think about.

While Weakland continually invites the client to practice restraint, and in doing so inhibits the client's tendency to dismiss progress, he also subtly searches for any possible changes that have occurred, with the intent of underscoring their importance.

Tom: Actually there is something I have just thought about. . . . There has been a new employee at work, em, that I have met and, er, I have sort of been fantasizing about him. Actually I was surprised that the two times that I fantasized about him, I got complete erections and I was able to masturbate thoroughly. It was really . . . it was quite amazing.

John: Um-hmm. Ah, it is certainly amazing to me, too.

Tom: It was very exciting thinking about him. I hadn't really had anybody as a fantasy model for a long time and, well, it was great. I couldn't believe it.

John: Okay. Are you aware of what you were doing or thinking during those times?

Weakland's expression of astonishment underscores the importance of the change, and his follow-up question implicitly attributes it to a shift in Tom's actions or thoughts.

Tom: Um, I guess I haven't run into anybody that so attracted me as much as he did. But it was a short-term type of situation in terms of him. He seems to have expressed an interest that he prefers black men.

John: [*after a telephone consultation*] A message from one of my colleagues and I'll just pass it on. There is a likelihood that fate is being kind to you because there are some things that are better in the imagination than they turn out to be in reality.

Tom: It's weird, it was that . . . [*laughing*] um-hmm.

John: Um, but on a somewhat different tack: I certainly see a potential connection of what you just said with one of the things you have been emphasizing here, which is, what counts is not just somebody else's interest, but equally, and maybe even more important, your interest is existent here. You may need both for things to be as good as they possibly can be. But your interest is certainly not to be discounted by putting all the focus on "Is somebody else interested in me?"

Tom: That is true. He is . . . he was really . . . he got me going.

John: Um-hmm. It must be, as always—like everything else—there is possibly a down side to that, and that is the possibility, that if you can recognize your own interest, that it may not work out in the way that you want, and therefore the disappointment would be greater than if you sort of had a way to mute your own interest. But it's sort of, do you prefer to keep things on a fairly modest level, or do you prefer, sort of, to go out and win?

Having just encouraged Tom to shift his focus from what others think about him to what *he* may want, Weakland immediately proposes a possible disadvantage of change: It might put Tom in the position of experiencing greater disappointment if things didn't work out as he'd hoped. In so doing, Weakland continues to intervene by restraining change.

Tom: A lot of times I really don't know if somebody interests me. You know, you can go by how good-looking a person is, but it doesn't work like that for me. There are interior qualities that are much more important and I don't always recognize them right away, and it comes out like when I had that erection with that guy. Other times it doesn't take an erection for me to be interested in somebody, but I don't always know what it is.

Erickson (in Haley, 1973) and Jackson (1967) described people's experiencing seemingly intransigent problems as having a limited repertoire of behavioral alternatives available to them. Therapy involves creating contexts, both in and outside of sessions, where the client can experiment with expanding this repertoire. Weakland's next statement infers this.

John: So things can develop from a variety of different paths.
Tom: Right. But he is the first person that just struck me like that. It was quite amazing, just like a bolt of lightening. Yeah, it's nice to know that I am not beyond that. That it can still happen to me. I've sort of, you know, in a way given it up or thought I'd given it up.

Rather than celebrate Tom's report of success, Weakland acknowledges that the change is amazing *and* takes steps to temper Tom's enthusiasm.

John: Well, that is amazing, and again don't be too sudden. It's possible it was a fluke of some sort. Certainly it is amazing anyway, and anything else that was going on that in any way seems different than the way you came here?
Tom: Since when I first started?
John: Yeah, we can use that as sort of a baseline reference point.
Tom: Um, no. June has been quite a great month for me; I have just loved the excitement of June. There has been so much that I have been interested in, I've been doing, and I feel—a lot of friends have come into town—so I have been feeling very much appreciated and supported. And there are a couple of friends that I have talked about the situation to and they are very concerned. They listen well to me. So . . .
John: That's perhaps a little different than you were doing before, talking to your friends?
Tom: No, I was talking about it with certain friends. I still don't want to talk with everybody about this. But they're understanding and concerned.

There are times they want to talk about it and I really don't want to. Pretty much since this happened, I've been feeling a certain amount of frustration—you know, what do I want to exercise for? Nothing is going to happen much more in my life. My life, part of my life is over with. So there is a whole feeling of loss that I was going through. And that is still a part of me, this feeling of loss. But there are times I can overcome it and still exercise to an extent.

John: Um-hmm. So you think you will get back with your exercise despite these bouts of negative thoughts?

Tom: Well, I feel I need to badly.

John: In the framework of "change takes place," you have come to make changes that are more important than you realize. Again, a basic principle is that change that is gradual is much more secure and lasting than trying to leap over a fence all at once. And therefore, again, my best recommendation to you would be: Go ahead much the same, don't push yourself, don't even . . . don't trouble yourself by even saying, "I've got to get out there . . . make a next step tomorrow." And, other than that, keep on much as you have been doing. Certainly keep observing more than acting, especially observing how other people seem to be interested or disinterested in you. And the same thing for yourself, "Who am I interested in? How much? How?" And I would say certainly we shouldn't meet next week; it would be too soon. I would say two or three weeks again would be best, and probably three I would say.

Weakland underscores the desirability of "going slow" by extending the time between sessions.

Tom: Well, any suggestions on the urination thing? Any way that you think that the feeling, the feeling of urination . . . do you think that is psychological?

John: Well, certainly, although it's hard to say how much of each. It's almost certainly both physical . . . physical and psychological. I could only make one suggestion to you about it. That is more in the nature of an experiment, but you might have the curiosity to try the experiment. And that is, if you could pick a time when either there is an exception and you don't have that urge, or when it is at its lowest rather than at its highest level, and make a point of going and attempting to urinate. I think you might get some useful information on that.

Tom: Well it's always there. I always feel that way.

John: Okay, always to exactly the same degree?

Tom: Yeah. Well, sometimes when the pressure is to, as I mentioned, the urge is always there, okay? It's only when it becomes overwhelming, that's when I need to urinate.

John: Okay. But sometimes, and correct me if I'm wrong, but I think I recall you saying that when you are busy with a daily task sometimes it may be there, but you are not that aware of it.

Tom: Right.

John: Um-hmm. I would say, sometimes in the middle of daily tasks that you are not aware of it, make a point of stopping and becoming at least aware of it. That would be step one. If you could take step two and go see if you could urinate then, that would be two things that you could experiment with until we meet again.

Once again, Weakland prescribes a counterintuitive experiment that reverses Tom's typical method for handling his urge to urinate. By asking him to focus on the problem when it isn't bothering him, he directs him to move toward, rather than away from, it.

Fifth Session

John: Okay, and I had also suggested that you continue the things that you have been doing, so we make sure that you got out some, not to rush yourself, and to observe two aspects of things: one, what you see about others' interest in you, and, not less important, how much would you be interested or disinterested in other people.

Tom: It has been good. I have a regular number of people who are interested in me and I'm initially interested in them. I mean this goes in an active stage right now. For various reasons I'm not sure that I want to pursue any of them, but it has been very nice. I really don't know why it is sort of happening all at once. I have no idea. I do know at different times in my life it has happened like this, not recently, but it has happened in the past.

John: And, ah, it could be cyclical; it could be a different sort of change. You are not aware of anything that you might be doing differently?

Tom: No, I really don't think it is anything that I have done differently. I think it could be maybe that I am just meeting people who seem to be affected by me in a nice way.

John: Anything else that might be significant or relevant during these four weeks that we haven't met?* Not necessarily immediately connected to the problem, just how things have been going for you.

Tom: Well, actually it has to do with a lot of the sexual responses that I've been getting. This one person that I have seen a couple of times, you know, he has a lover, so he's very uptight about having these feelings, as long as we can do anything other than have sex it will be okay. So we have spent a lot of time sort of being very . . . touching and you know, and sort of there are just certain sensations, my chest is extremely sensitive and so is his. So we have spent a lot of time, you know, playing around with that. And that's very exciting to me and he is very certain with all that he wants me doing based on, you know, what we have talked about, it's fine with me, you know. But I do have feelings for him. But, you know, I also understand about his other relationship. They've been together 16 years and I'm not a home-wrecker. But it has been very nice. There is someone else that I met who is very turned on to me and we've had sex and it has proceeded to a nice level as a mutual masturbation thing. But it is very sexy.

John: Um-hmm, you can't do that without an erection.

Tom: Right. Right. I had an erection. I had an erection. But there was a tremendous amount of foreplay, which is really needed. You know and I needed that.

John: Ah, you're not objecting to the foreplay?

Tom: No, no. I saw him a second time and didn't need foreplay. I was really aroused.

John: Really!

Tom: Yeah. It was quite amazing to me.

John: Huh! So there was a big difference between the two times?

In what turns out to be the final session, Tom's problems have improved dramatically. Using restraint-from-change strategies evident in earlier sessions and displaying astonishment when Tom describes his rediscovered ability for full sexual arousal, Weakland works to solidify constructive changes that have taken place.

Tom: Yes, well, you know I had the experience of knowing what it is like to be sexual with him and he really turned me on at the time. With

* The client had rescheduled the session for a week later than was originally planned.

this information that I have, I don't think it will be the same but I haven't seen him since that time.

John: Hmm, you can't be absolutely sure of anything in advance.

Tom: I know. Needless to say, it's been a . . . I went to that mixer that I told you about, but I didn't particularly like it. Two people called me wanting to get together and start a sexual interest. I'm sort of not sure if I'm going to. My habit is to pursue one person at a time. I'm not very good at multiple relationships, but I don't know if it might be advisable—that's why I need your advice. Do you think that maybe I should go against my patterns so I might see some kind of responses? But I am getting sexual.

John: Well, I think you at least start with, I don't think I could give you a yes or a no there, because it looks to me like it's something that has elements of both ways. I was still thinking that the basic principle is: Take your time, don't get in a rush. And if you got together more, with more than one person, and you tried to evaluate—other than maybe your own evaluation—is that tracking it on three fronts at once, or is it setting things out and not getting too involved too fast in any one place? And I don't think I am in a position to judge where the balance of that would lie. So the best I can say is that I still think you would be much better off moving rather gradually, but you are the one that has to evaluate what gradually means to you between those two situations.

Tom: [*overlapping*] Um-hmm, I see. Sure. It is interesting, to say the least. But well, it's exciting. It's very exciting for me. To feel appreciated and needed and especially when I've been feeling so badly for the last two and a half . . . two years now.

John: All right. And I can see also . . . I'm very struck and impressed by what you are describing almost in passing, that you don't feel like, "I've got to sit by the telephone hopefully, even if I have got something that I want to do." [*Tom nods yes.*] Sounds like you've got your independence.

Tom: Yeah. It's always been there. I guess I needed a shot of sexual adrenaline. You know I think that I mentioned it to you the last time, that's what I needed. That's what I wanted. That's what I missed. But you know, I haven't been out there. Maybe the time that I went out to that thing, but it just seems like instead of me going to them, they keep coming to me—for whatever reason they seem to find me.

John: Sounds not bad.

Tom: [*laughing*] No it doesn't sound bad. Yeah, I'm in a pretty good state of mind, for me.

John: Well, it sounds to me like a lot of change has already been set in motion. Ah, there comes a point where things are moving. To sort of actively work on them you may only get in their way, rather than just let them continue to progress for themselves. Really, what I am thinking is, should we at least have a recess and see what develops from here?

CONCLUDING COMMENTS

Tom was a desperate man when he entered counseling with Weakland at the MRI Brief Therapy Center. Preoccupied with a constant urge to urinate, he was severely depressed about an inability to perform sexually. After one and a half years of treatment, encompassing multiple medical evaluations, psychological counseling, pharmacological intervention, hypnosis, and acupuncture—all of which had failed to alleviate his problems—Tom declared to Weakland during the first session that this was his "last chance" to find a reason to keep on living.

Over the course of five hours of therapy, Tom regained a satisfactory sense of sexual adequacy, his depression was lifted, and he expressed confidence in his state of mind and social outlook. During a follow-up conversation, he indicated that he no longer experienced difficulty with depression, and he didn't mention any further problem with an atypical urge to urinate.

These impressive results were not accidental, nor were they the product of some magicianlike ability on the part of Weakland, who devoted much of his career to demystifying the process of therapy. With study and practice, the theoretical premises and clinical skills used by Weakland are learnable and teachable. Thank you, John, for leaving such discernable footsteps for others to follow.

REFERENCES

Bateson, G. (1955). A theory of play & fantasy. *Psychiatric research reports*, 2, 39–51.

Bateson, G., Jackson, D., Haley, J., & Weakland, J. (1956). Toward a theory of schizophrenia, *Behavioral Science, 1*(4), 251–264.

de Shazer, S. (1998). John H. Weakland—master of the fine art of "doing nothing." In W. Ray & S. de Shazer (Eds.), *Evolving brief therapies* (pp. 30–43). Galena, IL: Geist & Russell.

Erickson, M. (1967). Pediatric hypnotherapy. In J. Haley (Ed.), *Advanced techniques of hypnosis & therapy: Selected papers of M. H. Erickson* (pp. 420–421). New York: Grune & Stratton.

Fisch, R. (1965, Sept. 15). Proposal for a brief therapy clinic and evaluation project. Unpublished memorandum, from Richard Fisch to Don Jackson.

Fisch, R., Jackson, D., Weakland, J., Watzlawick, P., Bodin, A., Clemes, S., Sorenson, E.,

& McLachlan, B. (1968). Brief therapy center unpublished year-end report. Mental Research Institute, Palo Alto, CA.

Fisch, R., Weakland, J., & Segal, L. (1982). *The tactics of change: Doing therapy briefly.* San Francisco: Jossey-Bass.

Fisch, R., Weakland, J., Watzlawick, P., & Bodin, A. (1972a). *Focused problem resolution with families.* Unpublished audio recording.

Fisch, R., Weakland, J., Watzlawick, P., & Bodin, A. (1972b). On unbecoming family therapists. In A. Ferber, M. Mendelson, & A. Napier (Eds.), *The book of family therapy* (pp. 597–617). New York: Science House.

Haley, J. (1973). *Uncommon therapy.* New York: Norton.

Jackson, D. (1955). The therapist's personality in the therapy of schizophrenics. *Archives of Neurology and Psychiatry, 74,* 292–299.

Jackson, D. (1957). The question of family homeostasis. *Psychiatric Quarterly Supplement 31*(1), 79–90.

Jackson, D. (1961). Interactional psychotherapy. In M. Stein (Ed.), *Contemporary psychotherapies* (pp. 256–271). New York: The Free Press of Glenco.

Jackson, D. (1965). The study of the family. *Family Process, 4*(1), 1–20.

Jackson, D. (1967). Schizophrenia: The nosological nexus. In *Excerpta Medica International Congress: The origins of schizophrenia.* Proceedings of the first International Conference 151, pp. 111–120. Rochester, NY.

Jackson, D., & Weakland, J. (1961). Conjoint family therapy: Some considerations on theory, technique, & results. *Psychiatry, 24*(2), 30–45.

Trepper, T. (1995). Introduction. In J. Weakland & W. Ray (Eds.), *Propagations: 30 years of influence from the Mental Research Institute* (pp. xvii–xviii). New York: Haworth.

Watzlawick, P., Beavin, J., & Jackson, D. (1967). *Pragmatics of human communication.* New York: Norton.

Watzlawick, P., Weakland, R., & Fisch, R. (1974). *Change.* New York: Norton.

Weakland, J. (1960). *Therapeutic use of paradoxical injunctions.* Unpublished manuscript, Mental Research Institute, Palo Alto, CA.

Weakland, J. (1991, June). *Interview by W. Ray.* Unpublished manuscript, Mental Research Institute, Palo Alto, CA.

Weakland, J., Fisch, R., Watzlawick, P., & Bodin, A. (1974). Brief therapy: Focused problem resolution. *Family Process, 13,* 141–168.

Weakland, J., & Ray, W. (1995). *Propagations: Thirty years of influence from the Mental Research Institute.* New York: Haworth.

thirteen

Transforming Stories: A Contextual Approach to Treating Sexual Offenders

William C. Rambo

All sorrows can be borne if you put them into a story or tell a story about them.

—Isak Dinesen

SINCE THE MID-1980s, I have worked with over 1,000 men accused of sexual offenses against children, men almost universally referred to as "sexual offenders" or, increasingly, "sexual predators." My work owes much to the theorizing of the English anthropologist Gregory Bateson (1972, 1979, 1991; G. Bateson & M. C. Bateson, 1987) and to the clinical theory and applications pioneered by the Mental Research Institute (MRI) in Palo Alto (Fisch, Weakland, & Segal, 1982; Watzlawick, Beavin, & Jackson, 1967; Watzlawick & Weakland, 1977; Watzlawick, Weakland, & Fisch, 1974). The combination of my own clinical experience and the ideas of Bateson, the MRI, and some others (Flemons, 1991, 2002; Gilligan, 1987; Haley, 1973, 1986; Keeney, 1983; O'Hanlon, 1987) has led to my embrace of several basic assumptions concerning human behavior, therapeutic relationships, and change. In this chapter, I set out to delineate and illustrate these assumptions; however, before I begin articulating the details, I want to offer a guiding metaphor to set the tone for what follows.

I recently made a rare visit to a local mall for some holiday shopping. In one store, I came across a collection of about a dozen different angels, each with a different name. Of those being offered, I selected three: the *Angel of Grace*, the *Angel of Remembrance*, and the *Angel of Hope*. It struck me, once

I'd brought them home, that these three angels encapsulate everything I strive to do in therapy.

First and foremost, I endeavor in my clinical work to convey an unqualified acceptance of each client—not as he might be, but as he *is*. As an essential precondition for the therapeutic journey on which we embark, this acceptance is an invitation into *grace*, which I understand in Batesonian terms:

> I . . . argue that the problem of grace is fundamentally a problem of integration and that what is to be integrated is the diverse parts of the mind—especially those multiple levels of which one extreme is called "consciousness" and the other the "unconscious." For the attainment of grace, the reasons of the heart must be integrated with the reasons of the reason. (Bateson, 1972, p. 129)

Acceptance fosters the openness my clients need if they are to assume full responsibility for their acts of sexual abuse and to find a pathway toward integrated understanding and change.

Our therapeutic journey necessarily involves *remembrance*. Each man is expected and encouraged to recall and face the facts of what he did and to grasp the consequences of his behavior, not only for the child(ren) he abused, but also for the rest of the family. Because most of my therapy is conducted in a group setting, each client participates in helping other men go through the same process.

The expectations I bring into my work place demands on my clients, but they simultaneously affirm the possibility of change, and thus they embody *hope*—hope for the transformation that I believe is possible for most of the men convicted of sexual offenses.

Through the theoretical descriptions and stories that follow, I will elaborate on how grace, remembrance, and hope interweave throughout my work.

CONTEXTUAL UNDERSTANDING

All behavior, including sexual behavior, can most usefully be understood as existing in context and not necessarily as a sign of some deep underlying individual dysfunction or pathology. This assertion is certainly nothing new to anyone trained in brief systemic therapy, whether problem or solution focused. Most such therapists agree that a wide range of harmful or painful human behaviors, ranging from intensifying marital arguments and sexual dysfunctions, to domestic abuse, substance abuse, and even child physical abuse, can be approached by viewing the behavior as part of a more encompassing interactional cycle. In other words, these behaviors need to be understood in context. What many such therapists appear to balk at, in my experience, is extending such contextual understanding to child sexual abuse. This chapter addresses this omission.

Bateson (1972) defines context "as a collective term for all those events which tell the organism among what set of alternatives he must make his next choice" (p. 289). But, Bateson continues, "an organism responds to the 'same' stimulus differently in differing contexts, and we must therefore ask about the source of the organism's information. From what percept does he know that Context A is different from Context B?" (p. 289). Understood this way, relevant change—what for our therapeutic purposes can be defined as a significant decrease in the likelihood of a repetition of sexually abusive behavior—can be occasioned by a change in context. Wilk (1985) explains that

> the significance of anything for humans depends on the context in which we find "it." In another context, an experience or communication or piece of interaction would have a completely different significance and therefore would be something completely different. (p. 214)

Therapists who balk at applying this contextual understanding to the problem of sexual abuse are typically caught short by the commonly held notion that individuals who commit this offense are different from "normal people." This is evidenced by the label "sexual offender," a term that conjures up all sorts of assumptions about the type of person who would perpetrate such heinous acts. Bateson (1972) observes that

> in describing individual human beings, both the scientist and the layman commonly resort to adjectives descriptive of "character." It is said that Mr. Jones is dependent, hostile, . . . anxious, exhibitionistic, narcissistic, passive, competitive, . . . careless, careful, casual, etc. . . .
>
> [These] adjectives . . . which purport to describe individual character are really not strictly applicable to the individual but rather describe *transactions* between the individual and his material and human environment. No man is "resourceful" or "dependent" or "fatalistic" in a vacuum. His characteristic, whatever it be, is not his but is rather a characteristic of what goes on between him and something (or somebody) else. (pp. 297–298)

Bateson (1972) argues that these patterns of interaction result from ways the individual has learned to make sense of events, probably date from "early infancy," and are "unconscious" (p. 300). The sociologist Joel

Charon (cited in Pryor, 1996) offers a similar idea when he suggests that "past experiences of the individual are used to help determine the kind of action to take in a situation. . . . The past . . . provides us with the tools to define the present" (p. 257). The men I work with, like the rest of us, have character traits that developed long ago within the context of their relationship with others, and part of what we do in our groups is tease these patterns out.

But thinking about context is a difficult business, fraught with perils. Bateson (1979) makes the unequivocal claim that "without context, words and actions have no meaning at all" (p. 15). However, this does not mean that the context "causes" behaviors. If this were true, then a contextual understanding of sexual abuse would rapidly degenerate into yet another way to delimit responsibility and excuse culpability (as in, "The context made me do it"). Context can't be separated out as an "independent or determining variable" that produces an effect on some equally separated dependent variable (Bateson, 1972, p. 338). Rather, context must be understood as being woven of the very components that it in turn contextualizes.

Music is a helpful analogy for making sense of this (D. Flemons, personal communication, September 30, 1989). A melody contextualizes each of the individual notes composing it, but it can't be considered independent of the notes—it is nothing but the connection between them. Complex patterns of interaction cannot be reduced to simple causal summations.

This suggests that participation in the creation and destruction of contexts is an inevitable human activity—an activity undeniably influenced by our external situations and personal histories and experiences, but one for which we are ultimately responsible. And, as with all human activities, there is an ethical dimension. When I argue for a contextually informed understanding of sexual abuse, this does not mean the men I work with are to be viewed as puppets, as hapless pawns in the unfolding of their lives. Indeed, if these ideas about context are at all close to the mark, these men, in a sense, stand doubly condemned. Not only are they responsible for their acts of abuse; they are responsible for participating in the evolution of relationships, of particular contexts with their families, with children, and with themselves, where such abuse becomes possible.

This understanding exists in stark contrast to one derived from an assumption of internal pathology as the causative factor in sexually abusive behaviors. Bateson (1991) criticizes "the trick of drawing a generalization from the world of external observation, giving it a fancy name, and then asserting that this named abstraction exists inside the organism as an explanatory principle" (p. 76). This is the essence of what occurs when we label those men who sexually abuse children as "deviants," as different from the rest of us, and then proceed to explain their abusive behavior in terms of their "deviancy." Unfortunately, much of the literature on sexual abusers assumes such a difference and offers such a circular explanation. It is not surprising then, given this, that many sexual offender treatment programs place this assumed difference at the heart of their approach.

CONVENTIONAL TREATMENT APPROACHES: RELAPSE PREVENTION

Clients in many traditional sexual offender treatment programs are taught, first, that they are different from normal men. No attempt is made to understand their sexually inappropriate behavior—it is already assumed to be the result of their deviant sexual arousal. No further explanation is needed, and the larger context in which the abuse occurred is not a consideration. One influential treatment guide unequivocally states that "no existing therapeutic intervention eradicates, across time and situations, the offender's sexually deviant fantasies," adding that "few therapists who have experience working with sex offenders regard the sexual aggressor as 'curable'"(Salter, 1988, p. 139).

These basic premises concerning sexual offenders are obviously almost identical to the central tenets of most addictions programs in this country, in which clients are also taught that they are not like normal people. It follows that deviant individuals will always be considered at serious risk of relapsing, whether it be an addict falling off the wagon or a sexual offender once again abusing a child. In both cases, the "therapeutic" effort is directed toward preventing a relapse.

Relapse prevention continues to be the dominant model for sexual offender treatment programs in North America (Laws, Hudson, & Ward, 2000, p. 21); however, other models do exist. In a major edited monograph published by the Civic Research Institute in 1995, Schwartz mentions a recent "movement away from the single factor model (e.g., Relapse Prevention . . .) to a more integrated approach" (p. 1.2)—one that recognizes

> that sexual deviancy is a multifaceted phenomenon that must be treated using a multimodal approach. Thus, the field seems to be moving away from simple cause-and-effect explanations to an appreciation of the dynamic nature of human behavior. (p. 1.2)

CONTEXT-SENSITIVE TREATMENT

A contextual framework invites a more encompassing view of sexual offender treatment than is afforded by relapse prevention models. I have
never used relapse prevention as the defining part of my program, choosing instead to make relapse-prevention strategy decisions on a case-by-
case basis (see Rambo, 1999, pp. 191–204, for a more detailed discussion
of this issue). Obviously, someone whose primary erotic focus is young
children will need to employ such a strategy for the rest of his life if he is
to minimize the chances of reoffending. However, this has not been necessary with most of the men with whom I work, and with some it could actually prove to be counterproductive.[i]

Instead of teaching my clients that they will always be at risk of sexually
abusing a child, I work with them on developing individual strategies for
not placing themselves in compromising or risky situations (i.e., contexts)
with children, or with adult sexual partners for that matter. What constitutes "risky" varies from person to person, though with most, the emphasis
is not so much on the likelihood that they might act inappropriately as it is
on the danger their actions might be *perceived* as inappropriate. No registered sex offender can afford to do anything that could possibly be construed as sexually deviant. This is something all of my clients must learn to
live with, while still finding a way to lead lives as normal as possible.

My choice of this more individualized, nonpathologizing, and context-
sensitive approach to treatment is not lightly made. Both my clinical work
and research results fail to distinguish most (particularly incestuous) sexual offenders from "normal men." Surely, they have made agonizingly bad
decisions, but this does not mean that they are hopelessly deviant men
who, for the safety of children in their vicinity, must continually be closely
monitored and tightly controlled. I conclude a small qualitative study of
incestuous fathers by saying that "in general, there were no specific attributes of the men with whom I worked which differentiated them from me
or others" (Rambo, 1999, p. 209).

Support for this position comes from Pryor's (1996) study of 30 men
who sexually abused their own children or children known to them. He
surmised that "there does not seem to be much that differentiates these
men from men who are not offenders except that they crossed what appears to be a thin boundary between ordinary sexual relations and what is

---

i. See Flemons, 1991, pp. 104–111, for a discussion of the problems of focusing on *not*
doing something.

defined culturally as extreme sexual deviation" (p. 273). More specifically, as Pryor (1996) describes the process,

> the men became interested in sex with children for the same reasons they do with any other adult—they were curious, they began noticing, they responded to what they perceived as a sexual cue, they experienced an erection from non-sexual touching, they chose someone they perceived as accessible to them. They experienced sex in the same ways men generally experience sex—they enjoyed the touch and the feeling of ejaculating, it was exciting because it was something new, they felt young again, it helped them forget all the stress in their lives, it was a thrill, they felt closer and more intimate. They approached and engaged the other party in ways men routinely initiate sex—by trying to seduce the person, trying to talk the person into it, being a little forceful, grabbing at the person, attempting to introduce sex in stages, taking over if they thought the other person started things. (p. 2)

Below, I present a case study of a father who initially became aroused in what began as harmless wrestling and hugging with his teenage daughter. He began to touch her inappropriately, "copping feels" off and on for over a year before his abusive behaviors escalated and the abuse was reported. Pryor (1996) describes an identical phenomenon "in the cases of nearly all the men [in his study]," where "feelings of sexual arousal surfaced as the result of an *unanticipated erotic shift*" (p. 257):

> The offending process started when the men unexpectedly found themselves in the midst of an erotic situation, experiencing feelings of sexual interest, desire, curiosity, and the like, which they experienced as spontaneous, unexpected, and unplanned. The men were able to pinpoint exact situations in which feelings of sexual interest and desire surfaced for them, which caught them off guard and led them to reframe their victims in sexual terms. (p. 258)

According to Pryor (1996), "Each offender became immersed in a stream of experience, an erotic stage of awareness *not bounded by reflection* [italics added]" (p. 258). I, too, have noticed an absence of reflection in nearly all cases of child sexual abuse. My clients find themselves becoming aroused and seem almost compelled to act on those feelings, something else they share with the men in Pryor's (1996) study, who "became unable to turn those [erotic] feelings off and return to a non-sexual state" (p. 258).

Pryor (1996) goes on to contend that these "*unanticipated erotic shifts . . .* are not unique to men who molest children" (p. 258), that, indeed, they may be involved "in initial forays into behaviors such as swinging or group sex, sadomasochism, bisexuality, cross-dressing, or extramarital sex" (p. 259). While fully agreeing with this, I would take it a step further and argue that experiences of such spontaneous sexual arousal are common to all normally functioning males, in part because of male physiology. The external position of the penis results in its being highly susceptible to stimulation by mild or even nonsexual stimuli.

When the source of a sexual stimulus is another consenting adult, the individual may end up (at worst) in an ill-chosen relationship. When the focus is a child, the potential harm is immeasurable. But regardless of the source, it seems clear that many, if not most, men *make meaning out of their arousal*, associating the *fact* of an erection with the *idea* of sexual attraction, and then constructing an *explanation* for the attraction. They experience, *without reflection*, something similar to the following sequence of conclusions: "Given the arousal I'm feeling around this person, I must be sexually attracted to her or him, and that must mean that he or she is doing something to attract me." With the fact, idea, and explanation in place, it is but a short step to feeling justified in taking action. This, or some similar process of belief-building, appears to be at the heart of so many of my clients' confusing warm and *loving* feelings for a child with warm and *sexual* feelings for that child.

Popular conceptions of sexual offenders characterize them as having deviant arousal patterns (Leberg, 1997; Salter, 1988). However, if my clinical experience is accurate, then, ironically enough, the problem for most of my clients lies not in their sexual arousal per se, but in the particular conclusions they draw from it and the actions they believe the conclusions justify. This offers one way of making sense of Haywood and Grossman's (1994) finding that, in their study, "normal control subjects admitted to a nearly equivalent degree of subjective arousal to young girls as did girl-molesters" (p. 337). It is not deviant *arousal* that differentiates most sexual offenders from normal men, transporting them to "the other side of the moral wall" (Pryor, 1996, p. 258). Rather, it is the *meaning they make of their arousal* and, as a result, the actions they feel justified in taking. The normal controls in Haywood and Grossman's (1994) study did not *act* on their arousal. Much of my clinical work is devoted to deriving a contextually informed understanding of how and why some men make sense of their arousal in a way that renders them vulnerable to abusing children.

It is precisely this understanding—that our clients are not demonstrably different from ourselves—that lies at the heart of the approach to therapy pioneered by those at the MRI (Fisch et al., 1982; Watzlawick et al., 1967; Watzlawick, & Weakland, 1977; Watzlawick et al., 1974). I am indebted to their elegant understandings of the pragmatics of therapy, including the idea that problematic behaviors can be conceptualized as failed solution attempts.

My approach has also been informed by the work of Douglas Flemons (1991, 2002), especially his understanding of the importance of not attempting to sever ourselves from our actions. Flemons (2002) argues that therapists working from a "relational perspective" will steer their clients away from trying to banish a problem they despise, choosing, instead to

> facilitate *a change in their relationship to it*. If your clients' dissociative attempts to negate what they hate have created a *separated connection* with it—a negative relationship that has maintained, or even heightened, its significance—then your job is to facilitate the associative development of a *connected separation*: a relationship with the problem that allows for a comfortable connection and/or a relaxed letting go. Instead of helping to push your clients' problem away, you'll explore ways they can embrace and/or lose track of or interest in it, allowing it to become boring or irrelevant or otherwise unremarkable. (p. 178)

A primary goal of my work is to support and encourage my clients to accept and, ultimately, embrace their abusive actions as a part of themselves, at least as part of who they were at the time of those actions. And while few of these men are likely ever to have a "comfortable connection" (Flemons, 2002, p. 178) with their abusive behaviors, it is possible for them to reach a place where they can begin "letting go" of the idea of themselves as deviant, and move—through the process of remembrance— toward hope. With such a change, a different story can be told.

TRANSFORMATIVE STORIES

Having long been aware of transformative potential of a good story, and appreciative of Bateson's (1979) use of "story" as a synonym for "context," I have placed the construction of stories at the heart of my clinical work. My overall goal is to create a safe space for each client to be able to speak openly of his sexual offense and, working together in a group setting, to develop an understanding of the various factors contributing to the inappropriate behavior. In the process, I do my best to engage the client in participating in the creation of a story that explains how he came to act abusively and how he is fully responsible for those actions.

If the story is successful, it doesn't define the client in terms of his abusive actions, turning him into a deviant monster, but, rather, preserves his identity as a human being. This makes it possible for him to incorporate the abusive behavior into his life history, accepting it as part of his past and, in so doing, defining it as no longer having a place in his present or future. Crucial in achieving such an undertaking is the particular means by which the client, with the group's and my help, constructs his understanding. Because multiple stories are almost always possible, there are ethical implications in the choice of which one to tell. Perhaps a story is in order.

My Story

A number of years ago, when my daughter, Rachel, was eight, I decided it was time we dispensed with the training wheels on her bicycle. My memory is that she was in agreement with this, albeit with some trepidation. In any event, one autumn afternoon I removed the training wheels and we began the process of figuring out together how to teach her to ride, given this was a new experience for us both. We were fortunate to be living in one of the few neighborhoods in south Florida with sidewalks, thus enabling us to stay off the street. I helped hold the bike steady as she got on and then did what I suppose is the only thing one can do. I held onto the back of her bike seat, trying to keep the machine upright while she, pedaling and moving forward, wobbled from right to left and back again. In this awkward fashion we made it about two thirds of the way around the block, with each house passed and every yard traversed witnessing an increase in Rachel's confidence and skill.

This, along with an increase in speed, finally led me to let go of the back of her bike. For a brief moment, she was actually riding by herself. But then she realized that I had turned her loose. Do you remember the coyote from the old *Roadrunner* cartoons? Zooming off a cliff, he would keep running in thin air until he realized he *was* in thin air, at which point he would plummet to the ground. In coyote fashion, Rachel almost immediately fell over, half on the sidewalk and half on the grass. I remember running up and stopping just behind the rear wheel of the prostrate bicycle and rider. A quick glance revealed no obvious injuries. She turned and looked up at me with a somewhat puzzled, or perhaps bewildered, look in her eyes, searching for clarification of what exactly had happened and, more importantly, for guidance on how she was to interpret it. How was she to make sense of this uninvited and unpleasant experience?

Rachel appeared on the verge of tears, which itself would have constituted one species of interpretation. I, however, had a more helpful frame in mind. I have nothing against crying in general and have certainly comforted Rachel many times, making no effort to stem her tears. But in this instance, tears and comfort would have communicated the idea that something bad had happened and, more importantly, that riding a bicycle is a dangerous activity. Delaying a return to riding would also have created a space for fear and doubt to intrude. So, still standing just behind her, I proclaimed how glad I was that she had finally fallen off her bike, as this is the only way to learn. I recall her looking at me rather quizzically, still obviously prepared to cry if necessary.

I reached down and helped her get up and back on the bike so we could finish going around the block. I again held on to the seat, but this time she was noticeably more competent in her management of the handlebars, riding in a nearly straight line. I continued to hold on until we rounded the last corner and then, with our house in sight, I warned her that I was letting go, adding that she now could ride by herself. She did. I still have the snapshot I took soon after, a picture of a young girl with an expression of pride and self-satisfaction, with a small scrape on her right knee.

Rachel's Story

I have one further story I would like to share and hope in the process of doing so to render more transparent the point I am trying to make. This one also involves Rachel, but the bicycle has been replaced by a compact passenger car, a gift from her mother and stepfather on the occasion of her successfully passing the written test for her learner's permit. Several months after getting the permit, Rachel, along with her car, ended up at my home, with the plan that I would take my turn helping her improve her driving skills. She and I had been out before, but this was to be our first time venturing beyond the immediate neighborhood.

We ran some errands, and except for one or two rather unnerving maneuvers on her part, the afternoon went well. We were on our way back, almost home, with one last left turn to make from a dedicated lane in the median of a divided boulevard. Tired, Rachel had asked me to take over the driving at our last stop; however, despite a light rain that had started to fall, I told her I wanted her to finish out the afternoon, a decision I would later recall with regret.

I instructed Rachel to turn into the left turn lane, assuming she would pull up to the end of the lane and stop, at which point we could jointly decide when it was safe to complete the turn. The situation was complicated by some landscaping in the median in front of the lane, which partially obscured the oncoming traffic. Perhaps in part because of this, along with the rain and her being tired and inexperienced, Rachel didn't stop, continuing the turn until she was two-thirds of the way across the inside lane of the other side of the roadway. Unfortunately, this lane was occupied by a large van heading in our direction at a speed that precluded the possibility of its stopping or swerving. It hit us on the passenger side and knocked us back out of the lane.

No one was hurt, but the impact was understandably terrifying for Rachel, who immediately burst into tears. I was furious at myself for not doing a better job of guiding her, for not agreeing to drive home when she asked me, and for not preventing such a frightening and upsetting experience. I felt even worse when word came back a few days later that her car had been written off by the insurance company, the damage too great to repair.

These are still, in essence, my feelings when I think back to this episode. Rachel, however, chose to interpret the experience differently. She tells a different story. Within an hour of the accident, she was saying how glad she was it had happened, because there was no other way she could have realized how truly dangerous driving is. Nearly a year later, as I write this, her story has not changed. She still says that the accident was for the best, and she genuinely believes it will prevent her having a potentially more serious accident in the future. I very much want to believe this, especially as she is now driving on her own.

And so we have two stories, each involving a father and daughter, each intricately related to the human business of constructing understandings and interpretations. In the first instance, I was clearly in the more influential role when it came to giving meaning to the fall from the bike; however, it is important to emphasize that I still needed Rachel to buy into my version of the mishap. The business of creating stories is not something we do *to* another person. Fundamentally a cooperative process, it is done jointly *with* the other's concurrence.

By the time depicted in the second story, Rachel was clearly much more capable of taking an active, even decisive, role in making sense of her own experience, to the point of formulating and holding onto an interpretation very much at odds with that of her father. The lovely thing about this is that her positive interpretation continues to offer so much more potential for growth and learning than my more pessimistic and self-blaming one. She has learned well the art of constructing useful stories.

CONTEXT-SENSITIVE TREATMENT

Most of my work has been with adult males, and this will be the focus of what follows.[ii] The vast majority of the men referred to me are on felony sexual offender probation, and thus they face constant reminders of how they are viewed by state and local lawmakers and, by extension, society in general. Laws and ordinances establish curfews, they restrict where the men can live, work, and even visit, and increasingly, they stipulate electronic monitoring. Such measures convey the message that these men are dangerous, potentially violent, and unfit to live in the community. Many of my clients also condemn themselves for their abusive acts, expressing shame and remorse for having hurt someone whom they may care deeply about. A significant part of treatment involves helping them understand the potential depth of this hurt and its effect on the victim. The therapeutic approach I have developed encompasses these stories of abuse and harm, yet also embraces the potential for hope—hope for the lives of the men, and hope for the lives of those they have abused.

Almost all men on sexual offender probation are under court order to attend and complete sexual offender treatment, with failure to comply most likely resulting in a violation of their probation and potential incarceration. All new referrals are seen for an intake appointment, during which I gather basic information concerning their alleged sexual offense and their current living situation. I sometimes schedule additional individual sessions to permit a more detailed initial assessment. The client is then scheduled to begin coming to one of the weekly groups I run at the center. Most men will be in therapy a minimum of five years, with at least the first two years involving weekly attendance. Clearly, this work is far removed from that of voluntary clients seeking help for a specific problem, and thus this chapter is not an especially obvious companion piece in a book on *brief* approaches to sex therapy.

It is important to understand that any court mandated treatment program must be structured to address not only clinical concerns but also those of social control. My responsibility is not just to my clients, but also to the criminal justice system and, in a very real sense, to society. Consequently, the length of treatment in many cases has more to do with the need to provide ongoing monitoring of men on felony probation than with the actual time required to address the inappropriate sexual behavior.

---

ii. Over the years I have worked with several adult women, as well as male and female adolescents.

While, as with all therapy, some cases require a longer term of treatment, many can actually be clinically resolved in a fairly brief time period, given the assumptions about change held by the brief therapy model discussed earlier.

The significant exception to this involves those men who appear to be primarily, or solely, sexually attracted to prepubescent children or barely postpubescent teenagers, as well as those exhibiting certain compulsive sexual behaviors, most commonly exhibitionism and voyeurism. Such men make up no more than 5 to 10% of all the adjudicated sexual offenders with whom I work; however, they do require ongoing treatment and monitoring, as well as a more traditional "relapse prevention" program. The argument here is not that such offenders do not exist, but that they are a small minority, and should not be used as the primary model for working with sex offenders in general.

Unfortunately, this argument has one major flaw: No one, no matter how experienced in working with adjudicated sexual offenders, can ever know with certainty whether any given individual will, or will not, go on to commit another sexual offense. This work inevitably engenders an abiding skepticism and distrust—both of the clients and of one's own clinical judgment. Obviously, the safest course is the more traditional approach to sexual offender treatment already mentioned—to assume that all offenders harbor sexually deviant thoughts and must be treated as chronic sexual abusers. For reasons already expressed, this is not an option for me. Instead, I utilize all of my education and experience, along with the best guidelines we currently possess in the area of risk assessment, to make what I hope are informed judgments regarding each individual with whom I work. Since mistakes are inevitable, I always endeavor to err on the side of caution. This caution, born of uncertainty, becomes another clinical reason for a fairly lengthy treatment program and for the judicious use of variants on the relapse-prevention approach with nearly all clients.

There are two further clinical reasons for a longer course of treatment that should be noted. First, many individuals seem to struggle in fully disclosing the details of their sexual offenses, even in the relatively limited confines of a small treatment group. In some cases, this takes the form of a complete denial that any sexual offense took place. When this occurs, I have found that having such an individual sit in group for several years, listening to others talk openly about their offenses, can assist in helping him find the voice to disclose his own inappropriate behavior. Recently, one such man, after three years of weekly group sessions, announced that he was ready to stop denying his guilt and acknowledge what he did.

This is not to say I am always successful—far from it. A number of those who enter treatment denying any inappropriate sexual behavior maintain this denial throughout. Perhaps they just cannot admit, even to themselves, what they did, or perhaps they are completely innocent of the charges. This latter possibility can never be summarily dismissed. As I write this, today's paper carries a story of a man, imprisoned in New York for 21 years for an alleged murder, being released after new DNA testing exonerated him. I have no doubt innocent men end up on sexual offender probation just as they do on death row. The problem is that there is no way to distinguish them from the guilty. Most sexual assaults on children leave no physical evidence and thus no possibility of some future vindication. In any event, I find that when the client will not admit to having done anything wrong, I am usually not able to be helpful in any meaningful sense.

A second clinical reason for longer-term therapy involves the supportive and rehabilitative roles of the program. Many of the men referred to treatment have lost everything they had prior to their arrest—family, job, savings, home, respect. Thus, part of treatment becomes offering basic emotional support, as well as encouragement and, at times, guidance, as they go about the difficult task of rebuilding their lives.

Phases of Treatment

As a practical matter, with such long-term group treatment, all groups are set up as open ended, with new participants coming in on a regular basis. The other treatment programs of which I am aware permit the participants to gradually move from attending once a week to three times a month, eventually attending once a month. The individual remains in the same group for the whole time he is in treatment, meaning that the primary focus remains on his past sexual offense, no matter how long he attends. In contrast, the program I run has three distinct phases, each with its own focus.

In Phase I, during two years of weekly group sessions, the emphasis is on each participant accepting responsibility for his past actions, recognizing the cycle of problematic behavior that resulted in the sexual offense, identifying contributing factors, and developing empathy for the victim(s). This entails each man, when his turn comes, sharing the details of the criminal sexual behavior of which he has been convicted (the court mandated treatment equivalent of defining the "presenting problem"). Working together with the therapist and group, he develops an understanding of the various contextual factors (including thought processes, personal history, and external circumstances) that may have contributed to the inappropriate sexual behavior. And, when appropriate, he participates in the relapse prevention strategy mentioned earlier, identifying danger signs, and developing strategies for avoiding actions or situations that might increase the probability of a reoccurrence of the abusive behavior.

Phase II consists of bi-weekly group sessions for a minimum of one year. The emphasis is primarily on present-day concerns—on how the individual is progressing with life-goals previously identified and on identifying better coping mechanisms for dealing with stress and disappointment. There is also a continued focus (when appropriate) on remaining aware of the cycle of maladaptive behavior, identifying danger signs, and avoiding actions or situations that might increase the probability of a reoccurrence of the behavior.

In Phase III, individuals attend monthly group sessions for a minimum of two years. The focus is similar to that of the second phase but with increasing attention given to addressing each individual's future—his plans, goals, dreams, and aspirations. After two years of such sessions, if the individual evidences continued stability in his personal life and work setting, I usually recommend termination of mandated treatment.

These three phases function as clear context markers, or "signals whose major function is to classify contexts" (Bateson, 1972, p. 289), demarcating change and, by implication, progress in treatment. This is nothing new. The education system accomplishes something similar by establishing grades through which students gradually move on the way to graduation. It is also not unlike what often occurs in traditional brief therapy, with the therapist underscoring progress by gradually lengthening the space between sessions from one to every two, three, or four weeks.

The hope is that, by the time an individual completes treatment, his gaze, and that of the therapist, is towards the future—no longer mired in the past offense, though remaining aware of it. All decisions as to whether to move someone further along in the program rest with me.

The following case example illustrates some of the theoretical points I've made and demonstrates the degree to which attending to the details of clients' stories is essential in providing a context-sensitive approach to treatment.

Paul's Story

Paul, a distinguished looking man of average size, began therapy with me when he was 46. Having recently relocated to South Florida for a new job, he was referred by his community control officer for court-mandated sexual offender treatment.[iii] I met with him individually for several sessions and then referred him into a weekly sexual offender group of 12 men. One member of the group was in the process of trying to secure a plea bargain for his charges, while the others were already on probation or parole for felony sexual offenses. Five months after starting, Paul was ready to tell his story. He qualified his description by noting that he had a history of treatment for "depression" and a "poor memory" for dates. Nevertheless, over the course of several sessions, he was able to clearly relate the details of the abuse and of his personal history.

Paul told the group that he had been charged with "lewd and lascivious" acts on his then 15-year-old daughter, Alice. One night, when she was sick and running a fever, he went into her room and washed her face and chest with a cool, wet rag. He then fondled her breasts and vagina, but did not penetrate her. He went back to her room "four or five times" that night and repeated his actions. She pretended to be asleep. Paul said that he had "copped feels" before, off and on for about a year and a half. He described himself, prior to this time, as having been a "model father," with a "model family," consisting of himself, his wife, Jill, and three children—Alice, her sister Nancy, who was three years older, and her brother Calvin, 10 years younger.

Two days following this instance of abuse, Alice told a girl friend, who told her mother. The sheriff was called. Paul's wife phoned him at work in the evening and said she had to talk to him. She picked him up and told him the sheriff had said he would not embarrass him by arresting him on the job if he would turn himself in. He immediately complied, did not get an attorney, and made a full confession. He was bonded out in a few hours.

Paul moved out of the house so his daughter could come back home. The Children's Protective Services of what was then called the Florida Department of Human Resources (HRS) became involved, initially blaming Paul's wife for allowing the abuse to occur. After a few months, however, HRS backed out of active involvement with the family. Paul went to a psychologist, who gave him an MMPI and said he thought his behavior was "out of the ordinary" and "not likely to happen again." But he also said "we might never know" why Paul molested his youngest daughter. In re-

iii. This particular form of community supervision is colloquially known as "house arrest." An individual on community control in Florida meets with his probation officer weekly, submits a detailed schedule for the upcoming seven days, and is only allowed to leave his home for purposes of work, doctors' appointments (including therapy), and a few hours of shopping per week.

lating this to the group, Paul added that he then "fired" the psychologist, because he wanted to know "why" he had done it.

Less than a year after the abuse was reported, Paul did a final plea bargain to two years community control and 10 years probation. He was initially able to keep his job of several years as the "right-hand man" for a family-owned business. However, six months later, his boss, who knew of the abuse, landed a contract with some local schools, became nervous, and fired him. Soon after, Paul agreed to a psychiatric evaluation and was placed on Zoloft. After two months on the medication, he realized that he had not been himself "for eight years"—that he had felt "withdrawn and depressed."

The next week, Paul continued his account with a brief personal history. He dropped out of high school in the 10th grade and spent a year and a half in the military. After his discharge, he met Jill, his future wife, at a party: Both were 19. It was the first serious relationship for either of them. They got a place together soon after they started dating.

After living together for five years, they decided they wanted to have children, so they got married. Their first child, Nancy, a girl, was born a year later. Jill was working as an accountant, and they jointly decided she would give up her career to stay home with the baby. A second daughter, Alice, was born three years later. After bouncing around in a variety of menial jobs, Paul finally "lucked" into a mail clerk job with a large corporation and was encouraged to apply for a lab testing job. During this time, he and Jill developed friendships with other parents of young children. Family and marriage were going well.

Several years later, tragedy struck. Jill's parents, who lived close to them and were an important part of their extended family, both died within a year of one another, her father of cancer and her mother of grief. Looking back on this time, Paul described his wife as "depressed, withdrawn, and absent minded." At about this same time, Paul landed his first computer job. Although he liked the work, he had a difficult boss who ended up firing him. He became depressed and also started withdrawing.

Soon after, he found an upper-level position in the IT department of a major airport, an opportunity he described as "heart attack city." Telling the group about that time in his life, Paul surmised that he never came out of the depression that hit him after getting fired from his first computer job. His wife wanted to relocate to Florida from the Northeast where they had always lived, and, after a visit to the state, he agreed and gave notice. Both Paul and Jill, each in their own way still feeling the recent losses of family and of Paul's job, saw the move as an attempt to "make a new start."

At the next therapy session, Paul described the family's relocation, which both he and Jill believed at the time to be a positive change for all. Their son, Calvin, was born soon after the move, and they were pleased with the schools for their daughters. However, Paul continued to have difficulty finding satisfactory and stable employment, and the family's savings were soon exhausted.

By the time Calvin was two, Paul had found a job he enjoyed. Given that Jill was a full-time homemaker, money was tight, but it was adequate for their needs, and the children seemed happy and well-adjusted. In a short time, however, Paul would start molesting Alice.

At the conclusion of the session in which Paul described this family history, he added that he believed something in his early childhood was related to the molestation. We agreed to resume discussion of his childhood the following week.

The process of listening to someone's story is for me much like reading a murder mystery, something I used to do on a regular basis. One needs to be alert for clues buried in a lot of irrelevant (for the purposes of solving the mystery) information and potentially misleading subplots. However, the danger lies not in eliciting too much information, but in ruling out prematurely a particular line of inquiry.

I prefer to let the client structure his story however he wishes, both to help him be as comfortable as possible with what he is saying, as well as out of respect for each person's right to be his own autobiographical author. Paul had chosen to begin with a brief account of the molestation. Other men leave that for last, preferring to begin with more historical background. As the story unfolds, I gradually assume a more active role, asking for more information about various aspects of the individual's life. Had Paul not suggested looking at his childhood, I eventually would have made that suggestion, given how important I believe a person's personal history to be in helping to make sense of current behaviors and attitudes (Bateson, 1972; Charon, as cited in Pryor, 1996).

When the group met again, Paul told stories from his childhood. His father left when Paul was three and was never heard from again. His older sister went with their father, while Paul and his younger brother were placed for a couple of years with a family of "backwoods rednecks" on a farm in the country. Feeling "abandoned," he wondered about his mother's whereabouts.

Eventually, when she was able to get a job and an apartment in Washington, D.C., his mother brought the boys to live with her, but they spent a lot of time with a babysitter who, he remembered, watched soap operas.

Paul remembered contracting spinal meningitis and being hospitalized at the age of five, but couldn't recall how long he was there. He paused in his narration for a moment and then commented that his childhood had been "a history of one abandonment after another."

This was one time I failed to listen as carefully for clues as I might have. The theme of "abandonment" subsequently became central to the understanding of the abuse that we constructed, but at the time, it didn't register as significant. Later, when some other crucial pieces of information came forth, I was able to fit the abandonment into the larger picture of Paul's life, a picture that included his sexual abuse of his youngest daughter.

As Paul continued the story of his childhood, we learned that by the age of 12 or 13 he was becoming "rebellious" and was taken to a psychologist for "testing." When he was caught with a stolen car at 14, his mother became "fed up" and gave him up to the courts as "incorrigible." Between the ages of 14 and 16, he was in a series of foster homes. His adult understanding was that he was testing his mother to see if she would desert him again. His wife had told him "for 20 years" that he should get help, that he was "constantly testing her." He denied the accusation and worked hard to be "successful."

According to Paul, Alice, now 17, was the most like him of all three of his children. She too was "rebellious," and, as a result, he had been stricter with her. He informed the group that Alice had recently written her first letter to him since his arrest. He described the letter as "blaming" in tone. Alice asked why he had been so hard on her and, saying that she'd probably "blocked the memory," she wondered whether the abuse had started earlier than she was remembering. Paul felt that she seemed to be trying to blame him for "everything that had gone wrong in her life." In response, I observed that I did not see the content of the letter as being as important as the fact that his daughter had finally reopened some contact with her dad. He seemed somewhat less distressed as the group ended.

This is but a small example of the possibility for multiple interpretations for most of human experience. Such flexibility of response lies at the heart of the MRI notion of reframing (Fisch et al., 1982; Watzlawick et al., 1974). My intent here was not to deny Paul's initial response to the letter from his daughter. He had much legitimately to feel bad about. But I wanted to offer him a different way to contextualize the angry message contained in the letter, in part because I was concerned about how frequently he seemed on the verge of lapsing into complete hopelessness.

In our next group session, I asked Paul where he believed we should go next. He was unsure. The letter from Alice had really upset him, in part due to her mentioning that a year earlier she had sliced her wrist. Nevertheless, he was somewhat encouraged by her having initiated some contact. I reviewed some details from his childhood, to which he commented that he had "always shied away from getting close to people," making the assumption that they would "abandon" him. He related this to his need for "control" as the father in the family: It had to be "my way or no way." He used to "roughhouse" and "wrestle" with all three children, and, sometime during Alice's 13th year, he also began "copping feels" of her during these otherwise innocent activities. Fondling her breasts, he found himself becoming sexually aroused.

The following week, I created a crude time line on the dry erase board in the group room, highlighting the progression of his adult life, from his marriage and the loss of his in-laws, through details of his erratic job history, and on to the initiation of the sexual abuse of his daughter and his eventual arrest. The final detail included in the time line was Paul's decision to begin taking antidepressants.

I still lacked a working hypothesis of how Paul's abuse of his daughter fit into his life and his family's life at the time. But this is certainly what I was grasping for, and it is, indeed, what I aim to construct in my work with each of my clients. I look for a satisfactory solution to the mystery of the individual's sexually abusive behaviors, to fit them into an idiosyncratic scheme that makes sense of the man's actions within the particular context of his life. Much of my information gathering produces only background noise, but, if I persist, a meaningful pattern eventually emerges. Of course, the pattern has to not only make sense to me; it has to make sense to the client (Fisch et al., 1982).

At this point with Paul, I still wasn't picking up on the importance of his childhood being "a history of one abandonment after another." However, I began drawing in another important piece of the story—his realization that he had not felt like himself for years prior to the start of the abuse. I did not know exactly where this line of inquiry might lead, but I made the decision to explore any possible connection between the abuse and Paul's seeming chronic depression. I suggested that perhaps he had been trying to overcome a sense of "despair," a sense of what the Danish theologian Soren Kierkegaard referred to as "that sickness unto death," and I asked him to think about how the sexual abuse of his daughter might fit within this.[iv] I used the word *despair* rather than *depression*, be-

iv. I do not commonly use such literary allusions in therapy; however, Paul was a well-educated, extremely intelligent man. I assumed it was something he could understand and, possibly, relate to.

cause despair suggests an object. We despair over or about *something*, and I was curious as to what that something might be.

In next session, I asked Paul about his relationship with his wife prior to and during the abuse. He hadn't, as yet, volunteered much about his marriage, but I wanted to explore it. I have found that, in many cases, an erotically charged connection with a child (usually a daughter or step-daughter) serves a similar function for the husband as would an outside affair. Paul replied that he and his wife didn't, at the time, talk about each other or their relationship. They "would talk about the kids"; they "got along fine"; the marriage was "comfortable." What about the relationship with his children? He was "closer" to Nancy, who was "so easy." He "got pissed" at Alice for being so difficult, and he was scared that she would go off in the wrong direction, like he had done in his teenage years. He could "roughhouse" with Alice, but Nancy was a "lady." Alice was "tougher than Nancy."

Paul commented that he agreed with everything I had said the previous week concerning his experiencing despair, but he couldn't "connect it with the abuse." He added that, having lost his family, his despair was still with him: "I've taken the better part of my life and thrown it away." He knew he would always be Nancy's dad, but he wasn't so sure about whether he could ever be Alice's or Calvin's. I didn't take issue with his dismissal of the despair being related to the sexual abuse, but I still believed that it could help in deciphering his sexually abusive actions. The search for clues continued.

In a subsequent session, Paul described a Father's Day card he'd received from Alice. She wrote that she remembered the good times they'd had and said that everyone makes mistakes, some worse than others. She expressed the hope that he would get the help he needed so they could have good times again.

Facing the imminent end of his current job contract and not yet knowing where his next job would take him, Paul was having trouble focusing and was "getting back into depression." He was distressed about being away from his family and about the amount of time remaining before he could be released from community control. I encouraged him to resume taking his antidepressant medication.

After two group sessions in which he was not the focus of discussion, Paul, looking agitated, asked to speak with me privately for a few minutes. We stepped outside. "What I want to know," he said, "is why I got a hard-on when touching my daughter." This was the first time he had admitted so directly that he'd experienced full physical arousal during the abuse. I started to comment about the male sexual response and sexual arousal in general, but he cut me off. He hadn't been aroused by Nancy or by either of his daughters' friends, even when, sleeping over at his house, they'd wandered around in nightdresses and other skimpy clothing. It had only been Alice. Only Alice. I didn't have an answer for him, but told him we would find one. I was most aware that he'd fired the therapist who said that they might never know why Paul had molested his daughter.

In session the following week, I asked the group for their help. I told them that I felt "stuck," and, with Paul's permission, shared his comments about his focused sexual attraction toward Alice. Group members are often helpful in the search for understanding.

Paul volunteered that he was missing the closeness he had with his daughters when they were younger. He felt he had lost Nancy as she grew older, and he was afraid he was losing Alice as well. I questioned whether there could be a connection between his fear that he was losing his daughters, primarily Alice, and his becoming sexually aroused. Could the sexual arousal have led to an "imagined closeness" or an attempt to remain close? Also, I recalled that Paul had been sent to a foster home about the same age as Alice was at the time of the abuse. I speculated that perhaps he didn't know what a parent did with older teenagers, as he'd had no parent during those years and he'd been without a father since the age of three.

When Paul returned for his next meeting, he handed me a copy of a letter he had written to his family, asking that I review it because he was concerned that it not inadvertently convey any sense of self-pity. From what he said and how he said it, I recognized that he finally had the explanation he had been seeking. Here are some excerpts:

> To my family,
> I miss all of you very much. I love you all very much. Apologies I have given, yet I know that you each need so much more than that from me. My problem is that I do not know what you need, or what to do about it.
>   My therapy has been very helpful. . . . I would like to share with you what I have learned about myself, and how that has affected you and us.
>   I never had a family life. I never had a father. It is probably not imaginable to you what that means. I did not know many many things that you all take for granted. In spite of this I tried my best to learn how to father and did my best to contribute to making our family a loving one. . . . I did so without any role models. I went on my instincts and whatever I could learn from books. . . .
>   Then you girls grew into young women. First Nancy. Then Alice. Sud-

denly, I was not god anymore. You began to see my flaws. Everyone has flaws, I know—but beneath the surface I began to feel insecure again. In a way I was returning to a part I did not even want to think about. You of course did not know this, and I know you would never do anything to hurt me. But suddenly I found myself not knowing how to relate to you.

Meanwhile, Jill, I was failing you as a husband. I really wasn't even aware of it. I felt that I was supporting the family—what else does a husband do? I have no idea. Naturally you withdrew from me—perhaps unconsciously, perhaps not—as you realized that I was not satisfying the expectations someone who has been raised within a family has. I see now, as I did not then, that I withdrew even more so. Now I see I withdrew, because I did not know what to do. I did not see that then.

I found myself unimportant to my wife. My daughters were moving away from me, as is only natural. Again, I did not see this then but now I do. I was wondering, "Where do I fit in?" I was the guy who brought home the paycheck. I began to withdraw even more.

I see now that in an attempt to be "something," to play some role in my daughters' lives, I became an "authority figure." I did so to make myself more than just that guy who brought home the check. I didn't do that because I did not love you; I did it because I love you, and I wanted to have a relationship with you. This was the first step in my sickness.

A surprising issue came up in therapy about my own past and how it affected this time. Again, I was amazed at how I did not see this myself until it was pointed out to me. At 15, I went from having next to no family life and one parent to *no* family life and *no* parents. Of course I had no way of knowing how to deal with teenaged kids as a parent or within a family. . . . How could I have been so blind to these issues I see clearly now?. . .

You cannot realize—any of you—how much I miss my little girls. How empty it feels now that you are gone. How helpless I feel about what to be in your lives now. And this was the next step in my sickness. As my therapist explains it, touching brings feelings of intimacy. Watching you girls slip away, feeling useless in your lives, and in my wife's life—only "being there," "providing," I longed for intimacy. My mind, with its repressed problems, explained to me that now that you were young women, not just little girls, touching would gain me intimacy.

I never meant to hurt anybody. I never meant to sabotage my marriage. I only desperately wanted to be "something" to you. . . .

I love you all so very much. I am so lonely. I am trying to take my therapist's advice and not hate myself. The best I have managed is to survive, so that I can continue to provide. It is the only role I can see for myself. I have no map. I'm lost. I am sorry I have failed you. I am sorry I continue to fail you. None of you has ever failed me. I am proud of each of you.

I love you all.

ALTERED CONTEXTS, ALTERED BEHAVIORS

One of the interesting aspects of Paul's letter for me is a phrase that, with variations, almost becomes a refrain: "I see now, as I did not then." I'm not suggesting that "insight" leads to change; however, I think in our desire to distance ourselves from "insight-oriented therapies," we brief therapists may have sometimes failed to acknowledge that changes in meanings (i.e., reframing) can look very similar to such insight. It becomes, perhaps, a matter of semantics, perhaps something more.

All explanations are not equal. Some are empty or self-serving—a way of assigning blame to someone else and maintaining the status quo. Others, however, are able to dramatically influence present perception and future behavior. These tend "to change the conceptual and/or emotional setting or viewpoint in relation to which a situation is experienced and to place it in another frame which fits the 'facts' of the same concrete situation equally well or even better" (Watzlawick, et al., 1974, p. 95). One explanation of Paul's behavior is that he is a pervert, an incorrigible sexual offender who, because of being "wired" differently from "normal" men, was capable of monstrous behavior. Another explanation is the one layered in the letter.

This brings us back to the notion of context as delineated by Bateson (1979, 1991). If "contexts are but categories of mind" (Bateson, 1991, p. 76), and "it is the recipient of the message who creates the context" (Bateson, 1979, p. 47), then any time we come to an altered understanding of any particular past or present behavior (whether our own or someone else's), there is the strong likelihood that the context of which that behavior had been a part has also been transformed. And a changed context, as we saw in the two stories about my daughter, Rachel, shared earlier, can lead to our choosing different behaviors in the future—indeed, can even make such a change in choice inevitable. Furthermore, if the transformation is significant enough, it can, at the same time, render almost impossible our continuing to act as we did in the past. As Watzlawick et al. (1974) suggest, "We cannot so easily go back to the trap and the anguish of a former view of 'reality'" (p. 99).

A trivial example of how such an altered understanding can abolish old behaviors is readily found in the playing of tic-tac-toe. Young children can be entertained for quite some time, attempting to beat their opponent, but as soon as they realize that any match between two equally experienced players will always end in a draw, the game ceases to present any challenge; it becomes predictable, and thus stops being fun. Such a newly born "insight"—not into human nature, but into the nature of the "game"—brings a new understanding, rendering it impossible to continue as before. As Paul said to me after sharing his letter with the group, "I'm not ignorant anymore, and I can't get into trouble again."

Shortly after this session, Paul announced that, in search of a possible job, he was immediately moving out of the area. Had he not left, he would have continued in this particular group until the end of his second year. I would then have promoted him to the second phase of the treatment program, and, after a successful year there, to the third.

Although I would never presume to be certain, I'm reasonably sure that both the transformation in Paul's story and the associated transformation in his experience will sustain into the future, making it very unlikely that he will "get into trouble again." Thus, by conventional brief therapy standards, the case can be construed as a "success." But the contextual changes of an individual's therapy are themselves contextualized by family relationships and societal restrictions, and, given the schisms that sexual abuse creates within families, coupled with the current climate in this country, convicted sexual offenders such as Paul face limited opportunities for reconnecting with loved ones and for regaining the semblance of a "normal" life.

Over the following year, I had a few subsequent individual appointments with Paul and one with him and his wife. He continued to struggle emotionally over the loss of his family and he lived in constant fear that, because he was now listed as a registered sexual offender on the Internet, he would be identified by a coworker or neighbor. The last time I saw him, he had eight years of probation remaining, but he will remain on the publicly accessible Florida registry of sexual offenders for 20 years beyond that, at which point he will be nearly 80 years old.[v]

DISCUSSION

Although my client population may be unfamiliar to many brief therapists, the process of my work bears many of the marks of a brief, problem-focused (MRI) approach. The time my clients spend in therapy (usually a minimum of five years) is obviously much longer than the 10-session ideal that many brief therapists use as a benchmark, but often the number

---

v. Florida, along with most states, has established an Internet site containing the names and addresses of all registered sexual offenders and sexual predators in the state. This site became operational in October 1997. In July 2006, the U.S. Congress passed legislation creating a national registry. Florida has recently passed a law that extends the 20 years to life.

of group sessions devoted to constructing an individual's story is approximately that number. This was certainly the case with Paul.

But the number of sessions is, for me, much less important in defining a brief-therapy approach than is the theory underlying the work. Regardless of the amount of time I spend constructing a story with someone, I'm always informed by the basic assumptions I outlined earlier, namely an appreciation of context; a deep respect for my clients, born out of viewing them as not remarkably different from me; and an assumption that most problematic human behavior, including inappropriate sexual behavior, can usefully be understood as a failed attempt to resolve some difficulty. The challenge lies in defining the difficulty.

These same assumptions lie at the heart of the therapeutic approach pioneered by those at the MRI. The only difference I see in the work I do is one of emphasis. While an MRI approach encompasses both efforts to alter behavior (through behavioral assignments) as well as changing the meanings clients attach to those behaviors (through reframing), I have found myself increasingly gravitating toward an almost exclusive focus on the latter, on constructing different understandings of my clients' sexually abusive behaviors. With this altered understanding, a different context emerges. In that new context, as Wilk (1985) reminds us, "an experience or communication or piece of interaction would have a completely different significance and therefore would be something completely different" (p. 214). What changes for my clients is how they view their sexually abusive behaviors and, ultimately, themselves. In most cases, when this shift occurs, the work is largely complete.

When my daughter Rachel "reframed" how she made sense of her car accident, she became a better driver, in part by appreciating how dangerous driving can be. I fully expect she'll never forget the time she made a serious mistake, and this will improve her ability to make safe choices in the future.

I believe something similar occurs with many of my clients when they make contextual sense of the abuse they committed, develop an empathic understanding of the abused child's experience, and understand with certainty that sexual arousal is not itself a green light to act, however good they think it might feel at the time. And I believe that most of the men with whom I work, like Paul, are able to regain trust in their sexual desire and arousal and to do so safely, always mindful of the time they made a disastrous choice.

There is a major exception (and it is major) to this goal of assisting my clients to feel comfortable once more with their sexual feelings and responses. It involves those men (mentioned earlier in the chapter) whose primary erotic object is young, usually prepubescent, children. I have worked with a number of such men over the years, some of whom have gone so far as to marry an adult woman or to engage in adult sex with women or men, and despite their taking such measures, they have continued to desire children. I have also worked, more frequently, with men who have never had any sexual experience with another adult and yet have not realized this was because they were exclusively sexually attracted to children. In these cases, as their story unfolds in the group sessions, the process is not that different from the way it was with Paul or has been with anyone else. The goal is still to reach a contextual understanding of the abusive behavior. The difference is that we end up discovering that the sexual abuse was the result of the individual's basic sexual orientation, not the result of a unique set of circumstances, along with arousal and opportunity, as was the case with Paul.

But even here, it is possible to "normalize" this attraction, at least in a sense. This is done by acknowledging that the attraction is a part of who the person is, not a choice for which he bears responsibility. After all, otherwise normal adult men can also find themselves aroused by young children. The issue is not the arousal, but rather the choices made relative to that arousal. In some cases, an individual client is able to come to a genuine recognition and belief that regardless of the pleasure he associates with having sex with children, he will, if he were to act again on this desire and arousal, seriously harm the children to whom he is so drawn. Thus, in some cases, the affection the man feels for children can help him choose not to hurt them. Such normalization and empathy-encouragement is coupled, as already discussed, with relapse prevention strategies that involve his not placing himself in situations where opportunities for abusive behavior might arise, being aware of his previous patterns of assaulting children, and so on. Safety for these men is a lifelong process involving a daily choice of a celibate lifestyle.

Turning again to the discussion of how my work relates to more traditional clinical settings and client populations, I suspect that some brief, problem-focused therapists would probably assert that MRI-informed work cannot legitimately be done with court mandated clients, much less felony sexual offenders who are only in treatment because it is part of the terms of their probation. These therapists might argue that an MRI approach depends on a voluntary client seeking help to resolve some already identified problem. I would disagree with this, pointing out that rarely does a family therapist, at least, have the luxury of working solely with clients who want to be there and who all agree on the "problem." The primary difference, as I see it, is that my clients come to therapy (at least initially) because a judge ordered them to, whereas other therapists work with clients who are there because someone else in the family (usually a spouse or parent) pressured them. The goal in both instances is to get the "involuntary" client at least somewhat invested in the therapeutic process. In the vast majority of cases, I have been able to accomplish this.

One last assumption implicit in my work is best expressed by Bateson (1991):

> I can know something of the inner determinants of my own actions, and something of what the contexts of my actions look like to me. But how much egomorphism should I allow myself in interpreting the actions and contexts of others? No final answer can be given. . . . Only by use of introspection, empathy, and shared cultural premises—the products of socialization—can anybody identify how context appears to another. (p. 76)

This is, for me, the central challenge of the therapy I offer—and also the source of a crucial humility, because this business of constructing understandings of sexual abuse can all too easily become an arrogant enterprise. I try to live up to the promise I have made to myself that every story I participate in constructing must always be, in some sense, merely a tentative and incomplete, all too human, attempt at answering the question, "Why?" I partially console myself with the belief that trying and getting it wrong is still better than not having tried at all. In the final analysis, stories are really all we have. But stories, as a medium, are themselves morally neutral. They can sew the seeds of damnation, denial, and despair. They can also nourish the fruits of grace, remembrance, and hope. It thus behooves us to choose, with care and ethical sensitivity, the stories we tell.

REFERENCES

Bateson, G. (1972). *Steps to an ecology of mind: Collected essays in anthropology, psychiatry, evolution, and epistemology.* New York: Jason Aronson.

Bateson, G. (1979). *Mind and nature: A necessary unity.* New York: Dutton.

Bateson, G. (1991). *A sacred unity: Further steps to an ecology of mind.* (R .E. Donaldson, Ed.). New York: HarperCollins.

Bateson, G., & Bateson, M. C. (1987). *Angels fear: Towards an epistemology of the sacred.* New York: Macmillan.

Fisch, R., Weakland, J. H., & Segal, L. (1982). *The tactics of change.* San Francisco: Jossey-Bass.

Flemons, D. (1991). *Completing distinctions.* Boston: Shambhala.

Flemons, D. (2002). *Of one mind: the logic of hypnosis, the practice of therapy.* New York: Norton.

Gilligan, S. G. (1987). *Therapeutic trances: The cooperation principle in Ericksonian hypnotherapy*. New York: Brunner/Mazel.

Haywood, T. W., & Grossman, L. S. (1994). Denial of deviant sexual arousal and psychopathology in child molesters. *Behavior therapy 25*, 327–340.

Haley, J. (1986). *Uncommon therapy: The psychiatric techniques of Milton H. Erickson, M.D.* New York: Norton. (Original work published 1973)

Keeney, B. P. (1983). *Aesthetics of change*. New York: Guilford.

Laws, R. D., Hudson, S. M., & Ward, T. (2000). *Remaking relapse prevention with sex offenders: A sourcebook*. Thousand Oaks, CA: Sage.

Leberg, E. (1997). *Understanding child molesters: Taking charge*. Thousand Oaks. CA: Sage.

O'Hanlon, S. H. (1987). Taproots: *Underlying principles of Milton Erickson's therapy and hypnosis*. New York: Norton.

Pryor, D. W. (1996). *Unspeakable acts: Why men sexually abuse children*. New York: New York University Press.

Rambo, W. C. (1999). *Fathers who molest their sons and daughters: An inquiry into understanding*. Unpublished doctoral dissertation, Nova Southeastern University, Ft. Lauderdale.

Salter, A. C. (1988). *Treating child sex offenders and victims: A practical guide*. Newbury Park, CA: Sage.

Schwartz, B. K. (1995). Introduction of the integrative approach. In B. K. Schwartz & H. R. Cellini (Eds.), *The sex offender: Corrections, treatment and legal practice* (pp. 1.2–1.13). Kingston, NJ: Civic Research Institute, Inc.

Watzlawick, P., Beavin, J. H., & Jackson, D. D. (1967). *Pragmatics of human communication: A study of interactional patterns, pathologies, and paradoxes*. New York: Norton.

Watzlawick, P., & Weakland, J. (Eds.) (1977). *The interactional view: Studies at the Mental Research Institute Palo Alto, 1965–1974*. New York: Norton.

Watzlawick, P., Weakland, J., & Fisch, R. (1974). *Change: Principles of problem formation and problem resolution*. New York: Norton.

Wilk, J. (1985). Erickson therapeutic patterns: A pattern which connects. In J. K. Zeig (Ed.), *Ericksonian psychotherapy: Vol. 2. Clinical applications* (pp. 210–233). New York: Brunner/Mazel.

fourteen

Re-Membering the Self: A Relational Approach to Sexual Abuse Treatment

Martha Laughlin and Kate Warner

Then there was the pain. A breaking and entering where even the senses are torn apart. The act of rape on an eight-year-old body is a matter of the needle giving because the camel can't. The child gives, because the body can, and the mind of the violator can't.
— Maya Angelou, *I Know Why the Caged Bird Sings*

WHEN YOU THINK OF SEXUAL ABUSE, you probably have some picture in your mind—perhaps a father with his young daughter while he gives her a bath, a woman being raped, or a coach giving special attention to an adolescent boy. Certainly, the horrific accounts and suffering of survivors of sexual violations have led many therapists to consider such abuse to be something that "impacts" the victim—a thinglike cause that produces thinglike effects later in life: painful intercourse, intrusive memories, terrifying moments of spacing out, bouts of profound depression, self-harming, self-loathing, feelings of fear or disgust with sexual partners, and so on.

This perspective, reflected in both the popular and scholarly literature, extends to how many clinicians (and clients) conceive of therapy. The therapist's job is to counterbalance the perpetrator's violent impact with the helpful impact of therapeutic interventions, which are intended, metaphorically, to "heal the wound," "recover from the disorder," or "take back control" (e.g., Blume, 1991; Drauker, 2000; Foa & Rothbaum, 1998; Vanderlinden & Vandereycken, 1997). And one of the most accepted means of accomplishing such goals involves "getting out the toxins" by recalling or reconstructing the abuse (e.g., Ainscough & Toon, 2000; Bass & Davis, 1994; Courtois, 1999; Salter, 1995).

We hold to the premise that experience and language do not belong to the world of *objects*, where one piece of matter energistically collides with some other piece (Bateson, 1972/2000). Instead, they belong to the world of *relationships* (Flemons, 2002, 2004). Sexual abuse surely has a physical component to it—after all, the victim's body is violated. But the *experience* of the abuse and the subsequent response to it are not material things that act mechanistically on the mind and life of the client. And a therapist's words cannot physically install hope, control symptoms, banish an urge, amputate rage, or dissolve fear. Why? The effect of abuse is not a localizable thing that can be excised like cancer or destroyed like bacteria, and therapy isn't a talking-cure form of surgery or antibiotic treatment that can directly make problems disappear.

Thinking relationally, we keep our eye on the interactions between the abuser and the abused, between the abused person and others, and between the abused person and herself[1]—her sensations, ideas, emotions, perceptions, meanings, and behaviors (Flemons, 2002). Our treatment of sexual abuse is not directed toward making something (a problem) go away, but toward helpfully altering some relationship.

In this chapter, we describe our relational orientation and how it informs our ideas about symptoms, problem definition, and problem resolution, offering case vignettes throughout to illustrate our points. By the time you reach the end of the chapter, we hope that you, too, will find it possible and useful to think about sexual abuse, and sexual abuse treatment, in a relational way.

THINKING RELATIONALLY

A well-established principle of systems theory states that a part of a system cannot control the whole of the system of which it is a part (Bateson, 1972/2000; Keeney, 1983). Language, however, inclines us to believe otherwise. Language breaks the world (and ourselves) into pieces and sets the

---

1. For the sake of simplicity and clarity, we have chosen in this chapter to mostly use the female pronoun when referring to victims of abuse. Nevertheless, we recognize and acknowledge that boys, too, are frequently subjected to sexual abuse and that their suffering is just as significant.

pieces over and against one another, giving the illusion that one piece can control another (Flemons, 1999, 2003). For example, a client came to us after getting into a rage, complaining, "My anger got the best of me." Her description of what happened separated her "anger" from herself, as if they weren't both part of the experience of the same person. And when she went on to say, "I'm never going to let myself get angry like that again," her statement implied that one part of her could control all of her.

Such is the nature of reflexivity. To observe yourself, to reflect on yourself (as in, "sometimes I wonder about myself"), you must stand outside and look back in. Yet the "I" doing the contemplating is the same person as the "myself" being contemplated. Any part of you that seems in need of control (anger, depression, procrastination, anxiety, etc.) is as much you as the part that strives to do the controlling. Language and the reflexivity of awareness successfully fool us into thinking (and also experiencing) that such portions of the self are truly separate and apart, when in fact they are complementary parts of a larger whole (Flemons, 1999, 2002).

This whole is a world of relationships. It is impossible *not* be embedded in multiple connections simultaneously. We are in continual relationship with ideas (some of our MFT students fall in love with, and think deeply about, systems thinking and postmodernism), with material objects (Martha loves her piano, Kate loves her new saddle), with emotions (teenagers get angry at their parents for being angry at them), and with behaviors (a boy outside our window is mimicking the antics of his friend as they ride their bikes down the street). And, of course, we all are in relationship with ourselves ("Oh, blast," Martha chides herself in dismay, "I can't believe you forgot your appointment book!").

Can you think of something with which you do *not* have a relationship? Maybe something outlandishly irrelevant, like the 15th step of the Capitol building in Washington. No connection to you, right? But wait! By identifying the step as something with which you have no relationship, you can't help but establish a connection to it.

DIS-MEMBERING: THE EXPERIENCE
OF SEXUAL ABUSE

We subscribe to Maturana's definition of violence as "the holding of a view by one person or group of persons to be true such that another person's or group's view is untrue and must change": in short, the imposition of one's will upon another (as cited in Sanders & Tomm, 1989, p. 350). Violence is perpetrated by a violator against the person violated, the victim. A sexual violator forces his body into the victim's body and forces his will into her psyche.

Cathy Winkler (2002) wrote about a man who broke into her bedroom in the middle of the night and kicked her into wakefulness to beat and rape her. At one point he said, "I know you haven't had a black boyfriend before. I'm your first" (p. 21). By naming himself something he wasn't, he defined the rape as the opposite of what it was, implying that his act of force was actually one she wanted. In so doing, he robbed Cathy of her humanity and her dignity—her ability to choose and define her own experience. He also ensured that he would remain a considerable presence in her life. One of our clients, not a victim of sexual abuse, described the rage he felt at the unwanted relationship that he now had with his daughter's murderer: "I don't know who he is or where he is in this world but he is forever in my head now."

Those who impose violence on others sever the humanity in the relationship they have with the people they hurt. This is not lost on victims, who object to the use of the word *victim* and its ability to call forth a state of nonpersonhood, a time in their lives when they've been denied the most significant of human acts—the freedom to say no.

By declaring, "No, I don't agree," "No, I don't want to," and "No, you can't make me!" you proclaim the individuality, position, and integrity that arise from defining yourself as different from the person(s) you're opposing. This is essential in all human interactions, even those not perceived as ostensibly "violent" by those involved. Jasmine and her husband Will came to therapy to talk about their sexual predicament. Simply put, he wanted sex, she didn't. At the beginning of the first session, Will made clear what was at stake. Given, he said, that sex is normal, that lots of sex is normal for men, and that he himself was extremely sexual, there was nothing to keep him in the relationship if Jasmine could not or would not agree to have sex with him as often as he desired. If Jasmine agreed to sex she didn't want, she compromised her integrity and lost herself. If she said no to sex, she maintained her integrity and lost her marriage. Caught between these two polarities, she felt frozen, unable to act or choose. After several sessions, reiterating his conviction that Jasmine was the one with the problem, Will left therapy and, some months after that, the marriage. Jasmine was profoundly sad, but she went through the divorce with her dignity intact.

Without the freedom to assert difference, sameness becomes impossible, and agreement becomes suspect. In such a context, "I will" is, at best, meaningless and, at worst, a terrible betrayal of selfhood. It is only when you're free to say "No!" that you can willingly, even eagerly, say "Yes!"

When a child can refuse the request or demand of an adult and know that she is in no way threatening their relationship, she learns bravery and self-determination, and, with a clear sense of herself, she enjoys the possibilities of human connection that are found only within such relational freedom. When it is impossible to refuse an adult's violation of her mind and body, she learns that the world isn't safe. This can be a life-altering experience.

In Wendell Berry's (1988) novel *Remembering,* Andy Catlett, a farmer, loses his hand to a corn-picking machine. This loss in turn dismembers his relationship to his wife and children, to neighbors with whom he has farmed since he was a child, and to himself:

> His right hand had been the one with which he reached out to the world and attached himself to it. When he lost his hand he lost his hold. It was as though his hand still clutched all that was dear to him—and was gone. All the world then became to him a steep slope, and he a man descending, staggering and falling, unable to reach out to tree trunk or branch or root to catch and hold on. (p. 28)

Andy's hand "had imagined many things, [but] never . . . its absence" (p. 103). Andy

> remembered with longing the events of his body's wholeness, grieving over them, as Adam remembered Paradise. He remembered how his body had dressed itself, while his mind thought of something else; how he had shifted burdens from hand to hand; how his right hand had danced with its awkward partner and made it graceful. . . . Now the hand . . . had been cast away, and he mourned over it as over a priceless map or manual forever lost. (p. 28)

In his anger, grief, and shame, a bitter sense of self-betrayal took up where his hand left off, leading Andy to disconnect from his wife and children.

People who have been sexually abused do not usually suffer the material loss of a body part. However, like Andy, they lose the easy familiarity with and the take-for-granted comfort of their body and those around them. Sexual violation, particularly when it is perpetrated by someone with whom the victim has a loving relationship, is a dismemberment that can give rise to consequences at least as dramatic and far reaching as those engendered by the loss of a limb.

Of course, those who meet and know abuse victims don't see visible evidence of the loss, because there isn't some "thing" missing. What is lost is the essential trust that interweaves the contextual web of relationships we all embody. Whether small or grown, we are elementally dependent on each other for learning and experiencing love, safety, self-knowledge, and meaning. When this fundamental dependence on one another is damaged, it violates the basic human ethic (Freyd, 1998), and it severs not only social relationships, but also the relationships the person has with herself. The result is profound mental anguish and confusion, and the potential for troubling experiences with her body and her sexuality, as well as her thoughts, perceptions, meaning, sensations, emotions, and behavior—producing the sorts of symptoms that call out for therapeutic intervention.

A person who has been sexually abused often feels stigmatized. Out of helplessness, fear, or alarm, family or friends who might otherwise be compassionate and supportive attempt, instead, to explain the abuse away by denying its occurrence, its impact, their awareness of it, or their responsibility for it (Trepper & Barrett, 1989). They blame the victim or make it clear that she should "just get over it." As an uncomfortable reminder to those around her, the victim may be left feeling profoundly lonely and cut off, locked in her awareness or belief that she is perceived as tainted. Such perceptions can widen the gap between her and the people she loves, leading to further stigmatization and an exacerbation of symptoms.

SEXUAL ABUSE SYMPTOMS

As a child grows, one of her important developmental tasks is to develop a sense of competency, to become self-determined. Sexual abuse conveys the message that she is other-determined, with no say over what happens to her body. Someone else, perhaps a very compelling someone else, gets to decide. This message conflicts strongly with developmental lessons learned cumulatively and experientially since birth. Through tumbling, running, and curling up to sleep, she has discovered the comforts, joys, limitations, and possibilities of her body. But when a child's physicality is no longer her own, when an abuser breaches her boundaries, she may see him as all-powerful and all-knowing, able to see and have command over her existence.

The former national Poet Laureate Maya Angelou (1969) was raped at the age of eight by her mother's boyfriend, a man she referred to as Mr.

Freeman in her book *I Know Why The Caged Bird Sings*. She described what it was like to be completely under his control:

> I knew I was dying and, in fact, I longed for death, but I didn't want to die anywhere near Mr. Freeman. I knew that even now he wouldn't have allowed death to have me unless he wished it to. (p. 81)

One way for a child to cope when she cannot control access to her body is to separate from it and stop feeling anything. Angelou describes living for years in a sort of emotional fog, her senses muted, her sense of reality confused and distanced:

> Sounds came to me dully, as if people were speaking through their hand-kerchiefs or with their hands over their mouths. . . . Colors weren't true either, but rather a vague assortment of shaded pastels that indicated not so much color as faded familiarities. People's names escaped me and I began to worry over my sanity. (p. 92)

A beloved child experiences the value her parents place on her existence. She feels the joy they take in her person and her presence in their lives. She recognizes their concerns for her safety, her development, and her independence. She expresses her feelings, including anger, without fear of retaliation. These experiences—trust, safety, concern, connection, pleasure, independence, appreciation—make up the frame of reference that she transports to the development of her own, adult relationships. An abused child may have no such frame of reference with which to build wholesome connections.

One of our adult clients, Amber, relayed how her father had always been "short tempered" and would become aggravated when as a child she made known that she needed something. After he started molesting her, his anger became explosive, and she suffered beatings, as well. She learned to stay out of range and become "a wall"—solid, useful, requiring little maintenance, wanting nothing, and provoking no one's rage. She didn't understand his physical and sexual assaults, but she became adept at minimizing their effects on her. For her, life was at its best when, like a wall, she could be around but remain unnoticed.

Sexually abused children exist in a state of helpless victimization, without dignity, without recourse, without a voice in determining what happens to their bodies. They can neither fight nor flee the situation, and their elongated perception of time tells them that this is the way it is, without end, forever more. As a result, they experience some predictable symptoms.

Self-Blame, Rage, Shame, Self-Loathing

For many months after she was raped, Angelou (1969), sick at heart, fell mute. Describing how utterly vile and loathsome she believed she was, she said she feared that "just my breath, carrying my words out, might poison people, and they'd curl up and die . . ." (p. 87).

Placing blame locates a cause and creates a comforting illusion of control in a life that feels otherwise completely chaotic and incomprehensible. Despite the psychological anguish that comes with locating the fault for the abuse within herself, the child who does so is relieved of some of the profound confusion that arises when faced with unwanted sexual attention, which moreover may actually produce sexual pleasure. Rage at not being able to stop or comment on the violation, combined with self-blame at her body's response, can result in the child's feeling self-loathing and shame.

Sarina, who had been sexually molested by an older brother, described how the pervasive sense of confusion and upheaval in her head led to her "being unable to hold myself together." In high school, she "went into destruct mode," taking drugs, drinking, partying, and saying anything she wanted to, to anyone she wanted to say it. "I was scary to be around. If I thought it, I said it. If I felt like putting my hand on your crotch or your breast, I'd find a way to snuggle up to you and do it. I loved shocking people." When life's social rules and boundaries have been violated, it makes sense to respond by careening through life without observing them.

Dissociation, Confusion, Intrusive Memories

Some years ago, I (Martha) stumbled into a hornets' nest. As I turned in terror to run, I stepped on a board with a nail in it, driving it deep into my foot. Without stopping to think, I reached down, yanked off my sneaker, board and all, and ran like the devil. When I went back some time later to retrieve my shoe, still firmly nailed to the board, I realized that during the moment when the nail was piercing my foot, and the moment later when I frantically pulled it out, the pain I felt was so distant that it seemed almost intellectual. I remember that as it was happening, as I became aware of the puncturing, I thought, "Uh oh. That's going to hurt." But my focus, my concern, at that moment was how the board, nailed to the bottom of my shoe, *was going to impede my flight*. My body suppressed the pain in favor of the more important problem at the moment: surviving that swarm of hornets.

Sexual abuse can provoke an analogous experience. The recognition of betrayal by another person may be painful, but the focus, the greater concern, must be for survival (Freyd, 1998). For the survivor, the effect of choking off such awareness may result in terrible confusion and dissociated or confused memories.

One of the central tasks of the government in George Orwell's novel *1984* was to rewrite political and social events so that its citizens would "remember" a "preferred" version of history. This aptly describes what the person who has experienced sexual abuse may wisely do for herself. When the pain of the past is simply too excruciating to endure, people may simply erase or amend it to make living in the present bearable. Consider exactly what that agony may comprise by thinking for a moment about the position in which a young child finds herself. Given that her very survival depends on continuing a bond with a caretaker and receiving care, it may be in her own best interest to not notice, to postpone noticing, or to forget what is being done to her (Freyd, 1998). If noticing or remembering alienates or angers the very person upon whom she depends to survive, then dissociating or forgetting part of the abuse in order to keep the knowledge at bay may be singularly wise, because, at all costs, a relationship with the caretaker must be preserved (Freyd, 1998).

Phantom Pain, Fear, Unreality

People who have lost a limb sometimes experience pain in a leg or a hand that is no longer there. People who have been sexually abused suffer similar pain. When a child feels sick with fear, when she cannot feel safe in her own bed, when she can't leave home but can't stay, when she has shut off all that makes her human, when her perception is that the world is no longer patterned and predictable, when all she can do is adjust to a life that includes sexual abuse, when her own body feels unreal and not her own, she may experience very real feelings of disintegration and fragmentation. Disconnected from herself, she walks through life like a phantom, unable to make clear distinctions between who she is and who others are, what is real and what is not.

The sense of unreality that plagued Angelou (1969) led her to believe that she had not actually been raped, that "the nightmare with its attendant guilt and fear hadn't really happened to me. It happened to a nasty little girl, years and years before, who had no claim on me at all" (p. 159). A similar feeling of disembodiment was experienced by Jamie, a happily married man with four children who felt like he wasn't living inside his body. He came into therapy after remembering on his own nearly two years earlier that he had been sexually abused by his pastor. He was worried about not being able to stop crying.

I had no earthly idea that I had been sexually abused. After I remembered a couple of years ago, it was such a shock to me. I walked around in a daze for months. I thought a lot about the stuff he did to me and then I just decided I didn't need to think about it anymore. I thought I was okay but I felt just weird, like I wasn't me any more. I was outside of myself. I was like a ghost. I floated. Everything was slow. And I always felt really, really sad. The whole world felt sad. Something really bothered me, though, when last year I ran across an old photograph of myself and the other boys in my Christian Boys Club with Pastor Jim. Without logical reason, as I stared at that photograph, my gut tightened. I felt despair. And I felt such a deep, deep sadness. It was as if someone had come and told me my son was dead.

Jamie walked around for several months feeling intermittent bouts of profound sadness. For no apparent reason, he, on and off, would think about the boys in the choral group.

And then, one day, a long time after seeing that photograph for the first time, I remembered that I loved Pastor Jim. The night before I had dreamed some sort of weird dream about being in a hotel and singing to him this terribly sad lament, except that I was my current age, and I woke up realizing what had happened. I was closer to Pastor Jim than I was to my own father. I had loved him like a father. That's when I started crying. Now I cry a couple of times a week, and I just feel so sad.

Jamie described how Pastor Jim formed a Boys Club at the church, leading the members on field trips, camping trips, and visits to people in the community who needed help. Jamie loved the activities and was proud of their service work, cleaning up properties, building storage sheds, replacing rotting wood on porches, and so on. Their club was a "small local celebrity," and Pastor Jim was beloved by the community and his church.

I was raised in a really small, rural town where nothing happened. Pastor Jim was the guy that made things happen. He was the mover and shaker, the guy who made an otherwise dead town come to life. He truly loved his church and town. He really was a good, good person. He somehow brought the big world to us, and I admired him and looked up to him. I loved him. We all loved him.

As he made this last statement, Jamie was overcome with deep sobs that went on for several minutes. We waited until he was able to listen to what we had come to understand, and then we said the following.

> When you first recalled the sexual abuse, you thought about it in terms of "the *things* he did to you," in terms of the sexual acts themselves. And although that was a terrible shock of realization that left you dazed, you knew you were okay. But you kept feeling a bit sad, and then, nearly a year later, after discovering the photograph, you began to feel terribly, terribly sad. You were remembering the really, really deep hurt, not just the skin-level hurt. You had moved beyond thinking of what he had done to your body. Now you were thinking of the harm done to your *relationship* with him. And he had shattered it. Here he was, this truly nice guy, beloved by an entire town and parish. You loved him, he was a second father to you. That someone so cherished could do those things to you, you knew was a terrible betrayal.

Jamie started sobbing again.

Pastor Jim's abuse left Jamie with the unreal experience of not being inside his own life—a phantom floating through the world. The sexual acts imposed on him dismembered his admiration and love for his adult mentor and undermined his age-appropriate ideas about the world. And they forced upon him a riddle that was beyond his ability at the time to solve: the paradoxical notion that truly good people can do truly bad things. Pastor Jim's violations lived side-by-side with all his good works, his genuine love for his community and his congregation, and his Christian benevolence.

It is important to mention that despite the profound effect of the abuse on him, Jamie was put off by the idea that he had been traumatized (Freyd, 1998). He underscored that he was not forced, terrorized, threatened, or even physically hurt. As he put it, "I was lovingly abused." We thus focused our therapeutic efforts in this direction, helping him embrace the realization that Pastor Jim's Christian goodness did not negate his violation of Jamie, *and* his violation did not negate his Christian goodness. Jamie discovered that he could love Pastor Jim *and* recognize that his mentor had betrayed that love. This was the beginning of Jamie re-membering his relationship with himself, the beginning of therapeutic change. But we're getting a little ahead of ourselves. Before we get into talking about change, we want to address the relationship between maps and territories.

MAPS AND TERRITORIES

Up to this point in the chapter, we've focused primarily on making theoretical sense of sexual abuse and describing the sorts of ways it affects victims. Others, such as Maltz (2001, p. 260), have, more specifically, offered descriptions of the variety of sexual and other symptoms common among people who have experienced sexual abuse including:

- avoiding or being afraid of sex;
- approaching sex as an obligation;
- feeling intense negative emotions when touched, such as fear, guilt, disgust, or nausea;
- having difficulty becoming aroused or feeling sensation;
- feeling emotionally distant or not present during sex;
- having disturbing and intrusive sexual thoughts and fantasies;
- engaging in compulsive, risky, or inappropriate sexual behaviors;
- having difficulty establishing or maintaining an intimate relationship.

Such information can be helpful, if only by virtue of recognizing that experienced clinicians have identified patterns of sexual and other symptoms considered typical of people who have been sexually violated—rage, shame, distorted body identification, dissociation, self-injury, intrusive memories, fear, flashbacks, depression, and suicide attempts (e.g., Dolan, 1999; Sheinberg & Fraenkel, 2001). But however important this background is, it is not, itself, enough to assist therapists in knowing how to help.

By way of explaining what we mean by this, we want to share a disclaimer that we offer at the beginning of a course we teach called "Treatment Issues." It goes something like this:

> The term *sexual abuse* is one of many comparable categories of problematic human experiences, including depression, grief, eating disorders, anxiety, panic attacks, chronic illness, divorce, domestic violence, sexual addiction, sexual dysfunction, and substance abuse. The invisible assumption behind a course such as this is that if we learn the particulars about each of these problems, we then know how to treat them. This is inaccurate and misleading. Information about issues is one side of a coin, and knowledge about practicing therapy is the other. Each is necessary for and suggests the other, but neither can stand on its own or is the other.

This difference between these two areas of knowledge is reflected in Jay Haley's observation that "no traditional diagnostic category is a solvable problem" (1987, p. 38). Haley inspires us to remember that we're in the business of treating individuals and their unique experiences, not the categories that we use to classify problems and the people who suffer from them. We do not, for example, think of ourselves as working with "a battered woman" or "a sexual abuse victim." Our clients have had experiences that share the same name (such as rape or childhood sexual abuse) as those of others, but each individual makes idiosyncratic conclusions about herself, the world she lives in, the nature of people, and whether there is hope for her future.

We thus read the literature to discover what other clinicians have learned, we read the insights offered by survivors (and remember those provided by our previous clients), and we read good fiction—an excellent source of new perspectives, wisdom, metaphor, and inspiration. We then tuck all of this away, along with our ideas of how to help people, in our therapeutic rucksacks where maps are kept, and we listen intently to what the client in front of us is saying, working to cull from her talk a clear, solvable problem definition. We begin by asking how she (or others in her life) think the experience of sexual abuse in the past is posing or contributing to a current struggle. Oh, but wait. Go back. Maps?

Yes, that's right. To us, expert knowledge—the information that we bring with us into each session and that informs what we ask and what we say—is a map, and, as Bateson (1972/2000) reminds us, the map is not the territory. Clinical knowledge about the category "sexual abuse" is a map, not the Truth about an individual's trauma. We prefer that the client guide us across the territory of her life and experiences. We do our best to make sure our maps are comprehensive and relationally sensitive, but they still aren't objective representations of the human being sitting in front of us. We never want to forget this, as we don't want our ideas to become the Procrustean bed onto which we attempt to stretch or shrink our clients. If we get lost, we pull out our map as a guide, but our job is to adjust ourselves to fit the person with whom we're working, not the other way around. We saw a client once, Danny, who reminded us of the hazards of therapists' thinking they have all the answers.

When Danny came to our clinic, he was mad as a hornet. He and his partner of seven years, John, had been in therapy elsewhere to work on disagreements about money, sex, in-laws, parenting, and career decisions. Although he liked the therapist and wanted to keep seeing her, he was also angry at her insistence that before he could resolve his problems with John, he would first need to work through his "unresolved childhood sexual abuse." After holding her at bay for almost a year, he'd finally agreed to broach the topic with her, but, meanwhile, he'd come to us for a second opinion.

Danny wished that he had never told John about the abuse he'd endured as a child, because John, a social worker, wouldn't let it go. From Danny's perspective, it made no sense to dredge up stuff that happened long ago and that nauseated him to think about. He knew what had occurred and had put it behind him, so, he asked us, was he, as his therapist insisted, in denial about the sexual abuse? Or could it be that sexual abuse sometimes resolved on its own?

Despite his therapist's well-intentioned and gently delivered diagnosis, Danny heard the description "in denial" as an accusation. For him, the label implied that he was pathologically refusing to see reality. A realistic person would accept the facts, no matter how hard and cold, and this was necessary for acceptance, which could only be arrived at through openly delving into the gritty details. In fact, from the therapist's perspective, acceptance was the only possible "healthy" response. Danny's denial needed to be torn down so he could access the Truth.

The therapist's challenge to Danny placed him in a paradoxical bind from which he was having difficulty extricating himself. If he refused the label *In Denial*, it would mean he was in denial about his denial. Yikes! Double denial! This would demonstrate his "resistance" to and "poor motivation" for treatment. If, however, he accepted the label, he'd be accepting a description of himself as dysfunctional or pathological, requiring him to surrender his trust in his own perceptions. In short, Danny's choices came down to accepting that he was sick or accepting that he was wrong. And if he didn't make a choice, the therapist might view him as both.

During our single session, we did not directly answer Danny's questions. We recognized that if our answers rendered either him or the therapist wrong, we could end up undermining both of them. So, instead, we told stories of people who, against all expert advice and professional knowledge of the day, had stuck to their own ideas and triumphed. We mentioned people who were alive many years after being diagnosed with life-threatening illnesses and told by doctors they had only months to live. We identified historical legal and military instances in which someone had defied the advice of the upper brass and triumphed. We noted that during a time in history when alcoholism was seen as a terminal condition, Bill W. had refused to believe that he had to die, and AA was born. We talked of the many people who, despite horrendous childhood experiences of abuse, neglect, and poverty, had never gone to therapy and still managed to build meaningful and happy lives. In fact, we suggested, sometimes it was these very experiences that imparted a sort of wisdom, teaching important lessons about what to do and not do in relationships.

We offered our observation that Danny had enormous strength and the courage of his convictions. We noted that holding his own against his therapist's insistence for so many months was remarkable, particularly given the therapist's position as a professional. That he could listen to himself and decide for himself what was in his own best interests, rather than rely on the advice of an expert, was admirable and a testament to his extraordinary strength of character and his capacity to know his own mind. We wondered aloud whether it might have been these qualities that had allowed him to move beyond the sexual abuse, and we speculated about what new things he might discover if he were to bring these qualities more fully into his relationship with John and his therapist.

RE-MEMBERING:
THERAPEUTIC PROBLEM RESOLUTION

As anyone who has ever had a back injury will tell you, when you feel pain, you fight it. Your natural inclination is to tense *against* it as you battle to get control *over* it. If the pain continues, you may begin to feel anxious or fearful as your oppositional efforts fail. Even if the pain subsides, you may feel anxious as you anticipate the next wave. Anxiety and fear constrict muscles and restrict blood flow, which generates more pain, which generates more anxiety, and so on. In the beginning, the anxiety, fear, and tension are attempted solutions—efforts to solve the problem of pain by *severing the relationship to it.* But as the pain cycles back around, as "more-of-the-same" (Watzlawick, Weakland, & Fisch, 1974) gives rise to more anxiety and fear, problem and solution become hopelessly snarled and this entanglement creates further problems. Flemons (1991) summed it up this way:

> It is precisely this attempt to eradicate problems that . . . guarantees an exacerbation of the original situation. Solution and problem are mutually defined; it is impossible for one side of a distinction to destroy the other side—any oppositional response only highlights the relationship, thus intensifying the problem and reiterating its intractability. (p. 93)

When clients and therapists treat a personal problem as if it were a material, separate thing that can be plucked out and thrown away, they establish an oppositional relationship to it. If you experience yourself as depressed and view your depression as some "thing" of which you have too much, then the only course of action open to you is to go up against it, to declare war on it. If you guard against it, if you prod yourself into action, if you demand that you not succumb to it, then you erroneously assume that one part of you (your will, rationality, or ambition) can succeed against another part of you (your depression).

If problems were things, then it *would* be possible to destroy them, but if you try to negate a relationship, you only create another relationship (Flemons, 1991, 2003). The husband who can't stop thinking about the wife who left him will never succeed in forgetting her if he fervently demands of himself, "I am *not* going to think about her anymore. I'm wiping her from my mind." And just as clients can't rid themselves of their problems by trying to negate them, so, too, we can't help clients by simply telling them to keep themselves from engaging in such negating efforts. If we had told the husband in the above example to stop trying to stop thinking of his wife, then this would have amounted to asking him to negate his negating (Flemons, 1999, 2002). Instead, we must find ways to help clients change their experience. Consider two different clients, Andrea and Colleen, whose problems started out as attempted solutions, as efforts to protect themselves from pain.

Andrea, a woman in her late 20s who had been molested by her father, related that she had been "having sex with way too many men" because, as she put it, "I want to prove to myself that I am normal." A therapist working from a traditional treatment model might have explained to Andrea that she was going through a period of "sexual acting out," characterizing the behavior as a pathological symptom of the sexual abuse. From our relational point of view, however, Andrea's behavior was a solution to the problem of feeling abnormal, an effort to feel normal. But when she found that sex only provided temporary relief, that sex failed as a total solution, it had to escalate. Sex became more sex, eventually becoming "way too much sex." The original solution became a problem.

Regardless of how bizarre clients' behavior may appear to those of us on the outside, we don't believe that people wake up in the morning, deciding, "I'm going to live as erratically and unreasonably as I can" or "I'm going to make ridiculous choices today!" Bateson (1972/2000) long ago convinced us that all behavior makes sense in context, so we view our job—and a challenging job it can be—as a process of contextualizing, and thus making sense of, people's seemingly nonsensical, illogical, harmful, or unhelpful behaviors.

Colleen, who had also been molested by her father, suffered from profound tension, a result of the fearful watchfulness that accompanied her every waking moment. The tension was tied into her continually guarding herself against others viewing her as perverted. However, when we asked her to notice what others could sense about her, she discovered that "nothing showed on the outside, so nobody realizes how twisted I am." This observation led her to conclude that since the abuse was not outwardly apparent, it didn't have to be inwardly apparent, either. When she decided that she could just be herself, "not some freak who had sex with her father," the tension didn't turn into a more-of-the-same cycle of escalation.

The general treatment goals of many therapeutic approaches to sexual abuse are to help clients recover from symptoms and to restore power and control (Dolan, 1999; Sheinberg & Fraenkel, 2001; Trepper & Barrett, 2000). Many therapists assume that such recovery and restoration requires clients to be "healed" by recalling and "working through," in painstaking detail, long forgotten violations (Briere & Scott, 2006; Frederickson, 1992). However, because we aren't guided by metaphors of woundedness, pathology, and distortion, we don't seek to heal our clients. To us, the enduring harm of sexual abuse happens at the level of relationship and involves the rupture of living connections. Freyd (1998) calls it betrayal trauma. We call it relational dismemberment. Rather than encouraging clients to remember their abuse, we orient toward helping them *re-member* their severed connections with themselves, their sexuality, and other people.

When Andy Catlett, the farmer in Wendell Berry's *Remembering*, lost his hand in his corn-picker, "his trust in himself failed" (p. 35), and, overcome by anger and guilt, he withdrew from himself and from family and friends. Before the accident, Andy had always known that his arguments with his wife, Flora, were "about duality: they were two longing to be one, or one dividing relentlessly into two" (p. 34). But after "giv[ing] his hand to the machine" (p. 34),

> he had no faith in himself, and he had no faith in her faith in him, or in his faith in her. Now their quarrels did not end their difference and bring them together, but were all one quarrel that had no end. . . . It was no longer about duality but about division, an infinite cold space that opened between them. (p. 35)

The boundary-breaching of sexual abuse similarly creates cold divisions within and between people, destroying trust and forging guilt, rage, and confusion.

At some point in the novel, Andy finds the ability to trust again—to trust himself and to trust his wife. He realizes that his and Flora's life together, building their farm, raising their children, "has depended all on trust" (p. 110), and he recognizes that trust always requires a leap of faith, because "one cannot know enough to trust. To trust is simply to give oneself; the giving is for the future, for which there is no evidence. And, once given, the self cannot be taken back, whatever the evidence" (p. 110). Andy stops trying to "take himself back," stops withdrawing. He begins to forgive himself and seek the "forgiveness of everyone and everything from which he has withheld himself" (p. 113).

The development of trust and forgiveness has to do with the repair, with the re-membering, of relationships the person has with herself and with others. We consider re-membering a useful relational metaphor for understanding therapeutic change. Rather than rushing to help our clients get rid of personal and interpersonal symptoms with which they're dealing, we start with the assumption that there is a wisdom to whatever they are experiencing. So although we very much want our clients to feel better, we tend to move slowly, making sure we understand what's going on, and not setting ourselves up as "removal specialists." Flemons (2002) avoids this trap by thinking of himself as a disentanglement consultant. We like this idea, because it underscores that therapy is about unsnaggling problematic relationships, rather than getting rid of thinglike problems. From our perspective, the change that takes place for people who have been sexually violated is not the result of remembering the sexual abuse but rather a re-membering, a reconnecting between self and dismembered relationships.

It is in the best interests of our clients and society as a whole to find ways that connect people, rather than generate new separations. Those who have been harmed by sexual abuse seem to have a sense of this, which is often reflected in their fervent wish to have the harm acknowledged, particularly by the offender or by those who denied it. However unarticulated, they recognize that if the person who harmed them could acknowledge the harm, he would be accepting responsibility for hurting another human being, which would go a long way toward restoring (re-membering) the legitimacy and the sanctity, the inviolability of that person's humanity. Such acceptance reconnects basic human values shared by victim and offender. When a victim is able to witness her offender's regret, there can be movement toward restoring their shared humanness. With true apology, the offender acknowledges the relational rupture inherent in his willingness to sever the human relationship between them for the sake of his individual gain, and he cedes back to the victim her freedom to dissent and her right of self-determination.

Braithwaite (2002) writes of the Palestinian Sulha who "build the greater good of a loving community" (p. 3) through their present-day practice of an ancient form of restorative justice that reconnects offender and offended, families and community. When a serious crime, for example, murder, occurs, the offender's family approaches individuals respected as peacemakers and requests their help. The peacemakers visit the victim's family, and, if accepted, begin working out a peace between the two families, which may include *diya* (blood money), meant to symbolize that blood is priceless (p. 4). At the end of the process, the community celebrates:

> When all the details of the peace between the two families are negotiated, a process that may take more than a year, the beautiful ceremony of the Sulha occurs. A leader of the victim's family ties a knot in a white flag of peace and gives this flag to the offender, who carries it, surrounded by the peacemakers, as he moves along a line of the victim's family, shaking the hand of each. Community leaders then each make knots in the white flag to symbolize a peace that cannot be untied. (p. 4)

The ceremony includes reconciliation speeches by both the victim's and the offender's family and, often, the return of the *diya*. In the end, the violator, whose separative acts of harm put him outside and against the community, is reembraced through the recalling and reinforcing of common personal and community values, and the relationships severed by the act of violence are re-membered.

In the current therapeutic climate in our country, it would be almost impossible for a re-membering process such as this to take place. For the protection of victims and because of legal limitations, the treatment of sexual offenders is almost always conducted separately from that of the abused. This, of course, constrains the degree of relationship repair that can be accomplished. We, too, are limited in this regard. Within our work, we concentrate on clients re-membering all relevant intra- and interpersonal relationships; however, we don't bring violators and those they violated into the therapy room together.

When Paula was 10, her mother, a nurse, took the better-paying 4:00 p.m. to midnight shift at the hospital. Paula and her stepfather, Charley, whom she'd dearly loved since he'd married her mother eight years earlier, began to get even closer. They would make dinner together, check over her homework, and then cuddle on the couch to watch TV. She so enjoyed having Charley all to herself, she sometimes felt guilty for being glad her mom wasn't there.

Until one night, when Paula was 13. Her stepfather came into her room and, putting his hand under her nightgown, began to feel up and down the length of her body. Soon after, he escalated to penetration. He returned to her bedroom almost every night for nearly two years.

When Paula came to see Martha and her team of student therapists, she was 32, married, the mother of a child, and, like her mother, a nurse working on a surgical floor. She came to therapy to get rid of a persistent and unsettling picture in her head, an image of herself repeating "no, no, no, no, no, no, no, no, no, no, no," while her stepfather, lowering himself into her, crooned gentle, soothing words of comfort.

Paula found herself throughout the day chanting "no, no, no, no, no, no, no, no, no" under her breath. This sing-song mantra highly disturbed her, but, try as she might, she couldn't turn it off. Although she currently had contact with both her mother and stepfather, she had begun to entertain the idea that she should sever her connection at least with him, as previous abuse-recovery counselors had long ago advised; but part of her didn't want to.

Paula was adamant that her many years of involvement in the sexual abuse recovery movement, progressing through what they identify as three stages of recovery (from "victim" to "survivor," to "thriver"), had resulted in her being "healed." She had learned to take control of her life and gain mastery over any symptoms. And she had been successful, except for this "one last picture" that was consuming her days and nights. Once she got rid of it, she'd be good to go.

Asked by the therapist how she was attempting to deal with the picture, Paula described her efforts to reassure, comfort, and ground herself, as she had learned to do in previous therapy. She might murmur affirmations to herself, such as "You're okay. Nothing bad is really happening." Alternatively, she might touch something solid, say, the counter of the nurses' station at work, and then concentrate on the physical contact between her hand and the surface, reminding herself that she was in the present and the world was stable. Here is the heart of the third session:

Martha: In the picture that you have, what are you saying "no" to, as you repeat the word over and over?
Paula: (with a touch of annoyance) He was raping me! I was saying no to the rape, of course. I wanted him to leave me alone.
Martha: Yes, of course you did. And your words couldn't make that happen. Your repeated "no's" couldn't make him leave you alone. Can you recall the words of comfort that your stepfather would offer as he was hurting you?

Paula: Oh, you know, the stuff you say to kids to make 'em think everything is okay, to calm them down, you know, like "It's okay." "It
doesn't hurt." "Don't cry." "Wait just a minute, you'll like it, you'll
see." Stuff like that.

Martha: Did you ever like it?

Paula: (vehemently) No! I hated it. I hated him.

Martha: Was it ever okay?

Paula: No!

Martha: Did it ever not hurt?

Paula: No! No! No! It was all lies. It was horrible. No, it made me feel
dirty and confused. No, I was just a little girl. I didn't understand
anything about sex.

Martha: Of course you didn't, you were just a little girl. But even then,
even at that young age, you knew the truth of how it was for you. His
words of comfort were meant to deceive you about your own experience. His words were meant to make you turn from your self-
knowledge, from what you knew to be true—that what you were experiencing was awful and painful, and you hated it. Your stepfather's
words of "comfort" (Martha flicks the air with her fingers to indicate
quotation marks) were designed to make you experience rape as
okay, something pleasurable, even. But you never did that, did you?

Paula: (very thoughtfully and more quietly now). No.

Martha: You were just a little girl, and you couldn't possibly physically say
"no" to your stepfather, but you sure could and did say "no" to [his]
defining the experience, [to his defining] the relationship the way he
wanted you to define it. And you're still saying "no" to his definition
of the experience. Every day, all day long, "no, no, no, no, no, no, no,
no, no. . . ."

Paula: (crying) Yes. I am, aren't I?

Martha: So, in some ways, we wonder. . . . It seems like you are saying
"no" to the pain because you want him to stop and leave you alone,
and you are also saying "no" to his insinuation that you could feel
pleasure from this.

Paula: Yeah, if I had said "yes" to that, I would be crazy right now.

Martha: That's right, you would, wouldn't you? Because if you had gone
about the business of trying to convince yourself that it felt good,
you would have had to cut off that part of you that knew the truth.

Paula: No, I didn't do that. I always knew what he did to me. I always remembered it. I've never forgotten like some people do.

Martha: And we think you should go right on saying "No!"

In further conversation with Paula, we remarked that she would never say "yes" to her stepfather's crazy-making idea that sexual abuse could be okay or pleasurable. She would never betray herself by telling herself that it was anything other than hurtful and horrible. We complimented her on her wisdom, her "know(no)-yourself-ness," and observed that these qualities had enabled her come to us and tell us precisely what she did and did not want from us. She had shown considerable wisdom and strength of character when she said "no" to previous counselors who had insisted that she had to cut off her relationship with her stepfather in order to heal.

We supported her idea that she could continue to have a relationship with her father, pointing out that saying "yes" to an adult relationship with him did not mean saying "yes" to the abuse. She had always loved him, and she could go on loving him without compromising herself. She had shown herself capable of hanging onto a clear-eyed recognition of what he had done to her, and she had done a great deal of important work "recovering" from that. We thus trusted her wisdom to know how best to care for herself. Now she could say both "no" *and* "yes." She could say "no" to his attempt to turn pain into pleasure, "no" to his former definition of their sexualized relationship, and "no" to what he had done to her. And "yes" to her love for him.

Paula had been trying to negate the picture in her head, tensing against it, touching something solid to convince herself it wasn't real, and repetitively saying "no" to it. These efforts had set up a fight between herself and the symptom. Finding herself on the losing side of the battle, she'd sought out therapists (the big guns) and solicited their help in joining the battle against it. Our work with her aimed at helping her have a different relationship with the symptom, one that did not oppose it (Flemons, 1999, 2002, 2004).

Paula did not think she needed to come back after the third session, and we agreed. However, we asked if she would be willing to return one last time to tell us how she was doing and to teach us about what had and had not been helpful in our work with her. Paula agreed, so we saw her for a fourth and final session about three months later. She reported that the picture had returned twice since she had last seen us but the effect on her had been much milder and far less upsetting. More importantly, she said, "I spent part of that day *happily* chanting "no, no, no, no, no, no, no," because now I know that a "no" to him means a "yes" to me." We heartily agreed.

Acts of sexual abuse dismember relationships, disrupting or severing the connections to self and others that make us human, make us whole.

The more important the violator is to the person violated, and the more difficult it is (for reasons of development and survival) for the victim to say "no," the more strands of connection that are severed.

Our therapy with people who have endured sexual abuse does not focus on their remembering the details of what happened but rather on their re-membering relationships that have been severed. This is the beginning of trust and hope.

REFERENCES

Ainscough, C. & Toon, K. (2000). *Surviving childhood sexual abuse: Practical self-help for adults who were sexually abused as children* (rev. ed.). Tucson, AZ: Fisher Books.

Angelou, M. (1969). *I know why the caged bird sings.* New York: Bantam Books.

Bass, E., & Davis, L. (1994). *The courage to heal: A guide for women survivors of child sexual abuse* (3rd ed.). New York: HarperCollins.

Bateson, G. (2000). *Steps to an ecology of mind.* Chicago: University of Chicago Press. (Original work published 1972)

Berry, W. (1988). *Remembering.* San Francisco: North Point Press.

Blume, E. S. (1991). *Secret survivors: Uncovering incest and its aftereffects in women.* New York: Ballantine.

Braithwaite, J. (2002). *Restorative justice and responsive regulation.* New York: Oxford University Press.

Briere, J., & Scott, C. (2006). *Principles of trauma therapy: A guide to symptoms, evaluation, and treatment.* Thousand Oaks, CA: Sage.

Courtois, C. A. (1999). *Recollections of sexual abuse: Treatment principles and guidelines.* New York: Norton.

Dolan, Y. M. (1999). *Resolving sexual abuse: Solution-focused therapy and Ericksonian hypnosis for adult survivors.* New York: Norton.

Draucker, C. B. (2000). *Counseling survivors of childhood sexual abuse* (2nd ed.). London: Sage.

Flemons, D. (1991). *Completing distinctions.* Boston: Shambhala.

Flemons, D. (1999, Jan./Feb.). Making symptoms vanish: Hypnosis and the mystery of the sudden cure. *Family Therapy Networker, 23*(1), 56–65.

Flemons, D. (2002). *Of one mind: The logic of hypnosis, the practice of therapy.* New York: Norton.

Flemons, D. (2003, Jan/Feb). The psychology of the sand-pit: Clinical lessons from Winnie-the-Pooh. *Psychotherapy Networker, 2*(1), 32–37.

Flemons, D. (2004, May/June). The Tao of therapy. *Family Therapy Networker, 28*(3), 44–47, 68.

Foa, E. B., & Rothbaum, B. O. (1998). *Treating the trauma of rape: Cognitive-Behavioral therapy for PTSD.* New York: Guilford.

Frederickson, R. (1992). *Repressed memories: A journey to recovery from sexual abuse.* New York: Simon & Schuster.

Freyd, J. J. (1998). *Betrayal trauma: The logic of forgetting childhood abuse.* Cambridge, MA: Harvard University Press.

Haley, J. (1987). *Problem-solving therapy.* San Francisco: Jossey-Bass.

Keeney, B. P. (1983). *Aesthetics of change.* New York: Guilford.

Maltz, W. (2001). Sex therapy with survivors of sexual abuse. In P. J. Kleinplatz (Ed.), *New directions in sex therapy* (pp. 258–278). Philadelphia: Brunner-Routledge.

Salter, A. C. (1995). *Transforming trauma: A guide to understanding and treating adult survivors of child sexual abuse.* Thousand Oaks, CA: Sage.

Sanders, G., & Tomm, K. (1989). A cybernetic-systemic approach to problems in sexual functioning. In D. Kantor & B. Okun, (Eds.), *Intimate environments* (pp. 346–380). New York: Guilford.

Sheinberg, M., & Fraenkel, P. (2001). *The relational trauma of incest: A family-based approach to treatment*. New York: Guilford.

Trepper, T., & Barrett, M. J. (1989). *Systemic treatment of incest: A therapeutic handbook*. New York: Brunner/Mazel.

Vanderlinden, J., & Vandereycken, W. (1997). *Trauma, dissociation, and impulse dyscontrol in eating disorders*. Philadelphia: Brunner/Mazel.

Watzlawick, P., Weakland, J., & Fisch, R. (1974). *Change: Principles of problem formation and problem resolution*. New York: W. W. Norton.

Winkler, C. (2002). *One night: Realities of rape*. Walnut Creek, CA: Altamira Press.

Afterword

W HEN WE DECIDED TO PUT THIS book together, we had three goals in mind.
(1) We wanted to access the wisdom of creative, talented brief therapists and provide them with a forum to talk about their sex cases. Everyone we called said no one had ever asked before. (2) We wanted to introduce a new audience to the brief, nonnormative approach. Specifically, we hoped that those working in the more traditional sex therapy realm might, upon reading this collection, find that brief therapy is not about trivializing client concerns or "applying bandaids" and overlooking the "real" problems. (3) We hoped to stimulate conversations and further explorations of "brief sex therapy."

As we sit here with the completed book in hand, it's clear to us that our first goal was achieved. We were delighted by the range of new ideas and techniques we encountered, but we were inspired still more by the spirit, integrity, and levity of the authors. As you've recognized from reading their chapters, they all share a deep regard for their clients, honoring their wisdom and working collaboratively to find meaningful and helpful solutions. You've also no doubt noticed how much the contributors value humor and curiosity. A commitment to irreverence lends a sense of play to their respect for clients and makes it possible for them to creatively discover simple yet elegant resource-based responses to presenting complaints.

How well we achieved our second goal remains to be seen, and the third goal depends on you. Although we're glad our editing is finished, we'd like the conversation to continue beyond the pages of the book. Just as sex is generally improved when accompanied by good communication, therapeutic practices can be improved by good communication among professionals. We'd like to initiate conversations among and between brief therapists and sex therapists, and we see this collection only as foreplay. You can heat

305

things up by emailing us your responses, ideas, inspirations, and challenges. Let us know how the ideas and clinical cases presented here resonate (or fail to) with your own therapeutic assumptions. Let the conversations begin! We look forward to hearing from you.

—Shelley Green & Douglas Flemons
www.contextconsultants.com

Index